RE-MAPPING LAGERLÖF

Re-Mapping Lagerlöf

Performance, intermediality, and European transmissions

Edited by
Helena Forsås-Scott, Lisbeth Stenberg
& Bjarne Thorup Thomsen

NORDIC ACADEMIC PRESS

The publication of this volume
has been made possible by kind support from

The Anglo-Swedish Literary Foundation, London
Magn. Bergvalls stiftelse, Stockholm
The Embassy of Sweden, London
Konung Gustaf VI Adolfs fond för svensk kultur, Stockholm
Letterstedtska föreningen, Stockholm
Åke Wibergs stiftelse, Stockholm

Nordic Academic Press
P.O. Box 1206
SE-221 05 Lund, Sweden
www.nordicacademicpress.com

© Nordic Academic Press and the authors 2014
Typesetting: Stilbildarna i Mölle, sbmolle.com
Jacket design: Design för livet
Jacket photo: Photo of Selma Lagerlof by A. Blomberg,
Stockholm, 1906. Map by Fugazi form.
Print: ScandBook AB, Falun 2014
ISBN 978-91-87351-21-1

Contents

Preface

The conference 'Selma Lagerlöf 2011: Text, Translation, Film', arranged at University College London in June 2011 to mark the publication of the first three volumes of 'Lagerlöf in English', the series of new English translations of key texts, was the first international conference on Lagerlöf since 1997. Papers were given by twenty-seven speakers from seven countries. The structuring of the material in the present volume reflects the key areas of scholarship that emerged at the conference: Lagerlöf as a celebrity; films inspired by her texts; and her texts in relation to other cultures. In addition to selecting for this volume a representative range of material, the editors have commissioned further essays so as to present a more comprehensive coverage of current Lagerlöf scholarship. We are grateful to the contributors for their willingness to develop their research for this volume, for their co-operation throughout the process of editing the material, and for their patience.

The three main sections of the book are introduced by sectional portals, the first two written by Helena Forsås-Scott and the third by Bjarne Thorup Thomsen. The editing has been done by Helena with some input from Bjarne. Lisbeth Stenberg has been responsible for the illustrations.

The Embassy of Sweden, London, and Riksbankens Jubileumsfond kindly supported the 2011 conference. For generous financial support towards the costs of publishing this volume we would like to thank the Anglo-Swedish Literary Foundation, London; Magn. Bergvalls stiftelse, Stockholm; the Embassy of Sweden, London; Konung Gustaf VI Adolfs fond för svensk kultur, Stockholm; Letterstedtska föreningen, Stockholm; and Åke Wibergs stiftelse, Stockholm.

Finally, the editors would like to thank Nordic Academic Press for their professionalism and efficiency. Annika Olsson of Nordic Academic Press and Charlotte Merton deserve a very special thank you: their expertise, support, and enthusiasm have been essential to the completion of this project.

Helena Forsås-Scott, Lisbeth Stenberg, Bjarne Thorup Thomsen
Edinburgh and Gothenburg, spring 2014

I
INTRODUCTION

CHAPTER I

Re-Mapping Lagerlöf

The volume and its parameters

Bjarne Thorup Thomsen

The present volume aims to offer an international audience a variety of insights into a new interdisciplinary discourse on the Swedish world-literature writer Selma Lagerlöf (1858–1940), the first woman to be awarded the Nobel Prize for Literature, in 1909. It is the first English-language volume to present a comprehensive conspectus of current Lagerlöf scholarship, conducted by researchers representing a range of national affiliations. Taken together, the innovative investigations presented in the volume provide the reader with a new and multicoloured map of developments and connections in Lagerlöf's wide-ranging work, canonical as well as lesser known, of its ideological significances, contexts, and impact, of its multiple travels between media and transmissions across countries, and of the astonishing attraction and influence of Lagerlöf's public persona during her career and beyond.

The history of the critical approaches taken to Lagerlöf's work and authorial figure since the beginning of her writing career projects, broadly speaking, a development from what could be described as more 'confining' perspectives in various forms to much more expansive and diverse ones, and *Re-Mapping Lagerlöf* may be seen as a further advancement along this route. While earlier criticism tended to tie Lagerlöf's literary activity to her home region of rural Värmland in western Sweden, and to remove artistic agency from the author by constructing her as the voice of a tradition of oral storytelling, as a mouthpiece for the Swedish soil itself, or as an embodiment of moral values,[1] the subsequent critical 'turns'—from the textual turn of the 1950s and 1960s to the application of a number of 'beyond text' approaches thereafter—have shaped a much more multifaceted understanding of the complexities,

Illus. 1. Selma Lagerlöf *c*.1881.

innovative force, and impact of Lagerlöf's work and persona. *Re-Mapping Lagerlöf* may thus be viewed as a unique window onto the current proliferation of perspectives on a writer, the appreciation of whom continues to grow.

The perspectives on display in this book cover Lagerlöf in the context of the international feminist movement and as a writer whose work offers a richness of alternative discourses on gender. They position her as an international peace campaigner, but also as a celebrity and a literary 'star' whose status in her own time could rival that of royalty. They cover Lagerlöf's key contributions to nation-building and early welfare agendas in her own country and beyond, and to the national imagination as such, but also the transnational thought inherent in much of her output, of obvious relevance to present-day political and cultural concerns. The perspectives include illuminations of important strands of Lagerlöf's work with reference to intertextuality, canonicity, and generic hybridity. The perspectives provide, moreover, a range of insights into the vibrant, and continuing, re-mediation of Lagerlöf's output, including, significantly, the seminal role of her work in supplying plot lines, spectacles, and thematic concerns to the emerging and expanding cultures of national and global cinema, which would markedly increase her already considerable audience. A further segment of perspectives in *Re-Mapping Lagerlöf* concerns the transmission of Lagerlöf's work into different, mainly European countries and cultural contexts, demonstrating how its reception speaks to very varied cultural constituencies and domestic interests. These transmission and translation histories illustrate a remarkable ability of the 'cultural capital' that Lagerlöf's work and persona increasingly represented to retain its currency through paradigmatic shifts in ideology and cultural politics beyond Sweden's borders.

This plethora of perspectives has been gathered into three main sections, while at the same time recognising that the essays, precisely due to their interdisciplinary impulses and desire to establish new connections, may straddle sectional boundaries. Each section is introduced by a 'portal' which sets out a common framework for the section and presents the essays. The first of these sections, 'Readers, performance, constructions', examines the author's construction of her celebrity persona in texts, environments, and public performance, as well as investigating, complementarily, the understanding of Lagerlöf by members of the general public, as manifested, for example, in an extensive collection of letters to the author from very wide and varied segments of readers, both domestic and international. The second section, 'Intermediality and film', assesses the role of Lagerlöf's narratives in advancing early Swedish cinema in a cultural period that figured a productive dialogic relationship between canonical literature and the emerging art and entertainment form of film. The section contains, moreover, incisive new film studies of some of the most significant Lagerlöf adaptations or reworkings, which have achieved iconic status in international film history, along with gendered readings of illustrations and images in both print and film form. The third section, '(Trans)national narratives and European transmissions', contains five case studies which explore the transmission and translation of Lagerlöf's work into a variety of languages, contrasting cultural and political climates, and different periods. The main focus is on Europe, but Lagerlöf's important role in the US is also covered in one contribution. The cases have been selected with the aim of representing diverse regimes and ideological environments, ranging from Czechoslovakia/the Czech Republic before, during, and after communism, via Nazi Germany, to the Netherlands, the UK, and

Illus. 2. Selma Lagerlöf c.1891. She adopted a short hairstyle in the spring of 1889, at the same time as she experienced a stylistic breakthrough in the development of her debut work, *Gösta Berling's Saga* (1891).

the US. In addition to sketching this trajectory from east to west, the cases also capture the function of Lagerlöf's work and the fascination of her persona in linguistic environments that range from the Frisian 'minor'-language culture to the world-language culture of English. These case studies are preceded by explorations of the role of transnational thought and international and public space in Lagerlöf's texts, along with examinations of the formation of canon, the construction of gender, and the role of the uncanny in Lagerlöf, the latter with a particular emphasis on the internationalised climate of the First World War period, appropriate in a volume published on the centenary of the outbreak of the war.

Thus, overall, the present volume may be seen as a road-map to the multifarious ways in which Lagerlöf and her work have engaged with and impacted on culture and ideology, a new orientation in one of the most significant and influential world-literature writers to emerge from the Nordic countries. In keeping with the recurring emphasis in the volume on word–image relationships and on pictorial representation as such, *Re-Mapping Lagerlöf* is richly illustrated, with many of the images rarely or never published before. They include reproductions of archival material and a range of illustrations relating to film adaptations of Lagerlöf's work and her important role in early cinematic culture. With its incisive perspectives, reader-friendly structure, detailed notes, extensive bibliographical section, and innovative range of illustrations, *Re-Mapping Lagerlöf* is designed to provide a tool for future Lagerlöf scholarship. Given the plurality of approaches and the variety of theoretical underpinnings used in the book, it is hoped, moreover, that the volume may serve as a source of inspiration for further interdisciplinary research in the arts and humanities.

The publication of *Re-Mapping Lagerlöf* coincides with an ongoing series of new translations into English of seminal works by Lagerlöf, launched by Norvik Press of London in 2011 under the umbrella heading of 'Lagerlöf in English' (see Carbone & Forsås-Scott, forthcoming), which is fuelling a new international interest in Lagerlöf's work. So far, four translations have been published—*Lord Arne's Silver* (2011), translated by Sarah Death; *The Phantom Carriage* (2011), translated by Peter Graves; *The Löwensköld Ring* (2011), translated by Linda Schenck; and *Nils Holgersson's Wonderful Journey through Sweden* (2 vols, 2013), translated by Peter Graves—with further translations to come. *Charlotte Löwensköld*, translated by Linda Schenck, will appear in 2014, while *Anna Svärd*, likewise translated by Linda Schenck, is due to follow in 2015. The availability of new and more accurate translations will facilitate internationally further progress along the lines of enquiry presented in *Re-Mapping Lagerlöf*.

Notes

1 For a comprehensive study of the Swedish reception history of Lagerlöf's work, see Anna Nordlund's monograph *Selma Lagerlöfs underbara resa genom den svenska litteraturhistorien 1891–1996* (2005, 'Selma Lagerlöf's Wonderful Journey through Swedish Literary History, 1891–1996').

CHAPTER 2

Selma Lagerlöf in context

Helena Forsås-Scott

'Mårbacka was the centre of Selma Lagerlöf's world', writes Vivi Edström, her most recent biographer (2002, 24),[1] but as the remainder of the relevant section of Edström's introductory chapter indicates, Lagerlöf's lifetime was a period of such comprehensive change—economic, political, social, technological—that we may be justified in thinking in terms of a succession of Mårbackas, plural. There is certainly a world of difference between the red wooden building, a single storey with an attic, at the farmstead where Selma Lagerlöf was born on 20 November 1858, and the impressive white building in neo-classical style with its manorial roof, two storeys with a large attic, and the façade enhanced by a balcony and five pairs of elegant columns, which she left behind when she died on 16 March 1940, along with a sizeable, productive farm with scores of employees. The Mårbackas can be read as part of 'a process of personal myth-making' (Forsås-Scott 1997, 55); but most importantly, they need to be understood in terms of the contexts that helped transform Sweden during Lagerlöf's lifetime, contexts that were themselves part of the prerequisites of her success, and that were, to some degree, also changed by her work.

The Sweden in which Lagerlöf was born was a poor and marginal country, with agriculture the mainstay of the population of 3.7 million. The *riksdag* (Parliament) consisted of four Estates, the king wielded extensive power, and since 1814 the country had been in an uneasy union with Norway—a union ultimately dissolved in 1905. The social differences were extensive; and although single women above the age of 25 were granted legal independence in the year in which Lagerlöf was born, women lacked access to publicly funded education and training, and there were extremely few opportunities for employment open to them. To Selma Lagerlöf's father, a military man who had inherited a

Mårbacka requiring a considerable amount of investment and modern-isation, and to her mother, the daughter of a wealthy merchant, it was obvious that their two sons should be allowed to draw on the limited family assets for their education, and so the risk for Selma Lagerlöf and her two sisters of remaining stuck in the remote corner that Värmland was at the time, given the inadequate communications, was very real.

Major changes, however, were beginning to affect Sweden. Indus-trialisation was late but swift, yet emigration to the US remained the preferred option for many tens of thousands up to the First World War. One of these emigrants was Lagerlöf's brother Johan, who ended his days in Seattle. Johan had assisted Selma with money for a course in preparation for her training at the Women Teachers' College of Higher Education in Stockholm in 1882–5. She subsequently obtained a post at an elementary school for girls in Landskrona, in the south of Sweden. With her mother having been widowed in 1885 and Mårbacka sold at auction in 1888, the fact that Selma Lagerlöf was able to support her-self—and to some extent her mother and an aunt too—was crucially important; and although her ground-breaking first novel appeared in 1891, the early phase of her career as a writer was slow, leaving her dependent on her teaching post until 1895.

In 1866, the Swedish Parliament had been restructured into two chambers, and modern political parties were beginning to take shape in the decades before 1900. Universal suffrage for men was introduced in 1909, following a general strike, but the campaign for women's right to vote was drawn out and had to contend with many setbacks. Selma Lagerlöf was actively involved in this campaign, and Elin Wägner, herself a writer and suffragist and author of the first comprehensive biography of Lagerlöf, has described, with reference to the 6th Con-gress of the International Woman Suffrage Alliance in Stockholm in 1911, how wonderful it was 'to have on the rostrum a world-famous woman author and landowner who lacked the civic right that any male author and farmer possessed by virtue of his gender' (Wägner 1943, 85).[2] Lagerlöf's international fame in combination with her commit-ment to the cause made her the obvious icon of the Congress. While Lagerlöf's extensive international travels had been fundamental to some of her work, notably *Antikrists mirakler* (*The Miracles of Antichrist*), set in Sicily, and *Jerusalem*, her texts had also been widely translated; and she had received, as the first woman ever, the Nobel Prize for Literature in 1909. But as Wägner indicates, Lagerlöf at the time of the Congress

Illus. 1. Mårbacka before Selma Lagerlöf's renovations in 1908. Mårbacka had several different owners between the auction in 1888 and Lagerlöf's purchase of the property in 1907.

was also a landowner: having purchased Mårbacka with its garden in 1907, she had bought the land and the livestock in 1910, a move that not only made her responsible for the running of a sizeable farm but also for the farmworkers, numbering no fewer than fourteen families at the time (Wägner 1943, 77).

Lagerlöf's speech at the Congress in 1911, 'Hem och stat' ('Home and State'), analysed here by Lisbeth Stenberg, presents Lagerlöf's vision of a welfare state that is democratic and inclusive, with the extensive contributions by women as a transformative influence. However, full democracy in Sweden was still some way away, with parliamentarism introduced in 1917 and women granted suffrage only in 1919, later than in any other Nordic country. In the meantime the impact of some of Lagerlöf's works was becoming conspicuous, with the short story entitled 'Tösen från Stormyrtorpet' ('The Girl from the Marsh Croft'), 1908, made into an acclaimed film by Victor Sjöström in 1917, contributing to new and more humane welfare legislation introduced in Sweden not long afterwards. The novella *Körkarlen* (1912, *The Phantom Carriage*) originated as a short piece commissioned by the National Tuberculosis Society; again thanks to Sjöström, Lagerlöf's text subsequently inspired one of the most famous works of the Swedish silent film era. Arguably,

Illus. 2. Mårbacka following extensive rebuilding in the early 1920s. The photo, from the 1930s, shows Selma Lagerlöf in the loggia.

however, her schoolbook *Nils Holgerssons underbara resa genom Sverige* (1906–1907, *Nils Holgersson's Wonderful Journey through Sweden*), about a boy who is turned into an elf and travels the length and breadth of Sweden on the back of a goose, has had greater impact than any of her other works, having taught generations of Swedish children about the interdependence of humankind and Nature.

In one of the last chapters in the book, Nils arrives one autumn evening at a Värmland farm whose main building is 'small and modest' (Lagerlöf 2013b, II, 285).[3] Having bought Mårbacka in the year in which she described it in these terms, Lagerlöf immediately set about extending the main building, and while at first intending to live at Mårbacka during the summers and continuing to spend the winters in Falun, she moved back to her childhood home in 1911.

Here the main architectural transformation took place in 1919–21, with the old building effectively retained as the core of the imposing edifice that is Mårbacka today. But the remodelling of the main building, improvements to the outbuildings, and the day-to-day running of the farm were costly, and Wägner has described how Lagerlöf, during an interview in December 1920 and with the suffering on the Continent in the wake of the First World War uppermost in her mind, wondered if she ought to keep Mårbacka: were she to sell it, Lagerlöf pointed out, she would be able to help many more of

Illus. 3. Selma Lagerlöf in her study at Mårbacka, 1933.

those writing to ask her for financial assistance (Wägner 1943, 166). Lagerlöf's big anti-war novel had only appeared late in the war, but in addition to *Bannlyst* (1918, *The Outcast*), many shorter texts from the war years brought to the fore the role of peace and co-operation across national borders.

When Lagerlöf turned 70 in 1928 and was celebrated with a performance at the Stockholm Opera and a banquet at the Grand Hôtel, those sending their congratulations included writers such as John Galsworthy from Britain, Thomas Mann from Germany, and Carl Sandburg from the US. When she turned 75 in 1933, by contrast, she spent the day quietly at Mårbacka. But, as Wägner has emphasised, with her works performed at the Opera, theatres, cinemas, and on the radio, including a speech broadcast to the US, Lagerlöf, at home at Mårbacka 'knew that on that day she was present everywhere' (Wägner 1943, 291).[4]

Over Lagerlöf's lifetime Sweden was transformed, with the population almost doubling to 6.4 million by 1940, industry becoming the mainstay of the economy, growing numbers of women in the workforce, and the Social Democratic welfare state beginning to take shape from 1932 onwards. In 1938, Lagerlöf accepted a collective agreement on pay and conditions for her employees (Edström 2002, 24). Tourists visiting

Mårbacka today from all over the world easily forget that the famous author and the first woman elected to the Swedish Academy (1914) was also an estate owner and entrepreneur, but Wägner's snapshot of Lagerlöf at 75 in her study concretises her complex and multifaceted contexts. In addition to classic texts, books by herself and about herself, and several shelves of translations of her works, Lagerlöf also had a series of wooden trays into which her mail was sorted, with labels such as 'Baltic states, Belgium, Holland, Denmark, Norway, England, France, Italy, Finland, Germany, Sweden, Switzerland, the Slavic countries, Austria-Hungary, Bonnier [her Swedish publisher], Langen [her German publisher], the Swedish Academy, the Press, Relatives and friends, Valuables, Mårbacka oatmeal, Miscellaneous commissions' (Wägner 1943, 312).[5]

The contexts of Lagerlöf's work have only continued to expand and develop since her death in 1940. In the present volume's essays, a broad range of them are brought into focus.

Notes

1 'Mårbacka var centrum i Selma Lagerlöfs värld.'
2 'att på podiet ha en världsberömd författarinna och godsägare som saknade den medborgarrätt vilken den enklaste manliga författare och hemmansägare ägde på grund av sitt kön'.
3 'liten och oansenlig' (Lagerlöf 1907a, 410).
4 'visste hon att den dagen var hon allestädes närvarande'.
5 'Balticum, Belgien, Holland, Danmark, Norge, England, Frankrike, Italien, Finland, Tyskland, Sverige, Schweiz, Slaviska länder, Österrike-Ungern, Bonniers, Langens, Svenska Akademien, Pressen, Släkt och vänner, Dyrgripar, Mårbacka havremjöl, Diverse uppdrag'.

CHAPTER 3

A star in a constellation

The international women's movement as
a context for reading the works of Selma Lagerlöf

Lisbeth Stenberg

Selma Lagerlöf's career as a writer has close connections to the women's movement. Mentors who were literary critics and pioneers in the women's movement in Sweden gave Lagerlöf decisive support when she entered the literary field.

Social movement literature provides examples of the cultural spaces opened up for movement intellectuals (for example, Eyerman & Jamison 1991; Frascina 1999; Kaplan 1992; Peterson 2012). According to these theorists, social movements provide the cultural context for critical intellectuals, and draw attention to the role they can play expressing the collective identity of social movements. As I shall argue here, the women's movement at the turn of the twentieth century provided an important part of the context and preconditions for Selma Lagerlöf's authorship. After being awarded the Nobel Prize for Literature in 1909, Lagerlöf actively engaged in the campaign for female suffrage. In June 1911, by then an icon of the movement, she gave a famous speech, 'Hem och stat' ('Home and State') at the 6th Congress of the International Woman Suffrage Alliance (IWSA) in Stockholm. To use the term coined by Eyerman and Jamison (1998, 22), Lagerlöf with this speech took on the role of 'truth-bearer' for the movement. I am going to compare the ideological content and rhetorical style of Lagerlöf's speech to ideas held more widely within the women's movement at the time.

International congresses

When women entered the public sphere, congresses were one form of 'visualised politics', displaying an invention of tradition used to create an emotional energy that generated solidarity and commitment (Rupp 1997; af Petersens 2006). The International Council of Women (ICW) was founded at a congress in Washington in 1888, held to celebrate the memory of the declaration forty years earlier in Seneca Falls. The initiator was Elizabeth Cady Stanton, who had been one of the moving forces behind the first national congress. At the time of the initiative, Cady Stanton together with Susan B. Anthony were leaders of the American Women's Suffrage Movement (AWSM). But the issue of votes for women was controversial, and not only among men. The ICW did not have suffrage as a political demand, and for a long time the ICW was led by Lady Aberdeen, who represented the Establishment. At a meeting of the Council in 1902, suffragists formed a separate organisation, the IWSA, under the leadership of Carrie Chapman Catt (Crawford 2001, 301).

After the formation of the Alliance, major congresses were held in Berlin (1904), Copenhagen (1906), Amsterdam (1908), and London (1909). In 1911, the IWSA held its 6th Congress in Stockholm, where Selma Lagerlöf attended as an honorary delegate.

The sessions of the IWSA congresses consisted of reports from the suffrage organisations of the member nations; the sharing of strategies and methods; discussions of common goals; and the business of the Alliance's periodical *Jus Suffragii*. Ways to establish a common identity were prominent on the agenda, and competitions were held to choose both banners and hymns that could rep-resent the movement.

Rupp identifies different kinds of cultural practices at the congress-es that created visual images of the merging of discrete national loyalties into an international

Illus. 1. This logo was used in many contexts to signal the justness of the cause of the International Woman Suffrage Alliance.

Illus. 2. An IWSA banner donated to the organisation during the Congress by the Swedish poet and philanthropist Lotten von Kræmer.

identity. One of these was the use of national flags at international ceremonies. At the 1906 IWSA Congress, according to the official report as cited by Rupp, 'the international character of the meeting was indicated by little silken national flags which marked the seats of each delegation' (2010, 149).

During the Congress week in Stockholm, 12–17 June 1911, the Swedish suffragists were host to representatives from twenty-two countries. The proceedings were held at the Grand Hôtel, where the banqueting hall was decorated with flowers in yellow and white, the colours of the Alliance, and with the national flags of the participant countries. The board of the IWSA were seated on the dais and a number of guests of honour beside them. The foremost of these guests of honour was Selma Lagerlöf.

The week was full of other events related to the Congress such as meetings, cultural arrangements, and excursions, and on these occasions the leaders of the IWSA gave numerous speeches. These events were important for networking, building friendships, and creating a joint sense of purpose (Rupp & Taylor 2002). The newspapers in Stockholm followed both the international Congress and the supplementary activities closely. Most attention was focused on the Rev. Anna Howard Shaw (1847–1919), who was allowed to preach in Gustaf Vasa Church the Sunday before the opening of the conference. This was the first time a woman minister had given a sermon in a church in Sweden.

Lagerlöf's speech 'Home and State'

The most prestigious of the public events took place on the Tuesday evening at the Opera. The following day, an article in English appeared on the front page of the daily, *Dagens Nyheter*:

> It is 8 o'clock. The beautiful Opera Hall is full; more than a thousand women and several scores of men have assembled to hear the best speakers of the I.W.S. Alliance. At 8 ¼ the curtain is raised. On the beautifully decorated scene, surrounded with palm trees and flowers, we see familiar faces—the pride and glory of our Alliance: Mrs Chapman Catt, our 'uncrowned queen'—looking as majestic and handsome as ever … the famous authoress—Selma Lagerlöf—the pride of Sweden. … The whole audience rose to its feet and enthusiastically greeted Selma Lagerlöf when she was introduced by the president. (Mirovitch 1911)

The writer of this report was a delegate, Mrs Zenéide Mirovitch, who added in a footnote: 'Her [Lagerlöf's] speech being read in Swedish so we are, unable to give it.' The 'Home and State' speech was later translated and published in three English versions. The Swedish papers all highlighted Lagerlöf's speech as being the most impressive contribution to the programme, creating an atmosphere of *'andakt'* (reverence) (Anon. 1911b).

Lagerlöf's speech has been analysed by Vivi Edström (2002) and Birgitte Mral (1999), and it is with their analyses as my starting-point that I am going to revisit the speech, situating both the performance and the content of 'Home and State'. Recent analyses of women's rhetorical style have highlighted the significance of the gendered body. As

Carol Mattingly has pointed out, 'clothing and appearance constituted a major component in the ethos women presented, an element taken for granted by men' (2002, 5). When the journalists in Stockholm had the opportunity to listen to some of the world's foremost female public speakers, they showed, not surprisingly, an enormous interest in both dress and delivery. In the US at this time, women had a fairly long tradition of speaking publicly; one organisation, the Women's Christian Temperance Union (WCTU), even had national training schools as early as 1885 (Mattingly 1998, 62–3). Francis Willard, the prominent leader of the WCTU, stressed the importance of presenting a reassuring feminine persona, and gave the advice: 'Womanliness first—afterwards what you will' (65). When, for instance, Cady Stanton started her career as a public speaker, she adopted for a time a type of Turkish trousers introduced by Amelia Bloomer, but by the end of the 1850s she and most other speakers had already abandoned this controversial outfit and returned to a more traditional feminine style (Mattingly 2002, 58).

Lagerlöf had achieved great success with her Nobel speech, in which she had told a story with her father as the central character. She had thus established herself as non-threatening to the conservative gender hierarchy, which consisted on that occasion of the all-male Swedish Academy. The speech at the Opera posed new problems. Who was she addressing? Obviously she did not choose the delegates of the Congress, as the speech was given in Swedish. It must rather be judged as aimed primarily at the domestic press and audience. The delegates had to be content with watching her performance. The satisfaction of having a renowned author in their ranks helped strengthen the construction of a common identity. When the foreign delegates felt the enthusiasm of the Swedish audience, they knew this was adding to the interest in the common cause. As a Swedish media event, Lagerlöf's performance was a triumph, and, like the whole Congress, added goodwill to the struggle for women's rights. The latter was one of the expected outcomes of the international women's gatherings strategically arranged in various countries.

As for the content of the speech, Vivi Edström has pointed out that the Swedish papers and even the women's journals are contradictory, writing that the speech would have a great impact on public opinion, while at the same time failing to discuss its content. Edström writes: 'Her role as "the storyteller" is now so established that people are unable to view "Home and State" as anything other than a piece of elocutionary art. Her fame had disarmed her message—everyone was preoccupied with studying her person and registering her beautiful voice' (2002, 390).[1] Lagerlöf's celebrity and performance had defused her message—but what was her message?

Lagerlöf, I would argue, had been awarded the Nobel Prize largely thanks to the way she had transferred in her novel *Jerusalem* the symbolism attached to the concept of 'the home' to the birthplace, to the nation. By this move, she transcended the unsolved conflicts in actual homes at the time. In the novel, in my reading, the central character Ingmar Ingmarsson has to learn a new way of becoming a 'real man'; and the story is thus in line with the agenda of the early women's movement to change male behaviour. This message was probably not recognised by all readers. Instead it was the ways in which Lagerlöf succeeded in harmonising conflicts, in particular class conflicts, and elevating Nature and man to mythical levels, that won acclaim. When she made work the meaning of life in *Jerusalem*, work took on the proportions of a rite, becoming the central means of self-identification—for men. Stressing, as Lagerlöf did, the importance of men's work, the novel could appeal both to the men in the emerging labour movement as well to industrialists. *Jerusalem* was indeed an immediate success (Stenberg 1995).

Women's work is almost invisible in *Jerusalem,* but it is the focus of 'Home and State'. According to Mral's analysis of the speech, Lagerlöf has taken on

> the gently ironic mask of a deeply uncertain suffragette who considers a number of well-known arguments for women's suffrage—only to reject them as invalid. She uses, that is, a sort of self-opposing rhetoric. Apparently quite at a loss, she gropes after some way of justifying women's suffrage—and thereby happens to discover all the relevant arguments for it. The means that she employs here are rhetorical questions (which she hesitantly puts to herself), profound emotion, metaphor, and Biblical associations. (Mral 1999, 168)[2]

Mral also describes Lagerlöf's attitude as 'non-aggressive' and 'non-threatening'.

Among the arguments in favour of votes for women that the speaker dismisses is the fact that women were a growing part of the workforce. Lagerlöf clearly describes the problems women met on entering working life with regard to both social and economic discrimination. By raising the subject of unfair wages and the ridicule and harassment women often encountered, Lagerlöf is taking a radical position. She compares women leaving their homes to emigration. At this time, tens of thousands of Swedes were leaving for America, and this emigration was much debated. In Lagerlöf's opinion it was not only the hope of a better income that drove the emigrants to leave their old country: she also views emigration as a law of Nature, and states that as long as there is a patch of untilled land, there will be settlers. She ascribes a similar 'law of Nature' to the process of women entering the workforce: 'Woman shall perhaps once show that when she advanced into the man's field of work, she too wished to cultivate wildernesses and deserts' (Lagerlöf 1911e, 13).[3] At the end of the speech she addresses women directly: 'You have to get in everywhere, you have to be at hand everywhere, if the state is eventually to be as loved as a home.'[4]

Opening her speech, Lagerlöf, looking for something that would legitimise giving women the vote, calls to mind paintings of the faces of old women. In one scene she places herself in front of a picture by Rembrandt of an old woman with a wrinkled face. Lagerlöf asks the woman on the canvas why she has lived. And, including the audience, she provides the reply: 'We read the answer in her gentle and kind smile: "All I did was to make a good home."'[5] In a subsequent scene, Lagerlöf conjures up women from their graves who give the same answer. What women have done, 'generation upon generation', is fundamental to culture:

> we have tamed those among the wild animals that the home needed, among the plants on the earth we have chosen the cereals, the trees bearing fruit, the sweetest berries, and the most beautiful flowers. We have furnished and decorated our homes, we have devised its customs, we have created the art of upbringing, comfort, courtesy, the happy, pleasant manner.[6]

The dignified life in these good homes is presented in a language influenced by the Bible, and the parable of the Prodigal Son is used to illustrate the fact that everyone deserves equal treatment. The home is also explicitly referred to as 'a place to lay up our ancestors' traditions and songs'.[7] Lagerlöf thus opens up for memories that are not part of traditional history, including previously silenced voices.

The speaker, then, using pathos and parallel questions, compares man's foremost accomplishment, the state, to the qualities of the home. Men have failed to build a state, a community where all are respected and safe. Why? They have refused to rely on the help of women. Lagerlöf points to the fact that she has never said that women have managed their homes on their own, and underlines that women are no more perfect than men. She then ends with a plea for co-operation: 'The small masterpiece, the home, was our creation, with the help of men. The big masterpiece, the good state, shall be formed by man the day he takes woman as his helper in earnest.'[8]

When Lagerlöf opens up new domains of activity to women there are aspects of her argumentation that should be brought into focus. Firstly, she mentions women as mothers only in passing. Secondly, she gives women's work the same existential role that she had assigned to men's work in her novel *Jerusalem*. Indeed, the qualities ascribed to the good home, Ingmarsgården (Ingmar Farm), in *Jerusalem*, are attributed to women in 'Home and State'. Thirdly, in *Jerusalem* Lagerlöf uses Nature and, as a means of counterpoint, creates a mythical, symbolic perspective, endowing men with cosmic or elemental proportions, and transforming the individual into the universal (Lagerroth 1958, 71). In 'Home and State', by referring to one of Rembrandt's portraits and evoking generations of women, she lends women's work an eternal, almost mythical significance.

The claims Lagerlöf makes for the role of women in politics in 1911 can be compared to the bold ideas she held after her début with *Gösta Berlings saga* (*Gösta Berling's Saga*) in 1891. For a long time, her intention was to write women into history, a project which later became *Drottningar i Kungahälla* (*The Queens of Kungahälla*). In another project, it would seem that she was planning to compare the views of women in pagan religions with those in Christian religion. Some interesting short stories exist, but the grand design was left unfinished (Stenberg 2001, 268–86). Lagerlöf's political writings—her three suffragist speeches in 1911, 1917, and 1919, the last of these to celebrate the fact that Swedish women had obtained the vote—can be understood as a return to her early radical intentions. But how unique was Lagerlöf's argumentation in 'Home and State'? How did her rhetorical style compare with that of the leaders of the suffragist movement?

Argumentation within the women's movement

Karlyn Kohrs Campbell considers Elizabeth Cady Stanton (1816–1902), the main philosopher of the American women's movement, as its chief publicist and greatest speaker (1989b, 41). Cady Stanton was one of the authors of the Declaration of Sentiments adopted at the Seneca Falls Convention in 1848, where she also made the first speech of her long career. Similar conventions held in the following years were part of the process by which participants began to share an understanding of the ideas underlying their cause. During most of the early pre-organisational period, arguments based on justice, drawn from natural rights philosophy, dominated as they did in Cady Stanton's first speech. Another line of argument, based on expediency and dominating in the 1870s, presumed women to be different from men, and maintained that their influence would be beneficial both for politics and domestic concerns. In the home, women would, for example, be better mothers if educated. Arguments about beneficial influence could be understood as more 'feminine', in that they appeared unselfish and presupposed 'true womanhood' (Campbell 1989a, 14–16). Almost all of the leading advocates of women's rights mixed arguments based on natural rights and on benefits.

When, in 1911, Lagerlöf led with arguments that echoed the benefits approach, these were not very different from Cady Stanton's use of benefits in her 1848 speech. Cady Stanton had referred to great women of the past, especially Joan of Arc who had come to the rescue of the French army:

> She had a full faith in herself and inspired all those who saw her with the same. Let us cultivate like faith, like enthusiasm, and we, too, shall impress all who see and hear us with the same confidence we ourselves feel in our final success. ... 'Voices' were the visitors and advisers of Joan of Arc. Do not 'voices' come to us daily from the haunts of poverty, sorrow, degradation and despair, already too long unheeded. Now is the time for the women of this country, if they would save our free institutions, to defend the right, to buckle on the armour that can best resist the keenest weapons of the enemy—contempt and ridicule. (Stanton 1989, 68, 69)

The image is dramatic, highlighting the courage women needed to carry out a task where men had failed. Cady Stanton foresaw that 'contempt and ridicule' would meet the women dedicating themselves to women's rights, thus making the project a heroic 'moral crusade' (1989, 63). The argument for women's rights as a benefit to the nation and its less fortunate inhabitants resembles Lagerlöf's in 'Home and State', just as Cady Stanton's point about the courage to enter the state and correct the mistakes made by men dovetails with Lagerlöf's, lending women's contributions a heroic dimension. The passage about Joan of Arc appeared at the end of Cady Stanton's long speech. When Lagerlöf chose to focus on just one argument, she used her gift of fictionalisation and what I would call double positioning. At first she takes on the role of an uncertain suffragist, but having thus established a non-threatening persona or narrator, she transforms the position of the speaker. With the support of 'generation upon generation', the voice scrutinising the state develops a perspective from above, adding an almost religious touch. But as the speech ends, the more reassuring persona returns to affirm: 'Alas, we women are no perfect creatures, you men are no more perfect than us.'[9] In her fictional work, Lagerlöf's use of narrators, according to Sven-Arne Bergmann (1997), is unique. In her speech, she strategically employs this skill, to great effect.

At the time when Lagerlöf delivered her speech 'Home and State', the generation following Cady Stanton's had taken over as leaders and speakers in both the American and the international women's movement. They were having to tackle the problem of how to keep the arguments fresh, explain defeats, and meet a more organised opposition. Anna Howard Shaw was considered the best speaker (Campbell 1989b, 433), while Carrie Chapman Catt (1859–1947) was regarded primarily as an eminent organiser (461).

By the turn of the twentieth century, new arguments based on evolutionary theories were widespread. One of the radicals on the right was the Swedish writer and lecturer Ellen Key (1849–1926), a strong advocate of motherhood, who saw the home as part of a woman's sphere, in contrast to a public life that was synonymous with the world of men. As early as 1886, her arguments were dismissed by Lagerlöf's mentor Sophie Adlersparre, and placed among those threatening the progress of women's rights. As Key's international appeal grew nevertheless, women in the Swedish movement sharply opposed her. Tying women to their biological gender, as Key did, was considered a backlash, and her eugenic view of human nature was rejected as deterministic (Stenberg 2009).

A controversial radical on the left was Charlotte Perkins Gilman (1860–1935), whose books *Women and Economics* (1898), *The Home* (1903), and *Human Work* (1904) were hotly debated. The message she delivers in *The Home*, translated into Swedish in 1907, is that the family home of the day had not evolved in relation to other social institutions and must be changed. Eugenics is an important foundation for the social improvements Gilman describes. Like Key, she emphasised women's role with regard to sexual choice, but unlike Key she believed that women must take their place in the public sphere in order to evolve. Gilman opposed Key and judged her views antifeminist and essentialist (Allen 2009, 175–81). Gilman was so influenced by gynocentric theories, for instance those of Johann Jakob Bachofen (*Das Mutterrecht*, 1861; *Mother Right*) and Friedrich Engels (*Der Ursprung der Familie, des Privateigenthums und des Staats*, 1884; *The Origin of the Family, Private Property, and the State*) that she developed a new type of 'Reform Darwinism' (Määttä 1997, 110–33).

The view that women were the inventors of culture was not unique in 1911, but Lagerlöf's use of the perspective in her speech is worth commenting on. In her speech, there is also an idea of evolution that can be compared to Gilman's. A 'law of Nature' drives both emigrants and women to 'cultivate' new, previously untilled areas. Ulla-Britta Lagerroth has described Lagerlöf's view of evolution and the strong influence of Herbert Spencer's philosophy during the 1880s, when Lagerlöf together with her friends in Landskrona engaged in the struggle against poverty. Lagerroth argues that Lagerlöf's social conscience also was prompted by the general strike in Sweden in 1909, and that, drawing on Henry George, she formulated a view of life that runs through all her later writings—a social and ethical programme of an ideal, organic evolution of society (Lagerroth 1963, 125).

Both Lagerroth and Edström contrast Lagerlöf's ideas with Gilman's. I would argue instead that there are interesting similarities. Both use the idea of women as inventors of key areas of culture; both stress the need for women to leave the home to work outside it; both emphasise that evolution legitimises the 'emigration' of women from the home; and both stress a sense of community and communal responsibility. However, there are of course differences, but perhaps not the ones we might expect. Firstly, according to Gilman, women, secluded in the intimate home, have lagged behind men in evolutionary terms, and working life will make them more complete human beings. This is more in line with both Bachofen and Engels, who held that matriarchy at a certain stage was surpassed by patriarchy. In Lagerlöf's text, there is no indication that she believes women to be in any way less developed than men. Secondly, at the end of her book Gilman states her belief in a future in which the home will still consist of a father, mother, and children, 'the undying group' (1903, 347). Nothing is said of the close, heterosexual home as an ideal way of life in Lagerlöf's text. I consider this a silence charged with meaning, implying that Lagerlöf was open to other types of intimate bonds between people. Thirdly, in Gilman's work, one aspect of the eugenic argument is turned against mothers:

> *Who*, in the name of common sense, raises our huge and growing crop of idiots, imbeciles, cripples, defectives, and degenerates, the vicious and the criminal; as well as the vast mass of slow-minded, prejudiced, ordinary people who clog the wheels of progress? (Gilman 1903, 59, original emphasis)

There are close parallels here with texts by Frida Stéenhoff (1865–1945), a Swedish left-wing radical active at much the same time (Stenberg 2009, 201–206). In Lagerlöf's text there is no sign of exclusion. By contrast, she writes: 'There will be punishment—not, however, in order to punish, but to educate. All talents will be needed, but those who do not have any will be as loved as the geniuses.'[10] And in the description of the state's shortcomings, the sought-for qualities of the home are implied:

> Or where is the state, where no children roam around homeless, where no young person is wasted, but all young people are brought up in joy and gentleness, as is their due? … Where is the state, which does not contain foreign nationalities it cannot make happy? Where is the state, which gives everyone the opportunity to lead their own free life, as long as it does not upset the harmony of the whole?[11]

On the surface, Lagerlöf's argumentation, combined with her 'lady-like' performance when delivering her speech, was perfectly acceptable to the vast majority. But on closer scrutiny, there are claims here that differ from both right-wing and left-wing opinions at the time. This is the same strategy, I would argue, that Lagerlöf used in her fiction when she created symbols, using symbolic concepts but changing the content in ways that struck a chord among readers worldwide.

Social movements and their truth-bearers

Social movement literature discusses the cultural spaces opened up for the movements' intellectuals. Movements provide the cultural context for critical intellectuals, who in their turn play a role expressing the collective identity of social movements, functioning as truth-bearers for a specific movement. For theorists of social movements, the work and lives of movement intellectuals, termed 'movement artists' by Peterson (2012), provide the key to understanding the collective identity of the movement.

In the writing of women's history, the importance the early organisers gave to literature, art, music, and drama has often been marginalised. Women's struggle for the vote is one of the earliest examples of how a wide variety of methods were employed at a time when mass mobilisation was used to give groups influence in the wake of the ideas of democracy (see Tickner 1987). As in the case of Lagerlöf's speech, the words spoken, and the concepts and ideas conveyed, effected two complementary strategies—inwardly to build a common collective identity, and outwardly to influence public opinion. Lagerlöf embodied the women's suffrage movement.

Art as a cognitive praxis of social movements contributes to the ideas that movements offer, and to their challenges to the existing social and cultural order. While Selma Lagerlöf has long been seen as a star without a constellation (Williams 1997), I would argue that she was a star in the constellation of women's rights, by which she was influenced and to which she later also contributed. Lagerlöf was a truth-bearer for the movement, and her speech in 1911 is one example of the claims to truth expressed by the women's suffrage movement.

What were these claims to truth that challenged the social and political order at the time they were made in 1911? While Lagerlöf's performance and rhetorical style were well within the conventions of 'womanliness' at the turn of the twentieth century, the content of her speech in significant ways was at odds with the prevailing notions of both the family and the responsibility of the state. Lagerlöf only mentioned motherhood in passing, and she was tellingly silent on the heterosexual norm of the good family, which she claimed should be the model of the good state. Lagerlöf, however, was crystal clear as to the good state's moral of inclusiveness. The message of her speech went against the grain of the popular ideology of élitism, articulated on both the left and right, with regard to eugenics. She emphasised the state's intrinsic moral responsibility for all human life. In her vision of the good state, no one would be excluded from its nurturing embrace. The state must give equal protection to the human rights of all its members.

The vision in this political text by Lagerlöf is also found in her literary texts; and this type of ideal community, a welfare society, was in line with the ideas in the early women's movement. The transnational appeal of both Lagerlöf's text and her person can be understood as a real political force—for democratisation and the value of every human being.

Notes

1 'Hennes roll som "sagoförtäljerskan" är nu så etablerad att man inte kan betrakta "Hem och stat" som annat än ett deklamationsnummer. Hennes berömmelse desarmerade hennes budskap—alla var upptagna med att studera hennes person och registrera hennes vackra röst.' Edström (2002, 390). All translations are my own.

2 Where Mral uses 'suffragette' I would argue it should be 'suffragist', for the Swedish activists distanced themselves quite emphatically from any militancy.

3 This and all the following quotations are from Lagerlöf, 'Hem och stat', 1911. 'Kvinnan skall kanske också visa en gång, att då hon trängde in på mannens arbetsområde, ville hon lägga vildmarker och öknar under kulturen'.

4 'Du måste in överallt, du måste finnas till hands överallt, om staten en gång skall kunna bli älskad som ett hem'.

5 'Vi läsa svaret i hennes milda och goda leende: "Jag har ingenting annat gjort än skapat ett gott hem".

6 'vi ha gått ut och tämt dem bland de vilda djuren, som hemmet behövde, vi ha bland markens växter sökt ut sädesslagen, de fruktbärande träden, de välsmakande bären, de skönaste blommorna. Vi ha klätt vårt hem och prytt det, vi ha utarbetat dess seder, vi ha skapat uppfostringskonsten, trevnaden, hövligheten, det glada, behagliga umgängessättet'.

7 'en upplagsplats för fädrens sägner och visor'.

8 'Det lilla mästerverket, hemmet, var vår skapelse med mannens hjälp. Det stora mästerverket, den goda staten, skall skapas av mannen, då han på allvar tar kvinnan till sin hjälpare'.

9 'Ack, vi kvinnor äro inga fullkomliga varelser, ni män äro inte fullkomliga mera än vi'.

10 'Där straffas, men inte för att straffa, utan för att uppfostra. Där finns användning för alla talanger, men den som inga har, kan göra sig lika älskad som den mest snillrike'.

11 'Eller var finns den stat, där inga barn driva omkring hemlösa, där intet ungt människoämne förfares, utan alla unga bli fostrade i glädje och med saktmod, som barnens rätt är? …Var finns den stat, som inte hyser inom sig främmande folkslag, som den inte kan lyckliggöra? Var den stat, som ger alla tillfälle att leva sitt eget fria liv, så länge de inte störa harmonien i det hela?'.

II
READERS, PERFORMANCE, CONSTRUCTIONS

Illus. 1. Selma Lagerlöf advertising the throat lozenge Läkerol, *Vecko Journalen* 45 (1925).

CHAPTER 4

Sectional portal

'I have a feeling that I am becoming an institution, a non-being, ... some kind of trademark, given how many people are trying to use me to do business', Selma Lagerlöf wrote in July 1907 to her assistant and close friend Valborg Olander (quoted in Wägner 1943, 55, original emphasis).[1] At the time, Lagerlöf was still writing the second volume of *Nils Holgersson*, and had not yet entered the period that Vivi Edström has labelled 'the golden years' (2002, 362), from the nationwide celebrations of her fiftieth birthday in 1908 to the Nobel Prize in 1909 and on to her election, as the first woman ever, to the Swedish Academy in 1914.[2]

Lagerlöf quickly became a celebrity, the concept defined by P. David Marshall as 'a *system* for valorizing meaning and communication', with the power of celebrity status 'providing distinctions and definitions of success' within a specific domain, and also conferring on the celebrity 'a certain discursive power' (Marshall 1997, x, original emphasis). As Marshall has pointed out, the historical emergence of 'the celebrity sign' coincides with the rise of the 'audience as social category'; it is significant, moreover, 'that both are integrated intimately with the development of consumer capitalist culture' (61). Lagerlöf's career as a writer coincided with processes of modernisation that helped transform media and communications, created new audiences, and enabled members of the general public, including growing numbers of visitors from abroad, to travel to Mårbacka as 'celebrity tourists'. For her part, Lagerlöf simultaneously used the interaction with the audiences who read her books, flocked to her public readings, viewed films based on her texts, and pored over interviews and photos of her and her homes in Falun and at Mårbacka, as opportunities to construct her celebrity persona. As is clear from the essays that follow, it was very much a two-way process.

The large collection of correspondence, more than 42,000 letters, in the Lagerlöf archive in the National Library of Sweden in Stockholm, provides exceptional opportunities to find out who Lagerlöf's readers were, how they viewed her work, and how they perceived her persona. The essay by Jenny Bergenmar and Maria Karlsson is part of a research project about a section of this correspondence, encompassing 10,000 letters that have been digitised and categorised by their keywords. Drawing on work by Robert Darnton, Michel de Certeau, Jonathan Rose, and others, Bergenmar and Karlsson highlight the prominence of Lagerlöf as a 'biographical legend' and the great variations with regard to the readings of her texts, but also the constructions by many letter writers of the celebrity persona and her work in close relation to their own situations.

Anna Bohlin's essay reads *Mårbacka*, the first volume in the trilogy widely held to be autobiographical (1922–32), with a focus on the role of the auctioning of Mårbacka in 1888 as fundamental to the myth about Lagerlöf's authorship. The prominence in the text of the buildings at Mårbacka thus becomes an exploration of the auction, with Bohlin relating the motif to the extensive reconstruction of the main building taking place as Lagerlöf was writing, but also, on the basis of theoretical material from among others Mary Poovey on the late nineteenth-century novel, problematising the relationship between monetary value and moral and aesthetic value. While *Mårbacka*, on this reading, foregrounds the importance of rejecting the market economy, the commercial success of the volume, as Bohlin points out, enabled Lagerlöf to reinforce her position as a celebrity and, indeed, a commodity.

The essay by Git Claesson Pipping and Tom Olsson complements the other two essays in this section by exploring perceptions of Lagerlöf at meetings either at home or in public contexts. Demonstrating that interpretations of these types of encounter, usually as reported by journalists but in one case as recorded in a private diary, require multiple theoretical approaches, Claesson Pipping and Olsson here draw on Sara Ahmed's work to investigate how emotions, negative as well as positive, work in gendered politics. Spanning a number of encounters, beginning with the occasion of Lagerlöf's fiftieth birthday in 1908 and including her visit to Finland in 1912, where she was fêted like a queen, Claesson Pipping and Olsson pinpoint a range of views on Lagerlöf's celebrity persona, including significant differences between women's and men's perceptions.

Notes

1 *'Jag har en känsla av att jag håller på att bli en institution, något väsenlöst ... något slags firmamärke, så många människor söker göra affärer genom mig'*.
2 'De gyllene åren'.

CHAPTER 5

The reader in history and letters to the author

The case of Selma Lagerlöf and her audience

Jenny Bergenmar & Maria Karlsson

The most common source of information about reading in the past consists of documents written by professional readers. Authors, critics, and scholars conveniently leave behind not only traces of their reading, but complete, articulate statements and interpretations. A good example of this is the reception of Selma Lagerlöf's *œuvre*. Much has been written about how her work was received by reviewers, researchers, colleagues, the popular press, friends, and family. But how, where, and why ordinary people read and used her texts over the years is virtually unknown. This essay is about these people, or rather about the appearances they make in the many thousands of extant letters to Lagerlöf that are held by the National Library of Sweden.[1] The collection of letters will be described, and the theoretical and methodological issues to be faced when dealing with this kind of material will be discussed. Given the lack of sources useful for understanding the reader in history, the letters to Lagerlöf present an extraordinary opportunity to answer a number of questions about reading in the past.

An imagined reader in theory, an actual reader in history

In literary studies there has been no lack of interest in reading. Ever since the theories of reader response in the 1960s, the questions about how reading is, has been, and ought to be done have continued to capture the interest of researchers. However, assumptions about reader response in literary studies have often been based on imaginary readers who, due to, say, the narrative traits of the text, have been supposed to respond to it in certain ways. Literary critics, as Robert Darnton has put it, 'sometimes seem to assume that seventeenth-century Englishmen read Milton and Bunyan as if they were twentieth-century college professors' (2001, 174). In other words, the imagined reader often resembles the interpreter: educated, sophisticated, and distanced. Few everyday readers would recognise the responses constructed on this basis.

There are, however, more adequate ways of obtaining information about actual readers.[2] One approach is ethnographically oriented and common within cultural studies, such as Janice Radway's groundbreaking investigation into women's reading of romances (Radway 1987). More recently, empirical studies of reading in a cognitive perspective have gained prominence (Miall 2006). Studies of reading online is another growing field of investigation. Blogs, book circles, different kinds of online chat, interactive writing—all these spaces provide excellent sources for studying real reading today (Darnton 2009).

Needless to say, the scholar wanting to interview readers is restricted to interviewing her or his contemporaries. To track down historical responses from actual readers one has to use other kinds of material as well as different methods. Studies of everyday reading in the past are mainly performed within the still expanding discipline of history of the book, where the most common sources have been library statistics, sales figures and means of distribution, and reading lists for schools and other institutions. Less statistically oriented ways to gain information have also been used: the depiction of reading in literature or in art for instance, or the opinions of editors at publishing houses (Flint 1993; Radway 1997). Another approach is to study evidence of reading from people's private lives as manifested in diaries, autobiographies, and, not least, letters. A breakthrough for the latter was Robert Darnton's analysis of letters to Rousseau (1984). Since his study, the unique possibilities of reconstructing experiences of reading on the basis of similar sources have been pointed out, but such investigations remain rare. 'If the experience of the great mass of readers lies beyond the range of historical research, historians should be able to capture something of what reading meant for the few persons who left a record of it', Darnton writes (2001, 171).

However, in the case of Lagerlöf, many records exist. The National Library of Sweden holds more than 42,000 letters to the author. They were written by friends, family, and colleagues, but most of them came from the general public. An audience of impressive size manifests itself in the material, and does so over a period of fifty years, 1891–1940. The letters represent a cross section of society. Men and women of all ages, from all social strata, of many nationalities, from the country and the city, wrote to Lagerlöf. Their letters concern all kinds of things, reading included. The collection offers an opportunity to gain access to both micro- and macro-analytical levels of the history of reading. The single letter tells us how individuals expressed their own reading experience, while in the collection patterns appear which can help us reconstruct contexts of reading in a more general sense.

The general public, unattractive—and attractive

There are many reasons for the heterogeneity of the letter writers. One of them is the popularity of Lagerlöf, and the fact that her works were exceptionally widely spread is another. Most of her works were available in cheap editions and serialised versions, in libraries, schools, broadcasts on Swedish radio, films, dramas, and even opera adaptations. Other factors were the high literacy rate in Western Europe (Wittman 2003, 288; Lyons 2003, 313–15); the habit of writing letters; the notion of celebrity authors as approachable; and practical details such as postage rates and mail delivery services.

Whether the size of the collection of letters in the National Library of Sweden is unique or not is hard to tell, but it is unusual for letters to authors from the general public to have been preserved. Despite this, the letters have remained neglected, with the letters from friends, family, and the famous instead occupying the centre ground, as in many other cases. Selections of Lagerlöf's own letters have been edited and published, as has some of the correspondence with her friends (Toijer-Nilsson 1992, 2006; Carlsson 2009, 2010). The letters from the general public to Selma Lagerlöf belong to the same collection as the letters from well-known senders, and consequently there is no detective work underlying our effort to shed light on them. The letters are glued into binders in alphabetical order. Although indeed visible, the letters from the public have been unattractive both to Lagerlöf scholars and to those working in literary studies more generally. When referred to, they have been used to illustrate the burden they constituted for Lagerlöf: all those demands, all that begging. But an investigation into 'beggars' letters' reveals subject matter of interest to several disciplines today, for they contain short autobiographies, responses to Lagerlöf's media image, and, sometimes, explicit experiences of reading her work.

About one-third of the letters from the Swedish general public concern financial aid, which means that there is a wide range of other letters. People wrote about all kinds of things—from spiritual issues to the humdrum of their lives. Lagerlöf was often asked for advice: what school to choose, where to move, even what stocks to buy. Matters to do with morality, religion, upbringing, and politics were discussed, as were issues in which Lagerlöf was involved, such as education, the peace movement, and the women's movement. Lagerlöf received advice on what to read, and was provided with memoirs and anecdotes supposed to be of use in her writing. Beginners often asked her to read their attempts at writing literary texts. She received many letters from readers admiring her work, but when readers felt she had got something wrong in her writing or expressed an opinion not commonly shared, they did not hesitate to complain. Gifts such as handicrafts, dried flowers, works of art, and poems were often enclosed. Autograph hunters were numerous. Many of those writing to Lagerlöf wanted to visit her at home. Unemployed people asked for work, and some wanted access to her intellectual network.

The letters form a narrative of a Sweden far from the modern welfare state, yet on its way towards it. All the themes of modernity are represented: urbanisation, the restructuring of labour, technological advances, the mixture of hope and doubt. The letters convey the experiences of two world wars, and of women becoming voters and positioning themselves in the labour market. The collection reveals the extent to which letter writers from the working class believed in the importance of getting an education and improving their character. Their letters tell us about the breakthroughs of electricity, the motor car, radio broadcasting, and the cinema. Social norms change, and so do the ways in which Lagerlöf is addressed. And throughout this long, many-faceted, and polyphonous story, runs, more or less explicitly, the one about the significance of the author and of reading.

This overview illustrates just how multilayered and complex this type of material is. It highlights the necessity of a broad historical approach, but also the importance of the material as a source of information about individual experiences of the past. The letters contain stories about how, why, when, where, and by whom reading was performed, about how literature was used, and what literature and Lagerlöf meant

47

to the letter writers, but the letters also tell a more general story about the significance of these matters in society at large. The collection of letters to Lagerlöf opens perspectives both on history through reading and on a history of reading.

The growing focus on empirical evidence of reading in history will no doubt increase the use of archives such as Lagerlöf's, and more letters will be 'found'. But it takes a while before shifts in academic perspectives reach cultural heritage institutions. Still, the work of great authors, such as their manuscripts, gain most attention from archives, libraries, and elsewhere, as well as from editors of scholarly editions; letters to the author are not considered part of the *œuvre*, and they are rarely taken into account when, for instance, the reception of a work is described.

This lack of attention exemplifies what Michel de Certeau has called 'the ideology of consumption-as-receptable', a view of reading that distinguishes those who 'produce'—authors, educators, critics—from those who do not—for example readers in history (Certeau 2011, 132). The lack of interest in reader has also been called into question by Janice Radway: 'Are readers always already subordinated writers, incapable finally of writing their *own* experience because inevitably, they come *after* the privileged process of production?' (2008, 339, original emphasis). The readers writing to Lagerlöf do not conform to the notion of the unproductive, subordinate consumer. They demonstrate both agency and creativity, ranging from the active choice of writing to the author, to the expressions and discussions of their reading and their expectations of the author.

The collection of letters has in fact received a certain amount of attention over the years. Lagerlöf herself wanted it to be saved. According to her will, it was to be deposited in the National Library of Sweden. She knew that some letters contained sensitive information. Her will thus stipulated for the collection to be 'sealed on condition that it will not be opened until fifty (50) years after my death, and that letters from senders still alive by then are not to be made available to the public or to scholars until the letter writers have passed away'.[3] It may be that Lagerlöf primarily wanted to protect people she knew, but the letters from others are often of a strikingly private nature. Lagerlöf herself seems to have discerned the historical value of truly 'authentic expressions'. In a letter to her friend Elise Malmros, dated 26 August 1916, she writes:

I enjoyed what you wrote about the old diaries you are collecting and going through. Like you, I believe that it is very good to do an excerpt of the most interesting parts for ordinary people. But still, do not burn what you have been going through. The truly authentic expressions are of great value to someone who is interested in them. Every line of old handwriting with the simplest content can be of interest from a philological perspective. It is so much fun to get to know not only *what* earlier generations thought of, but also *how* they thought and expressed themselves. (Carlsson 2010, 524, original emphasis)[4]

Selma Lagerlöf died on 16 March 1940. Shortly after her death, the head of the Department of Manuscripts at the National Library, Nils Afzelius, went to the author's famous home to sort through her literary estate. The task was huge: 'Everywhere there welled forth new piles, new boxes, new packing cases of letters that had to be put in order, new manuscripts'.[5]

Due to the quantity of the material, Afzelius reduced it before it was catalogued. Where there were several letters from one sender, these were kept together. The correspondence from Sweden and Germany from 'unknown people' and autograph hunters, along with 'uninteresting letters celebrating birthdays, the Nobel Prize, or the election to the Swedish Academy' were separated from the rest of the letters. Obviously Afzelius thought that the letters from the general public were interesting, but he did not consider all of them equally important. He also arranged the letters in categories such as 'Swedish', 'German', 'Of great value', 'Family and friends', 'Seeking help', 'Needing help', 'Commissions'. It is clear that Afzelius was aware of the role of the letters as documents of social history: 'The collection as a whole is extremely interesting, not only because it provides insights into the author as a private benefactor. In addition it conveys some idea of the social and economic conditions both in Sweden and other countries (most of all in Germany) during a long period of time'.[6]

In 1950 the letters were handed over to the National Library, and the collection was made available to the general public forty years later. Afzelius' classifications were abandoned, and the entire collection was classified and catalogued in alphabetical order according to the surnames of the senders and chronologically for individual senders. The several thousand letters from children have not yet been classified.

The letters were mounted using Japanese tissue paper in special binders, the letters being glued onto the *recto* side of the binder page. More than 42,000 letters from over 17,000 letter writers filled 225 binders. The letter sheets were numbered in pencil from 1 onwards in each binder. Next to the name in the introductory index, the letter writer's country of origin was noted along with the number of the first sheet of the letter.

When the collection was made available on 16 March 1990, the Head of the Department of Manuscripts pointed out that this was the biggest collection of letters in the National Library and, probably, in the whole country. The National Librarian at the time, Birgit Antonsson, emphasised that it was rare for a letter collection to be so thoroughly organised when it was made available.[7] Clearly, by then, the letter collection was one of the most attractive in the library. Today the card catalogue has been digitised and you can search for the sender by surname as well as by country of origin.[8] However, the letters have not yet been digitised.

Approaching thousands of letters

So how, then, did we handle the problem of size? Our first delimitation was to focus on letters from the general public. We ignored professional letters, letters from family and friends, and financial transactions (for instance, invoices). This left us with about half the collection. However, 20,000 letters were still too many, considering reasonable time constraints. We therefore decided to concentrate on the Swedish general public. This decision was hard. The foreign letters are many and highly interesting, but they ought to be studied and interpreted within their specific cultural contexts of, for instance, translations and the book market. It has been estimated that one letter in four is from abroad. These letters are mainly from Germany, but also from the other Nordic countries, the US, and elsewhere. This last cut left us with approximately 10,000 letters. Now, this is a substantial amount too, and the best way to make this part of the collection available was to digitise it. The National Library did not have the resources to photograph them for us, but we were allowed to make our own digital working copies. Dirty, stained letters with poor handwriting could thus be enlarged and deciphered. In most cases it is also possible to draw conclusions about the quality of the paper used and about the specific writing tools.

The average letter is two to three pages long, but some can run to

En riktig
författarhustru
Selma Lagerlöf
skriver till Valborg Olander

Albert Bonniers Förlag

Illus. 1. The cover of *En riktig författarhustru* ('A Real Author's Wife'), Lagerlöf's letters to Valborg Olander, edited by Ying Toijer-Nilsson (2006).

twenty. The one-page letter is often a postcard, usually a grey-green cardboard card that had a reduced postage rate. We know that the letters were read and often answered because of the comments written on them, for example: 'Do not answer', 'Give 10 crowns', 'Say no', 'Kind words', 'Is this man crazy?'.[9] These notes are in Lagerlöf's hand and were intended for her partner Valborg Olander. Olander was deeply involved in Lagerlöf's authorship and handled most of the mail. Occasionally Lagerlöf answered herself, as proved by the fact that some senders refer to a previous letter by her or even enclose it.

The letters vary in legibility. Usually they are written in ink or in lead pencil. About a hundred were type-written. Sometimes the sheets are thin and fragile, the language poor, the writing tool has left stains, and the text fills every inch of the paper. Other letters are eloquent, with elegant handwriting and stationery with a letterhead. All these material factors speak, for they are markers of class and education, place, date, age, and health. Therefore it is important both to see the original letters and to work with them in digitised form.

The digitised letters are stored in a database suited to big collections with regard to functions such as viewing and classification as well as keywords. Our keywording is generous and includes the date when the letter was written, mentions of Lagerlöf's works, the letter writer's occupation, the city where the letter writer lived or wrote from, certain themes, the gender of the writer, and a number of reasons for writing. The choice of keywords is oriented towards the aims of the project, but it has also been based on the concrete contents and the materiality of the letters so that the database can be used for other purposes too.

For our decisions on keywording we were greatly helped by a pilot study. We went through letters sent to Lagerlöf in 1915, when her career reached its peak and the year after the publication of *Kejsarn av Portugallien* (*The Emperor of Portugallia*). While some of the results were expected, others were not, but, most importantly, we got some indication of what people wrote about, who wrote, and to what extent the letters included readers' responses to Lagerlöf's texts. Thanks to the pilot study, we were able to start constructing the database at an early stage, since many essential keywords had already been determined.

Reading the work, reading the author

As sources for reception studies, the letters require an empirical and historical approach. We have drawn on studies such as Jonathan Rose's *The Intellectual Life of the British Working Classes* (2001), about autodidact British readers. Rose used library records, educational archives, and early social surveys to track down the previously unexplored reading subject. His most important source consisted of autobiographical documents, such as memoirs and diaries. The autobiographical character of his corpus is similar to ours, since experiences of reading found in the letters to Lagerlöf are embedded, in most cases, in a life narrative. The difference in comparison with the memoirs and diaries used by Rose is of course that the letters have a specific addressee.

The challenges we have encountered when using letters to an author as a source for reception studies are largely theoretical issues to do with how to define 'a reading of a text' and 'a reader' in this context, and how to draw the line between responses to a text by Lagerlöf, and responses to her as a public figure linked to certain expectations.

Starting with the question of how to limit and specify the category of readership, this source material poses immediate problems. If 'a reader' is a person who clearly states that she or he has read at least something by Lagerlöf, what about those people who express admiration in general terms, or gratitude for all that Lagerlöf has given to the Swedish people? Variations of these tropes are more common than thorough accounts of how a certain text has been perceived, used, or interpreted. The most convenient way of dealing with this would be to single out letters which provide more articulate and specific reactions to one or more works. But this would lead to a significant loss of information. Letters in which an opinion of Lagerlöf's *œuvre* is only vaguely stated often conform to patterns that would be weakened within a more limited corpus. Sometimes people wrote to Lagerlöf for the sole purpose of setting out their opinions and feelings about one of her texts. But typically, this was just one of a number of reasons for writing to her.

The mixture of responses can be seen in many letters written in connection with various celebrations and anniversaries. The following example is from Lagerlöf's seventy-fifth birthday in 1933. The writer, a fairly young man, begins by saying that the press coverage of the birthday has made him long to speak to Lagerlöf personally, even though he is just a poor man from Lapland in the far north of Sweden. He expresses gratitude to Lagerlöf 'for the timeless treasures you have given us thanks to your books'.[10] But he does not go further into her work. Instead he asks if Lagerlöf can help him and his wife with some money, since they are on the verge of losing his parental home. The letter is handwritten on cheap, ruled paper. Although the letter writer has quite a wide vocabulary, he misspells some words, and there is no reason to doubt that he is indeed a person far from the cultural élite, lacking both economic means and education.

This letter does not contain much specific information on how Lagerlöf's work was received, but it informs us that this man had an understanding of what Lagerlöf represented as an author. The letter

Illus. 2. Letter to Selma Lagerlöf from Carl Grahn, Arvidsjaur, 18 Nov. 1933. Asking for money to save one's home is a common theme in the letters, and this letter writer has even included a photo.

refers to the celebratory coverage of her in the press as a person of both wealth and power, but also a woman with the goodness and charitableness of a mother. It is a representative response to this particular image of Lagerlöf.

Another typical aspect of the Lapland letter is that it was written to ask for money to save a home. This was one of the main reasons for letter writers to ask for financial help. The writers of some letters explicitly refer to the well-known fact that Lagerlöf herself had lost her home but eventually bought it back. The theme recurs in her works, and from the letter writer's perspective, Lagerlöf would undoubtedly understand his plight. It is also common for letter writers to add a spiritual dimension to their reasons for contacting Lagerlöf. The man from Lapland explains that he started thinking about getting in touch with Lagerlöf when he read about her in the press. But the final step of the process of putting pen to paper was beyond his control: 'I don't know why—but perhaps the Lord who guides the hearts of people made it happen'.[11] Here, the spiritual component is the will of God. In other letters, the senders claim that they have met the author in a dream, and that she herself has made them write.

If a 'reader' were to be defined in this context as someone who clearly states that he or she has read a text by Lagerlöf, this definition would exclude the Lapland letter. However, the letter provides a reading of the *image* of Lagerlöf, based on information in the press. In this case, the context of that information was Lagerlöf's seventy-fifth birthday, but in the collection of letters there are similar statements derived from a number of other sources such as her work, biographical facts, interviews, and rumours. Against this background, it is not surprising that the letter from Lapland hovers around many of the same themes as letters explicitly referring to readings of one or more of Lagerlöf's works, for example the lost home, the divine and spiritual inspiration to write, the empathetic and generous author. If the Lapland letter were not to be included in our study, the frequency of these themes would not be made visible. Consequently we have decided to work with an inclusive definition of 'reader'.

In other words, a 'reader' can be a person who refers explicitly to readings of one or more of Lagerlöf's works, but also someone referring to one of the paratexts of the authorship. Gérard Genette's concept of paratext is often defined as the written material in a book that is additional to the primary narrative. Although the concept in most cases is used in this sense, closely connected to the text itself, Genette's own definition allows for other applications. When describing the different kinds of paratexts, Genette states that 'the public epitext' is 'any paratextual element not materially appended to the text within the same volume, but circulating, as it were, freely, in a virtually limitless physical and social space' (1987, 334). Using this definition, it seems the concept of epitext would indeed cover the many different responses to Lagerlöf: comments on, for example, her life, background and experiences, or, put another way, 'paratextual scraps', to be found in the quite limitless scope of the epitext (346). Still, the examples of different epitexts provided by Genette are 'overwhelmingly authorial', with exception of the publisher's epitext and the semi-official allographical epitext, which lie beyond the declared responsibility of the author (351). The media epitext, let us say a radio interview, is clearly part of the public reception of Lagerlöf's *œuvre*. But other mediations, over which the author herself had no influence, are also important. It is impossible to decide whether a reader experienced a certain narrative by Lagerlöf as an expression of compassion and love because the author was publicly portrayed in these terms, or because Lagerlöf herself constructed this kind of public persona, or if the notion was the result of values expressed in Lagerlöf's books.

Seen in this light, the concept of paratext could be of use to distinguish different notions of Lagerlöf and her work expressed by the letter writers, but the fact that the concept privileges the literary text and the author makes it insufficient for our purposes. The common themes in the letters to Lagerlöf from the general public may well be products of different epitexts, for example interviews with the author, public readings, speeches, and so on, which may or may not also be connected to certain works. But it is obvious that the notions about Lagerlöf displayed in the letters also originate from other sources.

The letters to the author provide evidence of common knowledge of certain aspects of Lagerlöf's biography, which, inevitably, the writers were drawing on when responding to her *œuvre*, the home that was lost and regained being one conspicuous example. This was an event in Lagerlöf's life (to which we have no direct access), an event in her autobiography, a motif in her fiction, and a recurring narrative told by others in biographies, critical texts, and in the press. Using a concept from Boris Thomashevsky, it can be labelled as part of the 'biographical legend' about Lagerlöf. For Thomashevsky, the biographical legend is deliberately constructed from autobiographical documents such as letters and diaries, which are used to filter the understanding of the author's work (1978, 47–55). Lagerlöf clearly used different events from her life to create a narrative supporting certain readings of her work. One such narrative—or legend—is that the origin of her literary work was the childhood stories told by her aunt Nana. This narrative locates the source of her creativity to a specific place, the province of Värmland; a specific time, the past; and a specific situation, the oral transmission of stories. This particular narrative is a powerful part of the biographical legend, and still has considerable impact on the general opinion of Lagerlöf.

If the biographical legend of Lagerlöf can be described as a compilation of canonised anecdotal knowledge of her life, the separate events could be described as 'biographemes'. In Roland Barthes's use of the

Illus. 3. Selma Lagerlöf's biography was well known to her readers, including the loss of her childhood home Mårbacka. The photo shows Mårbacka following Lagerlöf's initial rebuilding in 1908.

term, it represents a separate event and its representations, as part of a larger biographical sequence (Barthes 1994, 109–110; Barthes 1997, 8–9; Claésson 2002, 13–20). Against this background, it becomes clear that those who wrote to Lagerlöf were addressing not only an actual person, they were also addressing 'Selma Lagerlöf': a construct made up of various canonised and commonly spread biographemes, with some of them deriving from authorial discourses, and others not.

The majority of the letters concern the biographical legend rather than any actual reading of any one of Lagerlöf's texts. In other words, the mediated image of the author is more prominent than are her works. Lagerlöf had a specific public ethos, but at the same time her public roles were quite diverse. Apart from the fact that she was a member of the Swedish Academy, she was also a literary celebrity, the owner of a sizeable farm, and the employer of a considerable number of people, and in addition she was politically involved in the peace movement and the women's movement, a contributor to modern teaching, and so on. In the letters, these various aspects of the public 'Selma Lagerlöf' are evoked for different purposes, while the letters also highlight a range of Lagerlöf's texts and the writers' interpretations of them.

However, there are also letters referring to one or more of Lager-löf's narratives in their manifestations as text, film, theatre, opera, or radio broadcasts. While a reading of the biographical legend cannot be separated from a reading of the texts, it is nevertheless interesting to single out the letters that express explicit opinions of the narratives, in order to see how the writers describe their use of and reactions to certain works, and to compare these reactions to those of professional readers. Although the latter aspect is our main focus, letters such as the Lapland one are part of an important context, making visible what kinds of biographemes permeated her reception as a whole.

The letter writers' readings of the texts, as they become apparent in the letters, vary greatly, and Certeau's description has proved to be apt: 'He [the reader] invents in texts something different from what they [the authors] "intended". He combines their fragments and creates something unknown in the space organized by their capacity for allowing an indefinite plurality of meanings' (2011, 133). This may give the impression that the reader is not only active, but also free to create his or her own patterns of significance in the text; simultaneously though, the individual reader is part of a hierarchical social system that makes her or him conform, to different degrees, to authorised meanings that are assigned to texts or authorships by a cultural élite. The interpretations of texts that are perceived as 'true' are articulated by people in positions of social power, for example reviewers, teachers, and journalists (Certeau, 134).

The potentially determining power of this social system is obvious in many letters. Certain articles about Lagerlöf generate direct reactions from the readers. It is very common for those asking for money to refer to articles in periodicals in which she has been described as generous to the poor. This is particularly striking in the mail Lagerlöf received following an article in the weekly magazine *Husmodern* ('The Housewife') in 1935, which had included examples of Lagerlöf sending money to people who wrote to her. The article resulted in a significantly larger number of letters from people asking for money.

The authorised meanings are also visible in letters from educated readers. Some of these, who elaborate on their readings and explicitly respond to aesthetic aspects of the texts, present interpretations remarkably similar to those of the critics. On the other hand, there are also examples of readings against these 'truths', with, for example, several letter writers finding the critical reviews of Lagerlöf's first novel unfair.

Different levels of reception often seem to be at work. The letters from less privileged readers, who might not have read reviews, often conform to the biographical legend that predominates in the press. But at the same time these readers view the celebrated author (and her works) in a direct, and often intimate, relation to their own lives, thoughts, and experiences, as we saw in the letter from Lapland. In these cases, the readings are totally unpredictable and indeed give proof of the wide range of usage and interpretations of literary texts that existed—or could be imagined—during this period of time.

Notes

1 This essay is part of the project 'Reading Lagerlöf. Letters from the Swedish Public to Selma Lagerlöf, 1891–1940', funded by Riksbankens Jubileumsfond (the Swedish Foundation for the Humanities and Social Sciences).

2 In education studies, interviews and inquiries have been carried out to explore responses to literary texts within a framework of learning (see Langer 1994, 2010); for the reception of Lagerlöf in a school context, see Molloy 2011.

3 National Library of Sweden, Dept. of Manuscripts, L1:335:1:2, Selma Lagerlöf's will (copy), 1932, § 9: 'förseglas med villkor att de icke får öppnas förrän femtio (50) år efter min död och att brev, som härröra från då levande personer, allt fortfarande icke få hållas tillgängliga för allmänheten och forskare, förrän brevskrivaren avlidit'.

4 'Det var roligt det du skrev om de gamla dagböckerna, som du samlar och genomgår. Jag tror också, att det är mycket bra, att göra ett utdrag av det intressantaste för vanligt folk. Men bränn ändå inte det, som du har genomgått. De verkliga äkta uttrycken ha ett sådant stort värde för den, som intresserar sig för dylikt. Varje rad gammal skrift av det allra enklaste innehåll kan ha sitt intresse ur språkhistorisk synpunkt. Det är så roligt att få veta inte blott *vad* de som levat före oss tänkte på, utan också *hur* de tänkte och uttryckte sig.'

5 National Library of Sweden, *Stiftelsen Föremålsvård*, ÄA F 1B, 225, Nils Afzelius, 'P.M. för ordnandet av Selma Lagerlöf's brevsamling'.

6 Ibid.

7 National Library of Sweden 225, Dossier *Stiftelsen Föremålsvård*, ÄA F 1B, 1989–90, Birgit Antonsson.

8 Department of the National Archives, <http://www.svar.ra.se>, National database SVAR.

9 'Svara inte', 'Ge 10 kronor', 'Säg nej', 'Goda ord', 'Är denne man galen?'.

10 Letter to Selma Lagerlöf from Carl Grahn, Arvidsjaur, 18 Nov. 1933. 'den odödliga rikedom ni skänkt genom ert skriftställarskap'.

11 Letter to Selma Lagerlöf from Carl Grahn, Arvidsjaur, 18 Nov. 1933. 'Jag vet ej varför—men kanske den Högste som styr menniskors hjärtan och tankar som vattenbäckar styrde det så.'

CHAPTER 6

Mårbacka: Larders, cow-houses, and other spiritual matters

Anna Bohlin

Large auction of fine furniture and household utensils etc.

By public auction, to be held at Mårbacka in the parish of Östra Emtervik on Monday and Tuesday 18th and 19th of June this year, starting on the first day at 3 p.m., the second day at 10 a.m., Mrs Louise Lagerlöf, on account of moving from the district, will dispose of most of her valuable domestic chattels and some of the farm property, namely: gold, about 800 *ort* [about 36 kg] of table silver, German silver, all types of utensils for the kitchen and pantry for a large household. Furniture: 1 good-quality piano, drawing-room furniture consisting of a sofa with armchairs, tables, chairs, sofas, mirrors, chandeliers, feather and horsehair beds, a sizeable highly valuable stock of linen including 25 table-cloths with table napkins. 1 coach with harness, carts, and sledges etc.

For trustworthy and well-known buyers, payment may be postponed until 1st September, others pay cash.

Skäggeberg, Sunne, 4 June 1888. PER JANSSON, instructed auctioneer

This announcement heralded the future celebrity of the writer Selma Lagerlöf—if we are to believe the myth about her authorship. The auction of the farm in Mårbacka in 1888 deprived Lagerlöf not only of a beloved childhood home, but also of the beautiful landscape of Värmland, leaving her to her work as a schoolteacher in the south of Sweden by the sea, far from the hills, the forests, the lakes and the people of her childhood province. But this loss also provided the necessary distance for the transformation of her experiences into text, for the

landscape and the stories of her childhood to become the body of her work.
At least this is the myth Lagerlöf herself
wanted us believe, and literary critics
and scholars have obliged.

The autobiographical trilogy consisting of *Mårbacka* (1922), *Ett barns
memoarer* (1930, *Memories of My Childhood*) and *Dagbok för Selma Ottilia
Lovisa Lagerlöf* (1932, *The Diary of
Selma Lagerlöf*), elaborates on the myth
of her authorship, a myth that Lagerlöf
had previously presented to the general
public and to which the critics were
to return again and again. In 1922,
when the first part of the trilogy was
published, Lagerlöf was a Nobel Laureate and a member of the Swedish
Academy, and she had also bought

Stor Auktion
å finare möbler och husgerådssaker m. m.

Genom offentlig auktion som förrättas
på Mårbacka i Östra Emterviks socken
Måndagen och Tisdagen den 18 och 19
innevarande Juni, med början förstadadagen kl. 3 e. m., andra dagen kl. 10
f. m., låter Fru Louise Lagerlöf, med
anledning af afflyttning från orten, för-
sälja större delen af sitt värdefulla inre
lösörebo och en del af det yttre neml.:
guld, cirka 800 ort bordssilfver, nysilfver,
alla möjliga i ett större hushåll förekom-
mande husgerådssaker för kök och ser-
veringsrum. Möbler hvaraf: 1 bättre
piano, förmaksmöbel af soffa med stolar,
bord, stolar, soffor, speglar, ljuskronor
sängkläder af fjäder och tagel, ett större
ytterst dyrbart linneförråd hvaraf 25 st.
borddukar med servietter. 1 droska med
selar, kärror och slädar m. m.
Vederhäftige kände inropare erhålla
betalningsanstånd till den 1 nästa September, andra betala kontant.
Skäggeberg, Sunne den 4 Juni 1888.
PER JANSSON,
anmodad auktionsförrättare.

Illus. 1. Announcement of the
auction at Mårbacka, *Nya Werm-
landstidningen*, 4 June 1888.

back her childhood home as well as the land. With *Mårbacka* she took
control over the making of herself as a female genius. The success was
immediate, with the five editions published in 1922–3 selling 30,000
copies, a very high figure for this type of book in Sweden at the time.
Surprisingly, Lagerlöf's trilogy of memoirs has not received much
attention from scholars, and those who have studied the autobiography have often focused on the third part, *The Diary of Selma Lagerlöf*.
When *Mårbacka* is mentioned, it is primarily because it foreshadows
the latter parts. As Jenny Bergenmar points out, the very first chapter,
'Strömstadsresan' ('The Strömstad Journey') introduces several of the
problems that will be explored throughout the biography (1998, 3).
Mårbacka is indeed part of a bigger project, but the audience at the
time read *Mårbacka* separately (the following parts appearing nearly
a decade later). It was well received and was Lagerlöf's greatest success since *Liljecronas hem* (1911, *Liliecrona's Home*) (Nordlund 2005,
170–7). Whether the trilogy should be read as an autobiography or
as fiction is of course an open question. There are strong arguments
for categorising the trilogy as fiction, especially since the first-person
narrative in *The Diary of Selma Lagerlöf* was presented, and to a certain
extent received, as an authentic childhood diary, although it is clear

that it was written by the author in her seventies. However, since my aim is to study how Lagerlöf crafted the myth of her authorship, I will regard *Mårbacka* in accordance with how the book was presented: as an autobiography. For the same reason, I will use 'the narrator' and 'Lagerlöf' interchangeably in this essay.

According to the myth, the auction is only one of several conditions for Lagerlöf's authorship (I will return to the others later). But it is the most important one since it accounts for the turning of life into literature, even if, while all the other formative conditions for her authorship are present in the autobiographical trilogy, the auction, conspicuously, is not. Yet in *Mårbacka* there is a curious obsession with the houses and buildings on the farm, not just the manor house but also the larder on stilts, the cow-house, the farm-hands' quarters, and the loom-house. Indeed, an entire section of the book is devoted to 'Gamla byggnader och gamla människor' ('Old houses and old people'), and every single hut is the object of the most detailed attention.

In my reading, the obsession with buildings is an exploration of the auction, with the entire book in fact exploring the complex of problems associated with the auction. The name of the manor is also the title of the book, and since the audience at the time was familiar with Lagerlöf's biography, the readers would interpret the title as being synonymous with the home that was lost and regained. Furthermore, the emphasis on the buildings makes for a nostalgic eulogy for the traditional, self-subsistent household, simultaneously formulating a warning against the market economy. These ideological values are expressed in reflections on, and stories connected to, the buildings and other objects, such as chairs and cutlery—exactly the sort of things that were specified in the announcement of the auction. The announcement transformed the objects that constituted Lagerlöf's childhood home into commodities by publicly listing them for sale. This essay examines the meaning of objects in *Mårbacka* against the backdrop of the auction, along with the importance attributed to this specific moment in the myth about Lagerlöf's authorship. However, before embarking on my analysis of how the motif of the auction is elaborated in *Mårbacka*, I will explore the origins of this myth in Lagerlöf's own account of the creation of her first novel. It had to be crafted with great care, as women and fame were supposed to be contradictory terms. Brenda R. Weber shows in *Women and Literary Celebrity in the Nineteenth Century* how the fame of female authors had to be portrayed as 'a matter of fate rather than of design, of rewards passively received rather than conquests actively pursued' (2012, 4). When, as early as 1902, Lagerlöf told her growing audience the marvellous story of how an impoverished girl from a provincial Swedish home became the author of *Gösta Berlings saga* (*Gösta Berling's Saga*), she opted for a very clever approach.

The myth about Lagerlöf's authorship

For the volume *När vi började* ('When We Began'), the Swedish Society of Authors invited a number of writers to tell the stories of how they started to write. Lagerlöf's contribution, 'En saga om en saga' ('A Tale about a Tale'), was to have a major impact on the representation of Lagerlöf up to the present day (Nordlund 2005, 95, 108). The device Lagerlöf used was to make her first novel, *Gösta Berling's Saga*, the subject of its own making: the story wants to be told, to enter the world, and the story itself forces Lagerlöf to write. The auctioning of Mårbacka is thus portrayed as the result of the agency of the story—an elegant solution to the tensions inherent in female celebrity. Lagerlöf is finally persuaded to write by an overwhelming emotion, planned by the story, who muses: 'I need once more to send this blind person a great desire that opens her eyes.'[1] I will quote it at length to show the crucial importance Lagerlöf attributes to this moment of loss:

> This desire arose because the farm where she had grown up was sold, and she went to see her childhood home for the last time, before strangers took possession of it.

> And the evening before she left the place, perhaps never to return, she decided in all humility to write the book in her own way to the best of her poor ability. It would not be the masterpiece she had hoped for. It would be a book people would laugh at, but she would write it all the same. Write it for herself to save what could still be saved of her home: the dear old stories, the happy peace of carefree days, and the beautiful landscape with the long lake and the hills with their tints of blue.[2]

The great desire opening Lagerlöf's eyes is the result of the auction; and a century later these lines still echo in the presentations of Lagerlöf's authorship. For example, the article on Lagerlöf in *Nordisk kvinnolit-teraturhistoria* (*History of Nordic women's literature*) reads the auction as 'the broken idyll' that will allow Lagerlöf to attain a 'world of memories' and 'a primitive language that permeates everything she will write'.[3] The announcement of the auction is even reprinted in the children's cartoon *Little Selma from Mårbacka* by Maria Bergström and Emily Ryan (2008).

However, in the quotation above, Lagerlöf is very precise as to the outcome of the auction, and there are several points to be made about how this decisive moment is portrayed. What eventually makes her write the novel is the decision to write it 'in her own way', but this decision is explained both as an act of reverence and as an act of rescue. The aim of the novel is to save the home that harbours the stories, the 'carefree days', 'the beautiful landscape'. Even so, this rescue plan is also a sacrifice. To give up the hope of writing a novel that would be appreciated by many is 'the heaviest sacrifice she had yet experienced'.[4] In 'A Tale about a Tale', Lagerlöf explains her authorship in terms of a sacrifice for Mårbacka, her work rescuing what remains of a home stripped of houses and possessions by encapsulating the stories, the happiness that used to prevail at Mårbacka, and the surrounding landscape. The pursuit of celebrity is rebuked, and celebrity is instead presented as a reward for the sacrifice for the family home, a most fitting act for a woman mixing passive submission with agency (Weber 2012, 112).

But before I turn to the issue of how the book *Mårbacka* reinvests the houses, buildings, and objects with meaning, I briefly want to pay some attention to the other three formative conditions for authorship in the Lagerlöf myth. The first is emphasised in the quotation above: it is the storytelling peculiar to the province of Värmland.

Lagerlöf's account in 'A Tale about a Tale' suggests that the loss of control of the buildings encourages her to let go of her control of the story. The story will then be free to act on its own, which is of course the fundamental device of the tale, effectively masking the active authorship. The text starts with the story being anxious to enter the world, because it is already practically complete: many people have contributed, and the only thing still missing is some kind of compositional principle holding it together. In one of Lagerlöf's early short stories, written not long after the publication of *Gösta Berling's Saga* but not published until after her death, she stages herself as a transmitter of an ancient tradition in a similar way: 'I know not how to compose, only how to narrate; not how to explain, only how to receive'.[5] This myth has subsequently been used to belittle her work from a misogynist perspective (the most spectacular example in recent years being Delblanc 1999, 395). But the notion of Lagerlöf's authorship as the vehicle of a tradition was initially the result of Lagerlöf dramatising herself and her genius, and featuring her aunt and her grandmother as her most important informants.

The second formative condition for authorship, according to the Lagerlöf myth, is the disabled hip. In 'A Tale about a Tale' the desire to become an author is fostered by a 'sickness' that prevents the future writer from running around with the other children and leaves her to concentrate on books and stories. In the autobiographical trilogy, this part of the myth has been considerably expanded, as has been noted by several scholars (Bergenmar 1998; Forsås-Scott 1998; Larsson 1996). Lagerlöf's hip makes her unfit for ordinary womanhood, setting her apart and giving her the freedom to praise women's work without having to perform it herself. Indeed, her hip makes her acquainted with the inexplicable magic of life and the wonders of the world.

The third formative condition for authorship, according to the myth, is, famously, her father and his carefree attitude to life. Lagerlöf returns to the importance of her father on many occasions, 'A Tale about a Tale' being one of these, but the most notable example is her speech on accepting the Nobel Prize for Literature in 1909. Vivi Edström (2002, 481) claims that if there is a central character in *Mårbacka*, it is the father, while Lisbeth Larsson (1996, 237–40) has pointed out that although his presence in the first part of the autobiography is overwhelming, it fades in the subsequent parts.

The storytelling, the hip, and the father—these, according to Lagerlöf, were the conditions that enabled an impoverished girl from a distant Swedish province to become a world-famous author. However, they would not have resulted in literature had it not been for the auction. Lena Kåreland (2008) has shown that Lagerlöf, from the beginning of her career, was fully aware of the strategies needed to gain maximum prestige in the literary field. But at the same time, she did not want to lose the appreciation of her big audience and the money to be gained from large circulation figures. She refused to choose between the Nobel Prize and readers of every social class; and in due course her very person became an institution in the Swedish public sphere (Claesson Pipping & Olsson 2010, 36–40). In *Celebrity and Power*, P. David Marshall analyses celebrity as a commodity that achieves its formative social power precisely in descriptions of the celebrity's private life in relation to her/his public life (1997, 51–61). The Lagerlöf myth of authorship was an integral part of her public persona and a lucrative part, too: *Mårbacka* was quickly translated into a number of languages and became highly appreciated abroad, not least in the US (Edström 2002, 477). Lagerlöf's publisher urged her to continue her autobiography, since it would be sure to sell well (Nordlund 2005, 177). Helena Forsås-Scott (1998) has analysed how Lagerlöf plays with the public image of herself in the third part of the autobiography; and in *Mårbacka* Lagerlöf does much the same thing with the myth of authorship already established in 'A Tale about a Tale' twenty years previously. As she presents her own unparallelled success story to the world in thousands of copies, she redistributes practically all of the characters from her novels, placing them in the setting familiar from her childhood, and recounts the roles of the storytelling, the hip, the father, and—if not the auction—all those buildings at Mårbacka.

The literary function of the buildings

In a letter to Sophie Elkan, Lagerlöf pointed out that the old buildings provided her with an excellent structure for the book, suggesting that the buildings were convenient for instigating narratives (quoted in Edström 2002, 478). Elin Wägner in her biography of Lagerlöf (1943) has high-lighted the fact that the construction of the new manor house at Mårbacka was taking place as Lagerlöf was writing the first part of her autobiog-raphy. In real life, the old house was disappearing while reappearing in the text—the simultaneous deconstruction and reconstruction of buildings, so to speak. Wägner, however, develops a different argument, contrast-ing the traditional ways of living and building to the modern ways. She points to the use of dynamite around Mårbacka to lay water mains as an example of one of the luxuries of modernity, running water, requiring the destruction of tradition (1943, 174–5). In *Mårbacka*, tradition is recalled and, indeed, praised while, in real life, it is being destroyed. In fact, Lagerlöf's ancestral manor house was being concealed within a new and more grand façade in the Swedish Caroline style, associated with 'masculinity and military achievements', and this has inspired Katarina Bonnevier, a specialist in architecture, to invent the term 'cross-cladding', meaning 'architectural cross-dressing' (2007, 277, 400).

However, the traditional buildings in the autobiography are not fact

SELMA LAGERLÖF

○
MÅRBACKA

STOCKHOLM

ALBERT BONNIERS FÖRLAG

Illus. 2. The cover of *Mårbacka* (1922). Illustration by
Eigil Schwab.

but fiction. Jan Brunius (1963) informs us that in many respects, Lagerlöf's accounts of these buildings are incorrect. One of the buildings that
Lagerlöf claims to be many centuries old had in fact been built at the
beginning of the nineteenth century; and the old byre that Lagerlöf's
father wants to tear down in order to build a new one certainly was not
in such a poor condition as claimed in *Mårbacka*. Furthermore, the new
cow-house, Lieutenant Lagerlöf's most imprudent yet favourite project,
taking many years to complete and costing him an enormous amount
of money if we are to believe the account in *Mårbacka*, was apparently built rapidly and without any problems, according to Brunius. He

draws the conclusion that the construction of the cow-house has been dramatised as a means of highlighting the relationship between Selma Lagerlöf's parents (10, 68–71). Vivi Edström has added another aspect to the function of the buildings as indicators of values: she has noted the solemnity with which the larder and its content are described, and concludes that Lagerlöf elevates women's work and the habits of the household to matters of the highest importance (2002, 478). Lagerlöf foregrounds the women's sphere and women's work in particular, as she does throughout her *œuvre*; but in *Mårbacka* the central role of the buildings themselves suggests another starting-point for our interpretation, namely the auction.

The importance of the auction reverberates in Lagerlöf's novels: inherited objects reformulated as commodities in the market economy invariably mark a crucial loss of meaning with far-reaching implications. In *Gösta Berling's Saga,* the auction is portrayed by means of a symbolism with sexual overtones, with the furniture symbolising Marianne Sinclaire's tarnished body. Following Marianne's flirtation with Gösta Berling, her father no longer controls her body: it has lost its family value and is therefore for sale to the highest bidder. In *Jerusalem* (1901–1902), the auction at the farm belonging to the Ingmarsson family illustrates the fact that the objects for sale define a family history covering many generations: the identity of the family is for sale. In *Charlotte Löwensköld* (1925) something even more valuable is at stake: the goods to be sold are children at an auction of inmates at the poorhouse (Bohlin 2008, 244–7). Thomas Steinfeld has drawn attention to the fact that real estate became a ubiquitous theme in nineteenth-century literature in the wake of the new market economy, *Gösta Berling's Saga* being one of his examples of a 'manifesto for real estate' (2011; see also Steinfeld and Lamm 2006, 111–15).[6] The auction is a special case of this interest in the new economic understanding of real estate. The auction transforms identifying objects and people into commodities, and it is a recurring motif throughout Lagerlöf's work. In *Mårbacka*, however, the motif of the auction has been reversed.

The market economy rejected

In the first chapter of *Mårbacka*, Lagerlöf's father subdues a whole community and brings it under the spell of his good humour, but he starts by challenging and conquering the market economy. His weapon is joy. On the journey to Strömstad, the Lagerlöf family reaches the city of Gothenburg and amuse themselves with window-shopping. Lieutenant Lagerlöf is not content with admiring the goods in the windows and enters a goldsmith's shop, asking to see everything for sale, despite the fact that he is not going to buy anything. The assistants are puzzled and embarrassed by his request, and the Lieutenant's wife and sister would prefer to vanish from the face of the earth. However, the goldsmith is taken in by Lieutenant Lagerlöf's personality and agrees to show all the items in the shop to the party.

This act of admiring the commodities without intending to buy, of enjoying the objects without spending money, has the effect of transforming them. Mrs Lagerlöf recognises the design of the silver spoons from her parental home; in other words, she recognises the commodity as an object to be inherited, as a matter of identification. This transformation of the commodities also brings out other qualities in the objects. The primary interest is not the price, since the objects are not to be bought, but the beauty and, of equal importance, the labour invested in each object, and the purpose of it: 'The shop-keeper and his wife took up each article and showed it to the strangers, explaining its workmanship and what it was for' (Lagerlöf 1924, 32).[7] The commodities are reintegrated into people's lives, regaining their appearance as articles to use. In the presentation of the articles, the production and the consumption of them, never leave the sphere of human needs to enter the market. The goldsmith summarises the visit when the family leaves the shop: 'One has to do something for one's own pleasure, now and then, though one does stand in a shop' (Lagerlöf 1924, 33).[8] *Nöje* ('pleasure') is the code in Lagerlöf's work for everything that makes life worthwhile. Clearly, objects can be a great source of pleasure, but this requires the exchange value to be replaced by the use value. The visit to the goldsmith's shop is an example of an auction in reverse.

The distinction between use value and exchange value has its origin in the late eighteenth-century political economy as part of a new analysis of commodities promoted by the credit economy (Guillory 1993, 315). In Marx's definition, a commodity is an object that satisfies human needs; its use value is decided by the properties of the object and realised in consumption. Further, it is an expression of labour and the material substance of wealth. The object is the material carrier of the exchange value, which is quantitative and relative: the object appears as equivalent to something else and is therefore reducible to, for example, money (Marx 1997, 31–6). Mary Poovey (2008) discusses the treatment of economic and financial themes in eighteenth- and nineteenth-century literature, highlighting the fact that during the second half of the nineteenth century, monetary values were increasingly portrayed as inferior to moral values. She connects this fact to the conception of aesthetic value as opposed to economic value: originally formulated in relation to the economic concept of value, the Romantic concept of aesthetic value had forgotten its origin and refused to acknowledge literature as a commodity. This idea of aesthetic value, she argues, is reflected in fiction, which features moral values as more powerful than market values (287–91, 373–83). In *Mårbacka*, the moral values are connected to the traditional, self-subsistent household.

The larder on stilts, in which all the food for a whole year was stored, is introduced at the beginning of the housekeeper's story. The housekeeper, however, got married. For a farm to lose the woman who held sway over the larder was a major blow; but the housekeeper had met a carpenter and moved to the nearby town. She was looking forward to the prospect of 'an easy life' (Lagerlöf 1924, 113), where everything could be bought in the market instead of being produced at home.[9] But the carpenter turned out to be a heavy drinker, and the housekeeper was longing day and night to return to Mårbacka, deciding, after just a fortnight, to do so. She left the immoral market economy and returned to the self-subsistent household, to the larder.

The larder itself is the very materialisation of the self-subsistent household; indeed, the very description of the building is an example of an allegory. The building is extremely simple, the narrator explains, underlining that despite the fact that it can be pretty inconvenient, it has never been modernised:

> [It stood on quite low posts and was entirely without ornamentation.] The door was so low one had to stoop to enter; but the lock and key were conspicuously large and strong. [They could have fitted a prison.] (Lagerlöf 1924, 110)[10]

A prison might not seem a very cheerful place, but the narrator quickly explains that the farmers kept their most precious property in the larder. It may look like a prison, but it is actually a treasure house. And you need to bend down, to be humble, to enter: the self-subsistent household fosters morality. The larder may not look attractive, but it contains all you need to survive, and it does not lure people into self-destructive behaviour, such as drinking.

Objects are also used to identify the protagonists in the autobiography. The children of Mårbacka are introduced by means of items that belong to them, namely three wooden chairs, which they 'regarded as their greatest treasure' (Lagerlöf 1924, 12).[11] These chairs are ever so useful, the narrator explains, but there is a special reason for the owners' love for them: 'Why the children prized those chairs so highly could be seen at a glance by turning them upside down. On the bottom of each chair was the portrait of its owner' (Lagerlöf 1924, 13).[12] In the biography, these portraits identify and name the children for the first time. Lagerlöf underlines that the children consider these chairs, 'which bore their likenesses' (1924, 13), to be their own property in a special sense, and will not part with them under any circumstances.[13] The owner identifies the property and the property identifies the owner.

Throughout this section Lagerlöf uses a vocabulary drawn from economics, which Velma Swanston Howard has retained in her translation: 'skatt' ('treasure'), 'satte ... värde på' ('prized'), 'egendom' ('property')— but this vocabulary is used mockingly. The value expressed in economic terms is exactly what *cannot* be translated into money. This property can never be prized by anyone else as a treasure, it has no equivalent, and thus it can never be traded, because these chairs are marked with the owners themselves. Their uniqueness makes them non-exchangeable.

The very act of constructing buildings, Lagerlöf tells us, is an act prompted by love and, indeed, desire. The original buildings on the plot of land were probably put up by a young couple, longing to live together but too poor to do so without moving out into the wilderness that this part of Värmland represented at the time. A building protects love as well as life and property, with the biggest, significantly, being the building for the animals. These values still apply when Lagerlöf's father plans to build the new cow-house: 'It would only be lacking a spire to look like a church' (Lagerlöf 1924, 169).[14] The cow-house is a sacred building, not only because it contains the most important property, the livestock, but above all because it is a token of love. Everyone is against Lieutenant Lagerlöf's project, including his wife, and as a result he is unable to complete it. Mrs Lagerlöf, however, understands that he will lose his self-respect if the cow-house is not finished, and so decides to support him: 'A great light broke in upon him. If the wife and he were of one mind there were no difficulties ahead. The foundation was solid and the walls rose firmly' (Lagerlöf 1924, 174).[15] This is the outcome of love in *Mårbacka*: it constructs a building.

The meaning of matter in *Mårbacka* is joy, survival, labour, honesty, identity, and love. The buildings, the chairs, and the cutlery in the announcement of the auction reappear as use value and become the material carriers, not of an exchange value, but of moral values that, by definition, cannot be exchanged. Maria Karlsson (2002) has shown that truth, in Lagerlöf's novels, is sought after by means of a 'melodramatic imagination', which is succinctly defined in relation to the autobiography by Joachim Schiedermair: 'Morality can no longer be regarded as metaphysical, i.e. externally guaranteed, but must itself lie concealed in the physical, i.e. in the world' (2005, 33). Morality and truth in *Mårbacka* are indeed to be found in that which is physical, even in larders and cow-houses, but my analysis has added a prerequisite to the investment of meaning in matter: the market economy has to be rejected. In accordance with the idea of aesthetic value, the market value is discarded and the status of literature as a commodity is concealed. The sales of 30,000 copies of *Mårbacka*, a book that told the story of the importance of rejecting the market economy, enabled Lagerlöf to finish the grand reconstruction of Mårbacka. The reversed auction, in other words, became a successful feature of her trademark, of the celebrity Selma Lagerlöf as a commodity.

Notes

1 'Jag måste åter skicka denna förblindade människa en stor längtan, som öppnar hennes ögon' (Lagerlöf 1902b, 148).

2 'Denna längtan kom öfver henne på så sätt, att gården, där hon vuxit upp, blef såld, och hon kom att se sitt barndomshem sista gången, innan främlingar skulle taga det i besittning.

Och kvällen innan hon reste därifrån för att kanske aldrig mer återse denna plats, beslöt hon i all ödmjukhet att skrifva boken på sitt eget sätt och efter egen fattig förmåga. Det skulle ej bli något mästerverk, såsom hon hoppats. Det skulle bli en bok, som människor skulle komma att skratta åt, men hon skulle ändå skrifva den. Skrifva den för sig själf för att rädda åt sig hvad hon ännu kunde rädda af det hemmet: de kära gamla historierna, de sorglösa dagarnas glada frid och det vackra landskapet med den långa sjön och de blåskiftande kullarna' (Lagerlöf 1902b, 148–9).

3 'Det är med den krossade idyllen som bakgrund som Lagerlöf kan börja forma sitt språk, sin *Gösta Berlings saga*, 1891 och det är genom själva bristen i tillvaron som hon kan stiga ned till sin värld av minnen och hämta upp ett urspråk som genomsyrar allt hon kommer att skriva och som kan uppfattas av hög och låg, av barn och vuxna' (Torpe 1996, 113–14).

4 'den tyngsta uppoffring hon ännu pröfvat' (Lagerlöf 1902b, 149).

5 'jag kan ej dikta blott berätta, ej förklara blott mottaga' (Lagerlöf 1949, 752).

6 'Selma Lagerlöfs 'Gösta Berlings saga' (1891) ... är [ju också] ett manifest för fasta egendomen' (Steinfeld 2011, 22).

7 'Men guldsmeden och hans fru, de togo upp varje särskild sak, visade den för de främmande och talade om vad den skulle brukas till och hur den var tillverkad' (Lagerlöf 1922, 37).

8 'Något kan man väl få lov att göra för sitt nöjes skull, fast man står i butik' (Lagerlöf 1922, 38–9).

9 'Hon skulle få leva ett så lätt liv, skulle varken behöva baka eller brygga, hon skulle bara gå på torget och köpa hem allt, som behövdes till hushållet' (Lagerlöf 1922, 142).

10 'Den stod på ganska låga stolpar och var utan all utsmyckning. Dörrn var låg, så att man måste böja sig för att komma in genom den. Men låset och nyckeln voro så mycket större. De kunde ha passat för ett fängelse' (Lagerlöf 1922, 137). The translations of the first and the last sentences of the quotation are mine, since they have been omitted in the published translation.

11 'räknade som sin största skatt' (Lagerlöf 1922, 11).

12 'Men varför barnen satte ett så oerhört värde på stolarna, förstod man först, då man vände dem upp och ner. Då såg man, att på undersidan av varje stol var ett av barnen avmålat' (Lagerlöf 1922, 12).

13 'som voro märkta med deras bilder' (Lagerlöf 1922, 12).

14 'Det var bara ett välvt tak, som fattades, för att den skulle komma att se ut som en kyrka' (Lagerlöf 1922, 212). In Swanston Howard's translation, 'a vaulted ceiling' has become 'a spire' (Lagerlöf 1924, 169).

15 'Och det blev ljust inom honom. Se, om hustrun ville som han, då fanns det ju inga svårigheter mer. Nu låg grunden fast, och murarna reste sig' (Lagerlöf 1922, 220).

CHAPTER 7

In the eyes of the beholder

Du coté de chez Selma Lagerlöf

Git Claesson Pipping & Tom Olsson

Meeting Selma Lagerlöf was an extraordinary event for most people. A number of biographies describe how touched people were, and how they wanted to celebrate the famous author. We have explored how this overwhelming interest, this enchantment with the author, functioned in connection with Lagerlöf's public appearances (Claesson Pipping & Olsson 2010).[1] We found that the accounts convey strong feelings of intimacy, even in the cases of wholly public encounters with Lagerlöf. Developing Lauren Berlant's theories (2008), we have argued that this was because individual emotional experiences of contact with Lagerlöf, resulting from reading her works, were re-enacted when she was seen and heard live on a podium. The reading experience had penetrated the bodies of the readers and touched their hearts. There was something heart-warming about the writer and the person Selma Lagerlöf, and she, too, was touched by the emotional involvement of her audiences. Furthermore, the craving for close emotional contact also led to a desire to touch Lagerlöf physically. We also discerned a degree of male anxiety about the public attention to Lagerlöf, as she and her female audience were perceived has having strong connections with the campaign for female suffrage.

For our 2010 study, our sources were newspaper reports from the encounters with Selma Lagerlöf, but in a second short study (Claesson Pipping & Olsson 2011) we compared and contrasted the accounts of a single meeting in two letters and one diary. In the diary we found something quite different from the other accounts. The writer, the Finland-Swedish Professor Oskar Fredrik Hultman, was introduced to Lagerlöf prior to her speech and was filled with disgust, finding her looking old and sallow and her eyes 'frånstötande'[2]. The term is interesting as today it means 'repugnant', but in those days it could also mean either 'forbidding' or 'dismissive'. The last two could mean that Lagerlöf actively sought to avoid contact, but the first (repugnance) is the most fascinating as it reinforces our earlier finding that Lagerlöf's public appearances could give rise to quite different feelings.

Thus our previous studies show that Lagerlöf's public appearances require multiple theoretical approaches to be fully understood. Berlant's theories focus on the reader's emotions, but we found that theories of emotions in the public sphere could also shed light on the encounters with Selma Lagerlöf (Hendler 2001). Furthermore, we compared our findings to studies of the European idolisation of heroes in the nineteenth century (Riall 2008) and to the attention paid to other Swedish authors during Lagerlöf's lifetime (Nyblom 2008). Since the context was one of public celebrations, we also tested our findings against theories of rituals (Althusser 2008; Collins 2004). Finally, Raymond Williams's concept of the structure of feeling (1977) also proved useful. Together, these theories enabled us to identify symbols and events that exerted an attraction, creating a sense of identification with and belonging to Lagerlöf. But we also found symbols and events that had the opposite effect, creating anxieties and alienation. In this study we will explore this double function of Lagerlöf's public performances, but in another context and within a different theoretical framework: Sara Ahmed's theories on how emotions work in gendered politics.

To us, the physical aspects of the meeting between Lagerlöf and the beholder are the most interesting. The contact zone in this case, Lagerlöf's home, is quite different from a formal gala dinner or a public lecture. In this essay we are going to explore close encounters of this kind. Our study is part of what Eva Österberg (2007) has termed the existentialist trend in research that focuses on the conditions and expressions of the experience of being a person in relation to other persons. How were experiences of meeting Selma Lagerlöf negotiated and communicated?

The term 'contact zone' has been adapted from Ahmed's *The Cultural Politics of Emotion,* in which she develops a model of how feelings of hate, disgust, and repugnance function politically.[3] Her theory is that 'the emotions of hate and fear are shaped by "the contact zone" in which others impress on us, as well as leave their impressions' (Ahmed 2004, 194). In the contact zone, persons or 'objects seem to have us "in their grip", and to be moving towards us in how they impress upon us, an

75

impression that requires us to pull away' (90). The objects or persons are sticky, and the stickiness becomes disgusting because '*what is sticky threatens to stick to us*' (90, original emphasis). In the present study, we focus on the hints of stickiness in accounts of meetings with Lagerlöf, and we will explore the extent to which the form this stickiness takes is dependent on the contact zone and on the gender of the person meeting Lagerlöf.

Ahmed's discussion of sticky objects focuses on the feelings created by and for politics aimed at stopping trends or movements perceived as threatening certain values and ideas. But what about the feelings created by and for politics aimed at changing society? By definition, these feelings cannot focus on disgust or fear, because this would mean experiencing the self as disgusting. [4] Feelings aiming to inspire change must be positive and affirmative. Yet, if Ahmed's theory holds, they must work in the same way as feelings aimed at stopping new political trends since, as she points out, 'desire pulls us towards objects, and open us up to the body of others' (2004, 84). Thus, we will treat both positive and negative feelings generated by meetings with Lagerlöf.

The emotional experience of meeting someone is a bodily experience. It contains a sexual dimension to which desire is central, thus demonstrating that our expansion of Ahmed's theory is not only possible but, indeed, inevitable: her theory can be used to describe positive as well as negative feelings. Also, intimacy calls for reciprocity: it is impossible to be intimate without a relationship. It takes the experience of Lagerlöf being generous, of opening up, for the relationship to arise. Only when the viewer/listener experiences her as present and accessible can she attract him/her in her stickiness.

We have restricted ourselves to contemporary accounts of meetings with Lagerlöf, concentrating in the first part on accounts of meetings with Lagerlöf in her home in Falun. These texts not only describe Lagerlöf, but rely on descriptions of the contact zone to enhance the intimacy of the meeting and the emotional experience.

Du coté de chez Lagerlöf

There are a plethora of texts describing Lagerlöf in her homes in Falun and, later, at Mårbacka, many written by journalists in connection with her birthdays from 1908, the year she was fifty, and onwards. When she turned sixty-five, Lagerlöf herself expected between 30 and

40 journalists from all over the world to want to interview her (Bonnevier 2007, 349).

The texts we use here are from newspapers, magazines, and in one case a radio programme. The writers wished for, and describe, private meetings face to face with Lagerlöf. In their texts these intimate meetings are shared with the readers. Each meeting becomes a close encounter, filled with emotions for the readers, too.

The most common way of achieving a sense of intimacy is by means of a mimetic text in which an 'I' experiences the meeting and provides a blow-by-blow account. An important feature is the author's presence in the story. The credibility of the text—leading to its emotional impact—is dependent on an 'I' experiencing a meeting with Lagerlöf.

A typical article of this kind was written under the pen name 'Yvette'[5] in the Swedish daily *Svenska Dagbladet*,[6] and describes how 'Yvette' walks through the snow to Lagerlöf's house in Falun and knocks on the door (Brunius 1908). As soon as it is opened, a sense of homeliness penetrates the cold, and the text goes on to describe the visitor's sensory impressions of the interior. Comfort is a key point here: the rooms are low-ceilinged and intimate, everything is snug and quiet, and these characteristics make the visit palpably intimate. 'Yvette' assures Lagerlöf that she will not ask many questions since she is aware of Lagerlöf's dislike of journalists' notebooks. Nevertheless, the article includes a long question-and-answer section, obviously constructed with the help of a notebook. The article concludes with an account of 'Yvette' leaving Lagerlöf's home, her impression that of a hostess radiating calm, but also with the potential of being haughtily dismissive.

Obviously, 'Yvette' had been aiming for a proper interview, a standard genre in journalism at the time: long, allegedly verbatim reports of the conversation were meant to convey a sense of authenticity.[7] Selma Lagerlöf's reluctance to be interviewed was emphasised in most articles about her, almost to the extent of becoming a genre requirement. Lagerlöf explained her aversion to interviews by pointing out that she had frequently been misquoted.[8] Being interviewed by 'Yvette', she questioned the veracity of the journalistic text, or, more precisely, the extent to which journalistic practice could achieve authenticity in the sense of being congruent with perceived reality—in other words, the 'truth'.

Nevertheless, the task of the journalist is to make the reader believe in the truthfulness of the story. Therefore the text by 'Yvette', and indeed almost all the articles about visits to Lagerlöf's homes, differ from most newspaper articles of the time in one important respect: they have bylines. The signature announces that the text is the record of the experiences of the subject. The name is a guarantee that the text is authentic.

Against this background, it is all the more remarkable that 'Yvette' breaks the pattern of Lagerlöf interviews (or perhaps, rather, non-interviews). Usually, the journalists restrict themselves to general accounts of what was said. Also, the journalists are normally subservient in tone, conventionally praising Lagerlöf's gentleness and her kindness in receiving them. But 'Yvette' actually uses the word 'förnäm' ('haughty' or 'superior'), which might be positive since it can indicate superior social status, but which, in combination with 'avvisande' ('dismissive'), is definitely not a compliment.

Clearly, this journalist's experience was not altogether pleasant. To apply Ahmed's terminology, something was sticky and repelling, but at the same time something was also sticky and attracting. Ambiguity is not unusual in the descriptions of Lagerlöf; and as we will make clear below, it is part of what makes the emotional impact so strong.

Lagerlöf's home as a contact zone

A visit to someone's home implies a relatively intimate relationship. Lagerlöf made herself accessible by admitting the visitor, and the contact zone became private. As the at-home interviews embedded Lagerlöf in a context that was the opposite of the large public assembly halls, the proximity between her and the journalist made her body all the more fascinating. A number of journalists wrote comparatively intrusive accounts, both of her home and of her home as an extension of her body.

Lagerlöf was deeply aware of the symbolic value of her home as a setting for herself. When she turned fifty, her successful career had made her wealthy, and she had the means to develop her homes into carefully planned contexts for herself. In addition to her childhood home of Mårbacka, in 1907 she bought a house in Falun, initially only living at Mårbacka during the summer. She renovated and redeveloped both houses extensively, and Mårbacka was transformed into a magnificent building recalling the era when Sweden was a great power in the seventeenth century, with distinctive connotations of masculinity and military success (Bonnevier 2007, 263–4). More than a home, Mårbacka became the place to worship Lagerlöf (Nyblom 2008, 24–5).

Although the word 'home' implies privacy, for successful women (and the wives of successful men) the home could be a very public site. The women's magazine *Idun* regularly published illustrated articles on women in their homes, and the magazine *Svenska hem i ord och bilder* ('Swedish homes in words and pictures') was entirely devoted to the subject.[9]

It is worth noticing that Lagerlöf's staging of herself at her home coincided with the first of her birthdays to be marked by a large number of at-home interviews. The large number was partly due to the Swedish tradition of celebrating the fiftieth birthday more than other ones, and partly of course to Lagerlöf's growing fame. Moreover, the at-home interviews coincided with Lagerlöf emphatically developing the notion of the home as a political site. The most famous example is her 'Hem och stat' ('Home and State') speech at the 6th Congress of the International Woman Suffrage Alliance in Stockholm in 1911 (see Lisbeth Stenberg's essay in this volume).

There are two aspects favoured by journalists for creating a sense of proximity to Lagerlöf's body and a sense of intimacy. One is their descriptions of Lagerlöf's eyes and voice, and the other is their descriptions of the feelings created by the interiors of her homes.[10] Thus, in an interview in the daily *Dagens Nyheter* on the occasion of her fiftieth birthday, the journalist Anton Karlgren emphasised Lagerlöf's warmth as expressed in her soft voice. Lagerlöf has 'clear and calm eyes that seize you with a peculiar power, these eyes of a seer'.[11] Another male journalist making the same connection between Lagerlöf's eyes and those of a seer is Ernst Högman who, writing in the women's weekly *Idun*, notes that her grey and blue seer's eyes had the expression of a dreamer, of someone able to see into the future (Högman 1908, 565). As far as we have been able to find, no female visitor described Lagerlöf in this way.

From the beginning, the terms 'siare' or the feminine 'sierska' (seer) were central to the characterisations of Lagerlöf's literary technique—or alleged lack of it (Nordlund 2005, 56, 76, 83, 107). But when Karlgren and Högman use it in their descriptions of Lagerlöf, it becomes a physical trait. Anna Nordlund and other feminist scholars have pointed out that the use of words such as 'sierska' and 'sagoberätterska' ('storyteller'), has the effect of diminishing Lagerlöf's intellectual ability, making her art the result of divine inspiration rather than of painstaking work. Whether the male commentators were aiming to diminish Lagerlöf or not, they turned her into an incomprehensible and slightly dangerous force of Nature. We know how carefully Lagerlöf staged her appearances, and such impressions might actually be the effects of deliberate acts on Lagerlöf's part.

In a radio programme broadcast in 1938, the film director and actor Victor Sjöström recounted his reading of a manuscript for a film in Lagerlöf's home in 1917 (Sjöström 1938). He made a point of the fact that high culture, in other words Lagerlöf and literature, was meeting popular culture, represented by himself and film. But he was flattered by Lagerlöf's apparent attention, especially as he found her home characterised by 'soft, warm comfort'.[12]

Like Karlgren and Högman, Sjöström especially noticed her eyes, but to him they were penetrating rather than clairvoyant: 'From the eyes meeting mine came no cold but a fascinating, calmly scrutinising gaze that made impossible any effort to bluff or put on a performance'.[13] Thus Sjöström is diminished, scrutinised, and stripped of his powers as an actor and director. He becomes a child in front of his teacher, the prototype of female authority, rather than his usual male self. This is quite different from the account by Karlgren who, when he refers to Lagerlöf as a seer, invests her with a power that goes beyond the moment, beyond Karlgren, and to other worlds. The experience may be unsettling, but it is not a threat to Karlgren.

Like many other visitors, Karlgren and Sjöström use the term cosy when describing Lagerlöf's home.[14] Home comfort was associated with conventional femininity at the time, and it would have been almost rude not to describe a woman's home as cosy. Furthermore, the notion of the well-kept home was fundamental to the campaign for female suffrage (Claesson Pipping & Olsson 2010, 63–4; Florin 2006, 236–7). To Lagerlöf, the home was created by women was as remarkable an institution as the state created by men. In 'Home and State', she emphasised that a good home was characterised by—cosiness: 'We [women] have ... created the art of upbringing, comfort, courtesy, the happy, pleasant manner'.[15]

The Finland-Swedish feminist Annie Furuhjelm also visited Lagerlöf's Falun home. She did not find it cosy. On the contrary: she refers to the bedroom as showy, and quotes Lagerlöf as saying that she had a weakness for that which was 'splendid and a touch palatial' ('praktfullt och en smula slottslikt') (Furuhjelm 1933, 459). Where Karlgren found Lagerlöf's femininity not only cosy but also enigmatic, Furuhjelm, on the other hand, perceived Lagerlöf as practical and independent:

Illus. 1. Selma Lagerlöf in her home in Falun. Are her eyes penetrating or farseeing? Whatever their impression, many visitors commented on her eyes. Photo by Birger Nordensten, taken at Christmas 1910.

> Seeing Selma Lagerlöf in her home makes you think of Swedish women at the time when Sweden was a great power, the women who ran their estates with a firm hand. There is plenty of power in her character, and she has a practical mind.[16]

Furuhjelm's comparison is with the women who ran not only their estates but practically everything except the formal government when the men were at war (Sjöberg 2001). On another occasion when Lagerlöf is associated with the era of the Swedish Empire, she was turned into a man. In her speech given at the party thrown by Swedish women to celebrate Lagerlöf's Nobel Prize in 1909, the historian Lydia Wahlström compared Lagerlöf to King Gustavus Adolphus (1594–1632), who successfully led the Swedish forces in the Thirty Years War and died at the Battle of Lützen. However, she modified this masculine and militaristic comparison by also referring to the warmth of Lagerlöf's home.[17]

There is a parallel here with Karlgren and Sjöström demasculinising their accounts of Lagerlöf, making meetings intimate by means of descriptions of her comfortable home, descriptions that—if Furuhjelm is to be believed—were highly questionable, even if the illustrations in an article in *Svenska hem i ord och bilder* indicate both home comforts and grandeur (Nathorst 1918). Bonnevier's study (2007) of Mårbacka's architecture also highlights Lagerlöf's predilection for the grandiose. Obviously, all these references to war and castles challenge the heterosexual norm and the concepts of relations between the sexes, as we shall discuss later.

The podium as a contact zone

The accounts of Lagerlöf in her home are intrinsically intimate because of their setting. But as we have pointed out, the emotional impact of her public appearances, despite the setting, also relies on experiences of intimacy.

Lagerlöf made numerous public speeches, but she mostly preferred to read one of her short stories or from *Nils Holgerssons underbara resa genom Sverige* (*Nils Holgersson's Wonderful Journey through Sweden*) when appearing on the podium, and she had spent a considerable amount of time learning to read aloud (Vinge 2000). Above, we mentioned Professor Hultman, who described Lagerlöf after meeting her and hearing her speak in Helsinki in 1912. Like Karlgren and Sjöström, he refers to her gaze, but instead of being enigmatic it is 'tired and rather forbidding', and she was looking 'sallow and old'.[18]

However, Professor Hultman changed his opinion when he heard Lagerlöf speak. To begin with, he noted her awkwardness and the fact that the lectern was too high for her so that she had to stand beside it. Her clumsiness made her human, and Hultman's description in his diary has traits of intimacy: he noted that she was right in front of him. On hearing her speak, he wrote: 'My perception of her now changed completely … Her presentation was modest, true, and sensitive, her voice sometimes breaking with emotion.'[19] When Lagerlöf is moved and moving she is perceived as accessible, and then intimacy becomes possible.

Lagerlöf's speech at the IWSA Congress in Stockholm in 1911 was a remarkable occasion, given its special dignity and political impact. It was extensively covered by the press, including the daily *Stockholms Dagblad*. Some days after the conference 'Sancho Pansa', in a light-hearted column in the popular *flâneur* tradition, claimed to have seen Lagerlöf in town, which explains the curious title 'Dem man möter' ('People You Meet'). The disposition of the text is as odd as its title. In the opening section, 'Sancho Pansa' describes Lagerlöf's person and posture. Then he describes her delivering her famous speech at the Opera. There is every reason to doubt his claim to have seen her in town, not least because he mentions her grey dress. The drawing illustrating the light-hearted column shows Lagerlöf in the grey dress she wore when delivering her speech, the same dress she had worn when receiving the Nobel Prize in 1909, a ballgown quite unsuitable for a city walk. We will return to his pretence later.

'Sancho Pansa' gave a different picture to Hultman's of Lagerlöf as a performer. While Professor Hultman found her voice weak, to 'Sancho Pansa' her words when she delivered her speech 'Home and State' were 'klangrika' ('resonant') and 'storvulna' ('grandiose'). The listeners were 'små' ('little') women. But not only were the members of the audience reduced in comparison to Lagerlöf. The other female speakers also emerged as smaller. Their speeches are referred to as cheerful and flowing like merry springs, whereas Lagerlöf's speech was like a 'brusande, [tung] vårflod' ('powerful, roaring spring flood'). Her tone was mighty when she preached her 'evangelium' ('gospel').

'Sancho Pansa' also compares Lagerlöf to a granite cliff on the coast, washed by waves, as in Viking days gone by. Firmness is a male virtue, and this trait is developed by means of further references to the Vikings. Lagerlöf becomes one of the heroic Viking shield-maidens who bore arms and fought alongside the men. 'Sancho Pansa' clearly wants to make Lagerlöf a hero, drawing on references to National Romanticism. Lagerlöf becomes a man or a masculine woman. 'Sancho Pansa' is obviously quite comfortable with admiring Lagerlöf. There is no negative stickiness, and his metaphors are freewheeling, probably because he was describing his own fantasies rather than a close encounter.

As an honorary male, Lagerlöf as perceived by 'Sancho Pansa' has a mighty head that 'would still seem to be growing, as is the case with great minds in literature and the arts, whose skulls have kept growing well beyond the normal period of growth'.[20] Her head, he claims, is as large as that of the Norwegian Nobel Laureate Bjørnstjerne Bjørnson. Both Karlgren and 'Sancho Pansa' find Lagerlöf enigmatic and distant; they note her eyes and use words such as 'siare' ('seer') or 'orakel' ('oracle') to describe them. Thus, the meeting is characterised by devotion—a devotion not untouched by fear, as the oracle has power over men's destinies.

Female spectators stress other aspects of Lagerlöf's appearance. The women who saw her in Helsinki (Claesson Pipping & Olsson 2010, 2011) emphasised their overwhelming sense of awe and joy, often expressed as tears. Anna Lindemann, the German secretary of the IWSA, noted that 'last but not least the presence of the woman all of us had long known and loved before we saw her, Selma Lagerlöf, made us feel at home in Sweden at once' (1911, 847).

Loving Lagerlöf as a woman or as Other

'A woman's place is in the home.' Lagerlöf used this tenet as the starting-point for her argument for female suffrage. Interestingly, however, she herself in her home could be perceived as threatening, but more so to men than to women. Ahmed points out that the narrative of love relies on an acceptance of heterosexuality (love of the difference) as a norm, but that Freud's idea of group love/group identification complicates this, not least when it comes to nationality as a group identity (Ahmed 2004, 130). We would like to suggest that this notion can be developed. As shown in our *Dyrkan och spektakel* ('Worship and Spectacle'), Lagerlöf's female audiences are typical examples of people who identify themselves as a group by their shared love of one another, of women's suffrage, and of the nation, all of which are seen as embodied by Lagerlöf. Her body is that of the mature woman, the mother figure. Many men were troubled by this fusion of nationalism and motherhood. As Lagerlöf was sticky with nationalism, the radical press chose either to ignore the festivities we have studied in *Dyrkan och spektakel* or to make fun of them.

The accounts of the close encounters show that the attraction of Lagerlöf's body, bound up with the notion of her home as cosy, focuses on her voice, her eyes, and, in one notable case, her head as the important features. We have also seen that males and females differ in their attraction to Lagerlöf. Not only are the men ambivalent, but they are also less likely to refer to her perceived motherliness. Following Sara Ahmed, we would like to suggest that these differences with regard to gender can be explained in terms of the prevalent heterosexual basis of the concept of love. In the case of women, their desire is described as the love for a mother. The only way to make Lagerlöf an object of sexual desire is that taken by Lydia Wahlström: in her speech, Lagerlöf becomes male.

There were also men who could turn her into a mother figure, for example Victor Sjöström. But this meant reducing themselves to boys (see Claesson Pipping & Olsson 2010, 99–106). They could possibly also make her their object of sexual desire; however, Lagerlöf's status as a genius prevented this. Thus, they had to reveal the ambivalence of their desire either by pointing out that she frightened them or, as 'Sancho Pansa' does, by turning her into a fictional historical heroine and force of Nature. In this way, they avoided identifying with the group as such—the women—but could still be part of the nation. The one exception, of course, was Victor Sjöström, who seems to have been cast in a different mould than the other men. At the end of his radio programme, he declared that he had fallen in love with Lagerlöf. But perhaps this was not surprising as he himself had developed on screen what could be perceived as Lagerlöf's own ambivalent desire for troubled male heroes, for example in his famous 1921 film *Körkarlen* (*The Phantom Carriage*).

One way of making nationalism, in Ahmed's terminology, stick to Lagerlöf is by comparing her to real or mythical heroes in Swedish history. We have mentioned that Lydia Wahlström and 'Sancho Pansa' made her male, while Furuhjelm likened her to the women who did men's work in wartime in the seventeenth century. The latter connection is also made by Lagerlöf in her speech 'Home and State', her examples being Kristina Gyllenstierna (1494–1559), who led the defence of Stockholm during one of the numerous Nordic wars, and Joan of Arc. However, to make the image of women doing men's work more palatable, Lagerlöf points out that women, if an enemy threatened their creation, the home, would defend it as men defended the state, albeit with different weapons: 'disktrasan' ('the dishcloth'), 'kvasten' ('the broom'), 'den vassa tungan' ('the sharp tongue'), and 'den klösande handen' ('the clawing hand') (Lagerlöf 1911e).

Given pre-war nationalism and the suffragists' usual wording of their arguments for votes for women, it is remarkable that this is Lagerlöf's only reference to the need to defend one's country, a concept common in nationalist rhetoric (see, for example, Stenkvist 1987). To Lagerlöf, the state was an institution constructed by the citizens. It contained states within the state (the Church, the universities, industry) that appeared to be human anthills, but that also harboured numerous reasons for grievances and bitterness. Homeless children, for example, were failed by the state, as were ethnic minorities. The state had to be reformed in order to become a home: 'The state has to be a tool for comfort, security, nurture, culture, refinement'.[21]

The notion of 'trevnad' ('comfort') is thus deeply political and part of the struggle to bring about political change. By extension, Lagerlöf's staging of visits by outsiders to her homes could be said to be bound up with her political vision.

Voice, eyes, and contact

Sara Ahmed claims that pleasure 'brings attention to surfaces, which surface as impressions through encounters with others' (2004, 164). Obviously, the pleasure of meeting Lagerlöf was sometimes tinged with fear, but this was hardly the effect of encounters with her body—with the exception of her eyes.

The descriptions of Lagerlöf written by men depict meeting Lagerlöf in person. Indeed, they stress the intimacy, Anton Karlgren by noting her wish for a conversation rather than an interview, Professor Hultman by claiming that he was the only one close enough to hear her speech,[22] and 'Sancho Pansa' by transferring her from the podium to the street, where he as a *flâneur* could watch her without others seeing what he observed. These claims to intimacy seem to be one way of handling the fact that Lagerlöf was superior to them. Only Victor Sjöström seems not to mind being diminished, but this may be because Lagerlöf's flattering interest in his film based on her novella 'Tösen från Stormyrtorpet' ('The Girl from the Marsh Croft') had enhanced his status. Perhaps there was also a connection here with Sjöström's role as an interpreter of the play of desire in Lagerlöf's work.

We started out by claiming that Sara Ahmed's theory of stickiness as a reason for disgust might just as well be the opposite: the sticky object attracts us and we get stuck. Attracting stickiness creates intimacy. Or, to reverse this statement: the experience of intimacy makes people emotionally stuck to Lagerlöf. And they stress what they are attracted to, or frightened by: her eyes. This focus on Lagerlöf's eyes is a male phenomenon, and is connected to the prevalence of the terms 'siare' and 'sierska' ('seer').

There are significant differences with regard to male and female perceptions of Lagerlöf. To the men, her stickiness is ambivalent: they feel trepidation and awe, in two cases having to construct intimacy in the crowd to avoid being feminised. But to the women, her power is regal rather than alarming. They can experience intimacy in the crowd or, as Anna Lindemann pointed out, feel at home in a foreign country. They are not diminished or disgusted by Lagerlöf's stickiness. Rather, they use the feelings created to energise their struggle to change the world.

Notes

1 Our research has been part of the project 'Enchanted Identities: Symbols, Rituals and Feelings around the Baltic Sea, 1860–1950', financed by the Foundation for Baltic and East European in Studies 2006–2010.

2 Hultman 1912, 6 Feb.

3 Ahmed provides useful insights into how sticky feelings work politically to inspire change through the sense of justice, but we hope to show that her theory on negative feelings can also usefully be applied to positive feelings.

4 This does not, of course, preclude the adversary being described as disgusting.

5 Journalists often took pen names. According to 'Signaturregistret' ('Journalists' pen names') at the Swedish National Archives, 'Yvette' was Celie Brunius. Two mentioned later in our text are 'Quelqu'une' (Märta Lindqvist) and 'Sancho Pansa' (Gustaf Uddgren).

6 The type of articles we use here, interviews with celebrated authors, were the same in all newspapers whatever their political affiliation. The newspapers that feature here are *Dagens Nyheter* (liberal) and *Stockholms Dagblad* (conservative). The third, *Svenska Dagbladet*, is difficult to label. Its readers belonged to the upper class, and the paper made a point of having no political affiliation, distancing itself from both conservatism and radicalism in spite of always defending the armed forces and other traditional institutions (Ekecrantz & Olsson 1994, 107–108). In the 1908 general election, *Svenska Dagbladet* supported the liberals, and in 1911 the conservatives (Lundström 2001, 65). Later it became the leading conservative newspaper in Sweden.

7 For an analysis of text forms and claims to truth in Swedish journalism in the twentieth century, see Ekecrantz & Olsson 1994, 21–39, 100–130, 164–93; and Olsson 2006, 49–100.

8 *Dagens Nyheter*, 15 Nov. 1908.

9 Including a lavishly illustrated article on Lagerlöf's Falun home (Year 6/3, 1918), in which the readers are reminded of Lagerlöf's reluctance to be interviewed.

10 This is the Falun home. We have only found one report from Mårbacka that uses the term *trevnad* ('comfort'), by Lindqvist ('Quelqu'une') in 1923. On the other hand, the term is found not only in the text itself but also in the headline and the front-page teaser for the article. It seems that this was the first article about Mårbacka in *Svenska Dagbladet*.

11 'klara lugna ögon, som gripa en med en underlig makt, dessa siarögon' (Karlgren 1908).

12 'mjuk varm hemtrevnad' (Sjöström 1938).

13 'Ur ögonen som jag mötte kom ingen kyla men en fascinerande lugnt forskande blick som gjorde att här inte lönade sig att komma med något bluffande eller teaterstycke' (Sjöström 1938).

14 The Swedish terms vary. Sjöström says 'inlindad i mjuk hemtrevnad' (lit. 'wrapped in soft comfort'); Karlgren mentions the 'varmt hemtrevna' ('warm and cosy') reception room were the interview took place.

15 'Vi har … skapat uppfostringskonsten, trevnaden, hövligheten, det glada, behagliga umgängessättet' (Lagerlöf 1911e, 8).

16 'när man ser Selma Lagerlöf i sitt hem, tänker man ofrivilligt på stormaktstidens svenska kvinnor, som med stadig hand styrde och ställde på sina gårdar. Det finns mycket kraft i hennes natur och mycket praktiskt sinne' (Furuhjelm 1933, 459).

17 For an analysis of Wahlströms speech, see Claesson Pipping & Olsson 2010, 31, 37.

18 'trött och tämligen frånstötande', 'gulblek och gammal' (Hultman 1912, 6 Feb.).

19 'Jag fick nu en helt annan uppfattning av henne … Hennes framställning var flärd-fri, sann och känslig; ibland svek rösten henne för idel rörelse' (Hultman 1912, 6 Feb.).

20 'måtte ännu vara statt i tillväxt, liksom fallet har med andra storheter inom dik-tens och konstens värld, vars kranier har fortsatt att växa långt utöver den vanliga tillväxttiden' (Uddgren ('Sancho Pansa') 1911).

21 'Staten måste vara ett redskap för trevnad, trygghet, uppfostran, kultur, förädling' (Lagerlöf 1911e).

22 'When she had finished and stepped down from the rostrum with the help of Schybergsson, there was of course enthusiastic applause. But I think that many, perhaps the majority, had heard little of her lecture as it was delivered in a voice far too low and mostly with a bent head—neither of which will allow you to be heard in that hall' ('Då hon slutade och, hjälpt av Schybergsson, steg ned från katedern, applåderades naturligtvis entusiastiskt. Men jag tror dock att många, kanske de flesta, just ej hört någonting av föredraget, som framfördes med alldeles för låg röst och för det mesta med nedböjt huvud—vilket man ej lär få ha, om man ska höras i den salen') (Hultman 1912, 6 Feb.).

III
INTERMEDIALITY AND FILM

CHAPTER 8

Sectional portal

The golden age of Swedish cinema, synonymous with the work of Victor Sjöström and Mauritz Stiller in the 1910s and first half of the 1920s, was heavily dependent on works by Selma Lagerlöf. As is clear from the essays in this volume, there was a range of reasons, from the visual quality of Lagerlöf's narrative to the authenticity that her texts brought to the medium of film, still relatively new and often regarded as providing little more than entertainment. Lagerlöf had a genuine interest in the new medium and worked creatively with Sjöström on his scripts based on her texts.

Lagerlöf's texts have continued to inspire film-makers, in Sweden and other countries, long after the era of Sjöström and Stiller, as illustrated by the analysis, in one of the essays here, of the Japanese animated series of *Nils Holgersson* from 1980. Lagerlöf's works have also inspired a string of illustrators, Swedish and non-Swedish; and a set of illustrations by the Finnish artist Albert Edelfelt is considered in this section.

Films based on literary texts have long been labelled 'adaptations', with comparisons between the two media taking their starting-point in the text and pinpointing the 'omissions' and other shortcomings in the film; and the relationship between literary texts and illustrations has been seen in a similar light. But the 'intermedial turn' has radically changed this relationship. 'Never before', Werner Wolf wrote in 2002, 'have there been such important and far-reaching blendings and interactions of originally separate media' (2002, 15). In a note, Wolf highlighted the sound film with its 'blend of moving pictures, dramatic dialogue and music', but he went on to emphasise that the notion of the 'intermedial turn' also referred to 'developments within the traditional arts: to innovative interactions between different arts, and to attempts at approaching the condition of other arts' (2002, 30). Taking Wolf's argument a step further, W. J. T. Mitchell, author of several influential texts on visual representation, has claimed that all arts are indeed '"composite" arts (both text and image); all media are mixed media, combining different codes, discursive conventions, channels, sensory and cognitive modes' (1995, 94–5). The result, applying Mitchell's perspective, is that the 'real question' to ask when confronted with image–text relations—such as those in Sjöström's and Stiller's films based on texts by Lagerlöf, subsequent films drawing on her work, and, indeed, illustrations of her work—is not '"what is the difference (or similarity) between the words and the images?" but "what difference do the differences (and similarities) make?" That is, why does it matter how words and images are juxtaposed, blended, or separated?' (1995, 91). With the notion of the 'intermedial turn' underpinning the contributions to this section, one of the essays also draws on the significant development represented by Mieke Bal's reading of images in narratological terms, an approach that is in itself intermedial and according to which images 'are not a retelling of the text but a use of it; not an illustration but, ultimately, a new text' (1991, 34–5).

The essay by Anna Nordlund provides a comprehensive survey of the role of Lagerlöf's texts for the work of Sjöström and Stiller, with the emphasis on Sjöström's *Tösen från Stormyrtorpet* (1917, *The Girl from the Marsh Croft*) and *Körkarlen* (1921, *The Phantom Carriage*), and Stiller's *Herr Arnes pengar* (1919, *Sir Arne's Treasure*), *Gunnar Hedes saga* (1923, *Snowbound* or *The Blizzard*), and the two parts of *Gösta Berlings saga* (1924, *The Story of Gosta Berling*). Foregrounding the notion of medial continuity inspired by, among others, Marshall McLuhan, Nordlund explores the interrelationship between established media such as the novel and drama and the new medium of film. While, in Nordlund's analysis, Sjöström and Stiller represent two quite different ways of relating to an understanding of Lagerlöf's texts—in other words, medial continuity— there can be no doubt that to a very considerable extent texts by Lagerlöf helped generate the golden age of Swedish cinema.

Drawing on Jonathan Crary and others, Christopher Oscarson's contribution investigates another famous Sjöström film, *Ingmarssöner-na* (1919, *Sons of Ingmar*), based on part of Lagerlöf's novel *Jerusalem* (1901–1902). Oscarson is particularly interested in Sjöström's use of the scenery from the province of Dalarna (the cinematographer was Julius Jaenzon), and in the ways in which the medium of film not only records but mediates and constructs views of the natural landscape, and thus also problematises spectatorship. Sjöström, Oscarson argues, played a fundamental role for Swedish cinema's longstanding interest in landscape—which, at the time, also had a nationalist dimension—and which, in a wider perspective, can be read as part of an ongoing re-evaluation of the human–Nature duality.

The essay by Helena Forsås-Scott spans illustrations as well as film: the Finnish artist Albert Edelfelt's illustrations of Lagerlöf's *Herr Arnes penningar* (1904, *Lord Arne's Silver*) and Stiller's *Herr Arnes pengar* (1919, *Sir Arne's Treasure*). The analysis also draws on the fact that stills from the film were used to illustrate an upmarket edition of Lagerlöf's novella published in 1919. Relying on Bal's gendered analysis of images as texts, the essay, in part a radical revision of the author's earlier study of Lagerlöf's text and Edelfelt's illustrations (1997), demonstrates the extent to which an investigation inspired by Bal can help problematise the dominant discourses on gender and power exemplified in the illustrations and the film respectively, and so indicate alternatives and the potential for change.

Tytti Soila's essay, which draws on work by Christine Gledhill and others, explores the film for which Sjöström is most renowned, *Körkarlen* (1921, *The Phantom Carriage*). Lagerlöf's novella of the same title had been published in 1912, and part of Soila's study highlights the collaboration between Sjöström and Lagerlöf as the script of the film was finalised. But the emphasis in her analysis is on the role of melodrama in *The Phantom Carriage*, a genre with roots in eighteenth-century theatre that was widely exploited in early film. Focusing on the representation of the unspoken, Soila demonstrates the extent to which the ineffable is conveyed using carefully chosen camera angles in shots of settings and characters, and especially hand movements.

Astrid Surmatz's contribution expands on the subject of Lagerlöf and film by considering a film not only made long after her death, in 1980, but one that is an animated series, made in Japan. Surmatz's starting-point is a study of the Sami chapter in *Nils Holgersson* from a postcolonial perspective, her argument being that while Lagerlöf's text represents different ideas about Lapland current at the time the book was written, these ideas were also adapted to the discourse on national identity in which the schoolbook was to play a central role. The Japanese animation illustrates both the international range and the continuing appeal of Lagerlöf's work, and with its focus on a Japanese representation of Lapland, this part of Surmatz's investigation opens up new perspectives on the significance of intermedial analysis.

CHAPTER 9

Selma Lagerlöf in the golden age of Swedish silent cinema

Anna Nordlund

Selma Lagerlöf's writing career coincided with the rise of the modern media, and she received a great deal of attention from the emerging new culture industry. The success of Swedish silent cinema depended to a considerable extent on adaptations of works by Lagerlöf, and her texts provide an example of the important role that prose fiction played for the emerging film industry. In this essay, I explore how the works of the enormously popular Nobel Laureate were used in the film industry during the period of international success for Swedish film often referred to as the golden age of Swedish silent cinema, defined both as the highly successful period between 1916 and 1924, and as a distinctive national style with characteristics such as austere and naturalistic settings, mastery of landscape, long shots and in-depth photography, and restrained and expressive acting.[1]

Lagerlöf remains underexplored in Scandinavian studies internationally, and this is also true of Lagerlöf in relation to Swedish silent cinema (the exception being Segerberg 1999). Swedish silent cinema as a field has generated considerable attention otherwise, the focus having been on the significance of the two leading directors, Victor Sjöström and Mauritz Stiller. What is needed, then, is a mapping and analysis of Lagerlöf's importance for the success of Swedish silent cinema, with special emphasis on fictional content, narrative techniques, and the prestige mediated by her work. But Lagerlöf's readiness to have the content of her work adapted to other media, demonstrated early on in her career, also needs to be explored.

This essay is based on the notion of medial continuity: new media take over, integrate and adjust their narratives from older fiction and drama, and adopt an audience that is trained in the interpretation of how narratives in novels and dramas are structured (McLuhan 1964; Bolter & Grusin 1999; Lury 1993). My study is dependent on the strong Swedish research tradition of the sociology of literature, in which aspects of the sociology of culture are combined with the analysis of literary texts in order to shed light on the complex connections between literature and society. This study also deals with the internationally expansive field of intermediality, and connects with the materialistic understanding of history, exemplified by influential media theorists such as Marshall McLuhan and Friedrich Kittler. Like them, I am interested in the extent to which fictional literature as a medium helped generate the new medium of film; the extent to which fictional narratives were the sources of new conditions of media techniques; and the extent to which these conditions, during Lagerlöf's active years, helped restructure the book industry into an extensive media industry, in which fiction in combination with a new awareness of 'star qualities' had begun to be seen as content with synergetic effects. More specifically, in this essay I shall analyse the dependence of Victor Sjöström (1879–1960) and Mauritz Stiller (1882–1928) on Lagerlöfian source material as two very different ways of relating to an understanding of medial continuity. The intermedial analysis undertaken here thus emphasises that comparison on its own is not a sufficient procedure in the study of intermedial relations. The necessary subject matter is the whole ensemble of *relations* between media. Relations between literature and film can be built on antagonism and dissonance, as well as on collaboration and harmony. Thus difference is just as important as similarity (Mitchell 1995, 89–90).

The films covered are Sjöström's *Tösen från Stormyrtorpet* (1917, *The Girl from the Marsh Croft*) and *Körkarlen* (1921, *The Phantom Carriage*); Stiller's *Herr Arnes pengar* (1919, *Sir Arne's Treasure*), *Gunnar Hedes saga* (1923, *Gunnar Hede's Saga*, aka *Snowbound* or *The Blizzard*), and the two parts of *Gösta Berlings saga* (1924, *The Story of Gosta Berling*). *The Phantom Carriage* and *Sir Arne's Treasure* are also analysed elsewhere in this volume, by Tytti Soila and Helena Forsås-Scott respectively.

Selma Lagerlöf as starting-point

The golden age of Swedish silent cinema began in 1917 with Henrik Ibsen and Selma Lagerlöf. She saw Victor Sjöström's film adaptation of Ibsen's epic poem 'Terje Vigen' (Sjöström 1941, 178). While in the process of reading Selma Lagerlöf's short story 'Tösen från Stormyrtorpet' ('The Girl from the Marsh Croft'), included in a collection of stories published in 1908, Alma Olsson, a young lady in the port city of Gävle, also saw the film *Terje Vigen* (1917, *A Man There Was*). Strongly touched by both stories, she saw they had something in common and wrote to Victor Sjöström:

> I admire your ability with film and I prefer to go to the cinema when Swedish actors appear. I have given a lot of thought to what Selma Lagerlöf's 'The Marsh Girl' might be like if it were to be filmed under your direction and with Greta Almroth in the role of Helga. Might this not become a popular show that everyone would like? I'm sure it would, if you were to take it on.
>
> I apologise for sending you a request like this, but I would be really glad if you made a film of 'The Marsh Girl'. I am a disabled daughter who lives with her parents, neither rich nor poor. If you could let me have a few words about the result of my humble proposal, I would be eternally grateful. (Quoted in Åhlander 1986, 367)[2]

By 1917 Victor Sjöström was quite an experienced film actor (Sjöström 1941, 175), but he had only just begun his career as a film director, and one can understand the feelings of ambivalence generated by Alma Olsson's letter. The work of a literary giant such as Ibsen was a safe undertaking for an inexperienced film director, because Ibsen was dead. But how might Selma Lagerlöf react when approached by Sjöström, given that she was the first woman to have been awarded an Honorary Doctorate from Uppsala University (1907), the first female Nobel Laureate in Literature (1909), and the first female member of the Swedish Academy (1914)? There were good prospects for capturing Lagerlöf's interest, but it is easy to understand Sjöström's nervousness when he travelled to Falun, at her invitation, for their first meeting. In 1917, the cultural status of film was still low, although in the space of just a few years this would be changed by Charles Magnusson, the managing director of the small firm Svenska Bio (Swedish Cinema) together with Victor Sjöström and Mauritz Stiller (Idestam-Almquist 1959, 521–5).

It is doubtful whether Sjöström, when he wrote his first letter to Lagerlöf, knew that she had received the first suggestion to adapt her work into film as early as 1909. This concerned *Nils Holgerssons underbara resa genom Sverige* (*Nils Holgersson's Wonderful Journey through Sweden*), which for a long time was Swedish literature's greatest international success ever, published in 1906 and 1907 as a pioneering schoolbook for Sweden's elementary schools. Swedish Cinema's managing director Charles Magnusson had been keen to create more ambitious Swedish feature films in the style of French *film d'art*, and hoped to turn Lagerlöf's acclaimed children's book into his first artistic feature film project; however, she declined the offer, realising the difficulties the filming of this particular work would pose. Moreover, even without the film, Lagerlöf's emphasis in the book on fantasy and entertainment had generated moral outrage in conservative circles, where such elements were regarded as part of the general superficiality of the time (Nordlund 2005, 96–102). But there is no doubt that the lure of the new medium for Lagerlöf was evident as early as 1909 (Sahlberg 1961, 190).

A tension between high culture and popular culture underpinned the use of film from the beginning. The same performance could include documentation of contemporary history and high-brow cultural events, slapstick, and trick-film, and feature sequences of a thrilling erotic or violent nature. Much of what was written about film in the Swedish press during the establishment phase, the first decade of the twentieth century, branded it an unhealthy form of popular entertainment, although the educational aspects of film were also noticed early on (Liljedahl 1975, 110–24). On the whole, the period 1900–1920 was characterised by a sense of moral panic about the distribution of sensational film and fiction. Also, notions of a revolutionary, uneducated 'mob' impelled the educational aspirations of both the Liberals and Social Democrats to even out the great class divide in society by giving the lower classes greater access to higher education and culture, which, until now, had been almost exclusively reserved for the upper classes (Boëthius 1989). In this respect, Lagerlöf provided an excellent alternative to sensationalism and mass culture. Her work was appreciated by the establishment, but also very popular. Lagerlöf's texts did not come close to print runs of hundreds of thousands, but her sales figures were considerably higher than those of her contemporaries in the literary establishment (Nordlund 2005, 72, 138, 170).

In the debates about mass culture, aestheticism, and decadence in the 1910s, Lagerlöf had several advantages thanks to the themes already established in her writing. Since her début, she had been read as a transmitter of narrative treasures from Swedish folklore. Perceived as isolated from the city and rooted in the countryside—and, moreover, in the province of Värmland, with its literary traditions going back to the canonical poets of Swedish Romanticism, Esaias Tegnér and Erik Gustaf Geijer—she was regarded as having a special bond with the 'Swedish national soul' and as having high moral standards, both phenomena perceived to be under threat from industrialisation, foreign influences, and urban expansion. Moreover, with her pedagogically radical schoolbook for elementary schools and her highly acclaimed suffrage speech 'Hem och stat' ('Home and State'), delivered at the 6th Congress of the IWSA in Stockholm in June 1911, Lagerlöf had positioned herself as a representative of the new ideals of democracy, with the ability to depict modern, industrialised Sweden from the perspective of working people, and with an optimistic vision of a caring welfare state. She was thus perceived as conveying a new Swedish identity, based on the assumed soundness and morality of the Swedish people. All of these notions associated with Lagerlöf in the 1910s were also important cultural values linked to the establishment of Swedish film.

The international breakthrough

When Victor Sjöström met Lagerlöf in January 1917, the medium of film was in a period of transition. Films of some sort had been screened in Sweden for twenty-one years. During the 1910s, the repertoire had developed from a mishmash of material to full feature films—often imported from Denmark, France, Italy, or the US. But in 1909, Swedish Cinema, headed by its far-sighted managing director Charles Magnusson, made the first Swedish feature films, one based on Johan Ludvig Runeberg's cycle of poems *Fänrik Ståls sägner* (*The Tales of Ensign Steel*), and two based on popular folklore plays.

When the long-standing debate about the harmful influence of cinema resulted in state film censorship in 1911, this encouraged the development of domestic feature films, with artistic as well as moral educational ambitions. In 1913, Victor Sjöström's full-length feature *Ingeborg Holm* (*Margaret Day*), about a mother who becomes mentally ill as a result of having to auction off her three children, was released. The film was praised in Sweden as well as internationally for its social realism, and for demonstrating that the new art of cinema could generate debate and empathy, and not merely entertain the audience. The film resulted in a political debate about the inadequacy of poor relief, and new legislation was introduced in 1918, banning the auctioning of human beings (Idestam-Almquist 1959, 492–5).

In the year before Sjöström made *Ingeborg Holm*, Selma Lagerlöf had written *Körkarlen* (*The Phantom Carriage*), in which the sense of social commitment is more explicit than in any other of her works. Set in the same kind of city slum as *Ingeborg Holm*, Lagerlöf's text highlighted the disgraceful living conditions of those suffering from economic and social deprivation. With *Ingeborg Holm*, Victor Sjöström showed that he shared Selma Lagerlöf's capacity to combine socially and psychologically oriented representation with effective, melodramatic aesthetics. These features also characterise the first film based on a text by Lagerlöf, 'The Girl from the Marsh Croft', similarly associated with a harsh social reality and changes to the legislation on social security.

The Girl from the Marsh Croft was conceived as a contemporary film portraying current social issues. Sjöström also highlights the chronological setting by means of precise details, setting the film at the time it was made. For example, in the courtroom, a key scene some way into the film, one can see how the portraits of the newly crowned King Gustaf V and his wife Queen Victoria have replaced the portraits of King Oscar II, who had died in 1907, and Queen Sophia. In the novel, the courtroom is the opening scene. The film follows the events of the novel chronologically, while Lagerlöf in the opening scene, by using flashbacks and the characters' thoughts, sets out the background and presents the main characters. These are Helga, the daughter of a crofter, and Gudmund, the son of a wealthy farmer; and after various complications, the two of them end up together.

The film was a great success. To meet demand, 14 copies were distributed in Sweden the year of its release, when the normal figure was 4–6 copies, and *A Man There Was*, the greatest success of Swedish silent film to date, had been distributed in 12 copies. Internationally, 69 copies of *The Girl from the Marsh Croft* were distributed, and following the American première in 1918, 42 copies were sold to the US (Idestam-Almquist 1959, 514–16).

I believe it is possible to discern three reasons for the success of *The Girl from the Marsh Croft*. Firstly, the issues concerning illegitimate children and the difficulties of unmarried mothers in supporting their children when the fathers refused to acknowledge paternity was a worldwide problem. It was of immediate interest in Sweden in 1917 when, following an extensive debate prompted by the women's movement, the legislation making it possible for men to deny paternity under oath was revised. The new law meant that the father could no longer renounce paternity under oath, as happens in the film; illegitimate children, moreover, were also given the right of inheritance.

Secondly, following on from that, I would claim that an important reason for the success of Sjöström's film has to do with what Ann Kaplan has defined as 'the woman's gaze': in part, and with its origins in Lagerlöf's narrative, *The Girl from the Marsh Croft* is a 'woman's film', in contrast to what Kaplan has called 'the maternal melodrama', which foregrounded the male gaze in which the woman was an idealised, all-sacrificing mother figure, and was common in Hollywood during the 1910s and 1920s (Kaplan 1987, 123–35).

Thirdly, and in addition to the film's relevance to the social debate, much of its success can be explained by the fact that Sjöström's ethical and aesthetic ideals, which included the importance to feature films of subjects that were socially absorbing, coincided with the visual dimensions of Lagerlöf's narrative technique, as well as with the drama and growing emotional tension of the story. At the same time, Lagerlöf's capacity to shift perspectives and to use inanimate objects to convey strong feelings and psychological sequences of events were clearly challenges to Sjöström's cinematic narrative.

Sjöström's film convincingly mediates between the emotional intensification and the psychological events and battles of conscience in Lagerlöf's story, the acting of the three main characters in the highly emotional court scene being markedly restrained for its time. In the short story, Lagerlöf initially outlines the scene by means of the judge's focalisation, subsequently alternating between the external focalisation of the narrator and the internal focalisations of the judge and Helga. Arguably influenced by Lagerlöf's narrative technique and the notion of transfer of focalisation, Sjöström, in the courtroom scene in particular, uses a more advanced technique for point-of-view shots than in his earlier films. The camera perspective switches between the points of view of the gallery, the judge, and Helga.

However, Sjöström made no attempt to capture cinematically Lagerlöf's flashback technique and the complex shifts in time and place in the opening sequence of her story. On the contrary, while remaining faithful to the events portrayed in Lagerlöf's story, Sjöström rearranged the sequence of events chronologically throughout the film. Only one scene is added, as a concession to the cinematic conventions of the day: a short comic sequence with women gossiping over coffee, occasioned by the cancellation of a wedding reception. Not until his later Lager-

Illus. 1. In the highly emotional courtroom scene, the camera switches between the points of view of the gallery, the judge, and the plaintiff Helga, possibly inspired by Lagerlöf's narrative technique.

löf adaptations did Sjöström experiment in depth with the cinematic possibilities of depicting more than one level of place and time and of visualising a complex plot rather than a chronological story, the outstanding example being *The Phantom Carriage*. All in all, Sjöström made five films based on Lagerlöf's work before he left Sweden for Hollywood in 1923. The three films based on Lagerlöf's *Jerusalem*, the two-part *Ingmarssönerna* (1919, *The Sons of Ingmar/Dawn of Love*) (analysed by Christopher Oscarson in this volume) and *Karin Ingmarsdotter* (1920, *God's Way*) were also successful with both critics and audiences in Sweden, but they had nowhere near the same impact abroad as *The Girl from the Marsh Croft* and, later, *The Phantom Carriage* from 1921.

The masterpiece

The Phantom Carriage holds its position as the foremost Swedish film before the era of Ingmar Bergman. Many challenges that occur in the transfer of a complex literary narrative to the medium of film were so skilfully overcome in *The Phantom Carriage* that the film's representation of the novel's theme and intricate narrative technique are just as artistically successful and effective. The film stands on its own as a great work of art, independent of the source novel, although Lagerlöf's narrative technique and distinctively scenic–dramatic portrayal of the subject matter undoubtedly played a part in Sjöström's artistic success.

Sjöström has described how he wrote the script while confined to a hotel in Dalarna for a week, and he marvelled at the fact that he was able to produce an elaborate script so quickly (1941, 182). One probable explanation is that he used Lagerlöf's novella not only as a source but also as an inspirational model, and this clearly helped him visualise the design of the film. Lagerlöf's influence can be found in most of the detailed descriptions of interiors and exteriors in the script, in the descriptions of actions and facial expressions, in several of the camera instructions, and in the descriptions of diegetic light sources. Sjöström's script is full of direct quotations from, and paraphrases of, Lagerlöf's original text.[3]

The plot of *The Phantom Carriage* centres on the self-absorbed alcoholic David Holm and his relationship with Edith, a young Salvation Army slum-sister, who is dying from tuberculosis. Lagerlöf's text is a socio-realist portrayal of how alcohol abuse, widespread in Sweden at the time, destroys a working-class family whose prospects of leading a decent life are otherwise reasonable. Lagerlöf (Lagerroth 1963, 66–7) and Sjöström alike drew inspiration from the temperance movement at the time. For example, in the instructions for one scene—Mrs Holm and her children search the streets to find the husband and father drunk in the gutter—Sjöström in the script refers directly to the temperance movement's propaganda picture *Avlöningsafton* ('Pay Day'), based on widespread copies of the popular French sculpture *La Paye* (1910) by A. Jacopin. But unlike Sjöström's previous powerful social dramas, such as *Ingeborg Holm* and *The Girl from the Marsh Croft*, Lagerlöf's *The Phantom Carriage* also has elements of religious mysticism and edification, and of ghost stories and legends. Like Lagerlöf, Sjöström integrates these elements into the social drama, although the sense of metaphysical mystery between David and Edith in Lagerlöf's novella has been considerably toned down in the film. Lagerlöf had been inspired by Dickens's *A Christmas Carol* and by a Breton legend that last person to die on New Year's Eve becomes 'l'ouvrier de la mort', Death's searcher, for the coming year (Lagerroth 1963, 132, 136).

The main theme and narrative of *The Phantom Carriage* are represented in terms of repeated shifts between the present and the past and between earthly life and the beyond. David Holm, the alcoholic, receives his chance of redemption by the presence of death, his own as well as the dying of Sister Edith, at the present level of the narration. The present is interrupted by flashbacks, explaining the situations of David and Sister Edith to the viewer and not least to David Holm himself. In *The Phantom Carriage*, Sjöström, for the first time, committed himself to illustrating the different narrative levels, crucial to the theme. Instead of reconstructing the intricately narrated plot of a novel as a chronological story line, as had most previous films, Sjöström thus created a plot based on different narrative levels. It is true that his *The Sons of Ingmar* (1919) had made some use of flashback, but without employing the shifts between different narrators found in *The Phantom Carriage*.

With impressive poignancy, Sjöström, together with the photographer Julius Jaenzon and the laboratory technician Eugén Hellman, used the technical means of photography to portray intricate spiritual movements in time and space, and movements between different times and narrative levels, making these both clear and persuasive. *The Phantom Carriage* is most renowned for its double exposures, the very prerequisite for the shaping of the film's theme. Lagerlöf's description of how David Holm's soul rises from his body in the churchyard on New Year's Eve (Lagerlöf 1912, 43) comes alive in the film, and the visualisation of the deathcart also follows Lagerlöf's descriptions in detail. Lagerlöf makes the point that one can see straight through the old carriage (17–18, 38), and this is also noted in Sjöström's script.

In film history, the artistic achievement of *The Phantom Carriage* has been attributed mainly, and quite rightly, to Victor Sjöström and Julius Jaenzon, but the outstanding performances by Astrid Holm (Sister Edith) and Hilda Borgström (Mrs Holm) have also been praised (Forslund 1980, 131–3; Furhammar 2003, 81; Idestam-Almquist 1939, 190–201; Waldekranz 1985, 508; Werner 1978, 51–5). However, given the iconic status of the film, there have been surprisingly few analyses of its cinematic style, and Lagerlöf's significance for the film has rarely been mentioned. Florin's dissertation offers the first comprehensive style analysis, but without making any in-depth comparisons between the book and the film, or any attempt to assess Lagerlöf's significance for the style of the film. As Florin has pointed out, Lagerlöf's colloquial

Illus. 2. The visualisation of the deathcart follows Lagerlöf's description very closely.

style is represented in the intertitles (1997, 162–4), which quote her almost verbatim. This closeness to the source is characteristic of all Sjöström's films based on texts by Lagerlöf.

However, as I have indicated, a comparison between the script and the novel suggests that Lagerlöf had a more extensive influence on Sjöström's film. For example, Florin (1997, 164–8) pays much attention to the aesthetically advanced tableau technique with its dynamic interpretation of the graphic lines in the shots. In *The Phantom Carriage*, camera movements are used very sparingly. The viewer instead experiences movement in space by means of clean cuts and frequent shifts between full view, American shot, and close-up. Thus intense emotions build up. In Lagerlöf's text, descriptions of the setting and tableau technique are achieved either by the extra-diegetic narrator making use of tableaux in representations akin to those in stage drama, or by a diegetic narrator using expressions that convey information about the setting. Several scenes in the film can be traced back directly to Lagerlöf's theatrical style of representation. These include the churchyard scenes, the scenes at Edith's deathbed, and scenes from the Holms' hovel with Mrs Holm preparing to take her own and her children's lives (for further analyses of the effects of the tableaux and scenery in the novel, see Karlsson 2002, 102–116; Lagerroth 1963, 193–4). The intense emotions generated by the actors' small shifts and dramatically restrained gestures in the highly charged scenes in the film had been well described by Lagerlöf and were reused in Sjöström's script. For example, Tytti Soila has drawn attention to the scene at the beginning of the film when Mrs Holm comes to Edith's deathbed (see Soila's essay in this volume): the scene, complete with all the dramatic emotional shifts and movements of the two women, is developed in the film in terms that have striking parallels with those employed in the novella.

Another notable stylistic feature of Swedish silent film is the atmospheric lighting, usually discussed in terms of the way in which daylight is used in the Nature scenes common in Swedish film at this time. *The Phantom Carriage* has attracted attention for its atmospheric lighting too, despite the fact that scenes set in Nature are almost non-existent in this film (Florin 1997, 178; Revault d'Allonnes 1991, 136). Most of the film takes place in dark, cramped rooms and alley-ways. Sjöström, however, aims to give the viewer the impression of natural, atmospheric light. The light in the film gives the impression of coming from sources visible in the shots, with oil lamps and street lamps used frequently, and the diegetic light sources described in detail in the script. The lighting in combination with the shades of white, grey, and black used in the film amount to theatrical effects with symbolic and dramatic significance for the events that unfold. Interestingly, Lagerlöf uses descriptions of light sources in a similar way in the novella. She makes the reader aware of the source from where the light emanates and thus lends the light as well as the contrasts of light and darkness a symbolic and dramatic meaning. The light sources pinpointed by Lagerlöf in the churchyard and in Sister Edith's home are also foregrounded by Sjöström in the film.

The complex narration of the novella includes several shifts between an extra-diegetic narrator and narrators within the diegeses, and between direct and indirect narration and flashbacks. Common in Lagerlöf and ingeniously implemented here, this technique is particularly suited to *The Phantom Carriage* in that it also becomes part of the novella's theme. The actual narrative emerges as a prerequisite for David Holm's

Illus. 3. Light sources pinpointed by Lagerlöf in the churchyard scene are foregrounded by Sjöström, aiming to create an impression of natural, atmospheric light.

conversion; the narratives of others around him and those close to him are prerequisites for his transformation from a self-absorbed alcoholic to a compassionate human being. The novella consists of twelve chapters, with diegetic narrators central to five of these: in three of the five, the narrative consists of representations of David Holm's life in a format akin to that of stage drama, and beginning once the extra-diegetic narrator has located for the reader David Holm as a listener/viewer of the narrative. In all, there are four diegetic narrators in the novella. While David Holm and his friend Georges, who drives the deathcart, function as diegetic narrators in the film, Sister Edith and a colleague of hers also have narrative functions.

Sjöström has kept the complex structure of three narrative levels intact, with David Holm setting the conditions for the story as a whole. He does this by telling his two drinking companions, in the churchyard on New Year's Eve, in the film's present tense, about his old fellow drinker Georges. This intra-diegetic narrative also contains a hypo-diegetic level: Georges's ghost story about the driver of the deathcart who is succeeded by the last person to die on New Year's Eve, a hypo-diegetic narrative which is thus located outside time both in the film and in the novella. As in the book, the interjection of the ghost story about the driver of the deathcart comes after the extra-diegetic narrator has set the scene of Sister Edith's death and the subsequent scene with the three drunk men waiting in the churchyard for the New Year. Thus, the novella and the film have a structure similar to that of a Chinese box: the narrative opens for a new narrative, and within this narrative yet another narrative appears. In the film, the narrative levels are, of course, materialised visually. Florin has conducted a thorough examination of how this is done (1997, 170–8). After Georges/the driver of the deathcart has met with David in the churchyard, the present tense is interrupted three times by the former's narrative about David Holm's past. It is an elliptical yet chronologically produced narrative of David's life, covering the years when Georges became his drinking companion and the previous year when he got to know Sister Edith, whose deathbed along with the churchyard are at the centre of the present in the film. In these long sections, Sjöström moves across time and space, and Florin has highlighted in some detail the stylistic confidence with which Sjöström exploits a variety of camera techniques in these transitions.

Thanks to Lagerlöf's intervention, greater variation between the present and the past was achieved in the definitive version of the film than in Sjöström's script. Sjöström has described his concern about the simultaneously entangled and tedious narrative technique of the script when, as was his habit, he visited Lagerlöf to read it to her (Sjöström 1941, 183). She suggested he rearrange the narrative so as to achieve greater variety. Following Lagerlöf's advice, the last of the three long flashbacks in the film was moved from the present in the churchyard to the present at Sister Edith's deathbed, where David listens to/sees Georges/the driver of the deathcart explain to Sister Edith why her efforts to convert David have been in vain. The film has certainly benefited from the fact that David Holm and the viewer now have this dramatic flashback, including his disastrous reunion with his wife, in juxtaposition with the profound transformation that David undergoes at the moment of Sister Edith's death.

With his Lagerlöf films, Sjöström, then, built relations between literature and film based on harmony and collaboration, relations that permitted him to develop exceptional cinematic qualities from the verbal imagery in Lagerlöf's work. The other leading director of Swedish silent film, Mauritz Stiller, who in his pioneering work drew on works by Lagerlöf, developed a wholly different approach to the relationship between film and literature, emphasising instead the new medium's independence of literature.

Form, design, and intermedial inspiration

In 1919, Mauritz Stiller made his first film based on a text by Lagerlöf, *Sir Arne's Treasure*. After *The Girl from the Marsh Croft,* this was the second big international success for Swedish film. Without doubt, his concentrated account of this tale of murders, love, and revenge, set in the province of Bohuslän in the sixteenth century, is more cinematically narrated than earlier Swedish feature films. Stiller's first Lagerlöf film thus fulfilled a wish, shared by many film critics at the time, that directors would stop illustrating books in film tableaux and start experimenting with the medium's unique means of artistic expression. The film imagery in *Sir Arne's Treasure* is certainly both confidently made and consistently developed, and Stiller's film soon positioned itself as one of the iconic works in film history.

Herr Arnes penningar (1903, *Lord Arne's Silver*) is one of Lagerlöf's more famous novellas, and it had given rise to adaptations that surely inspired Stiller to the same degree as Lagerlöf's original text did. The German author Gerhart Hauptmann's adaptation for the stage, *Winterballade* (1917, 'Winter Ballad') was highly topical in Sweden, having had its première in Gothenburg in 1918, in a translation by Lagerlöf herself. The translation was published in 1919, and from this drama Stiller borrowed not only the subtitle of the film, 'En vinterballad i fem akter' ('A winter ballad told in five acts'), but also aspects of the staging and the dramatic concentration, with its focus on the Scottish mercenaries who become murderers. In terms of design, several scenes are also heavily influenced by Albert Edelfelt's famous illustrations in the 1904 edition of the novella. The costumes also appear to have been inspired by these illustrations, and more pervasively so than in similar cases of attempted cinematic reproductions of paintings.[4]

Stiller was more interested in smart and stylish design than in psychological content or cinematic narrative techniques such as flashback, perspective, and focalisation. Tracking shots, panning, and spatial mobility are used to a greater extent than in Sjöström's *The Girl from the Marsh Croft,* but less so the potential of the camera to convey different subjective viewpoints. Stiller's rearrangements in relation to Lagerlöf's text are primarily to do with clarifying the narrative's chronological sequences and toning down of the ghost story in favour of the love intrigue and crime mystery. He centres the interest on the lovers, the Scottish mercenary Sir Archie and poor, orphaned Elsalill, just 14 years old. In this he follows Hauptmann's 'Winter Ballad'. Unlike Lagerlöf's text, where Elsalill is the catalyst of the sequence of events along with the poor fisherman Torarin, the focus in the film is on the perpetrator and murderer Sir Archie. While it is mainly Elsalill's psychology that is portrayed in the novel, in the film the subjective viewpoints of the camera are principally those of Sir Archie. Whereas Lagerlöf's complex portrayal of Elsalill and the love between her and Sir Archie might be relevant to a women's film, Stiller's film largely becomes a 'maternal melodrama' (as defined by Kaplan 1987, 124–5), in the sense that the focus is on Sir Archie's desire and need for Elsalill to forgive and liberate him. As Helena Forsås-Scott (1997; 2013) has pointed out, these key differences in terms of power and gender also exist between Lagerlöf's and Hauptmann's texts, and Stiller has obviously followed the latter.

Still, the subject matter of the film narrative follows Lagerlöf's story. In particular, Lagerlöf's portrayal of Nature—stormy winds, snow, and ice—in symbolic interaction with the dramatic phases of the murder mystery is well captured in the film. The intertitles are drawn from the novella and are mostly much more elaborate than in Sjöström's *The Girl from the Marshcroft* (or for that matter, *The Phantom Carriage*). Stiller has deleted a considerable amount of Gustaf Molander's script but virtually none of the intertitles, with the result that the numerous and extensive text frames often interrupt and slow down the film narrative. Possibly Stiller's lack of interest in the text in relation to the visual portrayal meant he simply did not realise that the long intertitles drawn from the novella were so disruptive.

Lagerlöf was very pleased with the film, which did well at the box office in Sweden, and was sold to 46 countries (Werner 1979, 25, 32–4). The reviews were also very favourable: Stiller's faithfulness to Lagerlöf's story, as well as his stylistically sensitive staging and flawless personal direction were appreciated (Åhlander 1982, 405–406; Werner 1979, 108–113). Stiller himself, however, was less pleased. He now claimed that the scriptwriter Gustaf Molander's respect for Lagerlöf's text had impaired the film—although Stiller had condensed and simplified it in the definitive version of the film, as Werner (1979, 128–40) has demonstrated. Stiller wanted to show that Swedish film could compete with the rapidly growing American film industry. But in this regard, he failed with *Sir Arne's Treasure*, which was considered too 'arty' and too dependent on Lagerlöf's novella. The unhappy ending was criticised by Swedish Cinema's director of exports and by distributors in France, the UK, and the US (Werner 1979, 118–21).

Perhaps the ending of *Sir Arne's Treasure* was one reason why a conventional happy ending was emphasised in Stiller's subsequent Lagerlöf adaptations, *Gunnar Hede's Saga* (1923) and the two parts of *Gösta Berlings saga* (1924, *The Story of Gosta Berling*). These films were also the results of increased financial demands from the Swedish film industry and adjusted to a more American way of production, following simple and clear conventions and readily understood character sketches (Werner 1991, 151–3).

The star quality of 'Selma Lagerlöf'

To avoid accusations of being dependent on literature, Stiller himself took control of the script for his next Lagerlöf film, based on *En herrgårdssägen* (*The Tale of a Manor*), a short novel from 1899 set in the 1830s. Here Stiller marked the distance to the novel by locating the film in a contemporary setting, with an old maid telling the story and harking back to the 1830s and the adventure of Gunnar Hede's grandfather. Moreover, he chose a new title, *Gunnar Hedes saga* (1923, *Gunnar Hede's Saga*, aka *Snowbound* or *The Blizzard*), and one that apostrophised Lagerlöf's début novel from 1891, *Gösta Berling's Saga*, the iconic work in Lagerlöf's output and the work in which she makes the most extensive use of the intra-diegetic narrative voice identified as that of 'the great storyteller persona'—in other words the persona on which Lagerlöf and her supporters in the literary establishment had built her celebrity status (Nordlund 2005, 29–125).

In Lagerlöf's *Gösta Berling's Saga*, the narrator is an active part of the fiction. The gathering of meaningful stories for future generations is one of the overall themes of Lagerlöf's novel. Stories have been told by 'de gamla', 'old people', to the narrator, who once listened as a child and is now retelling these stories for a new generation. Thus in *Gösta Berling's Saga*, the narrator spans three generations, just like the visible narrator, the old storytelling maid Stava, in Stiller's *Gunnar Hede's Saga*.

Arguably the old storyteller created by Stiller in the opening scene of *Gunnar Hede's Saga* was modelled on Lagerlöf's storyteller in *Gösta*

Berling's Saga, functioning within that novel as a mediator between the present 1890s and the retold stories from the romanticised world of Värmland in the 1830s, and within the film setting essentially starting the film and launching its plot. In the sequence, the hero of the film—Gunnar Hede—is introduced as a small schoolboy, gazing at a portrait of his grandfather and begging the old maid to tell once again the family legend of his grandfather, the fiddler who made his fortune by selling reindeer. The camera focuses on the storyteller and the boy kneeling beside her. A shot showing their heads inclined towards each other dissolves into a shot of a reindeer herd. However, Stava's story does not follow. Instead the sequence cuts back to the boy and then again to the portrait, partly dissolving to reveal the reindeer whilst the grandfather in the portrait suddenly comes alive and starts to play the fiddle. This complex sequence emerges as Stiller's metaphor for the relationship between film and literature in general, and between film and Lagerlöf in particular.

As Ebba Segerberg has argued (1999, 107–39), film for Stiller was the natural progression from the storytelling situation of which Lagerlöf was a master: cinema, much more than literature, holds the role as collective storyteller in modernity. Just as Lagerlöf envisioned the role of storytelling in literature as a collective bridge-builder between past and present, Stiller envisioned cinema's power to offer to modernity a sense of community and belonging which literature itself did not have. By staging storytelling as a form of interplay and mediation between past and present Stiller, arguably, thus paradoxically touched the mindset of Lagerlöf, while at the same time staging Lagerlöf's public persona as a folkloric great storyteller, the popular notion on which Lagerlöf's celebrity was based, and making use of this authorial persona rather than the literary and cinematic qualities in the work of the author. Clearly, the Lagerlöf persona is inscribed in the opening sequence of *Gunnar Hede's Saga*: at the time, the comforting and nurturing old storyteller luring her reader to become like a child sitting at her knee, was a powerful metaphor for Lagerlöf's emotionally poignant aesthetics and her mysterious ability to charm her listeners (Nordlund 2005, 78–87).

The main theme in Lagerlöf's *The Tale of a Manor*—a complex psychological novel seemingly simply narrated—is artistic creativity renewed in the encounter between madness and death by a female force who changes male egotism into altruism. However, judged by the surviving two-thirds of the film, it became a conventional romantic melodrama and adventure story centring on a reindeer herd, with the lead reindeer dragging Gunnar Hede through the mountain scenery and causing physical injuries that lead to insanity.

The film contains quite a few elements of what Kaplan has defined as 'maternal melodrama' (1987, 124–5) in the interpretation of Hede's saviour, the innocent young girl, Ingrid, typecast as an *ingénue* by Mary Johnson. In Lagerlöf's text, Ingrid is a character of a different kind of strength and originality, and with the power to make Gunnar Hede a real artist and a man. In Stiller's version, Ingrid cures Gunnar Hede from insanity, but judging from the closing scene, she also lures him into a petty bourgeois sphere: the camera views Ingrid and Gunnar obliquely, in a cosy living room, with Ingrid at the grand piano, accompanying Gunnar on the violin. His correct and harsh mother is sewing and looking very satisfied, while the pair of pantomime artists who used to take care of Ingrid and wanted to adopt her into their world of art, are sitting uncomfortably at the door, drinking tea. The artists get the film's final line: 'This is very nice and pleasant, Napoleon. But tomorrow we head out on tour.'⁵ Arguably the line can be read as Stiller's own meta-commentary on the entire project of *Gunnar Hede's Saga*: American production lines that called for the typecasting of simple and clear character sketches, along with bourgeois conventions of love and happiness, would cost him his artistic freedom.

There is no doubt that many intrinsic qualities in Lagerlöf's story about insanity and the power of art and love as psychological healing processes were lost in the film. By giving physical explanations for Hede's mental breakdown, and by erasing the central themes in Lagerlöf's key scene in which Hede watches Ingrid, seemingly dead and waiting in her grave for her funeral, return to life, the film annulled the entire psychological viability of her story. Stiller, moreover, only made limited use of the potentially cinematic descriptions of the settings in Lagerlöf's text, where they highlight different mental states and the theme of insanity and healing. But Stiller did make use of material for what would appear to be the film's most successful representation of fragile mental states and unconscious healing processes: the portrayal of Ingrid's mental struggle with Fru Sorg (Lady Mourning), one of Lagerlöf's most successful allegorical portrayals of depressive mourning, received a cinematic interpretation of double exposures. In the script, Lady Mourning also returns in the film's resolution, but unfortunately this scene has not been preserved, and it is difficult to assess the degree to which this segment might have balanced the conventional portrayal of Ingrid as an *ingénue*. In the portrayal of Lady Mourning and in the film's other dream scenes, Stiller comes closest to Lagerlöf's aesthetics, combining psychological realism with magical-realist audacity.

Gunnar Hede's Saga was not the big new breakthrough that the Swedish film industry had hoped for, in view of previous Lagerlöf blockbusters and the adaptation to a more Americanised, cinematic storytelling. The most influential Swedish film critics did not appreciate the deviations from Lagerlöf's text, considering them not a proclamation of independence, but merely the result of yielding to what the established film journalist Märta Lindqvist ('Quelqu'une') called 'banal foreign film taste' (Åhlander 1982, 154–6).[6] *Gunnar Hede's Saga* sold only 17 copies abroad, a lower figure than for Stiller's previous films (Åhlander 1982, 156). However, in the history of Swedish film, it has a place as the first truly independent cinematic version of a literary original, even if it was a failure in artistic terms (Furhammar 2003, 86).

In comparison with his work filming the short novel on which *Gunnar Hede's Saga* was based, Stiller's next task, filming *Gösta Berling's Saga* was almost insurmountably difficult. Selma Lagerlöf's début novel from 1891, inspired by Carlyle's *The French Revolution*, tells us about an entire region's transformations during a year in the 1830s. As in all Lagerlöf's subsequent works, the focalisation is well suited to the camera, with a great amount of theatricality and dramatic conflict. But the narrative thread is less clear than in any of her later works. With her first novel, Lagerlöf broke with the narrative unity of the nineteenth-century realist novel. Although the structure of the narrative incorporates varying styles, an explicit present-tense narrator functions as the organising principle of the novel, addressing the reader by means of exclamations and apostrophes. From the very first critical response to the novel, the apparent simplicity of the narrator-character was identified with the assumed *naïveté* of Lagerlöf 'the storyteller'.

What Stiller used as his starting-point and staged in *Gunnar Hede's Saga* as well as in *The Story of Gosta Berling* was thus not so much the subject matter and the narrative techniques in Lagerlöf's works, nor the antagonism between literature and film, but rather the popular notion on which Lagerlöf's celebrity was based. Thus he accentuated the role of cinema in marketing literature in general and the Lagerlöf persona in particular: in *Gunnar Hede's Saga* by cinematically staging a meta-filmic situation to open the film narrative with a stereotypical

'Lagerlöfian' storyteller at the centre, and in *The Story of Gosta Berling* by the presence of a narrator imitating Lagerlöf's narrator in the novel, but more dependent on the national and international popularity of Lagerlöf in general and *Gösta Berling's Saga* in particular, and on the folk culture that Lagerlöf was supposed to represent. By the 1920s, Lagerlöf was regarded as embodying 'Swedishness' and the soul of the people (Nordlund 2005, 169–91). Even to international audiences she was a symbol of Sweden and of the province of Värmland, and, like Ibsen's Peer Gynt, Gösta Berling was regarded as a Nordic archetype (Segerberg 1999, 31). Tourists were soon attracted by Lagerlöf's *œuvre* and the perceived Swedishness of Värmland, also promoted by travel films such as *Bilder från Fryksdalen* (*Gösta Berlings land*) (1907, 'Pictures from Fryksdalen (the Land of Gösta Berling)'), with impressive landscape photography. By repurchasing her childhood home Mårbacka and rebuilding it in the early 1920s into a monumental manor house suitable for a Nobel Laureate, Lagerlöf further encouraged tourism in Värmland. Thus there were plenty of reasons for choosing the emblematic *Gösta Berling's Saga* in an attempt both to reinvigorate Swedish film internationally, and to bring out aspects of the symbiosis between literature and film other than those involving a mere comparison between the film and its literary source.

In *The Story of Gosta Berling*, Stiller emphasised the celebrity cult surrounding Lagerlöf by drawing on the entertainment factor of the Värmland scenery, and by having the province and its associations with folklore presented by an authorial persona based on the notion of the stereotypical Lagerlöfian narrator. The film's first intertitle, accompanying a panorama of an imagined Värmland, apostrophises the audience in a fairytale and folksy tone clearly designed to suggest a quotation from Lagerlöf: 'Oh Värmland, thou beautiful, thou wonderful'.[7] As Segerberg (1999, 132) has pointed out, this text is not from Lagerlöf's novel but the opening line of a song about Värmland, sung in honour of Lagerlöf at innumerable formal occasions. Thus this song alludes directly to the star author. No intertitles in the film actually quote the novel directly and accurately; instead they evoke the storyteller persona as the core of Lagerlöf's celebrity, as an attraction in itself.

This dependence on Lagerlöf's celebrity in *The Story of Gosta Berling* and *Gunnar Hede's Saga* also needs to be interpreted in the light of the international breakthrough of the more commercially oriented American film industry around 1922, compounded by the general decline of the film industry as a result of the Great Depression and the abrupt drop in audience numbers which began the same year. Directors faced demands that they create commercially sound films, and were also made financially co-responsible (Idestam-Almquist 1939, 206–208). As a result also of the increased demands from the new type of financial investor who had no explicit interest in film as an art form, the Swedish film industry started to adjust to Americanised production methods and adapted the Hollywood celebrity cult. This cult, however, was not yet quite as strong in Sweden, where the film star who shone brightest of all was still Selma Lagerlöf.

Conclusion

A mapping and an analysis of Lagerlöf's importance for the success of Swedish silent cinema demonstrates that her texts helped generate the new medium of film in terms of narrative content, narrative technique, and prestige. Victor Sjöström's and Mauritz Stiller's dependence on Lagerlöfian source material are clear examples of two very different ways of relating to an understanding of medial continuity. They show that relations between literature and early film could be built on collaboration and harmony as well as on antagonism and dissonance, with either alternative being dependent on the source novel and/or representations of the author. Sjöström's ethical and aesthetic ideals coincided with the visual dimensions of Lagerlöf's narrative technique, as well as with the drama and growing emotional tension of her narrative content; with *The Phantom Carriage*, Sjöström made use of Lagerlöf's novella not only as a source, but also as an inspirational model for his narrative techniques. This clearly helped him visualise this remarkably efficient film, including the use of flashbacks, different narrative levels, and the restrained use of double exposures. Stiller, on the other hand, was more interested in smart and stylish design than in psychological content or cinematic narrative techniques such as flashbacks, perspectives, and focalisation. Consequently, Stiller capitalised on Lagerlöf's star quality by trying to shape cinematically the great storyteller persona, but without paying tribute to the distinctive cinematic genius of Lagerlöf's narrative techniques, which Sjöström had shown to be so compatible with cinematic *mise en scène*.

Notes

1 The research for this essay was made possible partly by funding from Holger och Thyra Lauritzens stiftelse för främjande av filmhistorisk forskning (the Holger and Thyra Lauritzen Foundation for the Promotion of Research into the History of the Cinema).

2 'Jag beundrar eder förmåga med film och gå hälst på bio då svenska skådespelare visas. Har mycket tänkt på hur Selma Lagerlöf's "Stormyrtösen" skulle bli om den blev inspelad under eder regi och med Greta Almroth i Helgas roll. Skulle det månne ej bli ett folkskådespel som alla tycker om? Förvisso, om ni åtar er det. Förlåt mitt tilltag att skriva en sådan begäran till eder, men jag skulle bli uppriktigt glad om ni ville spela in "Stormyrtösen". Jag är blott en ofärdig hemmadotter, icke rik och icke fattig. Kan jag få några ord om utgången av mitt ringa förslag vore jag oändligt tacksam.'

3 Swedish Film Institute, Stockholm. Victor Sjöström, 'Körkarlen', unpublished manuscript.

4 As Bo Florin has pointed out (1997, 100–107), this dependence on art is not unique to *Sir Arne's Treasure*. Sjöström was influenced by Christian Krogh's illustrations for Ibsen's epic poem 'Terje Vigen', and the influence from book illustrations is also evident in Sjöström's *Klostret i Sendomir* (*The Monastery of Sendomir*). Florin also emphasises inter-textual and intermedial relations between the film *Synnøve Solbakken* (1919) and famous genre paintings. One explanation Florin does not stress is the attraction audience members could feel when seeing famous paintings come alive in moving images, and the possibility of recognition that this medial continuity gave rise to through its connection with the common parlour game in which famous paintings and art motifs would be acted out.

5 'Det här är mycket fint och trevligt, Napoleon. Men i morgon ger vi oss ut på turné'.

6 'banal utländsk filmsmak'.

7 'Ack Värmland, du sköna, du härliga'.

CHAPTER 10

Jerusalem, Sons of Ingmar, and the transparent thickness of the cinematic view

Christopher Oscarson

Swedish film audiences enthusiastically awaited the release on New Year's Day 1919 of the first part of Svenska Bio's (Swedish Cinema) two-part *Ingmarssönerna* (*Sons of Ingmar*, aka *Dawn of Love*), because the film brought together for the second time the work of two of Sweden's most significant cultural figures—the author Selma Lagerlöf and the actor/director Victor Sjöström. Lagerlöf's reputation was well established, and her novel *Jerusalem* (1901–1902), upon which the film was based, had been a great critical and financial success (Nordlund 2005, 87). Sjöström too was a popular figure, having directed and acted in some of the most successful Swedish films to date, including *Terje Vigen* (1917), *Berg-Ejvind och hans hustru* (1918, *Eyvind of the Hills*), and the first Lagerlöf adaptation to film, *Tösen från Stormyrtorpet* (1917, *The Girl from the Marsh Croft*). Sjöström's *The Girl from the Marsh Croft* had been reviewed very favourably by critics (and by Lagerlöf) and did exceptionally well at the box office both in Sweden and abroad (Fullerton 2001, 59; Åhlander 1986, 367–8), which only heightened the anticipation for *Sons of Ingmar*. Furthermore, this was again a Lagerlöf story set in Dalarna, a region that had already by the turn of the century assumed a mythic aura for the country's emerging urban cultures striving to define what was prototypically Swedish (Näsström 1937, 9–14; Sporrong 2008, 193–202).

While not as popular as *The Girl from the Marsh Croft* internationally, *Sons of Ingmar* was nonetheless an overwhelming success in Sweden: 196,000 people reportedly saw the film in Stockholm alone, and this when the city had a total population of only 400,000 (Forslund 1980, 120; Åhlander 1986, 394). Contemporary Swedish accounts praised *Sons of Ingmar* not only because of Sjöström's perceived faithfulness to the original Lagerlöf text, but especially because of the striking landscape photography by Julius Jaenzon and purported realistic depiction of a quintessentially Swedish rural folk culture. One reviewer commented in *Svenska Dagbladet* that, 'You were truly proud to be Swedish during those hours when this incarnation of ur-Swedish temperament and ur-Swedish Nature unfolded before our eyes' (Lindqvist 1919).[1] Others too in the Stockholm press and trade journals praised *Sons of Ingmar,* hailing it as 'a document of great and lasting cultural-historical worth' (Anon. 1919a, 16),[2] and as a 'national treasure' (Zackarias Linberg 1919).[3]

These contemporary accounts suggest that a great part of the film's perceived cultural value derived from its ability to effectively capture and provide access to something that was otherwise geographically and temporally distant to many in the audience. Reviews went so far as to call *Sons of Ingmar* 'a piece of authentic Swedish Nature in summer finery' (Anon. 1919b),[4] and 'a living cultural-historical museum, a monument to traditional Swedish rural culture that lifts itself high over the dogged concern with the present found in most modern films' (Anon. 1919c, 28).[5]

Reading *Sons of Ingmar* strictly as a cultural-historical, documentary project that transparently records and represents Swedish Nature and folk culture, however, misses an important dimension to what is actually at stake in the work. Contrary to the claims of contemporary reviewers, who concentrated on the film's efforts to authentically portray the past and the nation's Nature with objective detachment, the film actually does have a 'dogged concern' with the present moment and a keen awareness of the way the cinematic medium not only records but mediates and actually constructs views particularly in regards to the natural landscape. While the film invokes the model of a transcendent, disembodied, detached spectator able to objectively survey and document the details and minutiae of a scene, it simultaneously counterbalances this by developing self-reflective and materially 'thick' viewing positions that refocus the perspective, and explores how even the most natural of views are mediated by both cultural and technological concerns. Thus this study will begin with a historical contextualisation of Lagerlöf's *Jerusalem* and Sjöström's *Sons of Ingmar* within the visual culture of early twentieth-century Sweden, and will focus on how Sjöström's adaptation—like Lagerlöf's own novel—draws attention to the problems of vision and knowledge as well as the significance of the embodied nature of the subject, especially in relation to Nature and landscape.

Cinema and the construction of Swedish Nature

The decades around the turn of the twentieth century witnessed an almost feverish desire to document and record the essence of national identity in a plethora of scientific, sociological, cultural, and artistic projects intent on mapping the boundaries and limits of Sweden and Swedish culture in an era of great technical, social, and cultural change. Alongside the work of authors and artists such as Lagerlöf, Verner von Heidenstam, Anders Zorn, and Richard Bergh were museological projects such as Artur Hazelius' Skansen and Gustaf Kolthoff's Biological Museum, the proliferation of reference works and scientific surveys about Sweden, atlases, and almanacs, the formation of tourist associations, and so on, which in various ways all attempted to provide an overview of essential aspects of national and regional identities. Gunnar Eriksson sums up the impulse of this age well by arguing that,

> taking inventory and mapping is a process of identification: it describes what Sweden is. In the industrial community, people were subjected to tremendous changes. More and more were forced to move not only from one geographical location to another but completely from one lifestyle to another. ... A people in transit are a people seeking their identity. (Eriksson 1978, 202)[6]

A wide variety of visual practices and technologies, including photography, were in place even before the advent of cinema, and they both fed and were fed by this desire for mapping and surveying, and taught viewers to see natural milieus organised as landscapes and as defining national character. The unique abilities of photography to record and disseminate an ostensibly objective view of the world invoked the actual presence of Nature while simultaneously maintaining a critical distance from the objects represented. The implied distance was important for photography's aura of objectivity, and this detachment was often explicitly incorporated into photographic practice, as evidenced in images reproduced, for example, in publications by Svenska Turistföreningen (the Swedish Tourist Association) (Erlandson-Hammargren 2006, 136–42), stereographic pictures (Snickars 2001, 60–72), and photographic postcards. They each tended to seek out remote vantage points that by virtue of their distance from the subject could give the viewer an overview of a given place. The photographic apparatus made possible certain idealised perspectives from elevated, removed positions that constructed and formed a vision of Sweden under a cloak of naturalness. As W. J. T. Mitchell has written, these images, 'naturalize a cultural and social construction, representing an artificial world as if it were simply given and inevitable, and [made] that representation operational by interpellating its beholder in some more or less determinate relation to its givenness as sight and site' (1994, 2). Photography was able to set up an empirical reality even at the same time as that reality was being constructed. In particular, Swedish topography was used as a blank screen against which images of native Swedishness and nationalism could be projected as if they were natural and given.

Cinema was born into this cultural milieu, and when domestic Swedish film production began in earnest in 1905–1907, filmmakers quite naturally drew upon their experience of still photography and used the new technology to record and document the nation—especially natural landscapes. In 1907, for example, Charles Magnusson—the future managing director for Svenska Biografteatern (better known as Svenska Bio), Sweden's most successful film company of the era—produced two short travel films, *En resa genom Dalarne* ('A Trip through Dalarna') and *Bilder från Fryksdalen (Gösta Berlings land)* ('Pictures from Fryksdalen (The Land of Gösta Berling)') that was part of an advertised larger project (never fully realised) to film the nation (Åhlander 1986, 14–15, 105). These particular locations were, of course, chosen for their cultural significance and because they already conformed to certain ideas about an idealised Swedish landscape. These actuality films of different locales and landscapes from around Sweden, referred to as 'naturbilder' (lit. 'nature pictures') came to form their own genre (Furhammar 1998, 54–6), and were a regular staple of typical film programmes, eventually becoming an important aesthetic precursor to fiction films like *Terje Vigen* and *Sons of Ingmar* a decade later.

The incorporation of landscape into narrative films was not absolutely unique to Swedish film, but the frequency with which Swedish Cinema features made use of on-location shooting after the success of

Terje Vigen in 1917 suggests that it was part of a very deliberate aesthetic strategy. These films (many of which were directed by Sjöström and photographed by the brothers Julius and Henrik Jaenzon) drew on photography's ability to attract the viewer's attention to the sight and site of the natural setting, and depended on spectators who were already accustomed to constructing landscapes out of natural scenery— especially out of the natural settings that seemed to be most Swedish and unique to the Nordic region. As landscapes they did not function as a setting in the traditional sense. The attention afforded them in the films gave them an aesthetic autonomy not completely subsumed by the narrative.

Embodied vision in *Jerusalem* and *Sons of Ingmar*

One of the effects of this attention to landscape was an increase in the perceived documentary value of the films, and this strategy was successful judging from the critical response cited previously. Both Lagerlöf and Sjöström make use of overviews to help orient their audience, but both complicate this transparent viewing perspective, although through different means. Lagerlöf's *Jerusalem* highlights, for instance, the insufficiency of a disembodied, transcendent model of vision in the beginning of the second chapter immediately following the part adapted for the film *Sons of Ingmar*. The local schoolmaster's young daughter engages in a decidedly cartographic task of building a model of the parish in the corner of her living room. After describing how she used soil from her mother's flowerpots for the fields, sticks and twigs for the forests, stones for the houses and buildings, and a long piece of glass for the river, the third person narrator states, 'The girl needed only to cast a glance over her structure of stone, earth, and twigs in order to see before her the whole parish. She thought that it was quite lovely.'[7] The reader is given a type of cartographic view, but this view is qualified. Instead of seeing everything 'directly' through the omniscient narrator, we see the parish quite literally through the girl's representation of the landscape. Lagerlöf is able to describe the layout of the parish without resorting to a disembodied perspective that floats over the site. Instead of 'seeing' the parish from a transparent and detached bird's eye view, the girl is shown looking at her own representation. There is even resistance from within the representation, as the reader is told that she could not manage to make the fields green and thus needed to compensate by imagining the model as representing the parish in early spring, before the crops had begun to grow.

By insisting on the girl's embodied perspective and the challenge the girl faced in manipulating the material pieces of the representation, Lagerlöf does not allow the perspective of the subject to unproblematically disconnect itself and hover above what is being viewed. The boundaries between subject and object are recognised as provisional and not entirely clear, as a significant degree of imagination is required to make the representation work. In essence, the passage in Lagerlöf's novel can be thought of as a clever end run which allows Lagerlöf to sit on both sides of a figurative fence: she manages to give the overview of the parish even as she calls the adequacy of that viewpoint into question. Unlike in film, the perspective in narrative fiction can be more easily manipulated, and here the perspective lies somewhere between the girl and the omniscient narrator, a manifestation of what Bjarne Thorup Thomsen has called the 'plurality of perspectives' in the novel (1997, 39). Both the embodied, contextualised view and the omniscient view coexist as alternatives, although they may still be seen to be in competition with each other.

Because of the nature of the medium, point of view in film cannot be as ambiguous and imprecise as in this scene in Lagerlöf's book. While Lagerlöf's invocation of bits of stone and glass is fundamentally different from the commitment of cinema to a material world, this scene in *Jerusalem* is nonetheless suggestive of the challenge that *Sons of Ingmar* takes on in making both a transcendent perspective and a subjective, embodied view simultaneously present for the viewer. The genius of the film is how Sjöström and the cinematographer, Julius Jaenzon, accomplish this, although through different means than the novel, as evidenced most plainly in the opening minutes of the film. In this sequence, the protagonist, Ingmar Ingmarsson—played by Sjöström—is ploughing his field and deep in thought about the beauty and bounty that surrounds him as well as a troubling decision he must soon make. He stops and rests on a bale of hay, and as he does so, he imagines his way into heaven so that he might ask his late father for advice about a particularly vexing question. The scene that follows is remarkable as it successfully combines competing modes of spectatorship that go to the heart of the concerns about vision, the subject's embodiment, and access to knowledge. Thanks to the use of a split screen, Ingmar remains sitting on the bale of hay while at the same

Illus. 1. After climbing a ladder (foreground) to heaven, Ingmar Ingmarsson speaks with St Peter at the Pearly Gates.

time he approaches and starts to climb a ladder reaching up to the sky. After showing that the ladder reaches up into heaven, the split screen then disappears and the camera follows Ingmar's ascent. Several times, he glances back over his shoulder, and the spectator is given Ingmar's progressively distant perspectives of the Dalarna landscape until the final creation of the unabashedly cartographic view from heaven. From this removed vantage point, Ingmar is able to see his entire home province (and indeed all of central Sweden) in a single, all-encompassing glance. Not surprisingly, this abstracted view is necessarily disembodied; to attain this perspective, Ingmar has needed to leave his 'body' behind, sitting on the haybale. His position for the final, cartographic, all-seeing, celestial perspective is decidedly not located in the space of lived experience: its vantage point is from everywhere at once without being anywhere in particular.

After reaching heaven and discussing with St Peter his desire to talk with his father (Illus. 1), he is allowed to proceed, and as he reaches the room in heaven where he will greet his father, the bird's-eye-view of topography is converted into a similarly all-encompassing view of history. Ingmar sees all of his Ingmarsson ancestors (or at least his male progenitors), 'from time immemorial' down to his recently departed father, gathered together into a single room (Illus. 2).[8] Just as the landscape was previously gathered together into an all-encompassing, cartographic view, here history has been similarly gathered into a single, surveyable moment.

By containing both time and space within the surveying gaze, the film implies a totalising perspective consistent with neo-Enlightenment paradigms of modern progress and faith in human rationality that led reviewers to praise the film as a cultural-historical document. The perspective of such an observer is necessarily placed at a critical distance so that the object of study can be seen in its totality. To survey one's own situatedness in time and history requires a disembodied perspective—illustrated marvellously in this case by Ingmar leaving his body behind for his journey—as the vision of space and time in their totality requires the subject to be posited outside of both. This is the model of the Cartesian *cogito* grounded in a fundamental split between the body embedded in time and space and the transcendent mind with objective access to reality. Ingmar's perspective, enabling the telescoping of topography and history, might thus be read self-reflexively as an articulation of cinema's transparency and power over the depiction of time and space in positing a transcendent, disembodied subject-viewer.

The appeal of this transcendent perspective is, of course, its presumed stability, mobility, and unencumbered access to knowledge. It avoids questions about the viewing subject's ontology because the boundaries shoring up identity are assumed to be secure; context is not important. There is a clear division between seeing-subject and seen-object, and the distance avoids the complications that come with recognising the limitations of embodied context. Jonathan Crary describes this visual paradigm in *Techniques of the Observer*, as a historical model of vision based on the mechanical mediation of the camera obscura dominant particularly in the eighteenth century. According to Crary, this model of vision was:

> congruent with [Descartes's] quest to found human knowledge on a purely objective view of the world. The aperture of the camera obscura corresponds to a single, mathematically definable point,

Illus. 2. Ingmar Ingmarsson (Victor Sjöström, in black in centre) meets all his Ingmarsson ancestors in 'heaven'.

from which the world can be logically deduced by a progressive accumulation and combination of signs. (Crary 1990, 48)

This disembodied vision presented itself as an objective truth about the world and a definitive perspective upon which one could ground sure knowledge. These assumptions about the camera obscura model of vision are strikingly similar to the cinematic apparatus described by Jean-Louis Baudry and others in the latter half of the twentieth century, an apparatus that he claimed started with Renaissance perspectivalism (which also led directly to the genre of landscape painting), and continued through to the modern faith in the 'reality effect' of photography and cinema (Baudry 1974–5, 39–44; see also Bazin 1967, 9–16). In this paradigm, photography and cinema together form the logical end-point of illustionistic representation.

Crary, however, contradicts Baudry's argument of continuity, and suggests a breakdown of this camera obscura model of vision early in the nineteenth century, before photography and cinema had even made their appearance. According to Crary, the idea that photography could provide an accurate picture of reality actually contradicted a subjective model of vision that was already in place before the technology enabling photography was developed. While Crary provides a convincing argument and Baudry's claims are not now commonly held among theorists, a potential deficiency in Crary's history of vision is that it tends to be too dichotomous, as it wants to see moments of rupture and transition from one model of vision to another when, in fact, films such as *Sons of Ingmar* suggest not a model of transition but of accumulation. In this film, the disembodied and transcendent perspective is counterbalanced, yet not replaced, with a re-embodiment of vision, and both modes coexist as viable alternatives.

With this as a background, it is thus not at all surprising to see another model of spectatorship implied by this significant scene at the beginning of *Sons of Ingmar*. Again, turning briefly to Lagerlöf's novel provides some hints as to a possible reading of this cinematic scene, developing multi-levelled spectating positions. By way of contextualising the relationship between the cinematic text and the literary text, it should be said that the film largely holds itself very close to its literary precursor. Just as the film went to great efforts in the naturalistic recreation of the period with the use of appropriate settings, it also adheres closely to the popular literary text as part of its claim to authenticity and legitimacy. Cinema was still very much fighting a battle for its artistic standing in the cultural sphere, and a large part of this film's prestige rested on its relationship to both the original novel and to Selma Lagerlöf's persona (Forslund 1980, 114–21). Much was made of Lagerlöf's contract with Swedish Cinema that allowed them to adapt her work, and the publicity for the film did not fail to take note of her approval of the final product (Anon. 1919d). So strictly, in fact, does *Sons of Ingmar* adhere to the literary text that even the intertitles come directly from the novel, and the mammoth two-part film only manages to adapt about forty pages of the first part of the two-volume novel.

Be this as it may, the passage from *Jerusalem* describing Ingmar's ascent into heaven highlights interesting differences when compared to the adapted film version, which in turn provides some compelling interpretive clues. As Ingmar is ploughing his fields at the beginning of the book, he is weighed down by a difficult decision he must make, and thinks about how much he would value his late father's advice on the question. As he begins to lose himself in his thoughts, he sits down, and the omniscient third-person narrator, describing the scene in the past tense, abruptly gives way to Ingmar's own thoughts in the present tense within quotation marks:

> The ploughman suddenly stopped in the middle of the field. He looked up and laughed. These thoughts amused him greatly, and he was so carried away by them that he hardly knew whether or not he was still upon the earth. It seemed to him that he had all of a sudden come all the way up to his old father up in heaven.
>
> 'And now as I come into the main room,' he went on, 'there are many farmers seated along the walls.'[9]

The film preserves Ingmar's interior monologue in the intertitles with the use of quotation marks, but it deviates from the source text by inserting a prolonged, special-effects-laden spectacle of the ascent into heaven not at all described in the book. This supernatural cinematic addition, which lasts several minutes and steps far outside the otherwise very down-to-earth, naturalist tendencies of the film, is, however, in a sense true to the text if one reads this cinematic embellishment in the context of the impossibility of a literal ascent into heaven. Ingmar, after all, is accomplishing the impossible by crossing the boundary between this world and heaven. Thus through this scene, Sjöström and Jaenzon underscore the transgressive nature of their decision to step outside of their own naturalist style; and not only that, but they seem to relish in the spectacle. Special effects and trick photography for a moment take over in a film that otherwise attempts to keep the apparatus hidden by maintaining a fairly rigid naturalist aesthetic. The stylistically unique nature of this scene calls attention to itself and to its own illusion-making power—a power that, judging from contemporary reviews, was deemed quite potent by most of the original audiences.

Nor is this self-reflexivity entirely absent in the written source. As indicated, Lagerlöf uses a third-person, omniscient voice to narrate this opening section of the novel. There are parallels between the transparency of this type of disembodied narratorial perspective and the transparent, cinematic apparatus discussed earlier. But in this passage, the use of quotation marks indicates an important turn. In the text, everything the reader finds out about heaven is filtered through Ingmar's perspective (as he is quoted directly), underscored by the abrupt change of tense from past to present. Ingmar steps forward to take on the role of the narrator. Not only, in other words, is the action of Ingmar's story presented, but the account also foregrounds Ingmar's telling of that story.

The film has to resort to several creative techniques to focus the narrative through Ingmar, and in doing so works against the otherwise detached, objective view of the camera. After the use of the split screen, the film crosscuts several times as Ingmar is climbing into heaven back to the sight of Ingmar still sitting on the bale of hay, as if to remind the viewer of the bifurcated view. Once in heaven, Ingmar starts to recount to his father the long backstory of how he has come to be in his particular predicament, and then a prolonged flashback sequence begins to fill in the back story, while the intertitles make use of quotation marks (as in the book) to remind the reader that the narration is all in Ingmar's own words. Furthermore, the intertitles also use an inset, a picture of Ingmar discussing with his father, to regularly prompt the viewer that this story is all being mediated through Ingmar.

This meta-fictive layer in the film suggests a more complicated visual dynamic than was assumed by contemporary critics focusing on objective views of landscape and folk culture. No longer is vision transparent; it is, in a sense, thicker, for now the reader is not only presented with a straightforward narrative or view, but also with a subject seeing and mediating the perspective. The chain of mediation goes even further, in that the film quite explicitly shows its relationship to the source novel, and the novel itself was widely known to have derived much of its material, in turn, from an actual group of Dalarna farmers who emigrated to Palestine in the late nineteenth century. The meta-fictive layers refocus readers/viewers on their own act of interpretation situated in a specific time and place, as they navigate through these various layers of the representations.

The choices of set design and location in the film further underscore the thickness of the view. While the representation of heaven's gates and St Peter in the film might be more or less recognisable Christian imagery, Ingmar's father's home fashioned after a typical Dalarna *gård* ('farm') is not. The imagery is consistent, however, with eighteenth- and nineteenth-century *dalmålning*, Dalarna's traditional folk art that often depicts biblical scenes entirely in the context of contemporaneous Dalarna social life. There is a certain opacity to this tradition, for the paintings incorporate the specific historical context in which they were painted as opposed to striving for an illusion of cultural-historical transparency. Wise men visiting the Christ-child dressed in Napole-onic military regalia, women visiting Christ's grave in Dalarna folk dress, and so on might have been more transparent for a naïve Dalar-na peasant—although this too might be disputed—but it is difficult to imagine it being so for even an early twentieth-century film-going audience. Thus, the invocation of Dalarna folk culture itself gestures towards a contextualised view influenced by the geographical and his-torical context. What on the one hand at first seemed to reach for a certain transparency, upon closer inspection refers more and more to its own power to create illusion and to the context of the point of view.

Conclusion

Both scientific and artistic attempts to map and document the nation in early-twentieth-century Sweden were working to establish defin-itions and boundaries, most fundamentally between the subject and the object, and more generally between Swedishness and Otherness. In so doing, it was hoped, Swedishness might be defined. The bifurcated vision traced here in both *Jerusalem* and *Sons of Ingmar* is born out of this somewhat nostalgic and backward-looking need to catalogue, record, define, and map the essential qualities of the nation, but also out of a recognition of the limitations and provisional nature of such attempts. The self-reflexive aspects of both works call attention to the ways in which even experiences of Nature and landscape are mediated by culture and technology, and they highlight the importance of con-text and the entangled networks in which the perceiving subject always finds herself. The thickening of vision complicates a simple Cartesian definition of subjectivity as a self-contained, disembodied abstraction. The radical implications of a dispersed model of subjectivity and group identity were, of course, not fully realised immediately, but would con-tinue to develop over the course of the coming century.

Sjöström's engagement with natural settings helped set the stage both for the Swedish cinema's long-standing interest in landscape and the ongoing re-evaluation of the human–Nature duality. Nature does not function as a passive backdrop in the service of narrative in his films, but bodies forth with an autonomy from narrative rarely seen before or since in mainstream narrative cinema. Each natural settings in his films is presented in what Martin Lefebvre has referred to as a 'spectacular mode' in which those who stand outside the narrative flow are thus transformed into something more autonomous by virtue of the fact that, for just a moment, 'the natural, outdoor setting is considered in its own right, as a landscape' (2006, 29). The characters must thus interact with it differently as they cannot be fully considered as separate from it, and spectators are invited to reflect upon their own relationship to those settings, the contingencies of their definitions, and the process by which they are transformed into landscape.

Notes

1 'Man var sannerligen stolt att vara svensk under de timmar, då denna inkarnation av ursvenskt kynne och ursvensk natur upprullades inför ens blickar'.
2 'ett dokument av stort och bestående kulturhistoriskt värde'.
3 'nationell egendom'.
4 'ett stycke äkta svensk natur i sommarfestskrud'.
5 'ett levande kulturhistoriskt museum, ett monument över gammal svensk bondekultur, [som] lyfter sig högt över de flesta moderna filmers rena aktualitetsvärde'.
6 'inventering och kartläggning är en identifikationsprocess: den talar om vad Sverige är. I industrisamhället drabbades människorna av stora förändringar. Alltfler tvingades i rörelse inte bara från den ena geografiska orten till den andra utan totalt från en livsstil till en annan. ... Ett folk i uppbrott är ett folk som söker sin identitet'.
7 'Flickan behöfde bara kasta en blick på sin byggnad af sten och jord och grankvistar, för att se för sig hela socknen. Hon tyckte, att det var riktigt vackert' (Lagerlöf 1901a, 55). All translations from Lagerlöf's *Jerusalem* are my own.
8 'ända från hedenhös' (Lagerlöf 1901a, 7).
9 'Plöjaren stannade med ens midt på åkern, han såg upp och skrattade. De här tankarna gjorde honom ett otroligt nöje, och de löpte i väg med honom, så att han knappt visste om han var kvar på jorden. Han tyckte, att han helt hastigt kommit ända upp till sin gamle far i himlen. '"När jag så kommer in i storstugan," fortfor han, "sitter där fullt af bondkarlar kring väggarna"' (Lagerlöf 1901a, 6–7).

CHAPTER 11

'Nothing about art is innocent'

Reading Edelfelt and Stiller

Helena Forsås-Scott

Lagerlöf's novella *Herr Arnes penningar* (1903, *Lord Arne's Silver*) and the versions it has inspired across a range of media provide exceptional material for intermedial analysis. Rooted in historical accounts (Weidel 1964, 210–14), and having as a precursor a short story by Lagerlöf published in 1897, 'Hämnd får man alltid' ('You Always get Revenge') (Lagerlöf 1943a, 174–80), the novella was first serialised in the quality women's weekly *Idun* from late autumn 1903 until early 1904 and published in the series *Iduns romanbibliotek* ('the *Idun* Novel Library') in 1903. It was then republished in 1904 in the series *Nordiskt familjebibliotek* ('Nordic Family Library') with illustrations by the leading Finnish artist Albert Edelfelt. The German translation of Lagerlöf's text, *Herrn Arnes Schatz* (1904), inspired Gerhart Hauptmann's drama *Winterballade* ('Winter Ballad'), which received its first performance at the Deutsches Theater, Berlin, in October 1917 (Cowen 1980, 192) and was published in the same year. Translated into Swedish and considerably adapted by Lagerlöf, *Vinterballaden* was staged at Nya Teatern (the New Theatre), Gothenburg, in September 1918 and published the following year.[1] On 22 September 1919, Svenska Bios Filmbyrå (Swedish Cinema's Film Unit) released a film based on Lagerlöf's novella with references to both Edelfelt's illustrations and Hauptmann's drama. *Herr Arnes pengar* (1921, *Sir Arne's Treasure*), scripted by Mauritz Stiller and Gustaf Molander and directed by Stiller, with Julius Jaenzon as the cinematographer, was sold to at least 46 countries, and had its première in London on 17 January 1921 and in New York on 26 November 1921 (Werner 1979, 28–34). Regarded as one of the iconic works of the Swedish silent film era, it is also considered by Anna Nordlund elsewhere in this volume.

In addition, Lagerlöf's text has inspired a Danish stage drama (1923); a Swedish radio drama (1953–4); a Swedish sound film (1954); and an opera by the Swedish composer Gösta Nystroem, first broadcast on 26 November 1959 and given its stage première at Stora Teatern (the Grand Theatre), Gothenburg, on 6 January 1961 (Werner 1979, 160–3). The German translation of Lagerlöf's text published in 1943 as a *Frontbuch* for the German soldiers in occupied Norway is analysed by Jennifer Watson elsewhere in this volume.

This essay focuses on Edelfelt's illustrations in the 1904 edition of the novella and on Stiller's film, and I am also going to pay some attention to the edition of Lagerlöf's text illustrated with stills from the film published in 1919. In my earlier study of Lagerlöf's text and the illustrations (1997), I developed a psychoanalytical reading inspired by Elisabeth Bronfen's *Over her Dead Body: Death, Femininity and the Aesthetic* that was dependent not just on extensive comparisons between Lagerlöf's text and Edelfelt's illustrations, but also on certain assumptions about the reactions of a male artist to the text of a female author around the turn of the twentieth century. I now prefer to distance myself from essentialism of any kind. The present essay approaches Edelfelt's illustrations and Stiller's film as texts. I have found very useful Mieke Bal's narratological approach that subjects images to 'readings' (and thus develops intermediality at the methodological level too): images, Bal writes, 'are not a retelling of the text but a use of it; not an illustration but, ultimately, a new text' (1991, 34–5).

Art, as Bal has emphasised in the Introduction to her *Reading 'Rembrandt': Beyond the Word–Image Opposition*, is

> both entirely artificial—that is, not 'natural'—and entirely real— that is, not separated from the ideological constructions that determine the social decisions made by people every day. Hence, nothing about art is innocent: it is neither inevitable, nor without consequences. (Bal 1991, 5)

So what ideological constructions and, more specifically, what discourses on gender were relevant when Edelfelt made his illustrations in 1904 and Stiller his film in 1919? In 1903, Swedish campaigners for women's suffrage had established a national organisation, and in 1919, the Swedish Parliament granted women the right to vote and full citizenship. But with regard to the representation of women in art, the discourse that had prevailed since the late eighteenth century remained firmly in place. As Linda Nochlin has underlined, representations of women in art were founded on and served to reproduce

> indisputably accepted assumptions held by society in general, art-
> ists in particular, and some artists more than others, about men's
> power over, superiority to, difference from, and necessary control
> of women, assumptions which are manifested in the visual struc-
> tures as well as the thematic choices of the pictures in question.
> (Nochlin 1991, 13)

In cinema as in pictorial art, the predominant gender roles were deeply traditional. To quote Annette Kuhn's summary of 'dominant cinema', 'Perhaps the only thing that can be concluded with any degree of certainty is that, structurally and thematically, the classic Hollywood narrative attempts to recuperate woman to a "proper place"' (Kuhn 1994, 34–5).

Who would have been the consumers of *Lord Arne's Silver* with Edelfelt's illustrations and of Stiller's film? When Lagerlöf's novella was first serialised in 1903–1904, and then published as part of the highly popular series of new fiction appearing as supplements to *Idun* (which, incidentally, supported the campaign for women's suffrage), the majority of the readers would have been middle-class and upper-middle-class women. While I have been unable to track down the circulation figures for the relevant years, the figure for 1909, 50,000 copies, can provide a rough indication; at the time, it was a remarkably high figure (Frostegren 1979, 13). The Nordic Family Library series in which Lagerlöf's text was published with Edelfelt's illustrations was a joint venture between the publishers Gyldendal in Copenhagen and Kristiania (the name of Oslo at this time) and Albert Bonnier in Stockholm, also targeted towards middle-class and upper-middle-class readers; women would most likely have made up a considerable pro-portion of these readers too (Svedjedal 1997, 36). In 1919, the year in which Stiller's *Sir Arne's Treasure* was released, Sweden, with a popula-tion of 5.8 million, had a total of 703 cinemas, and in 1919–20 more than 40 million cinema visits were made (Furhammar 2003, 45). The cinema appealed to audiences that were much more socially diverse than those at which *Lord Arne's Silver* had been targeted (although a low-cost edition, without illustrations, had appeared in 1917), with a large proportion of the cinema audiences belonging to the working class, and many women going to the cinema too (Sjöholm 2003, 48). The book illustrated with film stills, on the other hand, was intended for the upper end of the market, an example of a strategy by the publisher, Bonnier, to keep customers spending at 'a time of shortage and high living costs' (Bachmann 2013, 192).

There can be no doubt, then, as to the predominance of traditional gender roles in both pictorial art and the cinema at the time when Edelfelt's illustrations and Stiller's film were made—notions of gender roles that would most likely have been shared by the majority of the readers of the edition of Lagerlöf's novella with Edelfelt's illustrations. Given the impact of Hollywood films, it is likely that many cinema-goers shared it too. So what differences and new perspectives might readings of the illustrations and the film along the lines promoted by Bal provide? And, first and foremost, what would such readings involve?

Elisabeth Bronfen, central to my earlier analysis of Edelfelt's illustrations, draws not surprisingly on Laura Mulvey's 'seminal article on narrative and visual pleasure' (1992, 123); and Norman Bryson has provided a helpful introduction to Bal's approach by comparing it to that of Mulvey:

> In the [concept of the] Gaze, a single viewpoint contains the scene, and the viewer has no choice but to line up either inside it, as its subject, or as its exterior, its object, its victim. Resistance, as they say, is useless. Bal's reading agrees with Mulvey's and post-Mulveyan accounts of the Gaze in its sensitivity to vision as determined within institutions of masculinist, even rapist, power—yet the strategic outcome is different. Resistance is built into each point of the image's field. (Bryson 2001, 15)

With Bryson referring to Bal's analysis of Rembrandt's two paintings of Lucretia, the field in this particular case consists of the narrator (not synonymous with the artist), Lucretia, and the viewer. Given that each point of the field 'possesses powers of resistance', power in Bal's analysis is not monolithic 'but rather a set of relations ... such that the possibility of reversing the power relation is present at each node of the image's focalization' (Bryson 2001, 15).

In my earlier analysis, I was preoccupied with 'the feminine project' in Lagerlöf's text and its relationship to Edelfelt's illustrations (Forsås-

Scott 1997). To what extent might an approach along the lines pioneered by Bal help call into question the seemingly monolithic relations of gendered power in Edelfelt's illustrations, and so also begin to clarify the position of these illustrations in the context of the predominant discourse on gender in art at the time and, indeed, their potential for change? And to what extent might an approach drawing on Bal shed light on constructions of gender in Stiller's film too? When analysing the film, I shall also make use of a selection of the images in the upmarket edition of *Lord Arne's Silver* published in 1919, the stills inviting close study in much the same way as Edelfelt's illustrations do.

Albert Edelfelt's illustrations for *Lord Arne's Silver*, 1904

When the illustrations for *Lord Arne's Silver* were commissioned in early 1904 (Weidel 1960, 79–81), Lagerlöf and Edelfelt (1854–1905) were leading figures in Swedish literature and Finnish painting respectively. Lagerlöf had recently reinforced her position with the publication of the novel *Jerusalem* (1901–1902), commonly regarded as fundamental to the fame that was to result in a string of honours and awards, including the Nobel Prize for Literature. Renowned for his history paintings and portraits, Edelfelt was the first Finnish painter to achieve an international reputation. He was also a famous illustrator, best-known for his illustrations of the two-volume cycle of poems by Johan Ludvig Runeberg (1804–1877) celebrating the struggle of the Finnish troops against the Russian army in 1808–1809, *Fänrik Ståls sägner* (1848, 1860, *The Tales of Ensign Steel*). Following the defeat of the Finnish and Swedish troops, Finland became a Grand Duchy in the Tsarist Empire, gaining its independence only in 1917. Runeberg's cycle of poems was widely read in Sweden, and at one stage served Lagerlöf as a tentative model for what was subsequently to become her first novel, *Gösta Berlings saga* (1891, *Gösta Berling's Saga*) (Lagerlöf 1902b, 143–4). Edelfelt's illustrations of *Ensign Steel* were published in 1894–1900.

The illustrations of *Lord Arne's Silver* have been hailed as the most coherent set of illustrations in Edelfelt's output (Anttonen 2004, 216–17). They consist of sixteen gouaches or wash-drawings, varying considerably in size, with some of them very small. With their sparse details and somewhat blurred lines, they have been praised for conveying a sense of monumentality which, as Schaffer has pointed out (1989, 57), complements the fateful atmosphere generated by Lagerlöf's text about the sixteenth-century massacre and robbery in a parsonage, the pursuit of the perpetrators, and the conflict between love and the demands of revenge experienced by the sole survivor, a young woman, Elsalill. The atmosphere is reinforced by 'minor ornaments' (Anttonen 2004, 216) of six different types, small drawings printed as headpieces or at the ends of chapters or sections. Edelfelt had used a more limited range of 'minor ornaments' in a similar way at the ends of some of the poems in *The Tales of Ensign Steel*. In *Lord Arne's Silver* they include the seed-heads of poppies, three hour-glasses linked by a rope, a skull with poppies growing out of one eye socket, and, in a reference to the identity of the murderers, a bundle of thistles, denoting Scotland.

What do these images have to say about gender and power and, more specifically, what can readings of a selection of these images as texts, along the lines employed by Bal, contribute to our understanding of them and their effect in Lagerlöf's text? I am going to focus on four illustrations, all of them relatively large (Schaffer 1989, 57 notes that Edelfelt was not happy with the reduction in size and details necessitated by the format of the book), all of them developing the plot, and all of them relevant to the issue of gender and power.

The first of Edelfelt's illustrations to represent Elsalill is the headpiece for the second chapter, 'On the Jetty' (Lagerlöf 2011b, 26) (Illus. 1).[2] On the jetty in Marstrand, Elsalill is gutting fish, the sleeves of her grey dress rolled up to her elbows. The simple table in front of her is piled with fish, as are the two barrels next to it, and behind her are several other women, also gutting fish. Elsalill does not stop working, her hands busy with the fish, despite the fact that three men are standing in front of her. Occupying well over half the picture space, the male figures are wearing expensive cloaks and hats and armed with rapiers. Towering over Elsalill, the three male figures look down on her as she bends her slim body slightly sideways, away from them. But far from being overwhelmed by them, Elsalill is looking up and straight into their faces, and as she continues working she is clearly also speaking to them.

Read as a text in the context of rhetoric along the lines developed by Bal, the image can be seen to acquire further dimensions. The previous chapter, the first in Lagerlöf's novella, has told the story of the massacre at Solberga parsonage as three men, dressed in shaggy furs and entering at night through a hole in the roof, killed the occupants and made off with Lord Arne's chest of silver. Those arriving at the scene eventually

Illus. 1. The three Scots encounter Elsalill on the jetty in Marstrand. Illustration by Albert Edelfelt, 1904.

found a single survivor, a pauper maid whom Lord Arne had taken into his house, 'but she was so terror-stricken that she could neither speak for herself nor answer their questions' (Lagerlöf 2011b, 25).[3] In Lagerlöf's text, the scene on the jetty is represented by an omniscient narrator but with the focalisation frequently that of Elsalill. For the viewer of Edelfelt's illustration of Elsalill facing the three male figures there is no indication of her focalisation, but the image can arguably be read in terms of synecdoche, the scene effectively flagging up the plot so far and thus pinpointing the relations of gender and power. Armed and dressed in sumptuous outfits, the three men epitomise the massacre and robbery at the parsonage: it is thanks to Lord Arne's silver that they have been able to acquire the elegant clothes in which they are strolling on the jetty in Marstrand. But we also know from Lagerlöf's text about the sole survivor, the young girl. In the novella the first reference to her has been in connection with the evening meal at the parsonage, when she has been sitting at the foot of the table close to Lord Arne's granddaughter, 'and there seemed to be great friendship between them' (Lagerlöf 2011b, 18).[4] As one of the men says to Elsalill on the jetty, they had been unaware that anyone had survived the massacre; and as she faces the three men with their rapiers, the synecdochal reading can be developed further, the situation of Elsalill recalling that of her foster sister as she was facing the three intruders on the night of the mas-

137

sacre. The killing of her foster sister is central to Elsalill's commitment to taking revenge on the perpetrators. In Lagerlöf's text the three men merely laugh at her, but Edelfelt's image arguably also anticipates her act of revenge. A rhetorical reading of Edelfelt's illustration, in other words, brings out the tensions in terms of power between the points in the field and unsettles what would seem to be traditional relations of gender, contrasting masculine power with feminine agency.

These tensions are no less conspicuous in the second of the images by Edelfelt I want to discuss, the frequently reproduced one of Elsalill's dead foster sister pursuing the leading Scot across the ice (Illus. 2). In Lagerlöf's text the focaliser here is Torarin, a fishmonger who becomes a helper in the project of revenge demanded by the dead Lord Arne; and as Torarin travels across the ice at night, discerning the ghost of a young female that remains invisible to the male figure being pursued, the viewer of the illustration is allowed to share the perspective that is making Torarin so frightened. As in the image of Elsalill and the three male figures on the jetty, at first sight there would seem to be no doubt as to the relations of gender and power. The image is dominated by the big, dark bulk of the male character who is striding diagonally across the picture space, taking up more than two-thirds of it and with his headgear, legs, and cloak reaching well beyond it. The ghost of the foster sister, by contrast, takes up little more than one-third of the space on the left, the cloak of the male character, the ice, and the horizon partly visible through her. The image, however, can be read metaphorically, summarising the feminine project of revenge on the male perpetrators. As the ghost of the foster sister floats behind the male character, her face seen from the side, her hands folded across her chest and her slim body bent slightly backwards and contrasting with the indistinct dark shape of the male figure, the shape of her body to some extent echoes that of Elsalill on the jetty. So, too, does her outfit with its long, belted dress and tight-fitting cap. Although it is representing just one of the female characters, the image plays on the convergence of the figures of the foster sister and Elsalill, and points towards the prominence of liminality as, in Lagerlöf's text, each of them goes on to be mistaken for the other. And despite the discrepancy between the male figure and the female one, the latter is clearly in control, worrying and frightening the male she is pursuing across the frozen sea.

Two of Edelfelt's images form a pair, and I am going to conclude my

Illus. 2. The ghost of Elsalill's fostersister pursues Sir Archie across the ice. Illustration by Albert Edelfelt, 1904.

analysis of his illustrations by looking at them together. Appearing on consecutive pages, they need to be read metonymically, as examples of temporal contiguity; interestingly, the viewer/reader has to turn the page to appreciate the similarities and contrasts between them. In Lagerlöf's text both scenes are represented by the omniscient narrator, but the focalisation is mostly that of Elsalill, with her thoughts prominent. In the first of the illustrations Elsalill, having just promised Sir Archie, the leading Scot, to accompany him back to Scotland and become his wife, is walking with him along a snowy street in Marstrand (Illus. 3). In an echo of the illustration of the ghost of the foster sister pursuing the Scot across the ice, the big, indistinct male figure, here in the right half of the illustration, partly reaches beyond the picture space. Far bigger than the small female figure, he is also embracing her, his hands reaching around her arms. In a sense the image is Edelfelt's most intimate one of Sir Archie and Elsalill. But this is not an instance of lovers looking into each other's eyes. Instead Elsalill, who occupies the middle of the picture rather than appearing on the left-hand side as in the majority of these illustrations, is clasping and perhaps wringing her hands and staring ahead and down, her face deeply troubled. In

Illus. 3. Elsalill and Sir Archie. Illustration by Albert
Edelfelt, 1904.

a visual equivalent of her focalisation in Lagerlöf's text, her body and
her agony dominate this illustration, and the tension is enhanced by
the parallels with the figure of her dead foster sister pursuing the Scot
over the ice, the similarities consisting not just of their clothing and, in
particular, their tight-fitting caps, but also of the arrangement of their
arms folded or held across their chests. According to Lagerlöf's text,
Sir Archie has indeed just mistaken Elsalill for her dead foster sister,
and it is this encounter that has made him realise how he should act:
'Now I know what I shall do in atonement, so the dead girl will stop
haunting me' (Lagerlöf 2011b, 62).[5] In Edelfelt's illustration, however,
the echo of the image of the dead foster in the figure of Elsalill ensures
that the project of the female character/s predominates.

This feminine project is expanded and clarified as the viewer/read-
er turns the page to the second image, the headpiece of the chapter
entitled 'Her Restless Spirit' (Lagerlöf 2011b, 66) (Illus. 4).[6] Again,
Edelfelt has represented a snowy street in Marstrand, although there
is no longer a blizzard blowing. As in the image on the previous
page, Elsalill is walking along the street. She is wearing the same
outfit and cap, her hands clasped in the same way, and again, she is

Illus. 4. Elsalill and the bloody footprints. Illustration by
Albert Edelfelt, 1904.

looking down and staring in front of her. But this time there is no
Sir Archie beside her, and her figure has been placed in the right half
of the picture space—the half in which the male figures are usually
placed in these illustrations. The convergence with the figure of the
ghost of the foster sister (Illus. 2) is of course relevant here too; here,
moreover, the presence of the dead foster sister is further reinforced
by the bloody footprints in the snow, which Elsalill is staring at and
following down the street. While the positioning of the two images
with their conspicuous parallels has clearly been carefully calculated,
a view of them as contiguous brings out not just the fusion of the
figures of Elsalill and her dead foster sister but, most importantly,
the role of the female body, alone in the street in the second of these
images. The foster sister, in a symbolic act of rape, was stabbed to
death by Sir Archie in the parsonage, and in another symbolic act of
rape, Elsalill will soon make a watchman's spear penetrate her heart.
But this latter case will involve an example of the female body being
used as a weapon, with Elsalill's act, in conjunction with the work of
her dead foster sister, ensuring that Sir Archie and the other perpetrators of the massacre will be unable to escape.

To sum up, then, my readings of this selection of Edelfelt's illustrations, images which at first sight seem to reinforce relations of gender
and power of the kind that were predominant in art at the beginning

of the twentieth century turn out, when analysed along the narrato-logical and rhetorical lines developed by Bal, to be far more complex.

Mauritz Stiller's film *Sir Arne's Treasure*, 1919

On the borderline between the medium of pictorial art and the me-dium of film, it is worth recalling Walter Benjamin's contrast between the magician–painter on the one hand and the surgeon–cameraman on the other: 'The painter maintains in his work a natural distance from reality, the cameraman penetrates deeply into its web' (Benjamin 1973, 235). The resulting pictures are entirely different, for while the painter's picture is 'a total one', the cameraman's picture 'consists of multiple fragments which are assembled under a new law' (236). The notion of 'multiple fragments' has special resonances in the case of Stiller's *Sir Arne's Treasure*, for in addition to the 'permeation of reali-ty' to which Benjamin is referring (236), the fragments combining in J. Julius' cinematography also derive from Edelfelt's illustrations which serve, according to Bo Florin, as 'visual intertexts' in the film (1997, 107). Moreover the script of the film, by Stiller and Gustaf Molander, had made extensive use of Hauptmann's drama based on Lagerlöf's novella, 'Winter Ballad'. Such quotations, as Irina Rajewsky has pointed out, can serve as a means of paying homage to the other medium—or of rivalling it (2005, 60).

Mauritz Stiller (1883–1928) was born in Helsinki and had a career as an actor in Finland before settling in Sweden. As detailed by Anna Nordlund in her essay in this volume, *Sir Arne's Treasure* was the first of his films based on a text by Lagerlöf; in 1923 he was to direct a film based on *The Tale of a Manor*, entitled *Gunnar Hedes saga* in Sweden and released in English as *Snowbound* or *The Blizzard*, with his *Gösta Berlings saga* (*The Story of Gosta Berling*) launched in 1924. The script of *Sir Arne's Treasure*, written by Gustaf Molander and subsequently substantially revised by Stiller, was also approved by Lagerlöf before filming began (Werner 1979, 21–2, 25). The filming took place between February and May 1919.

Gösta Werner has interpreted the numerous and extensive intertitles in Stiller's film, largely verbatim quotations from *Lord Arne's Silver*, as an expression of Stiller's and Molander's loyality to Lagerlöf's text (Werner 1979, 25–6). As Sofia Bull has explained, the intertitles were the work of a calligrapher, Alva Lundin, and her use of specific lettering, in this

Illus. 5. The escape of the Scots.

case 'a beautiful blackletter font', to indicate the period in which the film was set was already common in Hollywood (Bull 2010, 117). But if the prominence of Lagerlöf's text was a sign of loyalty, this loyalty has to be qualified in light of the film as a whole.

While the subheading of Stiller's film, 'A winter ballad in five acts',[7] alludes to Hauptmann's drama, the film narrates a story of its own. Most immediately striking in comparison with Lagerlöf's novella is the fact that the film turns the fabula, the chronological 'sequence of events' (Bal 1999, 6), into the story. The film thus begins with a sequence that appears late in Lagerlöf's text and then in the narration of Sir Archie: the Scottish mercenaries are escorted from Swedish territory following a conspiracy, and the three leading figures are put in prison. The film, in other words, foregrounds male characters and action, a shift that is further reinforced by the intertitles which sanction Sir Archie's words from the novella as those of an omniscient narrator. The sequence detailing the intrepid escape of the three Scots epitomises masculinity and action, and their joint effort to move a big gun so as to get out through the opening in the wall of the fortress is not only proof of their resolution and strength (in terms laden with unmistakably phallic symbolism), but also—to apply Mulvey's terminology—of their roles in 'advancing the story, making things happen' (2000, 41) (Illus. 5).

The face of Sir Archie (Richard Lund), moreover, is prominent in the still as he and his two companions struggle to move the gun; and as Bo Florin has demonstrated, the camera angles throughout have the effect of turning Sir Archie into the central character of the film (1997, 88–94). The still, then, highlights the prominence of masculine power and action in Stiller's film.

Elsalill and her foster sister, on the other hand, have considerably reduced roles in the film. Stiller and Molander have done away with much of the supernatural material in Lagerlöf's narrative, including the key scene in which the ghost of Lord Arne gives the ghost of his granddaughter (not named in Lagerlöf's text but called Berghild in Stiller's film, just as in Hauptmann's drama) the task of seeking revenge on the perpetrators of the massacre, and as a result it is solely Elsalill's close relationship with her foster sister that drives her struggle for justice in the film. It is significant, too, that Stiller's Elsalill (Mary Johnson) is effectively confined indoors, in the hut of Torarin's mother and in the Town Hall Tavern. The exceptions are so rare (with one of them occurring in a dream), that Stiller's famous paralleling of Edelfelt with the women of Marstrand carrying Elsalill's body across the ice from the ship is in fact not well motivated in the film—for how could these women know about a female character who is hardly ever seen in public? The still of Elsalill in the taproom of the Town Hall Tavern is thus a typical example of the kind of context in which she is represented in the film (Illus. 6). Having been led in a dream to the tavern by her foster sister who has asked her to help with the washing up, Elsalill, unable to forget her dream, takes the same route to the tavern the following day (for once, going out of doors) and similarly finds herself helping with the washing up. From the taproom, she also has a clear view of the three Scots sitting at a table. But as she prepares to wash up drinking-cups and plates, the focus is on her face and upper body. At the centre of the still, her body in its high-necked, long-sleeved, and rather tight-fitting dress is at a slight angle to the camera. The white of her frilled collar and cap frame her face and draw the spectator's gaze to the beautiful symmetry of her features, but also to her serious expression, her face dominated by her big eyes, looking upwards as she appears lost in thought. This eroticised young female is a classic example of an *ingénue*. In Lagerlöf's text, Elsalill in the taproom is the focaliser and indeed the subject, but the filmic discourse convincingly represents her as an object.

Illus. 6. Elsalill in the taproom.

In a still that can be read as a metaphor for the relations of gender throughout much of Stiller's film, Sir Archie, aware that Elsalill has unmasked him as one of the perpetrators of the massacre and hearing the town guard approaching, picks her up and uses her as a shield to help him escape (Illus. 7). This abduction scene provides an extreme version of the objectification of the female body, her light-coloured clothing making her stand out against the dark background, and the eroticisation of it all highlighted by the fact that she is bent backwards (in a position that must have been extremely uncomfortable for Mary Johnson) as she rests on Sir Archie's shoulder. As Astrid Söderbergh Widding has pointed out, the film has been reinforcing the foster sister's identification with Elsalill following Elsalill's first encounter with Sir Archie in the hut belonging to Torarin's mother, when Elsalill has begun wearing a white cap like Berghild's instead of her original checked one (2001, 33); however, in my view there is a further dimension to the still of Sir Archie with Elsalill slung over his shoulder. It has a 'visual intertext' (Florin 1997, 107), namely Edelfelt's image discussed above of the ghost of the foster sister pursuing Sir Archie across the ice. Wearing seemingly identical outfits, the female bodies in both cases are bent

145

Illus. 7. Sir Archie prepares to flee, using Elsalill as a shield.

backwards, the perspectives highlighting the outlines of their bodies and, in particular, the very similar profiles of their faces. If we draw on the intertext from Edelfelt, in other words, the seemingly helpless female figure in the film is metaphorically related to her dead foster sister and still very much involved in their joint project to seek revenge.

The confirmation comes with the shot of Elsalill directing the watchman's spear towards her heart. Serving as Sir Archie's shield as he is making his way up the stairs of Torarin's mother's hut, Elsalill is close to enabling Sir Archie to escape from the watchmen. In Lagerlöf's text, in which the project of revenge thus has far bigger proportions and the relationship between Elsalill and her foster sister is much more elaborate, the thought of Elsalill highlighted by the omniscient narrator at this point concerns her foster sister and their joint project of revenge: 'Now I will serve my foster sister in such a way that the task is finally brought to completion' (Lagerlöf 2011b, 78).[8] With the reasons for Elsalill's agency far more limited in the film and her act here consequently much more unexpected, her thought at this point, represented in an intertitle, concerns not her foster sister but Sir Archie: 'I have been loving a wolf in the forest' (Lagerlöf 2011b, 77).[9] Yet the extreme act of violence that Elsalill's action is leading up to as Sir Archie's face, distorted by anger, is visible by her side, can be read synecdochically. There are parallels here with Rembrandt's painting of Lucretia, as analysed by Bal, with Bal showing how a metaphorical reading of rape as self-murder conveys the idea of the victim as somehow responsible (Bal 1991, 68), while a reading foregrounding synecdoche makes Lucretia's act 'stand for the entire story, the rape and its consequence' (1991, 70). In Stiller's film, the shot of the female figure directing the spear towards her heart with a male face contorted with anger next to her makes the figures of Elsalill and her dead foster sister fuse: this is another version of the night of the massacre when the foster sister was stabbed through the heart. Condensing in it this rape and its consequences, the shot simultaneously highlights the feminine agency about to bring the male perpetrators to justice. Again, a narratological reading drawing on rhetoric brings out the dynamics of the relations of gender and power.

Conclusion

In her analysis of the Rembrandt Lucretias, Mieke Bal emphasises 'the inextricable intertwining of verbal and visual representation' (1991, 69). She is referring to the role of rhetoric in shaping our perception of reality, our responses to it, and, ultimately, the potential for change. In my previous study of *Lord Arne's Silver* and Edelfelt's illustrations, I argued that the exceptionally wintry weather that is so prominent in Lagerlöf's narrative, with vast expanses of snow and the ice covering the sea throughout the extensive archipelago, provides a 'space for significant alternatives, its very transience adding weight and dimensions to the events and profiling them against the occurrences on firmer ground' (1997, 231). I then read the joint project of the dead foster sister and Elsalill as the most important of these significant alternatives—and I still do. But some aspects of my earlier interpretation of Edelfelt's illustrations now strike me as simplistic: I believe I have shown, drawing on Bal's approach, that a more sophisticated reading can bring out tensions in terms of gender and power that result in greater concord between Edelfelt's images and Lagerlöf's text than I observed previously. And as I have tried to demonstrate, an analysis along the lines pioneered by Bal can also help add depth to Stiller's film, the approach all the more relevant in light of the fact that some of the stills were reproduced in the edition of Lagerlöf's text published in 1919. In his subsequent film based on a text by Lagerlöf, *Snowbound* or *The Blizzard*, Stiller interestingly distanced himself quite emphatically from his source of inspiration, radically reducing the quotations from Lagerlöf's novel along with the role of the central female character (again played by Mary Johnson), who was thus confirmed in her role as *ingénue*. In this context it seems symbolic that his next Lagerlöf film, *The Story of Gosta Berling*, was to launch Greta Gustafsson (Garbo) on her Hollywood career. The fact that *Sir Arne's Treasure* is less adapted to the demands of Hollywood helps make it such rewarding material for the kind of analysis I have undertaken here.

Nothing, indeed, about Edelfelt's illustrations or Stiller's film is innocent. In the midst of their conformity to the dominant discourses on pictorial art and film respectively, they problematise, albeit to different degrees, relations of gender and power. In so doing, they also open up for alternatives.

Notes

1 For an analysis of Hauptmann's drama in relation to Lagerlöf's novella, and also some comments on Lagerlöf's translation and adaptation of Hauptmann, see Forsås-Scott 2013.
2 'På bryggorna' (Lagerlöf 1904b, 33).
3 'men hon var så förbi af skrämsel, att hon hvarken kunde tala eller svara' (Lagerlöf 1904b, 32).
4 'och det såg ut att råda stor vänskap mellan dem' (Lagerlöf 1904b, 17).
5 'Nu vet jag hvad jag vill göra, på det att den döda må bli försonad och upphöra att förfölja mig' (Lagerlöf 1904b, 102).
6 'Den fredlösa' (Lagerlöf 1904b, 108).
7 'En vinterballad i fem akter'.
8 'Nu vill jag tjäna min fostersyster så, att detta ärendet ändtligen lyktas' (Lagerlöf 1904b, 133).
9 'Jag har älskat en ulf i skogen' (Lagerlöf 1904b, 130).

CHAPTER 12

The Phantom Carriage and the concept of melodrama

Tytti Soila

Selma Lagerlöf was an early movie fan. She was fascinated by the possibilities of expression and storytelling beyond the written and spoken word. In trying to understand the specific meanings and emphases of Lagerlöfian storytelling when transposed to the medium of moving images, the aim of this essay is not to track the genealogy of the different elements in the film to be discussed. It is clear that the appearance of different components of the story and techniques of storytelling are of significance for popular cinema, and that the comparative aspect with, say, a novel may be useful in that this may highlight the moments of choice in the realisation of the film. But I think the most interesting feature in the encounter between Lagerlöf the novelist and Victor Sjöström the film director is to be found in their shared sense for the contradictions of human feelings and the expressive capacity of pathos.

I shall therefore focus on the organisation of the components of the story that reinforce the essential paradox of melodrama: the expression of what cannot be expressed in logical or verbal terms—the (allegedly) ineffable. A central notion for my analysis is melodramatic sensibility, a notion that derives from Christine Gledhill's suggestion that melodrama should be regarded as a mode of expression that combines realism, excess, and emotionality, since it by taking 'its stand in the material world of everyday reality and lived experience, and acknowledging the limitations of the conventions of language and representation ... proceeds to force into aesthetic presence identity, value and plenitude of meaning' (1987, 33). Being 'sensible' in such a way, melodrama utilises a plenitude of expressive means too, 'speaking' to the audiences in sensory modes (music, movement, words, gesture, colours) that reach them on an emotional level, often moving them to tears.

The genre

Melodrama has been a popular cultural form across the Western world for more than two centuries. Greatly loved by the audiences in nineteenth-century Europe, melodrama transferred into the cinema in the early twentieth century with equal success. The businessmen of the period realised that the best way to make a profit from the new medium of moving images was to exploit its inherent capacities: the potential for the spectacular, for emotional expressivity, and for narrative suspense. These all corresponded well with the characteristics of stage melodrama as it derived from the boulevard theatre in Paris at the turn of the eighteenth century. A hundred years later, theatrical melodrama reached the peak of its popularity in London and the large American cities, now ready to be transferred into the cinema (Vardac 1987, 68–88; Waldekranz 1976, 267–77; Gledhill 1987, 24).

Film historians have often stressed the kinship between theatre melodrama and film melodrama. However, it should not be forgotten that expressions of the melodramatic sensibility are easy to trace in other popular forms of nineteenth-century entertainment, most explicitly in vaudeville, dime novels, and the work of authors such as Charles Dickens, Victor Hugo—and Selma Lagerlöf (Waldekranz 1976, 245–8; Sahlberg 1961, 196). The edifice of melodrama has actually been characterised as a 'hotchpotch' in which many different forms of media or expression 'mesh' with each other (Gledhill 1987, 18–20). W. J. T. Mitchell seems to be right in stating that 'all arts are "composite" arts (both text and image); all media are mixed media, combining different codes, discursive conventions, channels, sensory and cognitive modes' (1995, 94–5). Mitchell has also pointed out that,

> the necessary subject matter is … the whole ensemble of *relations* between media, and relations can be many other things besides similarity, resemblance, and analogy. Difference is just as important as similarity, antagonism as crucial as collaboration, dissonance and division of labour as interesting as harmony and blending of function. (Mitchell 1995, 89–90)

One might actually say that the most genuine characteristic of melodrama is its capacity successfully to exploit other popular genres, a feature that was quite familiar to Selma Lagerlöf too. On an intuitive as well as on a professional level, Lagerlöf had a deep understanding of the 'melodramatic' qualities—such as uncompromised passion and contradictory impulses—of human experience (Furhammar 2010, 88). Her characters conform to the class and gender rules in society, facing the compelling impossibilities of life with equanimity. Yet, within the narrative frame of a particular story, the inner desires and suppressed feelings of the characters, often at odds with prevailing societal conditions, are acknowledged as real. The recognition of emotions that are denied, contradictory, and do not fit in is the basis on which the popularity of melodrama rests, and such qualities may also be found in *Körkarlen* (*The Phantom Carriage*).

Experience and expression

Melodrama is about sentiments and values. Originally, melodrama was developed by hard-working and inventive theatre directors as a mouthpiece of the rebellious bourgeoisie during the French Revolution. The idea was to teach the virtues and values of the new class to audiences. It undoubtedly had its supporters among the illiterate audiences in Paris, addressing them in a didactic manner that relied on illustration instead of verbal argument, and on the combination of music and gesture rather than logical deduction (Waldekranz 1976, 112–50; Gledhill 1987, 11).

In melodrama, the rhythm or pace of experience often establishes itself against the backdrop of moral or intellectual values. According to the film historian Thomas Elsaesser,

> the persistence of melodrama might indicate the ways in which popular culture has not only taken note of social crises—and the fact that the losers are not always those who deserve it most—but has also resolutely refused to understand social change in other than private contexts and emotional terms. In this, there is obviously a healthy distrust of intellectualisation and social theory, insisting that other structures of experience—those of suffering, for instance—are more in keeping with reality. (Elsaesser 1985, 170)

Thus, according to Bill Nichols, in the use of *mise en scène* and every-day actions—such as setting the table or lighting a cigarette—a melodrama can construct a powerful set of tensions between a character's physical embodiment and the (moral) expectations that the spectator or the other characters in the story may have of him or her. And Nichols continues:

> The films exhibit a 'contents under pressure' that usually erupts in moments of emotional excess on which the popular definition of melodrama depends. That excess reverberates with the basic historical tensions of class, race, and sex that are expressed more than they are resolved, as characters live out the impossible contradictions of their lives. (Nichols 1985, 165)

The 'impossible contradictions' often deal with forbidden desires and moral obligations.

The tensions between the (societal) constraints on the one hand and the desires of the characters on the other, are expressed in melodrama as a set of binary oppositions, for example evil versus pious, light versus darkness and, of course, male versus female. In the course of the narrative flow and by way of a causal economy of 'punishment' and 'reward', certain categories are depicted as respectable, others as reprehensible. According to Christine Gledhill, this is how melodrama manages to restore and promote values that are supportive of (bourgeois) society even if its power over audiences lies in its capacity to go against the grain and acknowledge the ineffable—the potentially subversive dimensions in society (Gledhill 1987, 33).

My aim in this essay is to explore some expressions of the desire felt by a Salvation Army worker, Sister Edith, for a wretched, married man, David Holm, as they appear in Sjöström's film, emphasised by the possibilities of the medium itself. As the storyline outlined below shows the audience, Edith's love for David is unfeasible and inappropriate. Yet it exists. In melodramatic moments of 'emotional eruption', Edith's feelings are acknowledged. First, in spite of the many indications that David Holm is the main character, Edith's desire is the prime mover in the story. She calls for David Holm, she sends her friends to look for him. The force of her character is further emphasised by the recurring images that, in the present tense of the story, centre her body as if her pleas were addressed from a throne.

Another significant feature of the film is the focus on the hands and the gestures of Edith and of David's wife, Anna, in key scenes.

The tale

The story in *The Phantom Carriage* is both simple and complicated. David Holm (Victor Sjöström), a working man and family father, gets into bad company, starts drinking, wrecks his life, and finally ends up in prison where he decides to reform. Once out of prison he finds that his wife Anna (Hilda Borgström) has left their home taking their children with her. Bitter and vindictive, David takes to drinking more heavily, contracts tuberculosis, and arrives in the city where Sister Edith (Astrid Holm) is working as a slum-sister.

The two meet when the homeless David looks for shelter at the Salvation Army hostel. Sister Edith contracts tuberculosis from mending the sleeping man's clothes and, as the story begins, on New Year's Eve, she is about to die—as is David Holm. On this night he gets into a drunken fight and is injured so badly that Death's searcher (Tore Svennberg) appears with his cart to fetch him, aiming to pass his pitiful task of driving the deathcart—the phantom carriage—to David until another wretch dies on a subsequent New Year's Eve and takes over the task.

However, Death's searcher is the same person, Georges, who once dragged David Holm down with him. He is willing to give David a respite to make amends. A journey begins during which David Holm has to face all the acts of betrayal and evil he has committed during his life. At the same time, Edith on her deathbed is begging for a respite too. She cannot die in peace unless she is allowed to see David Holm once more to find out whether he has had a change of heart, and whether her prayers for him have been heard.

The fact is that Edith, in her eagerness to reform David, has brought him and his estranged wife back together. But instead of reforming, David has continued the daily abuse of his family, driving his wife Anna to the verge of insanity. This very night Anna has decided to kill her children and then herself. However, the story ends, if not happily then at least in atonement: Sister Edith succumbs to her disease and, as David arrives home in time to prevent Anna from killing their children and herself, the spouses are united in tears and in David's newly realised mission to 'raise his own home from the ruin into which it had fallen', as Lagerlöf puts it in her text (Lagerlöf 2011a, 114).[1]

Illus. 1. Two of the skilful professionals at one of the emotional climaxes of the film: Astrid Holm as Sister Edith asking for a respite, and Tore Svennberg as the Death's searcher.

This is one way of summing up the story. However, by choosing to play the role of David Holm himself, Victor Sjöström, the director, gave the character an extra-cinematic significance hard to overestimate. He was a famous actor and one of the leading film directors in Sweden at the time. Just this one decision would make David Holm the centre of the story told. Hilda Borgström, who played Anna, was a celebrated leading actress at the Royal Dramatic Theatre in Stockholm. She had starred in Sjöström's film *Ingeborg Holm* less than a decade earlier, a successful role that would surely bring an air of suffering and tragedy to her performance in *The Phantom Carriage*. *Ingeborg Holm* (1913) was also directed by Victor Sjöström. It is the story of a woman who, following the death of her husband, loses the custody of her children and ends up insane in an asylum. The film had such an impact on Swedish audiences that the legislation concerning poor relief was reformed in 1918.

The Danish actress Astrid Holm, originally a ballet dancer, who played the lovable Edith, was contracted as a promising 20 year old in the Royal Theatre company in Copenhagen by the time of the shooting of *The Phantom Carriage*. She had made her début as a film actress in 1917 and Sister Edith was her sixth role after her role in the Danish film *Avalanche* (*Lavinen*, Emanuel Geregers), released earlier in 1920. Tore Svennberg who played the wretched Georges was known from the two Sjöström films *Ingmarssönerna* (1919, *Dawn of Love*), and *Klostret i Sendomir* (1920, *The Monastery of Sendomir*), and had had a long career in different theatre companies, touring in both Sweden and Finland.

All the main actors contracted for *The Phantom Carriage* were thus skilful professionals, familiar with the routines of their profession. The basis of an actor's career at this time was typecasting: once a hero, always a hero; once a crook, always a crook. Many actresses played old women from their youth, while others played young girls until they retired. Part of an actor's scene image was his or her clothing, which most often entailed a considerable investment for the individual. The theatre companies regularly provided only the stars, and those participating in historical plays, with costumes (Soila 1997b, 168–70).

Acting conventions were quite strict and some of them dated back to ancient Greece. A performance on the stage was governed by rules (and superstitions), and was largely based on recitation and bodily conventions. Aspects such as the position of the actors' hands, along with gestures and mimicry, were coded and often exaggerated. During the era of silent film, such movements became one of the cornerstones of film acting. In Paris, at the end of eighteenth century, two theatres had a monopoly on the spoken word, namely the Comédie Française and the Théâtre Italienne. This meant that other forms of theatre performance, such as the melodrama, had to rely on gesture, mimicry and sometimes narrators in order to convey the story. Of course, such conventions were also very useful during the era of silent film. Thus there is an historical explanation for the fact that gestures are given a central role in creating meaning in melodrama.

Successful teamwork

The Phantom Carriage was shot in the new studios belonging to Svensk Filmindustri (Swedish Film Industry) in Råsunda, just outside Stockholm. Planned as an elaborate and prestigious production for Swedish Film Industry, it became part of a series of successful films that achieved world fame.

The background to the success of Swedish film in the 1920s was

complex, but the fact is that this national achievement was also a tribute to Selma Lagerlöf, on whose fiction many classic Swedish films
of the period were based. Lagerlöf herself was interested in cinema
as a new medium and a narrative form. Very early, she developed the
idea of making the famous story of *Nils Holgersson* into a film. She
subsequently assigned the rights to make films based on a number of
her works to the Swedish production company Svenska Bio (Swedish
Cinema)—from 1919 Swedish Film Industry—and the two celebrated
film directors Mauritz Stiller and Victor Sjöström (Furhammar 2010,
86; Sahlberg 1961, 201).

Of the two directors, Sjöström appears to have been a kindred spirit
to Lagerlöf, not only because, like her, he had his roots in the province
of Värmland with its rich tradition of folklore and storytelling. He also
had a genuine ability to recognise the rhythm of words and sentences,
and to translate them into images. Moreover, he showed a willingness
to compromise and listen to Lagerlöf's ideas—most often to the benefit
of the work itself. Initially, Sjöström was hesitant about approaching
the Nobel Laureate, thinking that she would be taken aback by the
idea of transferring her novels to a medium considered no more than
a pastime for children and housemaids. But he really believed in his
ideas and met Lagerlöf for the first time after travelling all the way
from Stockholm to Falun with the script of *Tösen från Stormyrtorpet*
(*The Girl from the Marsh Croft*). He was planning to read it aloud to
her to make sure she would listen. She did, and the film, launched in
1917, became a success. Very soon, the two of them developed a close
working relationship, and their routines were well established when the
idea of making a film based on the 1912 novella *The Phantom Carriage*
came up (Sahlberg 1961, 193–6; Forslund 1980, 126).

The project, as already noted, was regarded as ambitious, even haz-
ardous. The story traced the consciousnesses and memories of several
characters who were likely to be difficult to illustrate. After reading
Sjöström's script, Lagerlöf, however, was quite pleased and had only a
few criticisms. The memory scenes were to be illustrated by a number
of flashbacks, but she wondered whether there were not too many of
these, making them confusing for the viewer. Also, she warned the
director about scenes and gestures that might be perceived as comical.
For Lagerlöf the film was supposed to be 'a powerful sermon', as she
put it, and the spectators should not be distracted from this generic
dramatic nerve of the film (Sahlberg 1961, 198).[2]

156

Sjöström listened to Lagerlöf and made some modifications accordingly. *The Phantom Carriage* was released on New Year's Day 1921 in both
Gothenburg and Stockholm. The date was of course no coincidence. The
story is set on New Year's Eve, with a number of ghostly elements. The
film was an immediate success and was soon hailed as a masterpiece. Its
intricate visual structure consisting of several stories within stories, levels
of consciousness, and multilayered chronologies expressed in flashbacks
and in elaborate *mises en scène*, represented the cutting edge of cinematic
craftsmanship at this time. The astonishing cinematography by Julius
Jaenzon (alias J. Julius) has been singled out as unique in the history of
Swedish cinema (Florin 1997, 31; Furhammar 1991, 59, 80).

The meaning(s)

At first glance, one might say that in *The Phantom Carriage* the basic
melodramatic oppositions are organised in terms of male, active, bad,
dark, hatred, and abuse—and female, passive, good, light, loving,
and caring. But a closer look reveals interesting contradictions in the
organisation of the film's basic emotional qualities expressed through
'polyvalence'—a kind of emotional instability of the characters (Nichols
1985, 165). Such an instability, expressed with film's visual and audi-
tive means, may be discerned in quite a few works in Selma Lagerlöf's
œuvre, and often opens the way for alternative interpretations.

Misrecognition and impossible love are recurrent themes in Lagerlöf,
as in *The Phantom Carriage* or, for instance, in 'Dunungen' ('Downie'),
a short story from 1894, made into a film by Ivan Hedqvist in 1919
(*Dunungen/ In Quest for Happiness*). Love and passion are the feelings
that are omnipresent in *The Phantom Carriage*, but without the characters recognising them as such. This is of course another central feature
of melodrama, as highlighted by Thomas Elsaesser, who holds that the
difference between tragedy and melodrama is the fact that the tragic
hero or heroine knows why he or she is suffering, but in a melodrama
does not (Elsaesser 1985, 169).

Bo Florin has emphasised the crucial role that Sister Edith's love
and desire for David Holm plays for his repentance and the reforma-
tion of his character (Florin 1997, 182). Indeed, the original novella
underlines the relationship between David Holm and Sister Edith,
but much of the verbal evidence of this has disappeared from the
film script. Instead, in the process of transferring the verbal discourse

Illus. 2. Sister Edith sets aside her feelings for David Holm.

to images, a dichotomisation seems to have taken place: the focus of narrative action concentrates on the male lead and the dynamics of his character development, while the emotionality in terms of consuming passion has been transferred to a visual level and to the female character (Soila 2000, 167–9).

Love in both the novella and the film is split into two. On the one hand, there is earthly and pragmatic love with the purpose of raising a family and leading a decent life. On the other hand, there is spiritual and passionate love: real but not always possible to achieve in this life, and obviously not compatible with the first category. Indeed, the term 'passion' encompasses both desire and pain, the pain of exceeding the limits of that which is appropriate and, by extension with regard to *The Phantom Carriage*, the disavowal of desire.

A large part of the set of values in *The Phantom Carriage*—in other words, the views on marriage, honour, faith, love, life and death as well as on gender and religion—need to be seen against the backdrop of the time when the novella was written and the film made. People alive in the 1910s and 1920s were perhaps better equipped to perceive this story and its tenets as Selma Lagerlöf wanted them: a sermon about atonement and reform. Religious revivalism, the temperance movement, and different socialist and labour groupings all had as their goal to reform and mould the characters and lives of people, and their inherent values were known and accepted in Swedish society. As a result, the most interesting scenes are the ambiguous ones in which Sister Edith's feelings are made manifest and acknowledged because, as feminist theorists maintained in the 1980s, the point of melodrama is the actual acknowledgement and enunciation of the otherwise ineffable: the female subject position (Soila 1997a, 24–5).

Framing the characters

As important as theatrical gesture at the turn of the twentieth century was the actor's place on the stage: the protagonists were meant to stand in the middle, facing the audience, and the less important characters at the rear and to the sides. In key scenes, the imagery of *The Phantom Carriage* places Sister Edith on her deathbed in the centre, in a *tableau vivant* not unfamiliar in film at the time (Florin 1997, 111–13). The importance of this kind of positioning lies in the fact that there would have been alternatives: a professional photographer might have thought it sensible to make use of the golden ratio, familiar from paintings, in which the focus of the spectator's attention is placed in relation to the proportions one-third to two in a rectangle. In this film the focus of the spectator's gaze, often reinforced by an iris, is frequently used in domestic images to underline the significance of the female characters in their environment. Thus for instance, as Anna Holm is conducting her daily routines, the photography reinforces her air of competence and proficiency.

In the present tense of the film, Sister Edith in her bed is attended by her mother and friends. Her deathbed becomes the central locus— in a sense an inner sanctum of the cinematic space. This impression is reinforced by the manner in which the other characters move about the room: they move quietly, as with reverence, attending to Edith and her slightest wish. Moreover, the two women who attend to her are placed on either side of her, their hands reaching out towards her.

The centred position of Edith is further accentuated by the lighting of her face and the way she is framed by headboard of the bedframe, with the pictures on the wall symmetrically arranged around it. One might say that Edith's bed is the central locus where desire, the driving force in the story, is generated. Also, her friends sent to look for David Holm keep coming back to her bedside and so create a centripetal move-

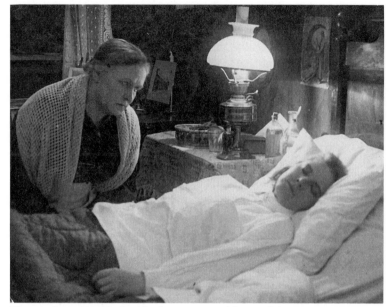

Illus. 3. Sister Edith's deathbed, a centripetal locus of the story.

ment of repeated returns. Finally, the story comes to a close when the ghost of David Holm arrives at Edith's bedside, and their hands meet.

Mediators of feelings

In *The Phantom Carriage*, the actresses' hand gestures express the inner feelings of those characters. By contrast, the male characters seem instead to gesture using the entire length of their arms. One might say that they speak a louder body language: they speak the obvious. The women's hand movements are more subtle but equally expressive. An example of this is Anna Holm who, in situations where she is in the process of making important decisions, wrings and clutches her hands: the tight knot that her fingers make expresses her inability to decide, but also conveys the kind of shrunken person she has become. Similarly, as she approaches Edith's deathbed, she wrings her hands fervently as if in agony and help-lessness. But when she stops at the bedside, looking down at Edith, she slowly spreads her crooked fingers as if she wanted to scratch the face of the sleeping woman or even strangle her. Her hands eloquently express feelings that perhaps are not quite appropriate at a deathbed.

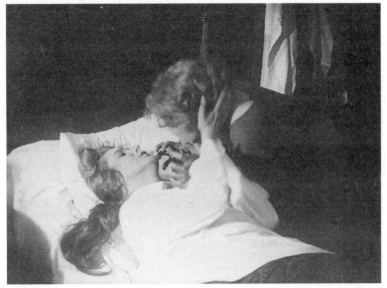

Illus. 4. The mixed feelings of the women are expressed in their eloquent gestures.

The movements of the women's hands also stand out because their hands look white against their darker clothing. Thus, for instance, in the scene in which Sister Edith tries to persuade David to give up his wretched life, her hands are like white birds by his chest, pleading silently for him not to leave. His spiteful glance at her hands makes her lower them as if in shame. Later, when Edith learns of the existence of David's wife, she quickly pulls herself together to disavow her feelings, deciding instead to bring the estranged spouses together. To quote from Lagerlöf's text, 'It was as if she had overcome her own feelings and had no further desire for earthly things' (Lagerlöf 2011a, 62).[3] In the moment of resignation, her hand rests motionless against David Holm's chest, his heart.

Conclusion

Montage is considered the privileged cinematic means of expression, based on tension and rhythm, often underscored by music. With regard to the differences and similarities with literary storytelling, the notable characteristics of the Lagerlöfian quality of storytelling are the emphasis on rhythm and pacing, and the velocity of the narrative voice and succession of sentences. These all come close to the suspense with regard to timing and rhythm that is crucial in film editing—montage. In order to establish a connection between the qualities of the Lager-löfian storytelling and the cinematic realisation of it, I have used the notion of melodramatic sensibility.

Melodrama is about expressing the ineffable. Forbidden feelings or nonconformist experience may be enunciated by means of the rhythmic imaginary created by montage, by means of music, by gesture, by mimicry, and by *mise en scène*. By studying some of the film's components—such as desire as a coercive theme, the framing of the characters, gestures as mediators of the true feelings of the characters—and by exploring the genre background, the production history, the collaboration between the novelist and film director, I hope to have highlighted the melodramatic potential of *The Phantom Carriage* and the way it 'speaks' to the audience by 'speaking out' experiences that, more often than not, many people have actually had.

Notes

1 'lyfta sitt eget hem ur förfallet' (Lagerlöf 2012, 140).
2 'den starkaste predikan'.
3 'Det syntes, att han hade övervunnit sig själv och ingenting begärde för egen del av något, som hörde denna världen till' (Lagerlöf 2012, 68).

CHAPTER 13

Nils Holgersson and a Japanese animated series

Astrid Surmatz

In recent postcolonial research, the emphasis has shifted from looking at dichotomies to analysing a variety of different voices in texts or other forms of representation. These voices may coexist on different narrative levels and are not necessarily hierarchic. Older models tend to show a clear and more or less dichotomist image of, for example, the dark, subdued other on the margins and the dominant, shiny self at the centre of a discourse. In more recent approaches, categories of the liminal and marginalised have, however, not been totally abandoned, and some of the dichotomous concepts can be extremely useful in order to shed new light on, for instance, established or canonical writers. Descriptions of Lapland by Linnaeus, Hans Christian Andersen, Kerstin Ekman, Elsa Beskow, or Selma Lagerlöf can be seen in the revealing light of postcolonial theory, but analysis would not need to be centred on a mainly black-and-white analysis of hetero-stereotypes. By granting that there can be several voices in a text, several layers of description, and that even within a stereotyped imagery one may find traces of voices counteracting and balancing one another in an interesting concurrent way, new readings and perspectives can be offered.

The image of Lapland presented by Lagerlöf in her novel *Nils Holgersson* (1906–1907), which depicts a boy's journey across Sweden, forms interesting material for this type of newer postcolonial reading. The image is a multifaceted one, showing an ambivalence and at the same time an openness not atypical of its time. Although intended as a narrative covering the geography and culture of Sweden for nation-wide school use, *Nils Holgersson* was quickly appreciated as a novel in its own right, both nationally and internationally. As the novel has seen countless editions, retellings, translations into other languages, and re-mediations into audio versions, films, plays, exhibitions, artworks, and other formats, aspects of transmediation and illustration will be taken into account in the following when analysing a central encounter in *Nils Holgersson* between Swedes and the Sami population of a village. Taking a postcolonial, intermedial, and gendered approach, the focus will be on the depiction of Lapland and the overarching impact of the Lapland imagery on the novel as a whole. The encounter of the girl Åsa with a group of Sami will be seen against the backdrop of concepts of Sami culture at the time.

As representations in different media tell us something about the shifting functions of this Lapland discourse, one of the best-known international re-mediations of the narrative in the form of an animation, a Japanese series made in the late 1970s, will also be considered.[1] Already in Lagerlöf's lifetime there were several transmediations of her works, and involved in different mediated forms of her works as she was, her interest is also mirrored in her letters and even in filmic documentation; however, not so much material has been accessible concerning the Lapland part of *Nils Holgersson*. Still, Lagerlöf's letters will be used as sources for her view on Lapland and on her journey there. In general, the definition of the reception of Lagerlöf's works over time within different media can be seen in the context of more recent trends in the development of the concept of intermediality and multimodality.[2] The rendering of Lapland in Lagerlöf's text might already mirror multimodal concepts of Lapland in its time. A central part of the analysis will focus on the textual version of the encounter in the Sami camp and its later filmic rendition.

Discourses on Lapland and the Sami

What *Nils Holgersson* seems to do is to represent different ideas of Lapland that circulated at the time and give these a specific turn, one that agreed with the general project of a national identity discourse in which her book was going to play a central role. Lars Elenius, Bjarne Thorup Thomsen, Gerda Lindskog, and others have investigated the redefinition in Lagerlöf of the national Swedish discourse of the time; an aspect of this redefinition is the embracing of a national identity in which Lapland was seen as an essential part (Elenius 2000, 2002; Thomsen 2007, 2011; Lindskog 2005).

The image of Lapland and the Sami population at the time was changing and diversifying into separate strands. There seems to have been no clear consensus as to whether the Sami were included in the idea of expanding the influence of the Swedish state towards the Arctic Circle and making the far North a vital part of modern Sweden. In the context of redefining borders and using borders for national self-definition, the perceived 'loss' of Finland in 1809 was still fresh in public memory at the turn of the century, and was reinforced because of the impending independence of Norway in 1905.

It is obvious from both the novel and from her letters that Lagerlöf followed the development of the mining industry in the north of Sweden with great interest and at least partly shared the optimism about what the modern colonial expansion of this industry in Lapland could mean for Sweden as a whole. Lagerlöf took pride in presenting the question of industrialisation, but did so in an ambivalent way, as the novel depicts how a child dies in a mining accident. References to the effect of the mines on the environment and the population are found in letters from Lagerlöf to her friend Elise Malmros, describing the mines in Malmberget, Gällivare, Luossavaara, and Kiirunavaara which she visited during her study trip to Lapland in 1904, undertaken together with her friend Sophie Elkan (Ahlström 1942, 52; Edström 2002, 328). However, the question of Sami inclusion or exclusion lingers on, and it seems unclear whether the Sami were part of this generally optimistic view of a more industrialised future for Sweden, which could turn the resources in the North into a vitalisation of hitherto marginalised areas (Sörlin 2013; Sandell & Sörlin 2005; Hansson, Lindgren Leavenworth & Pettersson 2010; Ryall, Schimanski & Waerp 2010).

This development required the situation and status of the Sami to be redefined. In several models, they would be further marginalised, having to move even further away from the new 'go West' mentality of industrial exploitation. According to some official policies, they should continue in what was seen as their ancient ways of life centred on nomadic or semi-nomadic reindeer herding. If they were to remain on the margins, they might be seen as a form of tribal group on the periphery of the rapidly modernising Swedish society, where technological development allowed for a totally renewed exploitation and accessibility of the land, which was seemingly devoid of inhabitants, or at least of properly recognised inhabitants. Such a phenomenon by which land to be exploited by the central government or authorised

Illus. 1. Selma Lagerlöf and Sophie Elkan during their trip to Norrland 1904.

settlers was declared empty, although there were obvious traces of land use by residents and even contracts with residents, would be a generally employed strategy within the imperialist or colonial appropriation of land.

The 'Sami should stay Sami' ('lapp ska vara lapp') debate started to gain momentum in Sweden at this time (Lindskog 2005). In contemporaneous discourse, it was beyond doubt that the Sami population should be missionised, Christianised, and thereby partly homogenised into state norms and the Established Church. Two different models of state interference were debated, although not necessarily part of the same public discourse: whether the Sami should be registered as Swedish citizens, and whether they should pay taxes to the Swedish state. However, there were some generally accepted strategies and restrictions; for instance, it was quite obvious to the respective governments that the Sami should have to respect national borders, irrespective of how these affected the traditional migratory routes of their reindeer. Such requirements impinged on the Sami way of life and on their symbolic cartography of the huge areas they were travelling through, with the result that long negotiations regarding their legal and political status ensued (Elenius 2000, 2002).

Within this discourse, the notion of desirable schooling for the

Sami population also had to be redefined. There was no self-evident solution, and different institutions on various levels were developing models and schemes to address the matter. The Sami children had been partly integrated into the Church teaching that was the earliest form of structured education in Sweden before the advent of the general schooling law in 1842, which was relatively early in a European context (Lindskog 2005). One of the main concerns of the 'Sami should stay Sami' advocates was that too much schooling would distance the Sami children from the nomadic way of life which at least the reindeer-herding Sami were used to. Idealists would claim it to be better to keep them in a museum-like state where they could represent a way of life close to Nature, provided that this did not prevent modern industrial access to the areas involved—a position that would seem to be somewhat contradictory (Elenius 2000, 2002).

There was clearly a strong and sometimes dubious scientific interest in documenting the Sami at this time, from phrenologists measuring skulls, both of living persons and skulls dug up, mostly illegally, from cemeteries, to the somewhat less invasive photographic documentation. Ongoing discussions about skull measurement, phrenology, and the status of the collections of Sami skulls in Swedish museums have resulted in the recent returning of skulls to the area (see Pikkarainen & Brodin 2008, 16–17). It has also been debated to what extent Lagerlöf herself might have been engaged in these racist positions.[3] Other activities at the time were linked to the collecting of orally transmitted stories of the Sami people and their artefacts and art. While early collecting and translation activities, including the intermedial translation of culture (Rajewsky 2002), had not primarily exhibited a nationalist tendency, they began to do so in the course of the nineteenth century.

When Skansen, an open-air museum of rural Swedish culture, was established in Stockholm in 1891, a Sami tent (*kåta*) was included. A kind of Lapland milieu was created, including a small herd of reindeer consisting of partly tame reindeer, but also of other animals whose iconographic status was perhaps less clearly connected to the Sami.[4] In 2010, a semi-modern Sami tent was still part of the park, where actors/employees either embody or demonstrate different handicrafts and lifestyles associated with the Sami.[5] Skansen represented a museological image of Sami life long before comparable institutions were established in Lapland itself.

Lagerlöf's novel as a network of voices

Nils Holgersson represents an up-to-date version of the ongoing discussion about the state of the Sami within the Swedish nation-state. But what are the ideological implications of the different voices and narrative levels in the novel, and what is actually going on in Lagerlöf's text? The layers of the representation of Lapland, and more broadly of Sweden and the nation's different regions, are enhanced by the special narrative voices employed in the text. The focus in the following will be on the encounter of the motherless girl, Åsa, who has travelled far up to the North in search of her father, with the Sami. The girl's northbound route runs parallel to Nils's journey with the geese, and from time to time their paths cross at narratologically suitable moments. The girl's father had earlier escaped towards the north, fleeing from a contagious curse or disease which, he believes, he has inflicted upon his family (in some ways also a parallel to Gerda's search for her brotherly friend in Andersen's fairytale 'The Snow Queen' from 1845, see Surmatz 2006). The fair-haired girl loses the last of her siblings, her younger brother, who has been her companion almost all the way on the trip north, in an accident related to the mining industry. In Lagerlöf's narrative, the mining accident is constructed as a fatal force, but also as a seemingly inevitable sacrifice to the modernisation of society. The girl pushes for a public burial for her dead brother, as if he had been a national hero, voicing her despair and showing a courage that is seemingly classless and admired by settlers and Sami alike.

As confirmed by the narrative voice, Åsa's intervention must be seen as quite a strong act by a young girl lacking parental protection and any kind of societal care in the rough and socially segregated mining community. She is an unschooled migrant from the south, and the class aspect is clearly emphasised in the representation of power as distributed between the agents in this story. The main differences with regard to power are between the child and the adult, between the farmer's daughter and the mining director, between southern countryside and northern urban mining setting, between unschooled youth and technically educated adult. However, the girl is self-educated to some extent, as she has learnt about the disease that killed part of her family and that could have been avoided with some simple precautions. One might say that her case is an example of enlightened propaganda for education and prevention. The prevention of tuberculosis seems to

Illus. 2. Illustration from the first edition of *Nils Holgerssons underbara resa genom Sverige*, II (1907): 'Lappkåta bland fjällbjörkar' ('Sami hut among birches'), photo: B. Mesch.

form part of an educational agenda in accordance with the genre of the schoolbook. From today's perspective it is highly problematic that a Roma woman is suspected of having brought the disease to the family. From a gendered, ethnographic perspective, the fair-headed innocence of the girl, on the other hand, clearly contributes to her white, almost superhuman and saint-like status.

In the search for her father, Åsa arrives at a Sami camp on the other side of the lake from the mining town, accompanied by a Swedish helper. Her focalised description of the Sami tent contains the usual prop-like elements, such as a seemingly crowded tent with an open fire, with the village giving the impression of a cluster of small, picturesque huts on the shore of the lake. The marginalised or liminal position of the village is clearly enhanced and symbolised by the fact that one has to cross water in order to reach it. The chaos of huts and objects conveys the non-fixity of the settlement, which can easily be moved to new pastures. This representation of the somewhat detached position of the Sami is later enhanced in a brief passage from the perspective of the Sami in regard to the imminent encroachment of urbanisation and the exploitation of mineral resources.

As the girl enters into a dialogue with the Sami, who are informed of her adventures so far, some typical roles in accordance with the stereotyped Sami–southern Swedish encounter are filled in and voiced. The wise older Sami man, Ola Serka, who oversees developments, has to some extent accepted that the Sami will be further marginalised in society, although, or perhaps because, he is described as 'the leading Lapp' (Lagerlöf 2013b, II 245).[6] Ola Serka is seen as the representative of the old generation and associated with what Lagerlöf seems to have classified as the common habitat of the Sami people, the mountains. He is regularly and rhetorically described as a man of the mountains, 'fjällmannen' (Lagerlöf 1907a, 363–7). As the Sami elder, he is willing to help the girl find her father and support her, although his intentions are only partly revealed to the reader at this point.

The energetic young Sami man, Aslak, voices the ideal of the noble savage and of living a life in Nature, which should be attractive also to the single Swedish woman incorporated in it within the frame of the story-within-the-story and possibly even within the plot Aslak has in mind concerning Åsa. Schooling in Swedish, however, seems an inevitable precondition for a civilised and thereby authorised voicing of the Sami interest according to the narrative frame, as is clear from the following examples: 'Aslak had been to school and he could speak Swedish' (Lagerlöf 2013b, II 245);[7] 'Old Ola understood more Swedish than he was prepared to let people know' (248).[8] As mediator, he is more secretive about his knowledge of Swedish, almost like a covert activist or a cunning sorcerer, making his image more complex than suggested at the beginning, when he seemingly agreed with the state policy of virtual segregation at the time. The boy Aslak, whose name is familiar both from Ibsen's play *Peer Gynt* and from the Kautokeino uprising, represents the younger Sami generation with a more regular Swedish schooling, and tells quite an elaborate story of a young woman in plague-stricken Sweden who, having stayed with the Sami for a year and enjoyed the free life close to Nature, decided to stay with a Sami man rather than returning to 'her own people'. The opposition between a healthy free life in the mountains and life in 'white' civilisation is thus emphasised. It is not entirely clear from the context whether Åsa, charmed by the boy's manner, reacts to this implied suggestion at all. Still, the narrative represents the clear-cut choices offered within the colonial discourse: either choose to retire from civilisation into native isolation, or choose 'civilised' life within the Swedish community. What is not discussed in this story is whether it would have been a realistic option for the boy to have followed the girl into her plague-stricken community.

Illus. 3. Illustration from the first edition of *Nils Holgerssons underbara resa genom Sverige*, II (1907): 'Renkorna mjölkas' ('Milking the reindeer cows'), photo: N. Thomas.

The wise old Sami man employs a different path and method, almost in a cynical way, for Ola 'cures' the girl's father who has been living in double liminality on the outskirts of the Sami settlement, by threatening to adopt the girl into the Sami community. When confronted with the idea that the brave Swedish girl should be integrated into the Sami 'clan', the father reveals his identity and promises to take care of Åsa again.

To put it crudely, free from all the other family members, having paid a high price for this final redemption, father and daughter can now, 'cleansed' by the meeting with the Sami, enjoy each other's company and return to society together. The girl may, just as in Andersen's fairytale 'The Snow Queen', return to childhood and hand her heavy responsibilities over to her father again, which seems to be a traditional ending to this part of the narrative, subduing the Sami voices and instrumentalising their voices for the main 'white' narrative strand.

The role of the Sami is a clear-cut one in this narration. The wise Sami man realises that his people are marginalised but prefer to live in splendid isolation. He will have to move his camp further to avoid too much contact with the settlers. His role can be described as that of an initiated shaman or perhaps what one today would ascribe to a guru, a psychotherapist, or a therapist. Ola Serka heals Åsa's father who has been vaguely attached to the camp, unselfishly reuniting father and daughter. But his actions could also be interpreted as manipulative, as his shamanist-inspired rituals cannot be seen as entirely trustworthy in the context. He does not really speak the straightforward truth, but bluffs by threatening adoption.

This episode has an obvious narrative function and marks crossroads in the girl's journey and development. It could be placed in the tradition of an earlier, canonical Lapland travel account by Linnaeus (1732), in which the narrator's encounter with a Sami woman appearing to him like a fury ('furia') forces him to turn. The turning-point in Linnaeus' diary might be compared to the dramatic turning-point in the girl's meeting with the Sami in Lagerlöf's narrative. However, Linnaeus continued his expedition northwards, whereas Åsa is reunited with her father and supposedly returns south, just as Nils Holgersson expresses his desire to return towards his home in southern Sweden leave the vast and—to him—empty northern land.[9]

However, this reunion of daughter and father is decisive in several ways, and may even be seen as the crux of a Sami sub-narrative, adding a tragic element. The Sami man is aware of his power to give the lives of the father and the girl a new direction, but to do this he wisely, almost cynically, utilises the low status of the Sami population as exotic and liminal, employing it as the threat he rightly foresees it will form in the father's mind, separating the identities of the girl and himself which for a time had merged into seemingly peaceful co-existence:

> 'She must be one of your people, I imagine, that girl?'
> 'No,' Ola said, 'she's not one of us, not a Lapp.'
> 'Perhaps she's the daughter of one of the settlers and consequently used to life up here in the north?'
> 'No, she comes from right down in the south,' Ola said, looking as if that had nothing at all to do with the matter. But now the fisherman was becoming more interested.
> 'Well, in that case, I don't think you can take her,' he said. 'She's unlikely to be able to tolerate living in a tent through the winter unless she was born and brought up to it.' (Lagerlöf 2013b, II 250)[10]

A central question is whether the Swedish father would have been equally provoked by a Swedish family offering to adopt his girl. Presumably not, and Ola Serka, supported by the focalising narrator, is very much aware of this hierarchic approach to the issue. To be adopted by an ethnic minority, described here in somewhat denigrating terms as a 'stam' ('tribe') by the Swedish father, or, in his Other-ing perspective, even as a foreign tribe, is perceived as the ultimate threat, in spite of the romanticised images which the young boy Aslak employs in his inviting tale about the free life of the Sami. How-ever, the narrative may also mirror the perspective of the majority of Swedes on the Sami, voicing the nationwide Sami-should-stay-Sami ideology discussed above.[11]

Father and daughter return home to Sweden proper, as it were, altered and reformed by their trip, in a new union triggered by their shared experience of the Other. The concurrent voices in the text seem to negotiate different identities, and the representatives of the younger generation especially temporarily enter a new form of dialogue. How-ever, their worlds stay separate, and the implied Sami–Swedish re-union of Aslak's story about reconciliation remains a utopia. In the end, trans-ethnic adoption is a less strong model than the parental love still heavily endorsed in societal ideology in Sweden at the time, with the Sami functioning as an ethnically marked seemingly rather passive helper in a condition of marginalisation.

However, as has been pointed out, Lapland is the native home of the nomadic geese in *Nils Holgersson* with their part-Sami, part-Finnish names; and the female leading goose Akka almost functions as a mir-ror figure of the brave young girl Åsa, who travels north in a parallel movement, leading her younger brother. It is debatable whether the names of Akka and the other geese are really of Finnish or Sami ori-gin (Elenius 2002; Ahlström 1942; Lindskog 2005). The wild geese in turn name the mountain tops they pass, calling them Porsotjokko, Sarjektjokko, and Sulitelma, which the narrator, addressing and possi-bly empathising with the audience, says are remarkable or even strange names, 'märkvärdiga namn' (Lagerlöf 1907a, 369). This might be an attempt to bridge the knowledge gap between the double addressees of child and adult readers, but it might also express a certain hesitance about names perceived as exotic.

Nils Holgersson's central Lapland episode at Luossavaara can be seen in the context of a general dichotomy in the text between the marginalised northern wilderness represented by the Sami and the wild animals on the one hand, and the civilised south with its towns, farms, and agriculture on the other. The moment when Mårten, the domesticated goose that is Nils's travelling companion, looks at the wild geese carefully for the first time, is crucial for establishing the contrast between the domesticated geese and the possibly ethnically marked nomadic wild geese:

> When the white gander looked at the wild geese he felt ill at ease. He had expected them to be more like tame geese and thought he would have felt a closer kinship with them. But they were much smaller than he was and not one of them was white—they were a grey colour with brown mottling. He found their eyes rather frightening—all yellow and gleaming as if there was fire behind them. The gander had been taught that a genteel goose should walk slowly and with a rolling motion, but these wild geese did not walk, they half ran. (Lagerlöf 2013b, I 39)[12]

In passages like this one, ethnic and gender aspects are mixed in an intriguing way that deserves to be looked at in more detail. In the focalised perspective of the domesticated goose, the wild geese are more different than expected; the white goose expresses a kind of distress or even disappointment at the gap opening up between him and the Othered wild geese. These are described in accordance with the standard repertoire of the ethnically Othered and marginalised: they are seen as smaller, darker, and overly agile, moving swiftly in accordance with their nomadic status. As for the different groups of human young moving north, their path is paralleled by that of the white goose. Åsa's younger brother Mats dies tragically; young Nils is reformed but has to leave his animal friends to return to civilisation, as does the young girl, who seems to travel south again with her father. For all of them, their stay in the north represented a short visit in a marginalised domain; it is a potentially deadly or at least life-threatening experience on the borderline, resulting in sudden personal development. By contrast, the Sami boy Aslak and his father, as well as the geese, do not change their ways. The rhetorical appeal of the animals of the north yearning for a preserved landscape for themselves, like a reserve, without interference from humans, could be seen as something more complex than another marginalisation, namely as a part of the redefinition and negotiation of a pluriform and utopian Swedish Nature and nation at the time:

> Wherever he had gone the country had been grand and splendid and he was truly glad to have seen it, but he had felt no desire to live there. He had to admit that Akka was right when she said that

the Swedish settlers would be better to leave this land in peace, leave it to the bears and wolves and reindeer and geese and snowy owls and lemmings and Lapps—all those who had been created to live there. (Lagerlöf 2013b, II 255–6)[13]

This quotation seems to articulate Nils's perspective, referring to the wild goose Akka speaking of a country that should be reserved for animals and humans equipped to live there, resulting in a narrative riddle on several levels. The plea seems to strengthen the claim of 'Sami should stay Sami', advocating national reserves and connecting the Sami to the wild animals among which they are living. Romantic notions of Nature, national ideology perceived within a hierarchical system, and a genuine feeling for the need for advocacy for the area all seem to inter-act here. Thomsen reads the episode as a victory of nature conservancy over mining colonialism, but also discusses the questionability of fixed boundaries (2007, 149). The description of the wild geese as a kind of almost aristocratic natives coincides nicely with the general image of the Sami population at the beginning of the twentieth century (Ele-nius 2010, 477). Thomsen is sceptical about this direct identification of the geese as Sami, since one of the central projects of the book, facilitated by the flying flock of geese, is to shape the Swedish nation as one, uniting the different symbolic animals that figure in the nar-rative (Thomsen 2007, 113–17). In conclusion, there is considerable narrative ambivalence within the story, voicing Sami interests and Sami voices on several symbolical levels, but also representing contemporary discourses from the national and educative contexts within which the novel was written. These voices seem to overlap, and allow the discur-sive entanglement of differing interpretations of the ethnic identities and conflicts of interest within the novel.

The representation of Sami culture

The description of the Sami village seems to be partly an *ekphrasis* of existing depictions of Lapland. Some of the inspiration for the novel apparently stems from Selma Lagerlöf's trip north with her friend and partner Sophie Elkan in 1904, and from written sources available at the time.[14] Moreover, the Lapland art and drawings by the two Tirén brothers, both of them painters, and material from the Svenska Turist-föreningen (the Swedish Tourist Association) may have contributed to the inspirational process (Erlandson-Hammargren 2006). Intended as a school book, *Nils Holgersson* included photography, some of which represented Lapland. The illustrations representing different media and their role in establishing Lagerlöf's iconotext and construction of Lapland are crucial, and should be seen in the light of new media contexts arising at the time, as the selection process of the photographs provided by different commersial photograph libraries does not show a direct causal relationship with the text's narrative.[15]

In the following, the intermedial reception of Lagerlöf's text will be discussed by a swift shift to a Japanese animated series from 1980 and its interpretation of Lagerlöf's concept of Sami life and the narrative devices employed in this context. We shall consider to what extent the film, made in a different culture and several generations after the book, represents changing attitudes towards the representation of Sami culture.

In the film, the North is introduced by the story about the climate getting ever colder as the plot advances northwards. As in other depictions of the far North, the cold climate is expressed in anthropomorphic form both in Lagerlöf's novel and in the Japanese film. The Ice King battles the sun, and like the sun, Nils in the film progresses far too optimistically, followed like the pied piper by a host of spring flowers and huge trees on the way north (*The Wonderful Adventures of Nils*, 1980, episode 22). Animals, plants, and the Sami people all are discussed with reference to their 'adaptability' to the cold of the far north, associating the ethnic minority with the animal kingdom. The gendered confrontation between the female sun and the male Ice King is a fierce one, but acted out differently in film and book (*The Wonderful Adventures of Nils*, 1980, episode 23). Flora, fauna, and landscape as represented in the film do not always conform to established patterns of depicting Lapland, to say the least. The galloping reindeer introducing each of the episodes of Nils's journey north in the film have a decorative iconic value: while they may have a narrative function prefiguring the goal of the journey, they mostly have an exotic appeal for younger spectators. The reindeer appearing in the introductory sequence and at the beginning of each of the 52 episodes function as a narrative icon but also as transmitters of clichés and stereotypes about the far north (*The Wonderful Adventures of Nils*, 1980).

Thus, while the film generates a different, almost pan-national interpretation of the northern theme, it certainly does treat the episode of the lonely blonde girl's reunion with her distraught father against the background of the Sami village (*The Wonderful Adventures of Nils*, 1980, episodes 34–8). It also seems, however, to merge general pan-Scandinavian Viking iconography with the specific depiction of the Sami. The plot is quite dramatically changed in order to answer to the needs of the young audience, and also to the pan-Atlantic and pan-Pacific global norms of children's media at the time. A standard mode of adaptation has been used.

Compared to the plot of the book, some dramatic changes have been made in the film. Åsa's younger brother Mats does not die. In the film, the girl and her brother travel together searching for their father and are rescued by the beautifully dressed Sami and taken to their village, and they return together with their father to civilisation. The younger brother does not have to be sacrificed to illustrate the demands and dangers of the modern exploitation of Nature. Being together, they are not depicted as existentially alone in the last phase of their long trip (*The Wonderful Adventures of Nils* 1980, episode 37 and subsequent episodes). The reunion of father and children in the film is as tear-filled and haunting as in the book, perhaps even more so, but the role of the Sami as traders in humanist values is subdued. In the printed narrative, the concise account of the girl's fight for her brother's burial, focalised from a Sami perspective, makes the episode admirable rather than sentimentally melodramatic or merely functional, a dimension which disappears in the film plot (on melodrama, see Karlsson 2002). In the film the Sami are more of a decorative element and represent themselves in these terms more so than in the book, the change possibly influenced by shifting ideas of native identities. The Japanese context of the late 1970s adds to the exoticism of the Sami, conserving folklorist elements and generalising them as Scandinavian.

The ideas expressed through this representation of ethnicity and belonging are quite different from those conveyed in the book, but within the film narrative they fill their own function, teaching morals and values with an exotic slant to a worldwide audience. The film was one of the first successful European–Japanese ventures informed by a Hollywood-style family-film ideology, adapting Lagerlöf to new contexts. The quest for an overarching narrative is solved differently in different periods and media forms, and the concurrence of voices in Lagerlöf's text is remediated in a different way.

Flora and fauna in the mediated text of the animated series display a globalised imagery. The introductory film sequence, which functions as a trailer, shows a reindeer herd storming forward in a vaguely northern European landscape. In the introductory sequence at the beginning of each episode, a reindeer lookalike appears, more reminiscent of a deer than a reindeer. The animal stands in a regal position high on a mountain cliff, rather Disney-like (although Disney was not part of this international film cooperation), generating the traditional image flow over the course of the screen page, similar to a picturebook because of the still effect in the animated series (Nikolajeva & Scott 2001). Here different image traditions overlap and clash with what would be associated with the etiology of the animal in question, where no single leader would be exposed. As the trip continues in the film, the adventurous and entertainingly dramatic elements dominate over the educational ones, adding further suspense to the plot.

The depiction of the Sami people differs from the classic picturebook mode (Lindskog 2005), avoiding showing Sami people in close-up. However, it seems that the depiction of the Sami is somewhat confused with the general imagery associated with the Vikings, with the Sami represented as blond with heavy beards. This counteracts the traditional colonial gap, but only has the effect of reversing the roles.

Internationally, the 52-episode series generated a renewed world-wide interest in Scandinavia, identifying Lapland as the general image of the North in Lagerlöf's world. Attention shifted from the printed work *Nils Holgersson*, which was read in Swedish schools well into the second half of the twentieth century and spread in countless international translations, towards animated films and their internationally appealing focus on the development of the boy and his animal friends on their adventurous trip. The image shaped of Lapland may differ from the one shaped in Lagerlöf's text, feeding from different sources and catering to the differing needs of an international audience. Yet the film tells a story about the North which, in the late 1970s, shaped a different medial representation of Lagerlöf's view of Lapland and adapted it to new audiences.

To summarise the image of Lapland in the book and the film, it is quite obvious that the film tries to avoid some of the contrasts developed in the novel. Instead, the Japanese film seems to merge Sami and Scandinavian characteristics. If one regards Lagerlöf's novel as consisting of different, sometimes oppositional voices, the depiction of Lapland can be seen in the context of its time, with the remediations as part of a rewriting of these images in more recent times. Lagerlöf was aware of the discourses of her time and ready to take quite a modern stand. The representation of Lapland in the novel is diversified by using different voices, skilfully employing focalisation and leaving space for different interpretations. There is a fascination with modernisation and the mining industry, which is seen as disastrous for the Sami. The blonde Swedish girl Åsa appeals to the reader almost as a modern-day explorer, but she is finally reintegrated into Swedish society, leaving behind the Sami village which, although still intact, may be threatened in the future. Certain ambivalences with regard to determining the genuine voices of the Sami are not resolved within the novel; but it is clear that the overarching project is to create a narrative with a national impact, integrating different ethnic and gendered approaches.

The image of the Sami is realised on different symbolic levels, including that of the nomadic geese, who travel towards Lapland as the ultimate goal of their survey of Sweden. The encounter in the traditionally depicted prop-like Sami village combines different temporal aspects, directing the narrative backwards into a mythic past, generating an encounter in the present, and fast-forwarding into a future linked to a dramatic, yet ambivalent appeal to generate a separate sphere for the Sami, connected to Nature preservation. The autonomous, energetic, and at times despairing Swedish girl, her encounter with the open-minded and reflective Sami, and the voicing of some Sami views are gendered and ethnicised, but are more multifaceted than might be perceived initially. The mediated encounter in the Japanese anime leads to what at first seems a mere role reversal, representing the Sami people in the village as Viking-like. The active girl is translated into the weaker half of a sibling pair, and the main interaction takes place between the Sami old man, the father of the girl, and the boy. The girl's lonely search for her father disappears in this picturesque interaction. The film shows less awareness of ethnic and local issues, instead creating an internationally legible tale based on icons rather than on differentiated depictions. Overall, Lagerlöf's text remains a multilayered narrative with countercurrent voices, capable of being retold and remediated again and again.

Notes

1 *The Wonderful Adventures of Nils*, Studio Pierrot, 1980, Japanese animated film series in 52 episodes.
2 Toijer-Nilsson 1992, 219, 271, 279, 281, 283, 285 and 291; for an early documenta-

tion of letters, see Desmidt 1997; for intermediality, see, for example, Bruhn, Gjelsvik & Frisvold Hansen 2013; Elleström 2010; Arvidsson 2007; Rajewsky 2002.

3 See, for example, positions by Düben 1873, and others. A certain renewed interest has focused on the photographs taken by the photographer Lotten von Düben, who was married to Düben.

4 See the Sami display represented on the Skansen website (accessed 1 August 2013) at <http://www.skansen.se/sv/artikel/samevistet-pa-skansen>.

5 See <http://www.skansen.se/sv/artikel/samevistet-pa-skansen> (accessed 1 August 2013). See also Sandberg 1995.

6 'den förnämste bland lapparna' (Lagerlöf 1907a, 358).

7 'Aslak hade varit i skola och kunde tala svenska' (Lagerlöf 1907a, 358).

8 'Gamle Ola förstod mera svenska, än han gärna ville låta någon veta' (Lagerlöf 1907a, 363).

9 See Surmatz 2004 on a gendered approach to the Sami encounter, as described in the travelogue by Linnaeus.

10 'Hon är väl av din stam, den där flickan?'—'Nej,' sade Ola, 'hon är inte någon av Samefolket.'—'Hon är kanske dotter till någon nybyggare, så att hon är van vid livet här i norden?'—'Nej, hon är långt söderifrån,' sade Ola och såg ut, som om detta alls inte hade något med saken att göra. Men nu blev metaren mera intresserad. 'Då tror jag inte, att du kan ta henne,' sade han. 'Hon lär nog inte tåla att bo i kåta om vintern, när hon inte är uppfödd med det' (Lagerlöf 1907a, 365).

11 Sundmark (2009b, 116) is quite optimistic about a potential interethnic utopia.

12 'När den vita gåskarlen nu betraktade vildgässen, kände han sig inte rätt väl till mods. Han hade väntat, att de skulle vara mer lika tamgäss, och att han skulle kände mer släktskap med dem. De voro mycket mindre än han, och ingen av dem var vit, utan de voro alla gråa med vattring i brunt. Och deras ögon blev han nästan rädd för. De voro gula och lyste, som om det hade brunnit en eld bakom dem. Gåskarlen hade alltid fått lära sig, att det var mest passande att gå sakta och rultande, med dessa gingo inte, utan de halvsprungo' (Lagerlöf 1906, 32).

13 'Vart han hade kommit, hade det varit grant och ståtligt land. Han var bra glad, att han hade fått se det, men inte hade han just velat bo där. Han måste medge, att Akka hade rätt, när hon sade, att det här landet kunde de svenska nybyggarna gärna lämna i fred och överlåta det åt björnarna och vargarna och renarna och vildgässen och fjällugglorna och lämlarna och lapparna, som voro skapade för att leva där' (Lagerlöf 1907a, 370, 373).

14 For Sami photography, see also Dahlman 2008 and Lundström 2008.

15 For the concept of iconotext, see Hallberg 1982, and Nikolajeva & Scott 2001; for the connection between photo and text in the first edition, see also Edström 2002, 357, and Schaffer 1989.

IV
(TRANS)NATIONAL NARRATIVES
AND EUROPEAN TRANSMISSIONS

CHAPTER 14

Sectional portal

This section explores European and transnational dimensions of Lagerlöf's work as well as mapping its versatile transmission into other countries, cultures, and languages. The section consists of nine essays in total, with four focused on (inter)textual investigations of Lagerlöf's work as such, and a further five essays centred on its international reception and adaptation.

The first four contributions trace the significance of transnational thought, internationalised settings, and public space in Lagerlöf's textual world from the very beginnings of her writing career until the end of the First World War. The lines of enquiry include the transnational formation of canon, the gender constructs, the creative force of generic hybridity, and the ideological role of the uncanny in Lagerlöf's writing. The literary material under consideration ranges, in regard to critical recognition and degree of familiarity, from the canonical, via the ambiguously positioned, to the highly 'peripheral' and little known.

These contributions to a new criticism of Lagerlöf's work are followed by five transmission-orientated essays that together demonstrate how various regimes or cultures can 'receive' or appropriate a writer on very different terms; how that reception can reflect conservative or progressive positions, or combinations thereof; and how national agendas and modes of national representation can 'travel' internationally and be applied to other countries and contexts. Moreover, these transmission studies shed specific light on translation strategies, on the role of publishing, and on paratextual features of the target-culture publications.

The section thus opens with an overview by Bjarne Thorup Thomsen in which he reflects on the role of transnationalised settings and peripheral locations in three decades of Lagerlöf's work by discussing texts which, although set in Sweden, display a desire to destabilise national parameters and/or use liminal zones as sites for the articulation of welfare ideas and for literary experimentation. Thomsen, moreover, sets out to identify continuities in terms of transnational and utopian thought between Lagerlöf's peripheral and canonical work. Theories of travel writing and of the role of mobility in modernism inform the discussion. Related interests in the function of international, and public, place in Lagerlöf's writing and in the early period of her production are displayed in Elettra Carbone and Kristina Sjögren's essay, in which they analyse the critically neglected novel *Antikrists mirakler* (1897, *The Miracles of Antichrist*), arguing that public space is used in the text to problematise issues related to identity, gender, and social class, concepts which, in line with the ideas of the Scandinavian Modern Breakthrough, were highly topical in Nordic literature at the time. The essay draws on theoretical work by Michel Foucault, Eric Hobsbawm, Sally Ledger, Henri Lefebvre, and others. The emphasis on Lagerlöf's breakthrough period is maintained in the subsequent essay by Ebba Witt-Brattström. Informed by theoretical work on canonicity (Bloom) and sketching an inner-canonical method, this essay explores the role of Sara Wacklin's *Hundrade minnen från Österbotten* (1844–5, 'One hundred memories from Österbotten') as an intertext to Lagerlöf's breakthrough novel *Gösta Berlings saga* (1891, *Gösta Berling's Saga*), highlighting issues of aesthetics and gender. The final contribution, by Sofia Wijkmark, to the first group of essays shares with Thomsen and Witt-Brattström an interest in the impact of war on art. Taking its starting-point in the claim that the uncanny can be regarded as a central element in Lagerlöf's work, Wijkmark explores one of the author's most complex short stories from the First World War period. Drawing on Freud, Tzvetan Todorov, and Terry Castle, among others, the essay develops a reading that focuses on gender, violence, and power, simultaneously contextualising the theme of destruction and the atmosphere of imminent disaster in terms of the approaching world war.

Moving on to transmission and translation, the second group opens with an essay by Dagmar Hartlová that looks at Selma Lagerlöf's stories in Czech from 1901 to the present day. Hartlová reads the early enthusiasm for Lagerlöf in Czech in its political and cultural contexts (with three translations of *Nils Holgersson*, published between 1911 and 1915, providing a case study), analyses the reasons why Lagerlöf, remarkably, was the only Swedish author to be translated and published during the Cold War, and concludes by outlining some current perceptions of her work. Travelling west, the next essay, by Roald van Elswijk, explores the reception of the national travelogue *Nils Holgersson* and other works by Lagerlöf in the Dutch-speaking area of the Netherlands and in the northern bilingual province of Friesland in the second decade of the twentieth century. The approach of the essay is discourse-analytical, and its corpus consists of newspaper articles, reviews, travel accounts and other material from Dutch and Frisian archives. Its discussion of journalistic reportage, which records visits to Mårbacka and its surroundings and encounters with Lagerlöf as a celebrity, exemplifies how contributions to the current volume can fruitfully straddle subject boundaries. A central focus of van Elswijk's essay is an assessment of the reception and role of Lagerlöf's national imagination in Frisian and Dutch literary circles. Continuing west, the interest in the influential travel narrative is maintained and developed in the contribution by Charlotte Berry. This essay contributes to emerging debates regarding the translation of children's literature and publishing history, and also demonstrates how these two disciplines can be used in tandem in interdisciplinary research by investigating the publishing history of the English versions of the *Wonderful Journey*. Crossing the Atlantic, the penultimate contribution to the section by Björn Sundmark continues the theme of English-language translation of Lagerlöf's work. It explores Lagerlöf's correspondence with her American translator Velma Swanston Howard (1868–1937), with a special emphasis on Swanston Howard's translation practice as seen in the context of cultural practices, financial constraints, and personal agendas. The relevant corpus of letters, in the National Library of Sweden, is only now beginning to attract analytical attention. The section, and indeed the whole volume, concludes with an intriguing investigation by Jennifer Watson of Lagerlöf in Nazi Germany, where she continued to be published, despite having distanced herself most emphatically from the Nazi regime in 1933. The focus is on the version of *Lord Arne's Silver* published in 1943 as a 'front book' for German soldiers in occupied Norway, and on the changes that made it into a propaganda piece that aimed to demonstrate the Germanic mindset of the Scandinavian people.

Elsewhere, the translation theorist Lawrence Venuti has argued that translations of foreign literature are usually designed for specific cultural constituencies, and that they feed into processes of identity formation that can de double-edged: in providing a 'position of intelligibility', translations contribute to the construction of an 'ideological position, informed by the codes and canons, interests and agendas of certain domestic social groups'; at the same time, however, translation and transmission can also 'create possibilities for cultural resistance, innovation, and change at any historical moment' (Venuti 1998, 68). In the case studies below, the dynamic contributions that Lagerlöf's work and public persona have made to the formation of cultural identities as well as to cultural innovation on the European and American scenes are illuminated.

CHAPTER 15

Text and transnational terrain, 1888–1918

Bjarne Thorup Thomsen

This essay will reflect on the role of what may be termed the transnational terrain and on peripherality in Lagerlöf by discussing texts—most of them 'marginal' in the author's output—which, although set in Sweden, display a desire to destabilise national parameters and/or use liminal zones as sites for the articulation of welfare and utopian ideas and for literary experimentation. The texts to be investigated range from the virtual exhibition pamphlet *Officiel Vägvisare vid Verldsutställningen i Landskrona 1888* ('Official Guide to the World Exhibition in Landskrona, 1888') to the wartime German-language mapping of Sweden entitled 'Lappland–Schonen' (1917, 'Lapland–Skåne'). Comparative consideration, moreover, will be given to some of Lagerlöf's canonical work from the period, primarily the key novelistic narratives *Nils Holgersson* (1906–1907) and, in particular, *Bannlyst* (1918, *The Outcast*), whose spatial ambition extends across, and indeed beyond, the national terrain. A common trait of all the texts under consideration is their affinity with travel writing, some theory of which will therefore additionally inform the discussion.

A laboratory for literature and welfare

When Lagerlöf in August 1885 took up a post as a schoolteacher in the southern Swedish coastal town of Landskrona, located on the narrow Sound between Sweden and Denmark, she arrived in a borderland setting—and an industrial, socially stratified sphere —that would prove a decisive environment for her personal, ideological, and literary development. The extent of Lagerlöf's early engagement with social, political, and pedagogical questions is documented retrospectively in an essay from 1923 on her literary mentor Sophie Adlersparre, republished in 1933 in a collection entitled *Höst* (*Harvest*):

> What interested me the most during these early Landskrona days were the many social questions which circulated at the time. Everything that concerned teaching, peace, temperance, the women's rights movement, poverty relief captured my attention. I had some vague notion of devoting myself fully to my calling as a teacher and channelling all my strength into creating a model school, in which all the shortcomings of the current pedagogical system would be rectified.[1]

The utopian impulse that informs this passage formed a general tenet of Lagerlöf's thinking and production in the period, evident, for example, in her 1897 novelistic enquiry into socialism and Christianity, *Antikrists mirakler* (*The Miracles of Antichrist*), and already figured prominently, as we shall discuss below, in the 'Official Guide to the World Exhibition in Landskrona'.

It can be argued that the utopian impulse is bound up with Landskrona's marginal location, offering proximity to the neighbouring Nordic nation and its capital centre of Copenhagen, which contributed to a culturally productive centre–periphery ambiguity in the environment in which Lagerlöf operated. In 'Thinking Landscape and Regional Belonging on the Northern Edge of Europe', Michael Jones and Kenneth Olwig (2008) argue that borderlands possess a particular innovative potential that can 'perhaps later provide inspiration for changes at the core'. This margin–core dialectic may be applicable, moreover, to the relationship between 'peripheral' and canonical, or 'minor' and 'major', in Lagerlöf's production, with Landskrona constituting a literary laboratory of sorts in which ideas and forms of expression could be tested in occasional forms before feeding into more prominent work at a later stage.

The significance of Landskrona's borderland status is emphasised by several Lagerlöf scholars, and by the author herself. In an informative monograph, *Lagerlöf i Landskrona* ('Lagerlöf in Landskrona'), Erik Eliasson stresses the special relationship between the Swedish town and the Danish capital the other side of the Sound as evidenced by the close traffic connections: 'The ferry connections were surprisingly good. In some months three daily crossings in either direction were advertised, and on some holidays no fewer than four'.[2] Eliasson views

Illus. 1. The teaching staff at the girls' school in Landskrona where Lagerlöf was employed from 1885 to 1895. Lagerlöf is standing second from the left, between her friend Anna Oom and the headmistress Josepha Ahnfelt.

Landskrona as a Swedish–Danish melting pot situated in a transnational crossover zone, in which Lagerlöf manoeuvred with ease and enthusiasm from the outset of her stay in the town. Her contacts with cultural circles of the neighbouring capital, especially connected with the Danish women's movement, were intensified around and after the publication in 1891 of her breakthrough work *Gösta Berlings saga* (*Gösta Berling's Saga*). Similarly, in a discussion of Lagerlöf as a national icon, Vivi Edström observes that, in the Landskrona period, the author was orientated as much towards Denmark as towards Sweden (2001, 62), while Ulla-Britta Lagerroth in a study of 'nordism' in Lagerlöf argues that the author's cultural encounters on the 'other' side of the Sound contributed to the formation of her pan-Nordic inclinations (2000, 130).[3] Poignant insights by Lagerlöf herself into her participation in the cultural mobility across the Sound can be found, for example, in a recollection from 1927 (republished in *Harvest*, Lagerlöf 1933b), not without irony, of her meeting with the influential Danish critic Georg Brandes in Copenhagen in 1893, concluding with an empha-

Illus. 2. The cover page
of the 'Official Guide to
the World Exhibition in
Landskrona 1888' was
printed in an arresting
purple colour, in keep-
ing with the festive, and
perhaps also the utopi-
an, dimensions of the
pamphlet.

Officiel Vägvisare

vid

Verldsutställningen

i

Landskrona

1888.

af

Selma Lagerlöf

LANDSKRONA,
H. F. ÖSTERBERG & SONS BOKTRYCKERI,
1888.

sis on the impact on her own career of multidirectional currents of
literary dissemination, reception, and recognition flowing across
national boundaries.

Published anonymously but attributed to Lagerlöf, the playful 'Official
Guide to the World Exhibition in Landskrona' renegotiates the relationship between town, city and world, applying a 'glocal' perspective
with utopian overtones. In respect of its generic and stylistic hybridity,
its interplay between the fictional and the factual, its properties as a
travel text, its use of miniature and model, its embrace of modernity
and industrialism, its interest in 'import–export' transactions between
'home' and 'away', the publication reads, moreover, as a 'guide' to or
catalogue of some of the characteristics of Lagerlöf's future literary
practice. The publication signposts a charitable event organised in aid of
local victims of poverty, thus reflecting Lagerlöf's social orientations in
the period. The event took place in Landskrona's *festivitetshus* ('assembly
rooms') on 1 December 1888 and was modelled on the international

exhibition culture of the time. In the guide, the charitable event is ironically measured against Copenhagen's 1888 Nordic Exhibition of Industry, Agriculture and Art, which 'to some extent has served as an example and a model', but outperforming this to become 'a colossal, indeed world-wide enterprise'.[4] This self-aggrandising rhetoric works as an apt imitation of the style and the dreams displayed, for example, in the Danish *Nationaløkonomisk Tidsskrift* ('Journal of National Economics') of 1888, where the Nordic exhibition is envisaged to become 'an event which could give a new reality to Copenhagen's faded dreams of being a world city'.[5] Echoing such ambitions, the guide transforms the peripheral regional setting into a continent and the exhibition space into a global magnet for a transnational gathering where 'the most civilised nations on earth decided to ... be represented'.[6]

In a similar vein, the central part of the guide, 'Orientering på terrängen' ('Orientation in the Exhibition Area'), evokes the modern metropolis and its bombardment of the senses, reminding the charitable visitor to 'accustom the eye to the multi-coloured mix of products, signs and people on display'.[7] At the same time, the orientation reads as a journey of adventure *en miniature* into a multicultural, exoticised, and erotisised landscape, populated by people, primarily women, from a range of nations and ethnicities. There is no shortage, either, of industrialists or representatives of the imperial powers of the day.

This tour of a virtual transnational terrain of attractions and diversity echoes the contemporary culture of entertainment and consumption. It is, however, framed by a consideration of the very real social hardship which the charitable event is designed to alleviate. This frame in part adopts, or imitates, a higher literary register. It consists of an introductory 'exhibition cantata' and a concluding account of a journey on foot through Landskrona. This second travel account, a counterpoint in several ways to the preceding exotic exhibition orientation, incorporates an additional poem, 'Sjöpromenaden' ('The Sea Promenade'), which reads as a statement on the literary potential of the 'periphery'. The frame as a whole seems to project a potential regional route that leads from a dystopian state to a utopian one, envisioning the marginal local community transformed into a role model and a dynamic centre reaching beyond national confines.

This trajectory informs, moreover, the composition of both parts of the frame in themselves. The crisis point in the cantata, its dystopian turn, is thus connected with closed borders. It occurs when a wondrous

Illus. 3. The members of the sewing circle who organised the virtual world exhibition in Landskrona, photographed in 1885.

and poeticised vessel loaded with treasures from around the world is, in what is also a clash of discourses, denied entry by, so to speak, customs and excise, because the local social misery makes 'joy … contraband'.[8] The key device in the poem from this point onwards is to redefine the implied 'protectionism' from a mercantile to a social strategy, which will eventually break down the barriers towards the fulfilment and enjoyment of life:

> There must be coal in poor people's hearths
> And food in the corner of the school bag
> Stocking on the foot which the clog wears

And rooms where cradle and bed can stand.
And therefore friends, oh good friends
Open your heart and purse and hand!
Because as long as need is felt
Will also joy be contraband.[9]

In the concluding part of the frame, 'En vandring genom Landskrona' ('A Walk through Landskrona'), the level of social ambition as articulated in the cantata is increased further: from a fulfilment of fundamental human needs to an embryonic notion of a welfare society. This ostensibly much more mundane travel text depicts how a female collective, the local sewing circle that is also organising the charitable event, dialogically decodes and, importantly, re-imagines the local townscape that the women traverse. This is reconstituted from a stronghold of poverty to the originating site of a vision of welfare provision: 'Would it not be a credit to our town if it were the first to establish, say, a welfare committee whose whole ambition was focused on prevention and sustainability'.[10] In a typical play with scale, the sewing circle then morphs into the welfare provider, aiming to abolish not only poverty, but also its attendant social ills of crime, disease, alcoholism, and 'evil' behaviour as such.

This notion of making the peripheral town a model, an attraction even, is reinforced in the climactic stanzas of the poem 'The Sea Promenade', recited at the appropriate point of the walk, right at the edge of the Sound, with mirror effects between the fictional and the factual that are characteristic of the 'Official Guide' and of Lagerlöf's writing more broadly. The poem vows in ways that would seem prophetic of Lagerlöf's literary career to strive to develop the local setting into a world literature location:

Oh, my fair friend, if only
I could write novels
You should become the scene of
Wonderful episodes
You should become as classical
As a street in Verona[11]

It is logical, therefore, that towards the end of the tour of the town it is Landskrona itself, and not just its fantastical exhibition, that emerges

Illus. 4. This photograph of Lagerlöf sporting an emancipated haircut was taken in Copenhagen in a high-street studio on one of her frequent visits to the city while based in Landskrona.

as a competitor, in terms of being emblem of the dynamic world, both to classical cities such as Athens and Rome and to Copenhagen. Using traffic and transportation as key tropes—again, favoured techniques in Lagerlöf's subsequent literary practice—the text sums up its prospective redefinition of the periphery and its innovating role in the following redirection of influence and illumination, dialogically achieved:

> The ferry from Copenhagen squeezed into the narrow channel between the public baths and Gråen, with a yellow lantern placed high up in the prow.
> 'That is the spark of life which the big radiant world sends into our darkness,' someone joked.
> 'It will soon be our turn to transmit sparks of life.'[12]

Utopian continuities

The welfare ideas which the 'Official Guide' introduces in a borderland context are developed in later, more canonical, and nation-orientated texts by Lagerlöf, for example in the seminal 'Hem och stat' ('Home and State') speech of 1911. This likewise links a women-led organisation, in this case the family household rather than a charitable circle, to a conception of the inclusive society, anticipating, perhaps, the notion of the Swedish *folkhem* ('People's Home'), as formulated politically in the 1920s and 1930s. If so, it may be argued, then, that seeds of this societal idea may be found in Lagerlöf's earliest work. In *Selma Lagerlöf efter Gösta Berlings saga* ('Selma Lagerlöf after Gösta Berling's Saga'), Bengt Ek (1951, 233) suggests that socially utopian ideas inform Lagerlöf's work throughout the 1890s and beyond the turn of the century, also impacting on *Jerusalem* (1901–1902), her major novel of emigration and the quest for an ideal spiritual community (although ambiguously portrayed in the text). And the utopian influence does not stop there, we could add, but is also evident in her subsequent 'macro' novels *Nils Holgersson* and *The Outcast*.

In a discussion of utopian literature, Fredric Jameson argues that, alongside wish fulfilment and the elimination of evil, utopian writing is fuelled by a further form of satisfaction, namely the creative stimulation of constructing models and designing miniatures:

> the pleasures of construction may not be so evident: you have to think of them in terms of the garage workshop, of the home-mechanics erector sets, of Lego, of bricolating and cobbling together things of all kinds. To which we must also add the special pleasures of miniaturization: replicating the great things in handicraft dimensions. (Jameson 2004, 35)

This analysis is clearly of relevance not only to the 'marginal' 'Official Guide' but also to the main work of *Nils Holgersson*, which could be said to present a utopian picture of national interaction—a picture in which the reworking of regions into models, miniatures, and components of the national machinery is a decisive device. This reworking, in turn, depends on the miniaturisation which the eponymous hero himself experiences at the beginning of the narrative to enable his, and the reader's, participation in a literal bird's-eye-perspective that can 'shrink' the national terrain into perceivable and aesthetically pleasing dimensions. The 'Official Guide' and *Nils Holgersson* share, moreover, the freedom of form and thought that the hybrid textual category of travel writing may, according to several theorists, afford, as it occupies a liberating borderland between the factual and the fictional. In *Defining Travel*, Susan L. Roberson (2001, 61) identifies what she calls a play of ideology and imagination (of obvious relevance to both the Landskrona guide and the national geography adventure) as central to the 'creative' qualities of travel writing. Similarly, in his own 'guide' to modern travel literature, *Resa och skriva* ('Travelling and Writing'), Arne Melberg takes travel literature to be a 'nomadic' form of writing that borrows freely from a variety of text types ranging from journalistic reportage to novel and poetry. Although it has often been marginalised by criticism and cultural institutions, he sees it as a freer form of writing and a 'joker' in the literary game, offering the writer room for innovation and experimentation (Melberg 2006, 9, 13, 32). Again, it would seem meaningful to consider both the Landskrona guide and *Nils Holgersson* as generic 'jokers' of this type, challenging traditional literary categorisation.

Moving on to *Bannlyst* (*The Outcast*), this combination of anti-war and romantic novel clearly contains its own dystopian–utopian agenda, while also having a transnational and welfare vision in common with the 'Official Guide'. The period around the First World War seems to provide the foundation for a renewed scrutiny in Lagerlöf's production of the national parameters and the validity of a singular national perspective. Whereas *Nils Holgersson*, its considerable interest in southern and northern borderland settings notwithstanding (see also Astrid Surmatz's discussion of its representation of Lapland elsewhere in this volume), has as its obvious ambition the demonstration of the attractiveness of the entirety of the national terrain, *The Outcast*, just like the 'Official Guide', is dominated by a drift of its imagination towards the sea, away from the solidity of the national terrain and national understanding, and towards a wider vision. This is not to say that *The Outcast* does not share features with the novel of nation. As several critics have pointed out, *The Outcast* draws on the nationwide approach to spatial representation that Lagerlöf developed in the *Wonderful Journey*, giving regions, whose locations range from the coastal south-west to the new industrialised north of Sweden, significant roles in the narrative, connecting them through character mobility and multiple modes of transportation. In particular, the novel activates, but also subverts, what Franco Moretti has identified as the plot

paradigm of the national marriage, the joining together in romantic relationships, especially in the nineteenth-century novel, of characters from
different parts of a country in order to create a deeper sense of the nation
as homeland (Moretti 2009, 18). In *The Outcast*, however, the national
marriage is an unhappy one (apart from its rescue in an unconvincing
happy ending), dominated by the territorial and oppressive behaviour
of the male party (mirroring at a micro level the belligerent behaviour
of aggressive states). Instead, real romance is invested in an extra-marital
relationship between the female party and the novel's 'new man' hero, two
sea-connected soulmates, who are both characterised by extra-national
experiences or aspirations and by their charitable and welfare activities,
which form part of the novel's utopian dimension.

As for the war theme, and the anti-war message, the west-coast region
of Bohuslän functions in *The Outcast* not only as the site of the national
marriage and the extra-national romance, but also as a transnational
contact zone, in principle not unlike the Landskrona of the 'Official
Guide', although in this instance the interface is first and foremost with
the gruesome consequences of modern military conflict, making any
sense of 'neutrality' illusionary. Inspired by Lagerlöf's 'touristic' trauma of witnessing scores of corpses of dead sailors drifting towards land
when she was holidaying on the Bohuslän coast in the summer of 1916
at the time of the largest naval battle of the First World War off the west
coast of Denmark, the novel shifts its perspective offshore, right into the
centre of the maritime crisis. Here, the macabre bodily performances of
the dead, scattered across the sea like so much refuse, create graphic and
uncanny slippages between life and non-life that shocked readers. The
novel's uncanny components are essential, however, not only in depicting the dystopia of war, but also in facilitating the breaking down of the
barriers between living and dead, national and foreign, friend and foe,
which is central to the novel's agenda of peace. Thus, the transforming
impact on a variety of characters (several of whom have occupied roles
of opponents in the narrative up to this point) of witnessing the manifestations of the carnage leads to a transnational burial scene, set in the
local cemetery, in which the rescued bodies of British and German sailors
alike are redeemed. Although the subject matter and the register are very
different from what we found in the 'Official Guide', the underlying
linkage of welfare and porous borders seems similar.

The ultimate vision in *The Outcast* of a world of continuities rather
than territorial hostilities is articulated by the contested character of

Lotta Hedman, who at times operates as an embedded narrator in the novel. A factory worker, and a visionary, from a Lapland in the grip of new industrialisation, she is a proletarian product of the periphery, yet set on a nationwide mission that eventually takes her to the west coast, in keeping with an overriding motif of female mobility in the text. And the range of Hedman's vision by no means stops at the national borders. It is from her perspective that the novel provides its most globalised, and most sublime, 'Google Earth' image of the joined-up nature of both geographies and destinies.

Global sentiments in local environments

While *The Outcast* was Lagerlöf's main work of the First World War period, several more marginal sketches, memory pieces, and short fictions reveal intense engagement with the urgent questions of the time in hybrid, experimental, and more fragmented forms, reflecting, perhaps, the 'splintering' of worldviews, beliefs, and ideologies that the global conflict itself entailed. Thus, in the so-called *Stämningar från krigsåren* ('Impressions from the War Years'), Lagerlöf seems to take a variant route, reminiscent of the 'Official Guide', to the promotion of transnational thought by downgrading, or simply bypassing, the national perspective that remains strong in *The Outcast*, in favour of a pronounced interlinking of local and global, typically capturing 'eruptions', reflections, or refractions of wartime events and moral dilemmas on the small screen of apparently sheltered environments and mindsets. Four of the impressions were published in periodicals during the War and republished, together with a further two texts, under their umbrella heading in *Troll och människor. Andra samlingen* (1921, 'Trolls and Humans: The Second Collection'), while others remained unpublished or were published posthumously. In a commentary, tellingly entitled 'Världsbrand i småstadsperspektiv' ('World Conflagration in Small-Town Perspective'), written in connection with her publication in 1960 of one of the manuscript impressions, Ulla-Britta Lagerroth proposes a modification of what she calls the critical axiom that Lagerlöf experienced a lack of creative vision and productivity during the War. Instead, she argues that Lagerlöf harboured an overarching ambition, although only fairly partially realised, of creating 'a boldly designed and envisioned work, joined together by short stories, sketches and sentiments, which should all prismatically reflect the light from the mighty world conflagration'.[13] In the following, two of these war impressions, one published posthumously, the other unpublished, will be used to sketch a route that leads from Lagerlöf's rural home region of Värmland in western Sweden down to Bohuslän and its coastal exposure to the world, as already encountered in *The Outcast*.

The manuscript version of the war impression which Ulla-Britta Lagerroth published in 1960 under the title of 'Patron Ivar Halenius' ('Proprietor Ivar Halenius') is itself entitled 'Första kapitlet' ('First Chapter'), which leads Lagerroth to interpret it as the intended opening of Lagerlöf's planned 'prismatic' project. Although probably written in 1915, the narrative is set at the exact time when the news of the outbreak of war spread through western Sweden, tracing its impact on local behaviour: from tourists fleeing the seaside resorts to a run on the banks and panic buying, all expressed in terms of excessive traffic and stifling congestion. The narrative resembles the 'Official Guide' in using a walk through a townscape as the frame for an ideological investigation and a transnational turn. During the course of the proprietor's journey on foot through his home community—its location revealed by the inclusion of the signage for the 'Bank of Värmland'[14]—it becomes apparent that any isolationist inclinations and tendencies to appreciate the 'cleansing' potential of war the protagonist may hold at the beginning of the narrative are unsustainable.

The strategy of this impression is to challenge the notion of local sites as disconnected from a world scene—even the proprietor's idyllic garden situated on the outskirts of the town is constructed as an international tourist attraction, echoing, possibly, the magnetic force that Lagerlöf's home at Mårbacka exerted on the wider public in the author's later career and her own status as a world-famous literary figure. As the proprietor makes his way through the town (which, not unlike Landskrona, is figured as a place of mutual familiarity as well as social stratification), each encounter seems to offer a new concretisation of the complex interconnections between countries, which make the separation of them into enemy states a tragic absurdity. This reinforces the proprietor's own earlier observations on the density and richness of inter-European cultural and economic infrastructure, which render its division and destruction by battlelines preposterous in both moral and logistical terms. This perspective culminates when a young schoolteacher reports how the news of the outbreak of war turned the gathering of an international group of pupils assembled at the renowned arts and crafts folk high school in

Nääs outside Gothenburg into a truly transnational manifestation, as the various anthems of the nations represented were sung in a distinctly serial and connected manner, making the pupils' status as members of enemy countries incomprehensible: '"We felt such agreement there … We were unable to understand why we should fight and be hostile towards each other"'.[15] The Ivar Halenius impression reads in many ways as a farewell to the idyllic ways of a dying culture, and concludes with sensations of nausea and strangulation, highly prescient of the bodily reaction against war which Lagerlöf intended *The Outcast* to provoke in its readers.

An intensified articulation of uncanny war impressions can be found in another of Lagerlöf's precursor texts to *The Outcast*, the unpublished Bohuslän narrative 'Den fridsamme' ('The Peaceable One').[16] This war impression is regarded by Lagerroth as approaching 'the artistic climax of the whole material'.[17] While both *The Outcast* and 'Proprietor Ivar Halenius' chart collective tourism, 'The Peaceable One' focuses on the individual experience of its eponymous seaside visitor, the author's male alter ego of sorts (even the ambiguously portrayed Ivar Halenius may to an extent be considered in a similar way). From the first, the description of the protagonist's approach journey by train towards the sea is punctuated by the warning sounds of a westerly storm penetrating through the natural defences of the coastal cliffs and into the valley where the railway runs. When the visitor immediately after arrival at the Bohuslän resort makes his way to the most prominent point of the shore and challenges the wind-swept sea to display its secret life of sublime mythical beings, what emerges instead is a futuristic mono-chrome display of the monsters of the living, but deadly, machinery engaged in combat on an industrial scale:

> The whole gulf in front of him was filled by the most enormous battleships engaged in combat. Dark, tall colossuses of iron, grey like the sea, not resembling ships but some never-before-seen monsters. Battle raged between them, one was in flames, another turned with its stern sinking while the bow rose. And among these snorting monsters that spat fire and iron, a sea full of dead and drowning, of pieces of wreckage, of boats broken and capsized.[18]

In this apocalyptic vision the battle zone itself and its animated warships have been transported right into the vicinity of the shore (in more of a close-up of the machinery of war than even *The Outcast* would provide), thereby creating a 'horror-of-scale' effect that works as a metaphor for the proximity of global conflict and the unavoidability of exposure and engagement. The impact of the visual shock is intensified by the fact that the scene only manifests itself for a moment. While the core of the narrative is a nightmarish fantasy, its frame signals authenticity (a combination of the fantastical and the actual also found in the 'Official Guide', although very differently modulated). The text opens with the temporal marker of '1916, early June'[19] and concludes with exact background information that emphatically roots the preceding vision in the real horror of war. In another instance of the impact of scale, the enlarged and doubly darkened graphics of the modern news medium of the telegram convey to the tourist the news of the same naval battle off the west coast of Jutland the consequences of which *The Outcast* would later depict: 'Many ships were lost, and on the surface of the stormy sea masses of dead were rolling at this moment'.[20]

Related reworkings of apparent local idylls into something much more sinister are found in the war impressions entitled 'Den lille sjömannen' ('The Little Sailor') and 'Dimman' ('The Mist'), both published in wartime, in 1918 and 1916 respectively, and republished in 1921. 'The Little Sailor' (dated July 1916 and thus sharing the temporal, as well as the locational, setting of *The Outcast* and 'The Peaceable One') is a much more understated impression than the two previously discussed texts. Played out in what seems a programmatically peaceful and secluded place, it affords the observing narrator (a further alter ego of Lagerlöf) the role of a detective of sorts as she listens in on the conversation conducted—and deciphers the body language displayed—during a near-by coffee party consisting of a young sailor and his mother and maternal aunt. Conveyed in a mode that has subtly gothic overtones, the conclusion of this 'detective story' (a genre which would experience a golden age in the aftermath of the war) finds that a fourth, foreign, party has been present at the table: the pale shadow of a German sailor, whose dead body has been washed ashore and buried in the local cemetery the same day, is preying on the young Swedish sailor's mind, as he contemplates his own departure by ship the next day. The narrative in its ending thus eerily dissolves the boundaries between dead and alive, local and foreign, as the two sailors turn into reflections of each other. 'The Mist', finally, reads as a more abstract metaphorical summing-up of the warning against isolationism and small-world self-sufficiency which the war impressions together articulate. It is a central piece that develops the psychological impact of a Nature-induced but symbolic shortened field of vision from painful and unsettling via aesthetically revealing and rewarding in its close-up perspectives to, finally, morally unsatisfactory in the context of global conflict and suffering.

Transnationalising a wonderful journey

We shall conclude our tour through some of the transnational terrains of Lagerlöf's work from the beginning of her writing career to the end of the First World War by briefly discussing a little-known but fascinating travel adventure, 'Lapland – Schonen' ('Lapland – Skåne'), which may be seen as a transnational take on Nils Holgersson's seminal journey through Sweden, while also displaying welfare and charitable concerns not dissimilar to those found in several of the previously discussed texts. This travel text will, moreover, bring us back to the southern Swedish region of Skåne, where we started our investigations. 'Lapland – Skåne' fronted the German-language pocket-sized anthology *Schweden* ('Sweden'), which was published by Norstedt in Stockholm in 1917. The anthology was sold in aid of, and handed out to, wounded German prisoners of war transported by train from Russia through neutral Sweden towards Germany. This type of train transportation in turn forms the foundation of the storyline of Lagerlöf's contribution itself. The narrative was never published in Swedish, although several variants or fragments of it exist in the author's Notebook 11.

The pedagogical challenge facing 'Lapland – Skåne' is to map out the long railway journey from Haparanda on the Finnish border to Sweden's southernmost town of Trelleborg in ways which would capture and retain the interest of its intended key readership of the war-wounded in landscapes they could be forgiven for regarding as merely an extended stepping stone towards a desired destination. Like in *Nils Holgersson*, Lagerlöf's answer is to invite the reader to participate in an embodied play with geographies, dimensions, scale, and types of mobility. In

Illus. 5. Lagerlöf's contribution to the German-language anthology *Schwea* ('Sweden') was illustrated with this map, the bold line indicating the railw route from Haparanda to Trelleborg which is covered by the travelogue. T illustration reads as a reworking of the intricate outline of an airborne mig tory route projected onto the national map, which, from an early stage of publication history, became emblematic of *Nils Holgersson's Wonderful Journ*

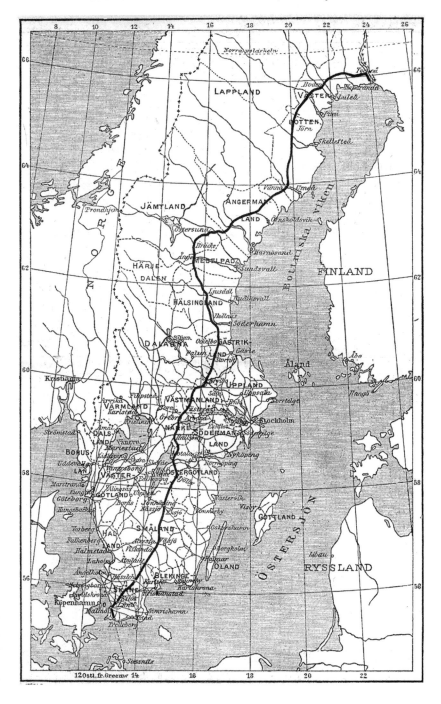

'Lapland – Skåne', however, this *Spiel* is of a distinctly transnational type. The narrative reads as a radical example of James Duncan and Derek Gregory's conception of travel writing as 'an act of translation' mediating between foreign and domestic to produce a 'space in-between' (1999, 4). It also seems to bear out Andrew Thacker's argument in his study entitled *Moving through Modernity: Space and Geography in Modernism* that modernist writing, in which he includes forms of travel writing in the modernist period, 'can be located only within the movements between and across multiple sorts of space' (2003, 8), which contributes to a sense of fluid boundaries and porous borders.

In a two-stage strategy, 'Lapland – Skåne' first turns to the lighter topic of tourism, a frequent theme in Lagerlöf's work, as we have seen. It depicts how a trio of Swedish hill-walkers playfully decode the various segments of a Swiss mountainscape through which they ascend by reference to regional landscape variations in Sweden. The tourists' continued grafting of Nordic geography onto the Alpine terrain offers them a scaling device, which enables overview and orientation in an unfamiliar terrain. At the same time, it introduces a method of miniaturisation in relation to the Swedish terrain, which the readers might find useful, while also inviting them to share a sensation of bodily command, including a superhuman ability to stride through entire lands. In the second stage of its strategy, 'Lapland – Skåne' (using the book itself as the communicating subject, a recurring device in the text) then returns to the train setting to encourage its travelling target readers to play a similar game to the one the tourists are engaged in, a game of familiarising the foreign, only reversed:

> In order now to return to the travellers on the hospital trains from Lapland to Skåne, the book would like to suggest to them that they play the same game ... Could they not imagine the whole of Sweden as a high mountain and compare it with an Alpine peak which they themselves have climbed or at least heard described?[21]

The narrative then goes on to stratify and decode the Swedish cultural geography through which the train progresses on these premises. Thus, 'Lapland – Skåne' takes a profoundly comparative approach to landscape depiction by which the two countries, Sweden and Switzerland, and their characteristics are superimposed onto each other to create a truly transnational terrain. The effect of this double mapping and its comple-

mentary 'translation' processes is to build a common, yet plural ground in natural and cultural terms and imbue it with a shared dynamic that combines historical depth with the restless 'traffic' of the modern times.
· While the immediate aims of the 'Lapland – Skåne' project are to provide entertainment and information on Sweden (also aimed at Lagerlöf's international audience more broadly), as the wounded make their long approach towards their homeland, its more profound ambition is to challenge the nationalistic causes of war by promoting the notion of countries as reflections of each other (not unlike the relationship between the German and the Swedish soldier in 'The Little Sailor'). This makes 'Lapland – Skåne' an important internationalisation of the idea of the wonderful journey, while also typifying the thrust of Lagerlöf's transnational sensibility as we have traced it over three decades of her writing career.

Notes

1 'Vad som mest intresserade mig under dessa tidiga Landskronadagar, det var de många sociala frågor, som rörde sig i tiden. Allt, som angick undervisning, fred, nykterhet, kvinnosak, fattigvård, fängslade min uppmärksamhet. Jag hade några obestämda funderingar på att helt ägna mig åt mitt lärarinnekall och att använda all min kraft på att skapa en mönsterskola, där alla det nuvarande pedagogiska systemets brister skulle vara avhjälpta' (Lagerlöf 1933c, 33–4). Unless otherwise indicated, the translations into English are my own.
2 'Båtförbindelserna var ... förvånansvärt goda. Vissa månader annonserades 3 turer dagl. i vardera riktningen och vissa högtidsdagar inte mindre än 4' (Eliasson 1958, 114).
3 See also Jørgen Ravn's study 'Selma Lagerlöf i Landskrona og København' ('Selma Lagerlöf in Landskrona and Copenhagen') which concludes that the author's intellectual contacts with Copenhagen in the Landskrona period profoundly impacted on her literary career overall (1958a, 150).
4 'i någon mån kunnat tjena till mönster och förebild'; 'ett kolossalt, ja verldsomfattande företag' (Lagerlöf 1888, 5).
5 'en Begivenhed, der skal kunne give ny Virkelighed til Københavns blegnede Drømme om at være en Verdensby' (Bauer 1888, 2).
6 'jordens mest civiliserade nationer beslöto att ... låta sig representeras' (Lagerlöf 1888, 5).
7 'vänja sitt öga vid det brokiga virvarret af exponerade varor, skyltar och menniskor' (Lagerlöf 1888, 5).
8 'glädjen ... kontraband' (Lagerlöf 1888, 4).
9 'Kol skall det finnas vid arma härdar | Och mat i skolväskans ena vrå, | Strump' på den foten, som träskon härdar, | Och rum, der vagga och säng må stå. | Och derför vänner, ack gode vänner, | I öppnen hjerta och börs och hand! | Ty ack, så länge man nöden känner, | Skall också glädjen bli kontraband' (Lagerlöf 1888, 4).

10 'Skulle det inte vara en heder för vår stad, om just den först inrättade en, låt oss se, en välfärdskomité, hvars hela sträfvan ginge ut på att förebygga och upprätthålla' (Lagerlöf 1888, 12).

11 'Ack, min fagra vän, om ändå | Jag romaner kunde skrifva, | Underbara episoders | Skådeplats du skulle blifva. | Du så klassisk varda skulle | Som en gata i Verona' (Lagerlöf 1888, 14).

12 'Köpenhamnsbåten kom inkilande i den trånga rännan mellan badhuset och Gråen med en gul lykta högt i fören. ... "Det är lifsgnistan, som den stora, lysande verlden sänder in i vårt mörker," skämtade en. "Det bliver snart vår tur att sända ut lifsgnistor"' (Lagerlöf 1888, 15).

13 'ett väldigt upplagt och stort tänkt verk, sammanfogat av noveller, skisser och stämningar, som alla prismatiskt skulle reflektera ljuset från den stora världsbranden' (Lagerroth 1961, 35).

14 'Värmlandsbanken' (Lagerlöf 1961, 20).

15 '"Vi kände oss så eniga där ... Vi kunde rakt inte förstå, varför man skulle strida och stå fientliga mot varandra"' (Lagerlöf 1961, 21–2).

16 The sketch is preserved in a group of manuscripts entitled 'Stämningar från krigsåren' ('Impressions from the War Years') in the National Library of Sweden, Stockholm (Ligg-pf, Sn-Sö, L1: 247).

17 'den konstnärliga höjdpunkten i hela materialet' (Lagerroth, 1961, 36).

18 'Hela viken framför honom var uppfylld av de väldigaste krigsskepp inbegripna i strid. Mörka höga kolosser av järn gråa som havet inte liknande skepp, men några aldrig hittills sedda vidunder. Det rasade strid mellan dem, ett stod i lågor, ett vände sig vacklande och sjönk med aktern medan fören reste sig. Och mellan dessa fnysande vidunder, som sprutade ut eld och järn ett vatten fullt av döda av drunknande, av vrakdelar, av båtar som bräcktes och kantrade' (Lagerlöf, 'The Peaceable One').

19 'År 1916 i början av Juni' (Lagerlöf, 'The Peaceable One').

20 'Massor av skepp voro förlorade och på det stormande havets yta vältrade i denna stund massor av döda' (Lagerlöf, 'The Peaceable One').

21 'Um aber nun zu den Reisenden, die mit den Invalidenzügen von Lappland nach Schonen fahren, zurückzukommen, so möchte das Buch ihnen vorschlagen, dasselbe Spiel zu spielen ... Könnten sie nicht ganz Schweden als ein Hochebirge denken und es mit einem Alpengipfel vergleichen, den sie selber bestiegen oder den sie wenigstens beschrieben gehört haben?' (Lagerlöf 1917b, 20).

CHAPTER 16

The many facets of a diamond

Space, change and identity
in Selma Lagerlöf's *The Miracles of Antichrist*

Elettra Carbone & Kristina Sjögren

In Selma Lagerlöf's novel *Antikrists mirakler* (1897, *The Miracles of Antichrist*), public space is used as a catalyst for social change. In this novel the fictional Sicilian town of Diamante (Italian for 'diamond') becomes the setting of great transformations that affect not only the characters' personal development but also that of the whole community.[1] In this essay we examine how public spaces are used to problematise issues related to identity, gender, and social class, all of which, in line with the ideas of the Modern Breakthrough, were highly topical in the Scandinavian literature of the time. Rural idylls, dramatic scenes of poverty, social conformism, women's struggle for emancipation, technological innovation, and workers' and peasants' uprisings—these are just some of the aspects that make this fictional Sicilian town one of the most multifaceted spaces in Swedish literature.

Four years after her acclaimed début with *Gösta Berlings saga* (1891, *Gösta Berling's Saga*), Selma Lagerlöf undertook a long Italian tour from October 1895 to the summer of 1896 with her friend Sophie Elkan. In 1897 she published *The Miracles of Antichrist*, a novel clearly influenced by her trip to Italy, and especially by the month she and Elkan spent in Sicily. They had followed in the footsteps of many Nordic artists who, particularly since the beginning of the nineteenth century, had travelled to Italy in search of direct contact with 'exotic' Nature and rustic life, classical culture, and Renaissance art. However, while most Nordic writers and artists travelled to Rome *en masse*, fewer ventured further south to Sicily like Lagerlöf and Elkan.[2] As Giorgia Alù rightly points out in her study on British women who lived in Sicily in the second half of the nineteenth and the beginning of the twentieth centuries, the island was geographically as well as conceptually set apart from the rest of Italy (Alù 2008, 22).

The Miracles of Antichrist received mixed reactions when it was first published and has so far been largely neglected by scholars. Some exceptions are Bengt Ek, with his important analysis of Lagerlöf's representation of socialism in *The Miracles of Antichrist* in his doctoral thesis *Selma Lagerlöf efter Gösta Berlings saga* (1951), and Vivi Edström, who in her *Selma Lagerlöf. Livets vågspel* (2002) dedicates a chapter to a general analysis of the novel in the context of Lagerlöf's experiences during her Italian journey and her general interest in Italy and its folklore. Ulf Olsson has contributed a sophisticated reading of the novel as an allegory in his essay 'I det svarta' (2007).[3]

However, *The Miracles of Antichrist* is a complex novel in which much can be discovered both about Lagerlöf's textual construction of spaces and about the different ways in which characters interact with these spaces. Lagerlöf represents Diamante as a 'social space', a space that—according to Henri Lefebvre's definition—is defined by social practices and implies and contains social relationships (Lefebvre 1974, 1, 26, 82–3). In other words, space and its inhabitants are linked by a dialectical relationship: 'society shapes spaces according to its needs, but equally, space plays a formative role in the construction of social life' (Thacker 2003, 17). How, then, does space change the characters in the novel, and how do the characters change the spaces in which they live?

The story opens with the arrival in Diamante of a copy of the statue of Christ preserved in the Basilica of Santa Maria in Rome.[4] The traditionally religious inhabitants rebel against poverty, and start showing greater interest in their material wealth and progress. The female protagonist, Micaela, goes through a classic journey modelled on that of the female *Bildungsroman*, progressing from a traditional subjugated housewife to an entrepreneurial leader and female hero.[5] In the process she engages in a passionate love story with Gaetano, who develops from a religious artisan into a working-class revolutionary leader.

Few Nordic authors from this period succeeded in placing their Italian characters in a setting as complex and detailed as the one Lagerlöf constructs in her novel. In *The Miracles of Antichrist*, Italy is not represented as a foreign and unfamiliar country, where the Italians remain mere exotic background figures to the main (usually Nordic) characters.[6] In *The Miracles of Antichrist*, the third-person omniscient narrator refuses

Illus. 1. The figure of *Il bambino* as displayed in Santa
Maria in Aracoeli.

to confine the Italian characters to the role of the Other and places them
in a realistic Sicily. The characters exist in a multifaceted Italian setting,
showcasing a variety of Italian spaces: idyllic depictions of the Sicilian
landscape go hand in hand with close-ups of the poverty of the lower
classes and of their struggle for survival, while colourful images of the
Sicilian local traditions are represented together with the arrival of technological innovations such as the railway. It is rather Northern Europe,
represented by England and English characters, which in this novel
becomes the Other: within the Italian domain England and all things
English remain a foreign dimension, whose intervention, whether positive
or negative, is represented as an intrusion. As we will demonstrate, this
small Sicilian town well beyond the main itinerary of foreign travellers is

represented as a quintessentially reactionary space. This natural idyll with its religious festivals and traditions masks a deeply conservative society affected by dramatic social problems. As Micaela and Gaetano try to find a balance between tradition and modernity one thing becomes clear: if change is possible in Diamante, it is possible anywhere.

Paradise and poverty

Sicily was famous among nineteenth-century travellers for its unique natural features: here the typical Mediterranean vegetation was enlivened by more exotic plants and dramatic geological and geographical features. The island, perceived as a 'liminal land, on the border between Africa and Europe', was often associated with an attractive yet dangerous fairytale world where idyllic landscapes were made more exciting by the sudden possibility of volcanic eruptions and earthquakes (Alù 2008, 22; de Seta 1992, 17–26). In line with this tradition, fascination and excitement are the keywords that characterise the very first representations of Sicilian Nature in *The Miracles of Antichrist*. The reader is introduced to the Sicilian landscape around Mount Etna by Donna Elisa as she tries to convince the young protagonist, the orphan Gaetano, to come to Diamante to stay with her. Mount Etna is portrayed as an imaginary world, where natural elements transform themselves into fictional characters. Etna, according to Donna Elisa, is the biggest mountain in the world; it is so big that it takes three days to reach its top; it is so big that there is space on it for fifty-one towns, fourteen big forests, and two hundred hills. The list of exaggerations continues until Mount Etna and Diamante become an irresistible world of adventure that the child cannot wait to see and explore, and Gaetano finally agrees to come and live there. Equally fantastic is the representation of the landscape that the protagonist Micaela sketches when, as a girl, she arrives in Diamante for the first time. In this case, the world surrounding the small Sicilian town is the anteroom leading to the gates of heaven. The beauty of the landscape, with Mount Etna silhouetted against the sky and illuminated by the sunlight, makes Micaela wonder if she has arrived in paradise, 'one of heaven's cities' (Lagerlöf 1910a, 63).[7] Diamante is thus represented as a kind of colourful and lively Arcadia, a location that, in the Romantic imagination, was perceived as an idyllic place, a wonderful utopia (Peucker 1980; Lewan 2001).

As lively, colourful and exciting as the representations of Sicilian

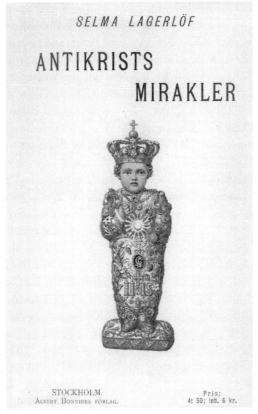

Illus. 2. Cover of *Antikrists mirakler*, 1897.

Nature are those of Sicilian folk life. Sicily is defined by the narrator as 'the noble island of Sicily, where there are more old customs left than in any other place in the south' (Lagerlöf 1910a, 48).[8] Scenes of folklore are often connected to the manifestation of the Sicilian characters' material religiosity. The inhabitants of Diamante are in fact often shown as engaged in parades, material offerings, and rituals, by means of which the saint, in Durkheim's phrase, is forced to 'come out and show himself' (2002, 40–1).

However, the representation of Diamante as a utopia does not remain unchallenged for long; it soon becomes obvious that more complex realities hide behind its fascinating appearance. The adjective 'fattig' ('poor'), often used about Diamante in the course of the novel, is an indication of this. Drawing on Michel Foucault's terminology, Diamante is not a 'utopia' but a 'heterotopia', a place constituted by the juxtaposition of a number of complex spaces that, at a first glance, might even appear to be incompatible with each other, but that are in fact closely connected (Foucault 1986, 22–7). Idyll and poverty are not antithetic, but blend into each other. The beauty of the Sicilian landscape cannot solve social problems. On the contrary, Nature, though fascinating, can inflict only greater sorrows on the inhabitants of this region, where people become poorer and poorer, and where want spreads like a plague:

> That autumn no clear, light October air lay over the Etna region. As if it had been in league with the famine, the heavy, weakening wind from the Sahara came over from Africa, and brought with it dust and exhalations that darkened the sky. (Lagerlöf 1910a, 128)[9]

As they become older, Gaetano and Micaela realise that Diamante is no paradise, and they become increasingly aware of the limitations of their surroundings. This realisation triggers changes in the protagonists that, in turn, have consequences for the social and technological development of the town itself. Sicilian conservative mentality cannot prevent the infiltration of modern ideals that threaten the pillars of this society, or stop the arrival of technological innovations such as the railway. Having grown out of Donna Elisa's representation of Mount Etna as an exciting fairytale world, Gaetano becomes aware that life in Diamante has its limitations, and undertakes a formative journey to England that will introduce him to socialist ideals. Micaela starts out as a traditional, patriarchal, submissive wife, but later becomes the initiator of a 'modern breakthrough' that connects Diamante with the outer world and opens it up to modernity.[10]

Leaving home

The Miracles of Antichrist was published at a time when gender roles were much discussed in the Scandinavian and other Western societies and first-wave feminism stirred up strong emotions. Micaela radically transgresses the gender boundaries of the time by changing into a modern New Woman.[11] The way space is represented in the text to promote feminism and more modern and equal gender roles is one of the most interesting aspects of the novel.

Until the end of the nineteenth century, public space had belonged almost exclusively to men. Come the *fin de siècle*, however, middle-class women started appropriating public space for the first time due to professional employment, suffragist politics, and increased consumption of factory-made goods. Middle-class women in public space were a controversial concept, and they were accidentally approached as prostitutes. At the same time, the competition with men in the labour market and in politics increased. Women did not only threaten men's domination of public space: by entering it they threatened masculinity itself. By occupying space both in the streets and in the public debate in the arts and the press, women displaced the very meanings of public space, writes Sally Ledger (1997, 150). Dichotomies such as the identification of private space (the home) with femininity and public space with masculinity were used to position and construct the genders in relation to each other. Griselda Pollock writes that this split into a private and a public sphere also *defined* the genders. To retain an acceptable femininity, women should not cross the border into the public sphere (2003, 96).

In literature at this time, a character often moving into public space was the New Woman: a professional, usually unmarried character, frequently represented as wicked.[12] Micaela develops from traditional femininity, living as a fragile young woman who has never left the house unaccompanied, into a New Woman working with traditionally masculine tasks outside her home and moving about in public space.[13] In Lagerlöf's text Micaela is not represented as wicked: her development is necessary, almost forced upon her by social change. At the same time Micaela is the motor of social change, a role traditionally defined as masculine. Prior to taking on this role, however, Micaela is constructed as the ideal middle-class woman of the nineteenth century, the representation of her recalling Ibsen's Nora: 'She had never been allowed to go alone on the street. She had never worked. No one had ever spoken seriously to her. She had not even been in love with anyone' (Lagerlöf 1910a, 77).[14] This representation of femininity involves confinement inside the home and removal from all public life, including professional work and serious discussion. To complete the picture of the passive woman in a patriarchal system, Micaela is married off to a much older man whom she does not love, for *his* benefit. As a deeply religious woman, leading her life between the walls of her home and totally dependent on her husband, Micaela is especially frightened of the socialist movement which, thanks to Gaetano, has by now reached Sicily.

The nineteenth-century patriarchal view that a woman is of little value without her husband is illustrated by Micaela sitting at the wake following the death of her husband, reflecting that a widow 'would be nothing, mean nothing; … because they no longer had a husband; because nothing any longer gave them the right to live' (Lagerlöf 1910a, 139).[15] Like a clinging vine, brought up within the confines of a traditional notion of femininity, she almost dies in her husbandless state.

Micaela secretly loves the young Gaetano and she now expects him to take over her late husband's role as her protector against the world: however, the text denies Micaela this patriarchal protection, demanding her growth instead. Gaetano is no patriarchal man, and before Micaela can have him, she must become his equal, the text implying that equality underpins the relationship between men and women in modernity. Micaela has to leave the obedient, self-sacrificing, feminine role behind and step into modern, active, and self-reliant femininity. A prerequisite for this is intimately connected with her use of space: in order to become independent, Micaela has to leave home. In text after text, Lagerlöf uses the concept of leaving home as a metaphor for her characters achieving freedom and emancipation.[16] It is not until Micaela summons the courage to walk out of her own front door and share public space with men that she becomes a free, emancipated human being who obtains both modernity and Gaetano as a lover.

Gaetano too must leave home. His skill in carving images of the saints as a way of serving God is not fully appreciated in the small town of Diamante, where nobody buys his figurines and nothing new needs to be added. Gaetano therefore emigrates to England, in the novel represented as the source of modernity. Here, thanks to his English master—an artist and a socialist—he not only develops his artistry but also finds the key to the solution of the social problems afflicting his hometown in Sicily.

Moving into public space

It is after Gaetano has been imprisoned for his socialist ideas that Micaela, left without masculine support, has to rely on her own strength. Her emancipation goes hand in hand with her decision to bring the railway to Diamante. The building of a railway should be seen as a philanthropic act, one of the few activities open to women at the time and a means of exercising political influence,[17] but also as a symbol of modernity, capitalism, enterprise, technology, and progress, all traditionally associated with masculinity. Micaela must cross several gender boundaries, and do so while Diamante's inhabitants resist her efforts by means of anger, unhelpfulness, and mockery:

> When Donna Micaela was gone they laughed at her. A railway, a railway! She did not know what she was thinking of. There would have to be a company, shares, statutes, concessions. How would a woman manage such things? ... Everyone was against her; no one would help her. They did not even like her to show herself on the streets or to talk business. It was not fitting for a well-born lady. (Lagerlöf 1910a, 188, 214)[18]

Diamante views business activities requiring movement in public space and interaction with men as improper for a woman of the middle or upper classes. The phrase 'How would a woman manage such things?' also indicates the low confidence in women being able to accomplish anything in the public sphere. Women's lack of experience, education, and money would effectively have stopped them at the time.

When Micaela finally gains the support of her old friend, Donna Elisa, the two women seem to throw all traditional femininity overboard. They not only move about in public space: they confront the most dangerous and powerful men in Sicily, and they set out to do business and make money to support the building of the railway. But not only do the women cross the boundaries of traditional femininity, they also cross the boundaries defining how business activities are traditionally handled. The goal of their entrepreneurialism is a typical socialist utopia: a non-profit cooperative between people for the common good. When they criticise 'the engineer and the fine gentlemen' (Lagerlöf 1910a, 253)[19] for driving up the costs of everything, they criticise traditional capitalism and its strong links to the upper classes. The people who end up helping with the railway are marginalised individuals who offer not money, but the work of their hands.

Micaela is gradually able to make use of any public space and even ventures to the old stone quarry, where no man dares to go, to talk to the robber chief. She facilitates the progress that, in the long run, will save her town from poverty. Her breaking of gender codes and developing of a new, modern femininity is represented as something positive: instead of punishing the New Woman protagonist by divorce or death, this text makes the change into modern femininity the prerequisite of a happy ending for Micaela. She, the female entrepreneur and New Woman, is the one who joins material spaces by building a railway that allows Diamante to connect with the outside world, to become modern.

In *The Miracles of Antichrist* entering public space is the trigger of social change, not only for women, but also for the working classes. Public space was traditionally controlled by men, but not just any men—by the men of the upper classes. The conservative establishment did not only fear feminism at the time, but also the working classes, often represented as large, anonymous masses threatening the status quo. In Lagerlöf's novel, the socialist leader Gaetano and his followers take over public space in Sicily to protest against their social conditions. On his return to Sicily, Gaetano is involved in a key historical event, namely the uprisings of 1893 and 1894, which were instigated by the Fasci Siciliani—organisations for the rights of workers and peasants—and which received extensive coverage in the local and international press (Ek 1951, 247–53). In the novel the uprisings fail, as in real life, and their leaders are executed, jailed, or exiled. Yet, in the long run the uprisings inspired a series of social reforms aimed at improving the conditions of peasants and workers (Hobsbawm 1971, 101–105).

By taking over public space, Gaetano and Micaela are able to change the society they live in. But although they are the initiators of this progress, they act inspired by their English role models, Gaetano's artisan master and the wealthy Miss Tottenham.

Two-way appropriation, or, Othering the English

In *The Miracles of Antichrist*, England becomes an idealised space, a symbol of emancipation and modernity. For this reason, the interaction with and involvement in the Italian way of life by the English characters always brings an element of novelty and progress to the plot. As mentioned above, Gaetano's English master is responsible for Gaetano's conversion to socialism, which, in turn, changes Diamante. Similarly, the immensely rich Miss Tottenham from England, who is travelling around Italy in her large coach collecting art, has a decisive influence on Micaela. When she arrives in Sicily, Miss Tottenham is already doing what Micaela must learn to do: she is moving confidently in public spaces and engaging in business. She is determined to bring progress to Diamante and to help battle poverty. Miss Tottenham's good deeds appear to be dictated by an egocentric drive to overcome her Otherness, to be loved and accepted by the locals. Yet, she remains a non-Italian, an outsider. The only way for the Englishwoman to be accepted by the Sicilian people is to sacrifice her innovative ambitions, get married to a local man, and become an ordinary Sicilian wife. Paradoxically, by the end of the novel, the Sicilian Micaela is on her way towards emancipation and independence from men, while the rich, independent globetrotter Miss Tottenham is confined to her home in conventional femininity and subservience.

As the Sicilian Gaetano longs for England as a different place where he can develop his art and learn about politics, English characters living in Italy, like Miss Tottenham, desperately try to establish themselves in this country by purchasing as many Italian holy treasures as they can. While the English in *The Miracles of Antichrist* try to appropriate part of Italian culture and traditions by gathering a great number of works of art, Selma Lagerlöf also had her own way of using the spaces she visited during her Italian journey. Lagerlöf was fascinated by Italy's local legends, which she used as the material of some of her short stories.[20] In addition, there are several cases of *ekphrasis* in the novel, with Lagerlöf transforming Italian works of art into narrative material.[21] Although the change and progress of the two protagonists and the town of Diamante can be seen as consequences of more general international trends related to technological and social transformations, in the novel they are all linked to the legend that opens the novel, about the Sibyl warning the Emperor Augustus not to build a temple in his own honour on the Capitoline Hill, as this would be an act of hubris. No matter where and when they happen, all the events that make up the plot of *The Miracles of Antichrist* refer more or less directly to this prophecy. The Sybil's words were not a specific warning to Augustus, but a universal message addressed to all humanity. Moreover, the Antichrist—a copy of the image of Christ preserved on the Capitoline Hill, commissioned by an Englishwoman—is represented in the novel as an 'English' creation. The image of the Antichrist, which bears the inscription *Mitt rike är endast av denna världen* (Lagerlöf 1897a, 20, original emphasis; Lagerlöf 1910a, 14,

'My kingdom is only of this world'), is said to urge people to seek material welfare and becomes the symbol of general socialist ideals such as harmony, philanthropy, and solidarity with the poor and disadvantaged. For this reason, when it finally arrives in Diamante thanks to Miss Tottenham, another Englishwoman, the influence of the Antichrist statue brings change to what had been for centuries a typical small Sicilian town set rigid in its traditions.

In Lagerlöf's novel the typical small Sicilian town of Diamante, initially represented according to recurrent topoi linked to the exotic natural and folkloristic features of the island, becomes the only place where progress, including social and gender equality, can be achieved, and where a profound and traditional Christian faith can be reconciled with socialist ideals (Ek 1951, 246). The Antichrist is the ultimate cause of transformations that are not destructive, but constructive. As Olsson has pointed out (2007, 88), Lagerlöf in her texts invariably returns to a confrontation between modernity and a conservative restoration. *The Miracles of Antichrist* not only promotes reconciliation between conservative and socialist ideals, it also opens up space for new gender roles.

Summary

In *The Miracles of Antichrist*, the fictional Sicilian town of Diamante is represented as a complex and dynamic space, combining features reminiscent of fairytales with terrible poverty, and strict and long-lasting traditions with progress. Particularly interesting are the connections between public space and individual and social emancipation. In this novel the two Sicilian protagonists, Micaela and Gaetano, embark on a process of development that will result in them taking control over their own lives while at the same time dramatically changing the space in which they live. Provincial Diamante therefore becomes the unexpected setting of radical social and technological changes that are linked to both local and transnational trends. With its all-Italian setting and characters, apart from Miss Tottenham, *The Miracles of Antichrist* discusses issues that were high on the agenda in Scandinavia in the late nineteenth century, such as the rights of the working classes, the position of women in society, and the role of religion in everyday life. Throughout the novel Lagerlöf maintains a difficult balance between local colour and her attempt to demonstrate that this remote region, considered by foreigners a specific geographical, social, and economic entity set apart from the rest of Italy, could be affected by the same social reforms and progress that pertained in nineteenth-century Scandinavia and other European countries.

Notes

1. Diamante bears a similarity to the small Sicilian town of Paternò on the Mount Etna, but also of other Italian cities such as Taormina, Palermo, and even Rome (Ek 1951, 214–15).
2. As Ek (1951, 249) points out, Sicily lay outside the traditional Grand Tour itineraries. The island became a more popular destination in the nineteenth century, especially after Italian unification in 1861 (Alù 2008, 22–3).
3. Others who have discussed *The Miracles of Antichrist* are Erland Lagerroth in 'Selma Lagerlöf som siciliansk hembygdsdiktare' (1971) and Henrik Wivel in *Snedronningen* (1988).
4. Fredrika Bremer wrote about the ceremony when the statue of Christ (*Il Bambino*) is displayed in the church of S. Maria in Aracoeli in her *Livet i Gamla Världen* (1860–2, *Life In the Old World: Or, Two Years In Switzerland and Italy*). There are several stories about how the crowned child has been subjected to thefts and forgeries. Hans Christian Andersen also refers to the image of Jesus in the Church of Aracoeli in his Italian novel *Improvisatoren* (1835, *The Improvisatore*). In 'En julbild från Rom' in *Ord & Bild*, 1893, Carl Bildt, Swedish Ambassador in Rome, retells a legend about the forged Christ child—'Selma Lagerlöf probably knew about this article, and also about Claes Lagergren's essay in the same issue of *Ord & Bild* about Pope Leo XIII and his view of socialism', writes Edström (2002, 199–200).
5. The literary female hero is characterised by agency, unlike the 'heroine', the term implying passivity and dependence upon a male hero. See, for example, Susan A. Lichtman, *The Female Hero in Women's Literature and Poetry* (1996).
6. In novels such as *Fra Piazza del Popolo* (1866, 'From Piazza del Popolo') by the Danish writer Vilhelm Bergsøe, *Nattevagt* (1894, 'Nightwatch') by Henrik Pontoppidan, also from Denmark, and *Jenny* (1911) by the Norwegian author Sigrid Undset, Italian characters are mainly used as a backdrop for the leading characters, who come from the Nordic countries. Lagerlöf was critical of her ability to represent the Italian characters in *The Miracles of Antichrist* adequately, claiming that she could not make them sufficiently credible (Lagerlöf 1936, 'Hur jag fann ett romanämne', in Edström 1996, 60).
7. 'en af himmelens städer' (Lagerlöf 1897a, 68).
8. 'den ädla ön ... där det finnes mera kvar af gammal sed än på något annat ställe i södern' (Lagerlöf 1897a, 52).
9. 'Och denna höst låg icke mera den klara, lätta oktoberluften öfver Etnatrakterna. Utan som om den skulle vara i förbund med nöden, kom den tunga och förlamande ökenvinden öfver från Afrika och förde med sig stoft och dunst, som förmörkade hela rymden' (Lagerlöf 1897a, 141).
10. Cranny-Francis et al. define 'patriarchy' as 'a social system in which structural differences in privilege, power and authority are invested in masculinity and the cultural, economic and/or social positions of men' (2003, 15); Connell points out that this

'massive structure of social relations' involves 'the state, the economy, culture and communications as well as kinship, child-rearing and sexuality' (2005, 65).

11 A very short definition of the New Woman is that she is a professional, financially independent, usually unmarried, and sexually liberated woman (see, for example, Witt-Brattström 2003 or Ledger 1997).

12 Examples of wicked, punished New Women can be found in texts by August Strindberg, Ola Hansson, and Annie Quiding-Åkerhielm.

13 Edström writes that *The Miracles of Antichrist* develops into a grand feminist novel where the naïve, upper-class girl turns into an independent, enterprising woman (Edström 2002, 203). Her comment is in line with the concept of the literary New Woman, where independence and personal development express feminine emancipation.

14 'Hon hade aldrig fått gå ensam på gatan. Hon hade aldrig arbetat. Man hade aldrig talat ett ord allvar med henne. Hon hade icke en gång varit förälskad i någon' (Lagerlöf 1897a, 85).

15 'ingenting skulle vara, ingenting betyda, … därför att de ej mer hade en man, därför att ingenting mer gaf dem rätt att lefva' (Lagerlöf 1897a, 152).

16 Examples of well-known texts in which Lagerlöf uses the theme of departure are *En herrgårdssägen* (1899, *The Tale of a Manor*), *Jerusalem* (1901–1902), *Nils Holgerssons underbara resa genom Sverige* (1906–1907, *Nils Holgersson's Wonderful Journey through Sweden*) and *Kejsarn av Portugallien* (1914, *The Emperor of Portugallia*). She also spoke of women's emigration and departures in 'Hem och stat' ('Home and State'), her speech to the 6th Congress of the International Woman Suffrage Alliance in Stockholm in 1911, in which she endorsed women's emancipation from the home.

17 It was common for middle-class women to do philanthropic work at this time (see Jordansson & Vammen 1998), and Selma Lagerlöf herself would sometimes help out at coffee mornings while working as a teacher in Landskrona, just as her fictional character Micaela does (see Carlsson 2009–2010).

18 'När Donna Micaela var gången, skrattade man åt henne. En järnväg, en järnväg! Hon visste icke hvad hon tänkte på. Det skulle vara bolag, aktier, stadgar, koncession. Hur skulle en kvinna kunna ställa med sådant? … Alla stodo emot henne, ingen ville hjälpa henne. De tyckte ej en gång om att hon visade sig på gatan, att hon talade affärer. Sådant var opassande för en fin dam' (Lagerlöf 1897a, 207, 235).

19 'ingenjörer och fina herrar' (Lagerlöf 1897a, 277).

20 In addition to *The Miracles of Antichrist*, Lagerlöf published a collection of short stories in 1904 entitled *Kristuslegender* (*Christ Legends and Other Stories*), with many of the texts based on Italian legends. Several other legends can be found in her works: 'Fiskarringen' ('The Fisherman's Ring'), which is inspired by a legend from Venice; 'Santa Caterina af Siena' ('Santa Caterina of Siena') and 'Ljuslågan' ('The Sacred Flame'), both of them inspired by legends from Florence, printed in collections of legends in 1899 and 1904; and the legend of Lucia, but never published it in her lifetime, and published posthumously in *Från skilda tider* (1943c). 'Kejsarens syn' ('The Emperor's Vision'), a legend from Rome, begins *The Miracles of Antichrist* and was later reused in *Christ Legends*. 'Den heliga bilden i Lucca' ('The Sacred Image in Lucca') was published in *Troll och människor* I (1915, 'Trolls and Humans') (Edström 2002, 194).

21 The scene with Augustus and the Sybil in the text is strikingly similar to a painting by Paris Bordon, *Augusto con la sibilla tiberina* (1535). The novel closes with an image from *La predicazione dell'Anticristo*, part of a bigger fresco known as *Il Ciclo dell'Apocalisse e del Giudizio Universale* (1499–1504) by Luca Signorelli. On this occasion the painting is clearly mentioned when Father Gondo and the Pope discuss it in the final chapter of *The Miracles of Antichrist*. Lagerlöf emphasised that seeing the painting had inspired her to write the novel (letter to Ellen Key, 15 Dec. 1897, in *Brev*, I: *1871–1902*, 1967a).

CHAPTER 17

Gender, war, and canon

Selma Lagerlöf and Sara Wacklin

Ebba Witt-Brattström

Gender, war, and canon are heavily symbolic and affect-ridden terms. In this essay I propose a loose definition of canon to include not only a classic author such as Selma Lagerlöf, but also a non-canonical writer such as the Finland-Swedish author Sara Wacklin (1790–1846), one of whose works I believe is an important intertext to Lagerlöf's novel *Gösta Berlings saga* (1891, *Gösta Berling's Saga*). I will proceed by sketching an inner-canonical method, which addresses the overall intertexual links 'within literature itself' with regard to plots, historical events, and the functions of gender negotiation in the narratives. The concept of war will be present in my discussion of the historicising function not only of the perception of 'Swedishness' in a given epoch, but also of the two authors.

Figuratively speaking, a war with gender implications is still being fought over the concept of canon. The notion of the classical canon, complete with an élitist aesthetics, has been under attack since the 1960s, when the aim was to expand the canon with 'working-class literature' and 'women's literature'. The issue was methodological, a critique of the 'theological' practice in literary studies. As Franco Moretti puts it: 'the theological exercise—very solemn treatment of very few texts taken very seriously' (2000, 57). According to Moretti, scholars spent their time on the close reading of an extremely limited number of canonical texts. In each epoch, these few (mostly male) *œuvres* were then turned into hegemonic prototypes, excluding other kinds of fiction presenting dissenting experiences and worldviews. The canon was thus associated with hierarchy, doctrine, exclusivity, masculinity, and so forth. There was an acute need for a manifestation of women's symbolical and actual presence in literary history.

To the first generation of Nordic feminist literature scholars, to which I belong, the solution was to add female *œuvres* to the existing, predominantly male canon, wishing for a dialogue between the male line in literary history and the female line now made visible. We were hoping for a different and more dynamic canon formation to emerge, focusing on the innovative aspects of women's literature and related to, but not subdued by, the prevailing forms of male literature. In 1993–2000, the five volumes of *Nordisk kvindelitteraturhistorie* (*History of Nordic Women's Literature*) were published. With the motto 'Now literary history is expanding!', this achievement has challenged the 'theological practice' in canon formation as well as the masculine élitist value-aesthetics. In addition to upgrading forgotten female *œuvres* and/or genres, the aim of the project was also to liberate the 'queens' of Nordic literature, Selma Lagerlöf, Sigrid Undset, Karen Blixen, Edith Södergran, and others, from their function as hostages to a male canon. However, the task of relating them to a 'literature of their own', to use Elaine Showalter's phrase, was the more compelling since the 'queens' tend to overshadow their little sisters as well as their more unknown forerunners. This essay can thus be read as a case study of the (proposed) importance of a minor author to a major classic writer.

I will not address the 'external canon'—the Swedish literary history in which Lagerlöf is the undisputable queen, whereas Wacklin is hardly noticed. Instead I suggest the term 'internal canon formation', defined by Gottfried Willems as a 'canon within literature itself', distinguished from what literary theory, pedagogics, and so forth have decided amounts to a 'canon', and focusing instead on, for example, the ways in which forerunners are made productive in subsequent authorships (Willems 2001, 260).[1] This kind of settlement between literary generations whose existence I am proposing is not a Bloomian Oedipal struggle with a strong predecessor (Bloom 1973), but an intertextual relationship between the Nobel Prize winner Lagerlöf and her unknown Finland-Swedish colleague Wacklin. A kind of symbolic sisterhood, a baton exchange, is at stake here, a phenomenon not unknown to the tradition of women's writing. My point is to show that an excellent literary achievement such as *Gösta Berling's Saga* could be influenced by a text whose characteristics are those of a cross-over genre, a mixture of witness literature and mentality history indicative of an historical epoch when being 'Swedish' meant something different from what it does today.

Illus. 1. Sara Elisabeth Wacklin, 1790–1846. Oil painting by Johan Erik Lindh.

Sara Wacklin's *Hundrade minnen från Österbotten* ('One Hundred Memories from Österbotten') provides a glimpse into the last days of the era when Finland constituted the eastern part of Sweden. Lasting for six centuries, this epoch came to an end in 1809 when the Finnish War concluded with Sweden's defeat by Russia. Wacklin's narrative connects the living and the dead, the Finns, the Finland-Swedes, and the Swedes, thus creating a dynamic, multi-voiced plot that Lagerlöf later transforms into mythical—and feminist—explosives. Wacklin herself was 18 years old when the last Swedish unit retreated in 1808 from the town of Oulu, and the soldiers of the Savolax Infantry Regiment walked almost barefoot through the snow and mud, their uniforms reduced to shreds. In a kind of eyewitness report, she describes this in the present tense, preventing or avoiding the past tense of history writing.

Inspired by Wacklin, Lagerlöf, I would argue, aimed in *Gösta Ber-*

ling's Saga to achieve what the poet Esaias Tegnér (1782–1846) had in mind for his poem 'Svea' (1812), namely an attempt, in literary form, to 'regain Finland within the borders of Sweden'.[2] This, as I shall show, is what Lagerlöf in her way does in *Gösta Berling's Saga*, with intertextual and compositional 'loans' from Wacklin.

Who was Sara Wacklin? Born in poor circumstances in 1790 in Oulu in central Finland, she fought her way up to become a teacher and founded no fewer than three girls' schools. Late in life, after having been ostracised for wanting to open a shelter for battered women in Helsinki, she moved to Stockholm, wrote her 'One Hundred Memories from Österbotten' (1844–6), initially serialised in the leading newspaper *Aftonbladet,* and subsequently published as a book in two parts in 1844 and 1846, the latter being the year of her death. Among the subscribers were leading Finland-Swedish authors such as Johan Ludvig Runeberg, Zacharias Topelius, and Frans Michael Franzén, as well as the Swedish novelist Fredrika Bremer.

Wacklin's book is a hybrid between mentality history, witness literature, and historical narrative: five hundred pages detailing actual events and human behaviour at different levels of society, structured by the kind of gender-sharpened perspective of the unmarried woman familiar from women novelists such as Jane Austen and Selma Lagerlöf. I had scarcely opened 'One Hundred Memories from Österbotten' and read the introductory accounts of the town and the landscape, the 'virgin' forest, the people, and the turbulent river with its treacherous ice, when I had an intense sense of déjà vu. This increased when, in Chapter Eight, the blond cleric Karl Saxa, equipped with a bright mind and a gentle character, ascends the pulpit. At the sight of the church filled to capacity, he is overcome by emotion. The scene is reminiscent of the opening scene in *Gösta Berling's Saga*, Lagerlöf's first novel.

'One Hundred Memories from Österbotten' represents a type of narrative that only rarely attracts the interest of literary scholars—and then perhaps merely as an historical curiosity. Nevertheless, such books, written across the genres and including a diversity of perspectives and *faits divers,* can of course inspire canonical literature. The reader definitely prefers Gösta Berling to Karl Saxa, but without Wacklin's cleric (who goes mad and is discharged from his post), Lagerlöf's defrocked priest might not have existed, and neither perhaps would the twelve cavaliers. Wacklin's Karl Saxa is also surrounded by twelve drinking companions: Keckman, Niska, Wackliner, Antell, Öberg, Juliner, Melliner and

Colliner, Nylander, Poviander, Ulbrandt, and 'the philosopher' Kant. Worth noting is also a tale of a romantic abduction accompanied by the howling of predatory wolves, just as in *Gösta Berling's Saga*.

Wacklin's narrative, like Lagerlöf's, includes a touch of longing, a desire for glorious times past, but also an ironic glance at the phenomenon when 'the battlefield of honour' in war included the ball where women and men could meet. Sara Wacklin names the captains Gegersköld, Taube, Stjernschants, Aminoff, and other Swedish officers, 'distinguished by their dancing at balls as well as by their courage on the battlefield'.[3] In *Gösta Berling's Saga*, set in a Värmland of the 1820s, some of the scruffy cavaliers are depicted, with a subtle irony resembling Wacklin's, as Sweden's last war heroes. As young officers, they could easily be imagined as having attracted the beauties of Österbotten at the ball in 1808. With regard to the post-Gustavians who inhabit the cavaliers' wing at Ekeby, the mansion in Lagerlöf's novel, I want to highlight Colonel Beerencreutz, Major Anders Fuchs, the drummer Klein-Ruster, the warrior and adventurer Cousin Kristofer, and Sergeant Örneclou. The womaniser Örneclou with his Gustavian scarf, his wig, and his maquillage, is on a par with Wacklin's vain Lieutenant E., who pays visits made up like a Gustavian officer, and who sleeps in a chair so as not to ruin his powdered *toupet*.

If my hypothesis is right, how could Selma Lagerlöf, who began her studies at the Women Teachers' College of Higher Education in Stockholm in 1882, have read a work by a teacher from Österbotten who had died 36 years before? Wacklin had been at the peak of her (brief) fame in 1844, 14 years before Selma Lagerlöf was born. The answer is that in those days, there were strong strands of feminine subcultural knowledge. And the Women Teachers' College was not just any institution. In the spirit of Fredrika Bremer, the staff worked hard to raise the status of young women, whose destiny without education and training Selma Lagerlöf was to describe so vividly in her eulogy to 'Miss Fredrika', where the plight of single women is outlined in the following terms:

> Sisters, sisters! We were the loneliest on earth, the most slighted at feasts, the never appreciated home servants. There was mockery and lovelessness around us. Our way through life was heavy, and our name was Ridicule.[4]

Miss Bremer inspired both Miss Lagerlöf and Miss Wacklin. Wacklin wrote in 1844 to her compatriot Bremer (born in Turku), that she had recognised herself in the lonely female figures in Bremer's novels.[5] In other words, Wacklin was an excellent representative of the educational feminism that was still an ideal when the young Selma Lagerlöf attended the Women Teachers' College in Stockholm in the 1880s. Most probably, the great Finland-Swedish pioneer of education for girls and star pedagogue (at her own expense, she even studied for a year in Paris) was still idealised by anyone with an interest in education for girls. Moreover, a new edition of 'One Hundred Memories from Österbotten' appeared in Sweden in 1887.

My hypothesis is that Selma Lagerlöf read Sara Wacklin. The fact that she was a far from canonical author, not even a novelist, but a 'storyteller', made the tactical Lagerlöf 'forget' or 'oversee' her as a forerunner. Publicly Lagerlöf claimed that Johan Ludvig Runeberg's 'good-natured warriors' and Carl Michael Bellman's 'carefree drunkards'[6] had inspired her to transplant the scruffy heroes of the male canon (from Runeberg's Finland and Bellman's Stockholm respectively) to the soil of Vämland.

But if this was so, Selma Lagerlöf, with no more than a collection of retired soldiers, drunkards, and unworldly geniuses, would not have got much further than the second chapter of *Gösta Berling's Saga*. The compositional principle was still missing, and this, too, she found in the narrative of Wacklin. Only then was she able to throw away her drafts in epic verse and begin to write more elaborate chapters consisting of self-contained stories. Only then did she realise that the ball, so central to Wacklin's narrative, could serve as a topos and symbolic place for a parable about gender relations, the heterosexual plot of (complex) infatuation that powers the narrative of *Gösta Berling's Saga*. Only then could she make the novel come alive, complete with its touch of nostalgia for a heroic, old 'Swedishness'.

And it was not *any ball* that Lagerlöf could read about in 'One Hundred Memories': it was 'the last Swedish ball',[7] the regulator of what Wacklin calls the 'war theatre' in 1808–1809.[8] At this last front section of Sweden's period as a great power, the young couples danced 'with eyes brimming with tears': 'It was the end of joy, everyone thought: you know what you have, but not what you will get'.[9] Reluctantly, the Swedish officers left 'their beauties to their impending fate':[10] the barbaric Russians. Sobbing, the 'disconsolate graces' took an oath never to take a dance step again.[11] As Wacklin dryly comments, this 'never' lasted no longer than six weeks. On 30 November 1808, the elegant officers led by General Kamenski make their first appearance: 'among formidable cannon and frightful soldiers ... [were] some handsome Russian officers, who could surely dance'.[12] Furthermore, some of them spoke Swedish and Finnish, which promised civilised behaviour.

Swedish stock falls visibly when the Russians make a brilliant offensive—speaking not only in terms of war, but of gender. Shaking with fear and without male protection, the town's young ladies are forced to attend their ball. However, in no time their mood changes and they dance all evening with the brave and polite Russian enemy. In other words, the negotiation between female and Swedish surrender on the one hand, and male and Russian dominance on the other, is carried out in the ballroom. My hypothesis is that it was precisely Wacklin's combination of war and gender, the symbolically charged topos of the ball with its special lustre, that attracted Lagerlöf. Seen in this light, it is no coincidence that the opening sentence of her prize-winning début in the women's journal *Idun* in 1891, was 'It was Christmas, and there was to be a ball at Borg' (Lagerlöf 2009, 50).[13]

Thus, Lagerlöf started out with a narrative about a ball with a subsequent abduction, stopped by wolves 'howling with hunger and blood-thirst' (Lagerlöf 2009, 59);[14] this later became Chapter Four in the novel *Gösta Berling's Saga*. Sara Wacklin has the same topic, as mentioned above. In Lagerlöf, this particular ball marks the true beginning of the novel. Here, Gösta Berling meets the first woman with whom he falls in love, Anna Stjärnhök. And he refrains heroically from her, possibly because Wacklin had so vividly described the consequences of such an abduction (the seducer's death in prison, leaving his wife and children destitute). A short chapter, in which the gout-ridden Sergeant Örneclou dreams of his successes at balls in his youth (perhaps in the Finnish War), is followed by the brilliant chapter 'The Ball at Ekeby', opening with the nostalgic words: 'Oh, women of bygone ages!' (Lagerlöf 2009, 66).[15] At this particular ball, Gösta Berling falls in love with the intelligent Marianne Sinclaire. Last but not least, if Lagerlöf's Chapter Ten in Part I were to be renamed 'The Last Ball in Värmland', the change would highlight the internal canon at work. Here Lagerlöf settles the score with Wacklin as a forerunner by using the topos of the ball for a more far-reaching transformation than that of the Russians replacing the Swedes in Finland: the cavalier of cavaliers, Gösta Berling, becomes a New Man. This process begins when his third beloved, the young countess Elisabeth Dohna, refuses to dance with him.

With this, we have come to the differences between Sara Wacklin and Selma Lagerlöf. The former is a teller of factual events, the latter a novelist. The bright-eyed irony that saw through the hedonistic graces from Oulu does not haunt the belles of the ball in Värmland. Lagerlöf saves her ridicule for male chauvinism and the homo-sociality of her cavaliers. She was part of the emancipated generation that had learned from the Modern Breakthrough with its conflict between Strindberg's misogyny on the one hand and the feminist struggle on the other. Belonging to an earlier generation, Wacklin could not permit herself to be as frank as Lagerlöf. When ruthlessly documenting male egotism, including reports of assaults on women and abuse of them, she followed up with conventional phrases about the virtue of female forgiveness. To a reader of today it is evident that Wacklin uses melodramatic strategies to disguise a female opinion on male misogyny that could not be stated explicitly.

Written at a time when feminism was becoming more prominent, *Gösta Berling's Saga* embraces the ethos of the women's novel, a genre which takes the young, passionate heroine seriously while treating the man of her heart as a charming but necessary reform project. Maria Karlsson has shown that Lagerlöf's use of melodramatic elements is related to her highlighting of gender relations (2002, 212). I would go as far as saying that the affects evoking melodrama in *Gösta Berling's Saga* amount to Lagerlöf's tool for convincing her readers of the fairness of the new and equal ideal of love that is launched in the novel, after the reform project directed towards Gösta Berling has succeeded. It goes like this: when the beloved Elisabeth, who used to love to dance with Gösta Berling, turns him down, he at first responds with a ritual male punishment—an abduction. As a consequence, Elisabeth is degraded to an ordinary maid and an unwed mother. The lovers later unite, not in a waltz, but in a conversation on equal terms. Full of self-pity, Gösta claims that he is bound for life by his code of honour as a cavalier. 'We cavaliers are no free men. … Woe to us all, if one of us fails!' (Lagerlöf 2009, 379).[16] Elisabeth says sadly:

'how well I recognize this! Heroic gestures, heroic ostentation! Always ready to stick your hands in the fire, Gösta, always ready to throw yourself away! How great such things once seemed to me! How I now prize calm and self-control! (Lagerlöf 2009, 379).[17]

Put another way, Elisabeth Dohna, having become a New Woman, effectively punctuates the male heroic rhetoric of yesterday. And Gösta listens. He understands. He changes. The 'poet' Gösta Berling becomes a responsible New Man who dismisses the notion of honour in order to share the prosaic everyday life with his beloved. The symbolic location of this union of a woman and a man on equal terms is a cottage, not a ballroom.

Thus, figuratively speaking, Wacklin's Finland-Swedish nostalgic heritage of 1808 leads to the Swedish reality of 1891. This was the era of the New Woman, and Lagerlöf creates a reformed New Man who distances himself from the warrior's honour, from male chumminess, and from the pranks of the cavaliers. However, in Wacklin, too, the status of real hero is reserved for men who have a heart for women. When the young sergeant of the Wasa Batallion (he was Wacklin's own brother) starves himself to death in the camp at Soivola in 1808 so as to be able to send money to his ailing mother and sister, Wacklin writes that his corpse was worthy of being buried together with those of the Finnish heroes who had fallen for their Fatherland, thereby recasting the patriotic project (Wacklin 1974, 134). And there is more of this in 'One Hundred Memories'. To both Wacklin and Lagerlöf, 'Swedishness' is defined in terms of collective memory. In Lagerlöf's *Mårbacka* (1922) we find traces of the mourning of the national trauma of losing Finland in tales such as 'The Militia Men', 'The Orchestra', and 'The Old Soldier' that come close to the composition principle of Wacklin.[18] But that is another story.

As I have shown in this essay, the historicity of *Gösta Berling's Saga* can be related to the tradition from Esaias Tegnér, who in his poem 'Svea' from 1812 transposed the Swedish war defeat to the level of aesthethics. *Gösta Berling's Saga* is one of only a handful of responses in Swedish literature to Tegnér's call. Lagerlöf's achievement, as I have tried to demonstrate, was dependent on some assistance from Sara Wacklin, whose province of Österbotten lies like a long-vanished continent under Selma Lagerlöf's fictional Värmland.

Notes

1 'von der inneren Kanonbildung der Literatur selbst, wie sie von der äusseren Kanonpflege durch Literaturtheorie, Literaturpädagogik und ähnliches zu unterscheiden ist.' Unless otherwise indicated, translations into English are my own.

2 'inom Sverges gräns eröfra Finland åter' (Tegnér 1919, 77).

3 'lika utmärkta för sin dans på baler som för sin tapperhet på stridsfältet' (Wacklin 1974, 141).

4 'Systrar, systrar! Vi voro de ensamma på Jorden. De tillbakasatta på gästabuden, de tacklöst tjänande i hemmen. Det var hån och kärlekslöshet omkring oss. Vår vandring var tung, och vårt namn blef åtlöjets' (Lagerlöf 1894a, 163).

5 'I den ensamme i Mams. B. Skrifter igenkände jag så ofta mig sjelf' (5 Nov. 1844, in Wacklin 1919, 41).

6 'Runebergs godmodiga krigsbussar och Bellmans sorglösa dryckesbröder' (Lagerlöf 1902, 143–44).

7 'Den sista svenska balen' ('Andra delen. 6.', in Wacklin 1974, 137).

8 'krigsteatern' ('Andra delen. 1. Besöket på sjukhuset under 1808 års krig', in Wacklin 1974, 125).

9 'Det var slut på glädjen trodde alla: man visste vad man haft, men icke om man hade att vänta någon glädje mer' ('Andra delen. 6. Den sista svenska balen', in Wacklin 1974, 137).

10 'de sköna åt det hotande ödet' (ibid. 137).

11 'tröstlösa damerna' (ibid. 137).

12 'mitt bland de fruktansvärdaste kanoner och rysliga soldater … [fanns] rätt vackra och nätta ryska officerare, vilka säkert voro gentila dansörer' ('Andra delen. 8. Ryska arméns intåg i Uleåborg', in Wacklin 1974, 140).

13 'Jul var det, och bal skulle stånda å Borg' (Lagerlöf 2013, 54).

14 'tjöto af hunger och blodtörst' (Lagerlöf 2013, 64).

15 'O forna tiders kvinnor!' (Lagerlöf 2013, 71).

16 'Vi kavaljerer äro ej frie män … Ve oss alla, om en sviker!' (Lagerlöf 2013, 421).

17 'hvad jag väl känner igen detta! Hjältefasoner, hjältestät! Alltid färdig att sticka händerna i eldbrasan, Gösta, alltid redo att kasta bort dig själf! Hvad sådant en gång synts mig stort! Hvad jag nu prisar lugn och besinning!' (Lagerlöf 2013, 421).

18 'Lantvärnsmännen', 'Orkestern', 'Den gamla soldaten'.

CHAPTER 18

Violence and the uncanny in Selma Lagerlöf's 'Gammal fäbodsägen'

Sofia Wijkmark

Selma Lagerlöf's strange short story 'Gammal fäbodsägen' ('An Old Tale from the Mountains'), published in 1914, depicts an act of violence and its consequences.[1] In what might at first glance seem to be a traditional Swedish folktale, elements of uncanniness create psychological depth. Being a text written on the verge of the First World War, its national and folkloristic character is further deconstructed by its historical resonances as a transnational narrative, a premonition of the horrors to come.

The uncanny, a special variant of horror, can be regarded as a central element in Lagerlöf's *œuvre*. Lagerlöf is probably the most prominent representative of the Gothic boom in Swedish literature at the turn of the twentieth century, but horror stories, or horror components, are also present in her later works.[2] In the last few decades, the uncanny as a concept has moved from psychoanalysis into the fields of, among others, literary theory, film theory, philosophy, sociology, religious studies, and architectural theory. Freud's essay 'The Uncanny' (1919) constitutes the foundation of the theoretical applications of the concept in the various fields; and from being a somewhat peripheral text in his production, it has assumed a central position over time. At the basic level, Freud defines the uncanny as the feeling of horror and insecurity that arises when something familiar suddenly appears foreign and strange. It is also 'that class of the frightening which leads back to what is known of old and long familiar', that is, the return of the repressed, which involves childhood repression as well as the primitive, animistic stage of the cultural evolution (Freud 1995, 220). In Anneleen Masschelein's *The Unconcept: The Freudian Uncanny in Late-Twentieth-Century The-*

ory (2011), a genealogy of the uncanny is presented, and Masschelein points out that the meaning of the concept has extended far beyond Freud's definition. This is apparent in the first monograph on the subject, Nicholas Royle's *The Uncanny* (2003), strongly influenced by deconstruction. Royle also links the uncanny to Russian formalism and its 'notion of defamiliarization, or "making strange" (*ostranenie*)', and argues that this literary effect means that literature per se has an innate quality of the uncanny (2003, 4).

Alone in a mountain hut, the protagonist of 'An Old Tale from the Mountains', the herdswoman Ragnhild, is accosted by a robber who threatens her with a knife. She wards off the attack by throwing boiling whey into the man's face, locking him inside the hut, and escaping. But she has the presence of mind to return to gather the cows. As a reward for her resolute actions, she is united in marriage with the son of the owner of the farm and the hut. On returning to the hut the next spring, the couple find the dead robber inside. Ragnhild flees into the woods and is later found to have become insane. In the analysis that follows, I will use the uncanny as a key to understanding the narrative and its effects.

The short summary of the tale above illustrates the very foundation of the concept of the uncanny: how the familiar becomes foreign and frightening. Royle describes this as 'a sense of homeliness uprooted, the revelation of something unhomely at the hearth and home' (2003, 1). The hut in the woods is the substitute of the safe home, but the event that takes place in it transforms the homely and safe into its opposite (*heimlich* becomes *unheimlich*, see Freud 1995, 226), and this is manifested at the end of the story in the form of a decomposed body and madness. However, as we shall see, additional forms of the uncanny are manifested in 'An Old Tale from the Mountains'. Following in Freud's footsteps, Andrew Bennet and Nicholas Royle have listed the following motifs as the most important: strange forms of repetition such as déjà vu and the idea of the double, 'Odd coincidences and, more generally, the sense that things are *fated* to happen', animism, anthropomorphism, automatism represented by, for example, mechanical behaviour such as sleepwalking, epileptic seizures, trance and madness, 'uncertainty about sexual identity—about whether a person is male or female', fear of being buried alive, silence, telepathy; and, last but not least, 'Death. In particular, death as something at once familiar … and absolutely unfamiliar, unthinkable, unimaginable' (Bennet & Royle 2004, 34–5, original emphasis).[3]

The primary aspects of the uncanny are insecurity and ambiguity, and 'An Old Tale from the Mountains' is permeated by the insecurity generated by its balancing on the border of the fantastic. Repeatedly, the text alludes to the strange and the supernatural—a speaking pot, trolls, omens, and telepathy—while retaining the possibility of rational explanations. Freud emphasises insecurity related to the supernatural as an example of the uncanny, and this notion has been adopted by theorists of the fantastic, notably Tzvetan Todorov. In his book *The Fantastic: A Structural Approach to a Literary Genre*, he defines the uncanny as a genre bordering on the fantastic, or as the supernatural explained: 'In works that belong to this genre, events are related which may be readily accounted for by the laws of reason, but which are, in one way or another, incredible, extraordinary, shocking, singular, disturbing or unexpected' (1975, 46). For Freud, this aspect of the uncanny illustrates the fact that the concept involves something that appears to affirm old, discarded, primitive conceptions: 'Nowadays we no longer believe in them, we have surmounted these modes of thought; but we do not feel quite sure of our new beliefs, and the old ones still exist within us ready to seize upon any confirmation' (1995, 247).

As the title signals, Lagerlöf's narrative starts in the style of the tale or fairytale, but soon the traditional genre is infiltrated by psychological realism because the fairytale elements—the speaking pot and the trolls—are only represented as figments of the central character's imagination. We first meet Ragnhild, the herdswoman, when she is making cheese in the hut. It is autumn, and normally she would have returned to the village in the valley by that time, but she is having to wait for a cow to start calving. In her 'deep solitude' she regards the boiling pot of whey as 'company'.[4] Soon, however, she thinks that the seething pot is beginning to sound differently, moaning as if warning of imminent danger. But Ragnhild seems to take the warning lightly as she begins to laugh and banter with the pot. She associates the moaning with Sigrid, the old mistress at the manor farm, who liked to warn of the perils of the forests and in particular to tell stories about the man-eating trolls. Like Ragnhild, Sigrid used to work in the hut at the summer pasture in her youth, and on one occasion she heard the trolls calling to each other in the forest. To Ragnhild, this story is now being repeated in the murmuring of the pot.

This scene opens with phrases indicating a subjective perspective on events: Ragnhild 'thought' that she heard a moaning sound; and 'It still sounded as if [the pot] was having a bad time'.[5] When Ragnhild imagines that she is hearing her mistress, free indirect discourse is used, and the internal focalisation is evidently hers:

> Really, it was the voice of the old mistress, who wanted to instil in her how dangerous were the trolls in this forest. For she, the old mistress, had once in her youth stayed behind at the mountain pasture when the others had left to wait for a cow, just as she was doing now.[6]

Since Ragnhild's experience of the supernatural can be construed as the product of her imagination, there is a possibility that Sigrid's experience can be interpreted in the same way. Both cases involve strange sounds that need to be decoded:

> one evening when she had been out to milk the cows, she had heard a roaring from a mountain to the north of the grazing ground. It was repeated again, and again, and eventually she had understood … that it was the troll on the Norrfjället, who was asking another troll, living in an ant hill, when they were going to move into one of the huts.[7]

Sigrid has found it difficult to understand troll speech. They 'have such raucous voices, so it's hard to catch the words among all the other noises',[8] and she has had to listen to the strange sounds being repeated many times to make out that the trolls have been planning to eat her. Ragnhild's associations with Sigrid's story about the trolls seem logical. In both cases, the women have remained on their own in the mountain forest well into autumn, at a time when the hut would normally be vacated. Back at the farm, Ragnhild had always found it difficult to suppress her laughter when Sigrid was talking about the trolls, but now, alone, she shivers at the thought of what her mistress has claimed to have experienced: 'Like many others, the lass had heard that the trolls were in the habit of moving into the huts as soon as the people had moved out in the autumn'.[9]

As is often the case in Lagerlöf's works, fantasy and fairytale, reality and realism, are at odds in 'An Old Tale from the Mountains'. The speaking pot and its evocation of the account of the roaring trolls can be understood as products of Ragnhild's imagination thanks to the narrative strategies used. But even if the fairytale elements are given a logical explanation, it seems a strange coincidence that Ragnhild, shortly after thinking that she has heard the pot warning her of danger, is surprised by the robber. The uncanny in this scene lies primarily in her premonition of the event, but the effect is reinforced by the allusions to inanimate objects coming to life. One of the principal examples of phenomena capable of evoking a sense of the uncanny is represented by 'doubts whether an apparently animate being is really alive; or conversely, whether a lifeless object might not in fact be animate', if we are to believe Freud as well as his predecessor Ernst Jentsch (Jentsch quoted in Freud 1995, 226).

'An Old Tale from the Mountains' is divided into two parts. The first part depicts the incident in the hut, Ragnild's confrontation with the robber, and, once she has gathered the cows, her return to the farm to tell her story. We understand from the reactions of the people at the farm that Ragnhild will be rewarded for her courage and resolve and achieve her dream—to marry the farmer's son. At the opening of the second part, it is spring and Ragnhild and her husband Egil are on their way to the hut. 'She was now no longer a herdswoman but a well-to-do farmer's wife',[10] yet she has insisted on working at the hut although there is no need for her to do so. The second part presents the conversation taking place between the couple on their way through the forest. Psychological realism predominates, while there is a growing sense of impending disaster.

The conversation soon reveals that Egil does not approve of Ragnhild's plan to stay in the hut over the summer, but she laughingly dismisses his objections:

> I can assure you it's necessary for me to tend to the summer grazing this very year. The herdswomen would only think of the robbers and I hardly think that they'd have gone to the forest if I hadn't gone to stay in the hut myself.[11]

She also speaks of her wish to meet the robber to thank him for making her happiness. But Egil has misgivings and calls attention to the risk of revenge. Confidently Ragnhild again dismisses his concerns: 'Don't you worry ... you know that fortune is with me'.[12] The husband is not to be swayed, however, and warns against trusting fortune blindly: 'it is like the meat I put out as wolf bait to make them come close enough for me to shoot them'.[13] The truth behind Ragnhild's carefree façade is then revealed. The whole winter the robber has haunted her dreams, on one occasion transformed into the strange creature of a dog with the face of a man, and on another even making her walk in her sleep:

> He sometimes came in my dream and put the knife to my throat, ordering me to give him food. One night I dreamt that a dog was barking outside our door. I opened it, but then the dog had got at the man's face, and I hurriedly closed the door to shut him out. He wailed so horribly with hunger that the sound was still in my ears when I woke up. ... One day I walked as if in my sleep, unawares. Without anyone noticing I put some food in a knapsack and went into the forest. It was not until I reached the slope above the farm that I woke up.[14]

The narrative pace is intensified from this point on. On hearing her story, her husband makes the party hurry towards the hut, where his wife's nightmares turn into reality. Inside the hut, there is a rotting body: blinded by the hot whey, the robber has been unable to find his way out and has starved to death.

Here the effect of the uncanny reaches its climax. Ragnhild's dreams turn into omens, or strange messages from the hungry man, and the hypnotic somnambulist state afflicting Ragnhild seems caused by telepathic contact. In view of this, it also seems reasonable to interpret Ragnhild's experience of the speaking pot as an omen. The narrative, however, resists the supernatural. The series of events is certainly strange, but they still lend themselves to natural explanations. Ragnhild has been aware of the risk of being attacked while staying alone in the hut, her awareness taking the form of hallucinatory phenomena of fear repressed. There are also indications in the text that the circumstances leading to the robber's death have been clear to Ragnhild. For instance, she realises that he is severely injured and will be unable to get out of the locked hut on his own. We have been told how she saw him fumbling blindly and heard him screaming from the pain caused by the boiling whey in his eyes. She saw his gang of robbers flee into the forest, terrified by his screams, and although she suspected that they would not return for him, she persuaded herself that they would do so. They seemed to think, she thought at the time, that there must have been 'a dangerous enemy' in the hut,[15] thus indicating her awareness of having caused his death. But she has repressed this, and it returns in nightmarish visions and psychological phenomena. Read in this way, the narrative clearly suggests that her madness, with which the story concludes, has been present from the start. Hallucinations and changing states of consciousness are, after all, signs of psychosis.

Yet another strange coincidence foreshadows the discovery of the dead robber. When the party approaches the hut, the cows start behaving oddly. They act as if mad, butting one another, 'not playfully, but in a wild rage, as if wanting to kill one another. They were attacking each other in a great hurly-burly, fighting and knocking each other down in total madness'.[16] With great difficulty, the herd is moved on, and as soon as the cows have left the hut's yard, they become completely calm and behave as if nothing had happened. The incident seems extraordinary and suggests that the place may be haunted. But a herd of cows fighting, on the other hand, does not necessarily indicate the presence of something supernatural.

Ragnhild persists in her denial for as long as possible. When her husband turns on his heels in the doorway and returns to her, his face ashen, she sits down as if all strength has drained from her, saying: 'Pray tell me, Egil, what is that stench I smell up here? ... This is not how the forest smells? ... Why is there such a long row of ravens on the roof, Egil?'[17] When Egil tells her the truth, she rushes to the door and looks inside. Her reaction is strange but the reader has a feeling of déjà vu: 'Soon after her loud and shrill laughter could be heard. She came out into the yard roaring with laughter, her arms held high. "Have you seen happiness as great as this?" she cried.'[18] Ragnhild's laughter appears in crucial scenes in the text as a sign of her inability to listen to her inner self or to the warnings received. The repetition of similarities is an aspect of the uncanny that Freud links to the small child and to the compulsion for neurotic repetition (Freud 1995, 238). In 'An Old Tale from the Mountains' this phenomenon is also present in the similarities between the events experienced by Ragnhild and Sigrid while alone in the forest, and in the repetitions of events that can be construed as foreshadowing the impending disaster. But as Royle has pointed out, there is also an element of humour in the uncanny: 'the uncanny is never far from something comic: humor, irony and laughter all have a genuinely "funny" role in thinking on this topic' (Royle 2003, 2). 'An Old Tale from the Mountains' is, in fact, also a narrative with elements of irony and humour. Indeed, in the first part, the reader can easily join in Ragnhild's laughter, an effect that intensifies the ironic and uncanny impact of her mad laughter at the end.

We have seen how Lagerlöf in 'An Old Tale from the Mountains' mixes legend and psychological realism, traditional folklore on the one hand and modern realistic prose on the other, thus facing the reader with a sense of insecurity. The mixing of genres can be placed in the context of the shift taking place in fantastic literature in the nineteenth century, described by Rosemary Jackson as 'the juncture when readings of otherness as supernatural ... were being slowly replaced and disturbed by readings of otherness as natural and subjectively generated' (2003, 62). The traditional fairytale elements can be explained in rational terms and the reader is confronted with psychological phenomena, yet these seem to confirm the same primitive conceptual world that gave rise to trolls and animism. Back to square one?

In *The Female Thermometer: Eighteenth-Century Culture and the Invention of the Uncanny* (1995), Terry Castle has explained how the uncanny emerged during the period of the Enlightenment. When ghosts and other supernatural phenomena were gradually perceived as hallucinations, the psyche was transformed into an uncanny sphere and thinking into a process that could project ghosts, developments that rendered ourselves and our reality strange and unfamiliar. In 'An Old Tale from the Mountains' the supernatural is produced by one of the characters, a projection of her subconscious fear on to the environment. The central message communicated in the text, and also generating the most uncanny insight, is the fact that the trolls have been replaced by something far more dangerous, namely mankind. This brings the issue of violence to the fore, while also reminding us of the violent opening of Lagerlöf's short story and the questions of its function and meaning.

If we are to understand the representation of violence and the power structures linked to it in 'An Old Tale from the Mountains', we cannot ignore the issue of gender. There is no doubt that the violence with which Ragnhild is being threatened is rape. This is clear from the symbolism of the events and from the robber's attributes, a spear and knives: 'all of a sudden, he stretched out a big, ugly, hairy hand, gripping firmly the shaft of a long knife. "Have you seen a sharper knife?" he asked with the kind of facetiousness that a cat would show to a mouse he knows is at his mercy.'[19] This is a symbolic echo of the speech by the man-eating trolls about the young Sigrid as a piece of meat which, in the text, precedes the events in the hut: 'Scratch'er with claws, Fry'er on the fire! Seventeen-year-old maiden, healthy and plump, Tasting better than year-old goat'.[20]

Ragnhild's fear of the robber turns to fury when he points his knife at her, and she counters his *verbal* threat of violence with an *act* of violence:

> 'Have you felt hotter whey?' she cried back and threw a whole scoop of boiling liquid into the robber's face. Knife and spear fell from his hands and he stumbled backwards until he reached the wall. There he remained standing, the backs of his hands pressed against his eyes, uttering desperate screams. The lass quickly picked up the knife and tucked it inside the waistband of her skirt.[21]

Violence is linked to power. Here this is symbolised by the knife, which Ragnhild takes from the robber when she has dethroned him from his position in a symbolic act of Freudian castration. The acts of actual violence in this short story are performed by Ragnhild, who thus also assumes the position of power. As a result, she moves up socially and achieves long-term power. Ragnhild is a character who transcends social norms and rules, both as a woman and as a servant.

Lagerlöf deals with violence in many of her texts. Violence, Nils Afzelius has argued, is a characteristic feature of her works, an ethical imperative saying: '*violence destroys the perpetrator of violence, mercy helps the helper*' (Afzelius 1961, 54, original emphasis).[22] The novellas *Herr Arnes penningar* (1903, *Lord Arne's Silver*) and *Körkarlen* (1912, *The Phantom Carriage*), the novel *Bannlyst* (1918, *The Outcast*) and short stories such as 'De fågelfrie' (1892, 'The Outlaws'), 'Riddardottern och hafsmannen' (1892, 'The Knight's Daughter and the Man of the Sea'), 'Tale Thott' (1895) and 'Frid på jorden' (1917, 'Peace on Earth') are examples of narratives involving acts of violence or portrayals of violent characters. The violence actually exercised in 'An Old Tale from the Mountains' is in fact comparatively mild. However, several critics, including Afzelius, have singled out this short story as especially unpleasant and disturbing (Afzelius 1961, 60). Ulla-Britta Lagerroth has studied Lagerlöf's works during the First World War, and in her doctoral dissertation pinpointed some distinctive characteristics of her writing belonging to this period: 'the colours were more uniformly dark, the narrative voices more consistently dissonant, the "abominable" more abruptly foregrounded' (1963, 26).[23] Lagerroth has referred to 'An Old Tale from the Mountains' as an example of these dark features.

GAMMAL FÄBODSÄGEN
BERÄTTAD AF SELMA LAGERLÖF

et var en valljänta, som stod i en fäbod och höll på att göra ost. Hon hade båda händerna nere i ostkaret och klämde till, allt hvad hon förmådde, för att få vasslan ur osten.

Bredvid henne på spisen stod en stor gryta, som var full af vassla. Den puttrade och porlade, och flickan tyckte, att den var som ett sällskap i den djupa ensamheten. Vallpojken var borta i skogen med korna, och jäntan, som hon hade haft till hjälp i fäboden under sommaren, hade för ett par dar sen dragit hem med en del af böskapen. Med rätta skulle hon ha varit nerflyttad till bygden, hon också. Hösten var redan kommen, och alla andra fäbodar voro utrymda, men så hade hon blifvit tvungen att stanna kvar i skogen, därför att den bästa kon hade fördröjt sig med kalfningen.

Medan hon stod och lyssnade på grytan, tyckte hon, att den helt plötsligt bytte om ton. Från att ha porlat vänligt och lugnt lät den orolig och klagande. Det var alldeles som om den skulle vara missnöjd med något.

»Hvad är det åt dig?» sade hon, som stod och klämde på osten. »Står du inte stadigt på dina ben, eller har du inte nog bränsle under dig?»

1. *Svenska Turistföreningens Årsskrift. 1914.*

Illus. 1. Illustrated first page in *Svenska Turistförenings-ens årsskrift* ('The Yearbook of the Swedish Tourist Association'), 1914, where Lagerlöf's short story was first published. Vignette by Arthur Sjögren.

Vivi Edström has indeed singled out this text as 'one of Lagerlöf's most alarming stories' (2002, 450).[24]

On a general level, the short story's theme of violence and the atmosphere of imminent disaster can be seen as expressions of pre-war anxiety. In its historical context, the short story emerges as a version of the premonitions iterated in it: the moaning of the pot, the warning of the trolls, the robber haunting the herdswoman's dreams; all of which contribute to the uncanny effect. 'An Old Tale from the Mountains' was written at the end of 1913 and was published in *Svenska turistföreningens årsskrift* ('The Yearbook of the Swedish Tourist Association') in

1914.[25] In the following year, it was included, slightly revised, in the first volume of Lagerlöf's anthology *Troll och människor* ('Trolls and Humans'). The first published version was introduced by a vignette by Arthur Sjögren, showing a hut in a mountain pasture with three ravens hovering overhead, the image framed by stylised pine cones and ravens. The illustration has strong symbolic implications and reinforces the impression of impending doom. The ravens are particularly prominent and, as Erik Erlandson-Hammargren has pointed out, ravens are 'often associated with wisdom, a secret message, or omens of disaster' (Erlandson-Hammargren 2006, 353).[26]

As the narrative of 'An Old Tale from the Mountains' makes clear, human beings pose greater danger to themselves than do the mythological creatures of the forest. The robber is more dangerous than any other being Ragnhild might have encountered: 'This was quite different from that troll Trillibacken that had wanted to eat the mistress'.[27] The short story also highlights meaningless violence and suffering, and blind evil afflicting victim and perpetrator alike. No one can question the right to self-defence that the resourceful female protagonist exercises in this story. So why is she doomed? Ulla-Britta Lagerroth has argued that the key to 'An Old Tale from the Mountains' is the fact that Ragnhild 'has been gripped by *hubris* and become overly confident in her fortune' (1963, 432).[28] Lagerroth has also modified Afzelius' claim that this short story is a representative example of the saying that violence invariably destroys the perpetrator. Ragnhild has the right to defend herself as she has done, according to Lagerroth. It is because she ignores the voice of her conscience, thereby killing the robber, that she has to be punished. Lagerlöf never equates the right to self-defence with the right to kill (Lagerroth 1963, 432).

The discussion above has illustrated how Lagerlöf in 'An Old Tale from the Mountains' masters the depiction of the uncanny in its various forms, using advanced narrative strategies to create the uncertainty necessary for this specific kind of horror to erupt from the text. It has also made clear that the ethical dilemma, activated by the discourse of violence, is not easily resolved. At the end, the perpetrator has also become a victim.

Notes

1 All translations from the Swedish are mine. 'An Old Tale from the Mountains' has not received much critical attention (which is generally true of all Lagerlöf's short stories). Erik Erlandson-Hammargren has contributed the most detailed discussion to date, offering an analysis of this short story as the depiction of 'a conflict between Paradise/civilisation and wilderness/Nature' ('en konflikt mellan paradiset/civilisationen och vildmarken/naturen') (2006, 354); see also Wijkmark (2009, 222–3) for a brief discussion of this short story and its depiction of random evil and cruelty in relation to Lagerlöf's 'Frid på jorden' (1917, 'Peace on Earth').

2 For the Gothic and the uncanny in Selma Lagerlöf's pre-war output, see Wijkmark 2009. I define the Gothic as a genre, dealing with the experience of reality expressed by the concept of the uncanny.

3 Freud mentions the same motifs, broadly speaking, in his essay, but he picks out the double as the most illustrative representation of the uncanny.

4 'djupa ensamhet', 'sällskap' (Lagerlöf 1914a, 1).

5 'tyckte', 'Alltjämt lät det som om [grytan] hade det svårt' (Lagerlöf 1914a, 1, 2).

6 'Det var sannerligen gammalmoras egen röst, som ville inpränta hos henne hur farliga troll det fanns i den här skogen. För hon, gammalmora, hade en gång i ungdomen stannat kvar efter de andra på fäbodvallen för att vänta på en ko, alldeles som hon själv nu' (Lagerlöf 1914a, 3).

7 'en aftonstund, då hon hade varit ute för att mjölka, hade hon hört ett rytande från ett berg, som låg ett stycke i norr om betesmarken. Det kom tillbaka gång på gång, och till sist hade hon uppfattat ... att det var trollet i Norrfjället, som frågade ett annat troll, som bodde i en myrstack, när det skulle flytta in i någon av stugorna' (Lagerlöf 1914a, 3).

8 'ha sådana skrofliga röster, så en har svårt att få tag i ordena mellan alla de andra ljudena' (Lagerlöf 1914a, 3).

9 'Jäntan hade ju hört, hon som andra, att trollena brukade passa på och flytta in i fäbodstugorna, så snart som folket hade utrymt dem om hösten' (Lagerlöf 1914a, 3).

10 'Hon var nu ingen valljänta längre utan välbeställd bondhustru' (Lagerlöf 1914a, 9).

11 'Var du viss, att det är rätt nödigt, att jag sköter fäboden just i år. Vallhjonena skulle bara gå och tänka på röfvarna, och jag tror knappast, att vi skulle ha fått dem att följa med till skogen, om jag inte hade åtagit mig själf att stanna där oppe' (Lagerlöf 1914a, 9).

12 'Det ska du inte bry dig om ... Du vet väl, att jag har lyckan med mig' (Lagerlöf 1914a, 10).

13 'den är då ofta bara som ett sådant där köttstycke, som jag lägger ut åt vargarna för att de ska komma mig så nära, att jag kan räcka att skjuta ner dem' (Lagerlöf 1914a, 10).

14 'Han kom ibland i drömmen och satte knifven på strupen på mig samt befallde mig att ge honom mat. En natt drömde jag att det stod en hund och skällde utanför vår dörr. Jag öppnade för den, men då hade hunden med ens fått den där karlens ansikte, och jag fick brått att stänga honom ute. Han tjöt då så hemskt af hunger, att jag hörde ljudet i mina öron, när jag vaknade. ... Det var en dag, då jag gick som i sömn och inte visste till mig. Jag stoppade oförmärkt mat i en ränsel

och hängde den på ryggen och gick till skogs. Först då jag kom i backen ofvanför gården, vaknade jag opp' (Lagerlöf 1914a, 12).

15 'en farlig fiende' (Lagerlöf 1914a, 6).

16 'inte på lek, utan vildt och ilsket, som om de ville döda hvarandra. De foro samman i en enda röra, kämpande mot varandra och knuffade omkull hvarandra i full galenskap' (Lagerlöf 1914a, 13).

17 '"Säg, Egil, hvad är det för en stank, som jag känner här oppe? ... Så brukar det väl aldrig lukta i skogen? ... Hvarför sitter det en sådan lång rad korpar på taket, Egil?"' (Lagerlöf 1914a, 13–14).

18 'Strax efteråt ljöd hennes skratt högt och gällt. Hon kom ut på gården storskrattande, med armarna högt upplyfta. "Har du sett starkare lycka?" skrek hon' (Lagerlöf 1914a, 13).

19 'rätt som det var, så stack han fram en stor, ful hårig hand, som höll hårdt om skaftet på en lång kniv. "Har du sett vassare knif?" frågade han i detsamma med en sådan där skämtsamhet som en katt brukar visa mot en råtta, som han vet, att han har helt i sitt våld' (Lagerlöf 1914a, 5).

20 '"Rif'a med klör'a, Stek'a på glör'a! Sjutton års jänte, frisk å fet, Smaker bättre än fjolårs get"' (Lagerlöf 1914a, 3).

21 '"Har du känt hetare vassla?" ropade hon tillbaka och slängde en hel skopa kokande vätska rätt i ansiktet på skogsströfvarn. Knif och spjut föllo ur händerna på honom, och han raglade baklänges, till dess han fick stöd mot väggen. Där blef han stående med båda handbakarna tryckta mot ögonen och uppgaf vilda tjut. Jäntan tog hastigt opp knifen och stack den innanför kjortellinningen' (Lagerlöf 1914a, 5).

22 'våldet bryter ned våldsverkaren, barmhärtigheten hjälper hjälparen'.

23 'färgerna var mer förtätat mörka, tonfallen mer ihärdigt dissonantiska, det "avskyvärda" mer oförmedlat framlyft'.

24 'en av Lagerlöfs hemskaste historier'.

25 Erlandson-Hammargren (2006) has shown that Lagerlöf corresponded with the editor of Svenska turistföreningen, Ezaline Boheman, about 'An Old Tale from the Mountains', and has dated the writing of the short story to October 1913 (351).

26 'ofta [förknippade] med vishet, hemligt budskap, eller omen om ofärd'.

27 'Detta var annat slag än den där Trillibacken, som hade velat äta opp gammalmora' (Lagerlöf 1914a, 4).

28 'har gripits av hybris, av övermodig tilltro till sin lycka'.

CHAPTER 19

Selma Lagerlöf's story in Czech

Dagmar Hartlová

Selma Lagerlöf's work—that is, almost all her novels, short stories and legends—were translated into Czech during the author's lifetime, in the period between 1901 and 1938. After the Second World War, the orientation of Czech culture changed completely, and the impact of ideological criteria on culture in general, and on translations from Western literature in particular, was devastating. Selma Lagerlöf's prose fiction provides one of the best illustrations of how Swedish literature was received in Czech culture throughout the whole of the twentieth century, with one—but very significant—exception that indicates the prominent position of her work even under communism: in the 1950s, when censorship was at its most effective, Lagerlöf was the only Swedish author deemed acceptable by the powers-that-be. This essay will discuss the history of the reception of Lagerlöf's prose fiction against the background of the crucial role of translations in Czech culture, including early Czech theories of translation. In a case study of *Nils Holgersson* in Czech, I will explore in more detail both the different versions of the text and a range of approaches to translation.

Selma Lagerlöf's reception in Czech can be divided into three very distinct periods. The first period, dating roughly from the 1880s to the end of the 1930s, is considered as the golden age of translation in general. It was the result of the continuous and goal-oriented efforts of Czech opinion-makers to support the emancipation from German language and culture, and to develop local literature in Czech through the exploitation of impulses from cultures regarded as being more advanced. Desirable models were soon found in the small, progressive, and independent nations of northern Europe. Hand in hand with the boom in translations, a considerable amount of attention was paid to translation studies and theoretical academic discourse in this field.

This period was characterised by a warm, enthusiastic, and almost uncritical reception of contemporary Nordic literature (Nordic was and still is a common—and vague—term for literature from northern Europe), although with the exception of August Strindberg and several other writers perceived as more experimental or decadent. The number of novels translated from Swedish, Norwegian, and Danish was growing throughout the period and culminated in the 1930s in what was called 'Nordomania'. These translations generated a new interest in and a massive demand for deeper knowledge of the countries behind these popular literary texts. Various educational or friendly societies and clubs organised trips to Sweden and other Nordic countries, and arranged lectures and seminars on social and political life in Sweden. Swedish began to be taught at various levels in schools and at universities. All these activities in turn subsequently reinforced the interest in translations from Nordic literature.

In the period between the two world wars alone, about 170 Swedish novels were published in Czech and frequently reprinted. The most popular Swedish authors during this period were Emilie Flygare-Carlén (1807–1892)—as many as 27 of her love and adventure stories were published in 73 editions (1870–1939), most of them in the 1920s—and Frank Heller (1886–1947), author of adventure stories set in casinos and the international business world. Both authors are almost forgotten today. These novels satisfied the taste of a middle-class audience that favoured realistic, sentimental, and didactic novels, adventure stories set in a thrilling modern milieu, and novels located in what was, to a Czech reader, exotic settings such as untamed Nature or the open sea. The novels of Selma Lagerlöf were the only ones to compete with those of Flygare-Carlén and Heller.

The second period extends over the whole communist era—that is, from 1948 to the Velvet Revolution in 1989—and is characterised by a general decline in the quantity of translations from Western literature. The third period, covering the decades from the fall of communism up to the present, shows a continuing decline in translations from Swedish, with the exception of detective and crime fiction, which is a completely new phenomenon of the last few years and which has again created a new and very strong Nordic cultural presence in Czech culture.

It is obvious that the differences between the three phases are significant and mirror the changing cultural and political situation on the home ground. Before we look more closely at the first four decades of the twentieth century, let us make a brief excursion into history in order to be able to judge the significance of translations in the Czech cultural context, and also to examine the roots of the enormous popularity of Nordic literature.

The historical background

Between 1516 and 1918 (the year Czechoslovakia was established), the country known today as the Czech Republic was part of the Austro-Hungarian Empire. German had a dominant position in all spheres of society: administration, higher education, and literature. Although the National Revival movement in Bohemia and Moravia (the area of the Czech Republic today) was most prominent in the period 1770–1848, it was only towards the end of the nineteenth century that Czech opinion-makers made consistent efforts to strengthen the cultural identity of the Czech language by promoting modern literature written in Czech, mainly by means of translations of modern world literature into Czech. In 1936 Jan Mukařovský, Czech literary theorist and leading representative of Czech structuralism, argued that 'translation is one of the ways in which national literature can be transformed, since they seek and develop equivalents for foreign texts' (quoted in Pym 2009, 5). Or as Venuti later points out:

> Because translation can contribute to the invention of domestic literary discourses, it has inevitably been enlisted in ambitious cultural projects, notably the development of a domestic language and literature. And such projects have always resulted in the formation of cultural identities aligned with specific social groups, with classes and nations. (Venuti 1998, 77)

The majority of translations of Swedish literature before the end of the nineteenth century, and even those thereafter, were done from the German, as all educated people spoke German and knowledge of Swedish naturally was rare.[1] German translations were frequently available before translations into Czech. Paradoxically, the efforts to break free from German dominance had to go via German. Thus even the choice of literature to be translated was influenced, for a considerable period of time, by what was available in German translation. As late as the end of the 1920s, publishers would insist on the Czech translation following exactly the German version already published.[2]

Early discourses on translation

According to Josef Durdík, writing in 1873,

> A translation can be true (which is a more primitive method, that respects the word), or free (then the translator follows the idea), it can be true to the meaning or true to the sound ... But the main guideline for a translation is that it makes the same impression on the reader as the original.[3] (Quoted in Levý 1996, 165)

Twenty years later, one of the most influential Czech literature critics, F. X. Šalda, in his article 'Překlad v národní literatuře' ('Translation in national literature'), described the function of translation as being not that of bringing people together, but that of highlighting that which was specific to the nation—in other words, cultural differences (Levý 1996, 192). By highlighting the characteristic features of another culture, a translation helps to emphasise the specific features of one's own nation. Vilém Mathesius (1882–1945), one of co-founders of the Prague Linguistic Circle, in his article 'O problémech českého překladatelství' ('On the problems of Czech translation methods'), published in 1913, stressed the importance of 'free adaptation' as 'the fundamental goal of literary translation ... to achieve, whether by the same or by differing devices, the same artistic effect as in the original' (quoted in Gentzler 1993, 82).

Opinions on 'true' versus 'free' changed rather quickly during this period, in some cases even those of the same author:

> F. X. Šalda in the 1890s struggled for accuracy as true and punctilious as possible, but a quarter of a century later ... defended freedom to an extent that was almost alarming. ... A real translator/poet takes the original only as a starting point and stimulus for his independent creation: it is something that opens the door of his imagination so as not to translate a poem but to create a real parallel in his own language. (Levý 1996, 192)

Anyway, the debate on translation concerned mainly highbrow literature and, first and foremost, poetry. But on the other hand, more and more works of prose fiction were translated into Czech for the constantly growing group of readers from the urban classes, a much broader and less critical audience than the academic circles. Translating was turning into a craft with a considerable social impact. Nevertheless, the above-mentioned discourses were intuitively applied in practice, as will be demonstrated later in this essay in an analysis of the approaches used in the early translations into Czech of *Nils Holgersson's Wonderful Journey through Sweden*.

A Swedish cultural identity in Czech, 1880–1939

At the turn of the twentieth century, modern Czech-language literature was supposed to address contemporary problems in urban society—not just the motifs from peasant and rural life that had been typical of literary works in Czech up to this point. By 'modern', scholars meant first and foremost novels and drama in prose, and not just poetry or short stories. However, Czech literature towards the end of the nineteenth century was not very advanced in this respect, and was not able to offer deep reflections on ethical and moral values or insights into social problems and conflicts of the types found abroad, especially in the literature of the Nordic countries. Nordic literature was 'socially conscious, ethical and positive', wrote F. X. Šalda in a review in 1893; and, he continued,

> On the basis of a similar political and social situation, it is possible and easy for us to understand [Nordic literature]. These literatures are fierce-tempered, heartfelt, sincere and deep as few living literatures in Europe … and, in particular and most fortunately, they are capable of injecting fresh blood into our modern art of the future. (Šalda, 1893)

Literary criticism and reviews in periodicals at the beginning of the twentieth century, in the years before and after the Czechoslovak Republic was established, accentuated values such as the freedom of the individual, high moral and ethical values, and individual responsibility. This value-based approach towards literature was predominant, and may to a great extent explain why translations of realistic prose that was socially aware were given precedence over decadence and modernism.

Literature was supposed to be educative and constructive, with a clear moral commitment.

On the other hand, the constantly growing numbers of middle-class readers of modern translated fiction required popular entertainment, adventure stories, dramatic events, romantic narrative, strong emotions, and monumental descriptions of Nature. As if that which was foreign guaranteed better quality than that which was local, translations soon became so popular that some Czech authors of detective stories and adventure fiction passed their own work off as translations in order to make them more attractive. The quantity of translated novels and short stories was such that, as early as 1899, complaints were appearing in critical literature. The prominent Czech literary critic F. X. Šalda expressed his feelings in *Lumír*, a weekly literary magazine: 'we are deluged and suffocated by translations' (Šalda, 1899). Nevertheless, the flood of translations grew steadily, culminating in the 1930s.

The works of Selma Lagerlöf fulfilled both criteria mentioned above: she offered serious literature illustrating high moral standards, which simultaneously provided romantic, dramatic, and entertaining reading. There was, however, another aspect that made Lagerlöf's status as one of the most translated authors so unassailable: she actually wrote about themes that were considered outdated in Czech literature, and she was not despised for doing so—quite the reverse. Her work provided a kind of self-confirmation for Czech literature. In the foreword to the translation of *Jerusalem,* published in 1910, the translator, Emanuel Miřiovský, pointed out:

> Nowadays our writers quite often resort to the farmer hero, in whom they see the idea of the independence of our nation personified. But look at the farmer in Lagerlöf's novel! He is tough, prudent, distrustful, clings to the old traditions, but at the same time burns for novelties and meditates on religious questions. (Miřiovský 1910)

Surprisingly, the first translation into Czech of a novel by Selma Lagerlöf came as late as 1901. Despite her famous debut with *Gösta Berlings saga* (*Gösta Berling's Saga*), Selma Lagerlöf remained unnoticed in Czech literary circles in the 1890s. Why was Lagerlöf not translated until 1901, when the demand for contemporary European prose fiction had begun to develop at least a decade earlier? And why was *Antikristovy zázraky* (*Antikrists mirakler, The Miracles of Antichrist*) the first work by Lagerlöf to appear in Czech? Maybe it was something to do with the theme of *Gösta Berling's Saga*, set almost a hundred years previously, in the Swedish countryside, and with a priest as one of the central characters. This was definitely not a modern novel. The Czech translation of *The Miracles of Antichrist* was published only four years after the Swedish original, and it could of course have been the author's popularity in Germany that made the Czech publisher choose her latest work, looking only afterwards at her previous output. But most probably the answer is to do with the personality of the translator. Behind the pseudonym 'O. S. Vetti' we find a real enthusiast, the parish priest Alois Koudelka (1861–1942), who had taught himself about thirty languages and translated from all of them. Sometimes he even had to create his own dictionary via another, better-known language. We can assume that this particular translation resulted from the dedication of a single individual and not from the customary 'German model' that subsequently was to enable Czech readers to discover Selma Lagerlöf.

With the boom in translations, a couple of big publishers on the Czech book market were established in the first decades of the twentieth century. Selma Lagerlöf's work was ignored, albeit only for a short time, by those publishers favouring decadent literature, but was well represented in all other important publishing houses: in Leichter's realistic series *Sbírka krásné literatury* ('Collection of *belles-lettres*') that existed (according to its own declaration) 'to promote eternal ideas of the good, truth and beauty', and fight the 'modern pathological nature of foreign and domestic literature'; in Topič's *Bílé knihy* ('White Books') that presented books as accomplished pieces of art and concentrated also on children's literature, explicitly specialising in Nordic literature; at the publishing house Otto, one of the three greatest Czech publishers at the beginning of the twentieth century; and at Alois Hynek, where a considerable number of Selma Lagerlöf's books, 16 out of 51 during this period, were published. Alois Hynek concentrated at first on rather trivial literature, but then changed his profile by publishing educative and entertaining books for families and children, including works by both Lagerlöf and the Norwegian author Bjørnstjerne Bjørnson. A number of Lagerlöf's short stories and novels were also serialised in magazines and daily papers.

Selma Lagerlöf represented all that the Czechs admired and found interesting in the Nordic countries. She was warmly welcomed by both critics and readers, and we can hardly ever find a single word of reservation in the press. She was admired for her 'uncomplicated faith in God' and for 'the victory of her altruistic love'. In a review of *Jerusalem* in 1910, her narrative was compared to 'fairytales created by the rich imagination of her strong, wild and bold people', and her style was praised for being 'almost masculine, solid, and concrete, the phrases characterised by a remarkably strict Nordic modesty' (Hikl 1910).

The lens of communist ideology, 1940–1989

Strikingly, Selma Lagerlöf was acceptable even to the communist regime, despite its strict ideological control in the 1950s, the period of political trials and capital sentences. In fact, no work by any other Swedish author than Lagerlöf was published in Czech throughout the first decade after the War. In 1957 a new translation of *Nils Holgersson's Wonderful Journey through Sweden* was published, in 1958 a new translation of *Poklad pana Arna* (*Herr Arnes penningar*, *Lord Arne's Silver*), and in 1959 a new translation of *Gösta Berling* (*Gösta Berling's Saga*). The last of these was then republished under the communist regime no fewer than four times, and in large editions.

In contrast to the period before the War, when at least 10 Swedish novels, short stories and dramas were translated and published annually, in the period between 1945 and 1989 the number of Swedish translations fell dramatically. However, by today's standards the print runs were enormous: 10,000 to 75,000 just in the case of Selma Lagerlöf.

In the years of *détente* and the Prague Spring in the second half of the 1960s when, for a short time, it again became possible to publish much that had been banned in the previous years, new translations of principal works by Selma Lagerlöf appeared. This is indisputable evidence of the author's significance in the Czech cultural milieu. Although there was a great number of key works by outstanding contemporary Scandinavian authors written between 1939 and 1969 to choose from, the publishing houses still found the resources to publish new editions and new translations of Lagerlöf. (Besides five editions of *Gösta Berling's Saga* and two editions of *Nils Holgersson*, *Lord Arne's Silver*, *Liliecronův domov* (*Liljecronas hem*, *Liliecrona's Home*), *Löwesköldův prsten* (*Löwensköldska ringen*, *The Löwensköld Ring*) and *Císař z Portugálie* (*Kejsarn av Portugallien*, *The Emperor of Portugallia*) also appeared during this period.)

One logical explanation for this publishing policy may be the great demand for Nordic literature, a demand that had not been satisfied for a long time. The publication of Nordic literature had been brought to a halt by the War, and now Czech readers were eager to get more of the kind of literature they had been enjoying previously. The second explanation may be to do with the influence of several enthusiasts—people who had studied Swedish and succeeded in promoting their favourite books with the publishing houses. The publication of Lagerlöf's Löwensköld trilogy, *The Löwensköld Ring*, *Charlotta Löweskóldová* (*Charlotte Löwensköld*) and *Anna Swärdová* (*Anna Svärd*) at the beginning of the 1970s echoes with the general tendency to avoid the rigours of ideology by escaping to adventure, entertainment, comedy, or detective stories, in translated literature as well as in domestic films.

In the periodicals published under communism, only a few reviews of books by Selma Lagerlöf and a couple of general articles written, for instance, to celebrate Lagerlöf's birthdays, can be found. Without exception, they are all very appreciative, if not to say effusive. The reviewers, fans of Nordic literature, made a real effort to present the author in as positive a light as possible, safeguarding her against potential ideological objections. It is necessary to emphasise that neither the reviewers nor the authors of prefaces were communists. These texts about Lagerlöf are examples of a kind of inevitable self-censorship: everyone knew what had to be done in order to achieve the goal—publication. Hence the sheer number of paratexts in the form of explanatory forewords and afterwords in order to prevent any possible reservations: once the author had fallen into disgrace, it would be almost impossible to get him or her approved for publication in the future. Nevertheless, the truth is that Swedish literature in general was far more acceptable to the regime than any other Western literature as it was perceived to be sincere in its treatment of social issues. One does not need to look far to find synergies between certain aspects of Lagerlöf's writing and the proclaimed values of communism: an interest in and a solidarity with hard-working people, a responsibility for higher common goals including a preparedness for self-sacrifice, a sense of social justice, and an engagement for peace. As František Branislav (1900–1968), a Czech poet who spoke Swedish, wrote in an article in a Czech daily in 1958: 'Selma Lagerlöf's works of art give us much of the humanism so needed in our epoch for the victory and implementation of the new human order and progress' (1958). Lagerlöf, in other words, was perceived as struggling for a new human order, and there is no doubt what kind of order this was. Commentators could even sound apologetic when they tried to explain why Selma Lagerlöf could not become a proletarian writer, as illustrated by an anonymous author in another daily in the same year:

> She did not become a revolutionary writer fighting against class exploitation as she was too firmly bound to a Christian-philanthropic morality, but for her noble-minded humanism, her understanding of and love for working people she rightly deserves a central place in world literature. (Anon. 1958)

The authors of the foreword to the Czech edition of *The Emperor of Portugallia* in 1962, the aforementioned poet František Branislav and translator Radko Kejzlar, did their best to defend Selma Lagerlöf who, 'although having another philosophy of life than we have, is near and dear to us because of her humanity, conscience, and moral emphasis', and because of her 'desire for peace'. She must, the authors conclude, have been interested in socialism, 'although her concept of socialism was Christian but not religious', and they excused her for this deficiency by referring to her isolation and partly also to the influence of Viktor Rydberg (Branislav & Kejzlar 1962). As this Swedish writer was totally unknown in the Czech cultural milieu, we must take this reference as an attempt to blame someone else for this regrettable shortcoming in Lagerlöf's character. Moreover *The Miracles of Antichrist*, which had not been reprinted following the edition in 1901 and which, with its mixture of religion and socialism, would have harmed Lagerlöf's reputation irreparably in the Czech context, was presented in this foreword as evidence of the author's interest in social rights and the idea of modern socialism. And when no such convincing arguments for conformity to the approved ideology could be used, as was the case with *Lord Arne's Silver*, the praise was rather vague, with references to 'the ethical beauty' or 'mastery of style and form', or to the author's 'unbound imagination that manages to free fiction from barren naturalism', as we can read in the same text.

From 1990 to the present

The period since 1990 shows only very modest results in terms of translations, and almost no response in the media. Four titles have appeared, three of them reprints of older translations, with one of the three, somewhat surprisingly, *Legendy o Kristu* (*Kristuslegender*, *Christ Legends*) in a translation from 1915; the most recent one is the Bonnier edition of Kathrine Aurell and Tage Aurell's shortened version of *Wonderful Journey*. While the first three titles received almost no attention at all, the last one initiated an indignant discussion in the press about the right to make such extensive revisions to a well-known work of art. This suggests that *Wonderful Journey* has become better known in the Czech context than any other work by Lagerlöf, and can still arouse strong emotions. Nils's adventures can thus demonstrate the reception of Selma Lagerlöf in Czech throughout the twentieth century better than any other of her works. Indeed, the history of *Wonderful Journey* in Czech gives a very good picture of different approaches to translation,[4] and also provides evidence of the popularity of Swedish literature in general. The first three translations had appeared in short order between 1911 and 1915.

The first translation was published by the Federation of Teachers' Union in the Czech Monarchy under the title *Podivuhodná cesta Petra Nezbedy s divokými husami* ('The Wonderful Journey of Peter the Urchin with the Wild Geese'). The translator was T. E. Tisovský (1863–1939), himself a writer of stories for children about Nature and animals behaving like human beings. In his handling of the Swedish schoolbook written as a fairytale, he had to cope with the problem of how to make it intelligible to Czech children. The result was an inspired free adaptation, and Tisovský himself did not call it a translation, but an 'echo'. As he explains in his foreword to the book in 1911:

> This is a study of a homeland presented with real and charming artistry as a fairytale. But to our children it could be difficult and hard to understand. This book about Peter the Urchin is a kind of Czech echo of the original. In some places it is a translation, although with local references; otherwise it is a freestanding story, but created in the spirit of the original. And just as other purposeful imitations of great epic works are not regarded as crimes, let us hope that Peter will not be condemned either. (Tisovský 1911, 1)

'Peter the Urchin' was far from being condemned: in 1930 this adaptation was published for the third time. But Tisovský was a writer, and the book was published by an authorised teachers' organisation, and it could very well have played exactly the same role as a compulsory schoolbook as Lagerlöf's had in Sweden. Tisovský does not let the wild geese fly as far as Lapland: they simply decide that this time they will spend some time in Southern Bohemia, a region known for its plentiful and beautiful lakes. In other words, the first Czech mediator of *Nils Holgersson* deleted most of the facts concerning Swedish geography and history as difficult or boring to Czech children, and concentrated on the fairytale story with its moral appeal.

Tisovský also shortened the book to 150 pages, in fact in a manner very similar to that of Kathrine Aurell and Tage Aurell in their Swedish version published in 1967. Tisovský's book has 16 chapters, all situated in the Czech countryside with real geographical settings and place names. Swedish historical facts are replaced by South Bohemian Hussite traditions. Only one chapter is set in Sweden, a story told by the grey geese to their white domesticated sisters. Without an in-depth analysis, it is difficult to say whether Tisovský understood Swedish and used the Swedish original. Most probably he did not—but in this case it is not relevant. His Czech story is beautifully written and provides children with plenty of facts about Czech history and geography, and about the animal kingdom. An interesting change is the replacement of the hymn printed prior to Lagerlöf's text in the Swedish version by a text 'On children's obligations towards their parents'—religion is replaced by secular morality. Another shift from the original seems freely inspired by Lagerlöf's concern for the very poor: Tisovský incorporates his own story about a marshy Bohemian region from where the population is forced to emigrate, but he suggests that the marshes can be drained and turned into fertile land, and so the old woman left behind by her children can write asking them to return home.

Czech literature for children, even for the youngest, has for a long time had a strong cognitive function, aiming to assist the children in exploring the fantastic and amazing big world. Tisovský's work fits very nicely into this tradition. Two years after Tisovský's version, in 1913, a complete version of *Nils Holgersson* was published in the translation by Karel V. Rypáček (1885–1957) and included in an edition labelled 'Selection of nice books for children and young people'.

Rypáček's translation is true to the original and does not omit a single thing. But at the same time the translator is very much aware of the difficulty of a text full of information that is new and perhaps unintelligible to nine- or ten-year-old children. Thus he has provided plenty of explanatory comments and also gives information on the pronunciation of proper names of both places and people. The book contains many pictures of elk, Sami huts, and so on, accompanied by the translator's own comments. Rypáček took upon himself the teacher's role that Selma Lagerlöf clearly counted on, and he added a whole system of explanatory notes and footnotes covering everything that he assumed to be unfamiliar to Czech children.

In 1915, a new translation by Emil Walter (1890–1964) was published. This, too, was a complete version with 55 chapters, but without any supplementary information or explanations to help the reader understand the text. The book was equipped with illustrations in a Romantic style, and the text sounds more poetic than that of the previous schoolbook. Emil Walter undoubtedly spoke Swedish, and he also lived in Sweden for a period of time. There are not many obvious mistakes in his translation. However, we cannot trace any clearly defined pedagogical concept underpinning his translation.

In 1957 *Nils Holgersson* appeared in a fresh translation by Dagmar Chvojková-Pallasová, and this time we may speak of a new conception of translation compared to the three previous versions. The 1957 translation is neither a pure fairytale nor a text book about a homeland as before: it is a book adapted for children, omitting some details regarded by the translator as unnecessary and too demanding for Czech children. Explanations have been incorporated into the text so as to make the reading easier for children. The translator's afterword to the book emphasises Lagerlöf's imagination, moral strength and 'the sense of romanticism that we so often miss in our lives' (Chvojková-Pallasová 1957), with the reviews highlighting much the same aspects. This translation had a very positive reception and was published in a new edition in 1967. Pallasová's approach is fairly balanced. It may be that the translator also applied ideological considerations so as not to provoke the censor when she omitted some religious motifs and some passages about the nobility. We can only speculate as to whether she was focusing on the reader who had no religious education and therefore insufficient knowledge, or whether she was adapting the text to conform to communist ideology in a country where religion was regarded as the opium of the people.

The last translation, from 2006, is not of the book written by Selma Lagerlöf, but of the shortened Swedish version adapted for much younger readers than those she had had in mind: small children between the ages of four and six. First and foremost it is a fairytale, in the Czech

Illus. 1. 'Rosenbom'. Illustration by Jiří
Sopko in *Podivuhodná cesta Nilse Holgerssona Švédskem*, tr. Dagmar Hartlová (2005).

edition with beautiful illustrations by Jiří Sopko, and it suits perfectly
the Czech fairytale tradition with its emphasis on a positive and educative way of exploring the world. But published fifty years after the
previous Czech edition, this is not Selma Lagerlöf: it is even more of
an 'echo' of the original than Tisovský's version was.

Looking back and forward

At the very beginning of the past century we can see a concerted effort
to develop Czech-language literature and its readers by means of translations. A very important aspect of this process was the search in the
texts to be translated for the same moral values as those the Czechs
appreciated. The key goal was emancipation from the German language,
and thus any other national literature was a welcome influence. Small,
independent nations with advanced, respected, and progressive literature
were highly appealing to Czech audiences. Very soon, cultural identities
emerged, Sweden's included. Translations initiated and established a
strong and persuasive image of Sweden containing exactly the same

values as we can find in reviews on Lagerlöf's books which mention, for example, 'a stable ethical code based on basic human values, such as purity in the relations between people, altruism, and real love' (Vodák 1984). This image has lasted up to the present, although its roots may not be widely recognised today.

We can only speculate about the reasons for the dramatic decline in the quantity of translations since 1990. Why has an author so warmly received by readers throughout the whole of the twentieth century, regardless of the variations in politics and cultural policy, now faded into obscurity? Is it to do with bad timing, old translations, or with the author appearing to be outdated? It is also worth remembering that since the fall of communism in 1989, the Czech book market has changed dramatically, with many Czech and foreign authors who had been prohibited for a very long time suddenly being published in immense variety and large editions by hundreds of newly established publishing houses. The supply was in the beginning so enormous that it exceeded demand and almost paralysed both the readers' interest and the book market.

How to reconstitute the cultural legacy of Selma Lagerlöf so that it can again address a broader audience? The answer, to begin with, is by means of new translations. The most recent one in Czech is from 1984. Some of Lagerlöf's key works were published only once, and more than a hundred years ago—*Jerusalem* is a case in point, having been translated into Czech in 1910, almost certainly from German, with many misunderstandings, errors, and clumsy expressions that must have been considered painful even at the time. Finally, the choice of what works to offer to the readers is crucially important. Today, this would mean presenting this almost forgotten novelist anew.

The overall picture of the history of translation from one small literary tradition (Swedish) to another small culture (Czech) shows a striking discrepancy. At least four times as many Swedish works have been translated into Czech than vice versa. The periods of interest in the other culture do not coincide, but on either side their roots are political. For more than a century, foreign literature has been thought important to the development of Czech culture, and at every point, cultural ambition had been underpinned by politics. Sweden served as a model—culturally, socially, politically—and once this image was established it continued to lead its own life. Swedish literature was read because it was from Sweden. And this may be so even today. Czechs have never been especially fond of detective stories. Today the best-selling literature in the Czech Republic is not detective novels in general, but especially those from Sweden (or Norway), now as before commonly labelled 'Nordic'. It is not impossible that this newborn interest might inspire a new and more wide-ranging interest in Swedish literature.

Notes

1 For example, the translation of *Jerusalem* from 1910 by the poet, novelist, and translator of German literature, Emanuel Miřiovský (1846–1911) shows at first sight, without any deeper analysis, plenty of German-like constructions and formulations. For instance, the name of the river Dalälven, translated into Czech as 'Dalelf', can be interpreted as a phonetic transcription of the German consonant 'v' into Czech.

2 'The book must be composed exactly as the German version published by G. Müller, Munich, with the title *Das Buch der Liebe*', demands the publisher of Strindberg's *En blå bok* in 1927 (Vimr 2006/07).

3 All translations from Czech are my own.

4 This topic is analysed in detail by Linda Kaprová (2009) in her excellent study, 'Translating Swedish Literature for Children into Czech'.

CHAPTER 20

Nils in the Netherlands

Selma Lagerlöf in Dutch and Frisian, 1911–1921

Roald van Elswijk

Works by Swedish writers have been enjoyed by children all over the world, examples being *Pippi Långstrump* (1945, *Pippi Longstocking*) and *Bröderna Lejonhjärta* (1973, *The Brothers Lionheart*) by Astrid Lindgren, and *Nils Holgerssons underbara resa genom Sverige* (*Nils Holgersson's Wonderful Journey through Sweden*) by Selma Lagerlöf. Published in Sweden in two parts in 1906–1907, *Nils Holgersson* was written as an educational text, commissioned by the Swedish National Teachers' Society. It has been a favourite among children and teenagers for several generations, including my own. Who would not be enthralled by this tale about a boy who, riding on the back of a goose, flies the length and breadth of Sweden, can talk to animals, and has all sorts of exciting adventures?

However, there is much more to this book than one might suspect. Here I am going to analyse the reception of *Nils Holgersson* and other works by Selma Lagerlöf in the Dutch-speaking area and also in the bilingual Dutch province of Friesland.[1] In 2011, to mark the centenary of the first Dutch translation of *Nils Holgersson*, I assembled a text corpus covering the period 1911–1921, consisting of newspaper articles, reviews, travel accounts, and other material from a number of Dutch and Frisian archives. By means of a discourse-analytical approach, explained below, I will use it to concentrate on possible constructions of Selma Lagerlöf as a nationalist author, and on references being made to national, for which read unifying, elements in her work. More specifically, I will follow up Bjarne Thorup Thomsen's theory put forward in his works of 2004 and 2007, that *Nils Holgersson* was not just intended to inspire children and young people to respect their local culture, but rather that the work's geocultural plurality and pedagogical ways of mapping the country were aimed at establishing a sense of the nation, quite literally through a bird's-eye view of the Swedish nation. I would like to take this a step further by analysing to what extent this sense of the nation is also touched upon in non-Swedish literary criticism, *in casu* Dutch and Frisian newspapers and journals. I will explore these interpretations of Lagerlöf in potentially national and nationalist contexts against the backdrop of research into language and nationalism. This essay also offers an outline of the early twentieth-century reception of Scandinavian literature in the Dutch- and Frisian-speaking area, thus following little Nils's early adventures in the Netherlands.

Scandinavian literature in the Netherlands

In modern literary criticism, two periods are discernible during which there was a marked interest in Scandinavian literature in the Netherlands and Flanders. The second of these started around 1994, when authors such as Peter Høeg and Kerstin Ekman had their breakthroughs in the Dutch-speaking area, a success which is still ongoing given the popularity of contemporary Scandinavian crime fiction. The first breakthrough, however, came as early as around 1900, when a great number of trans-lations were published and reviews spoke of Scandinavian literature in terms of 'young, fresh, and progressive'.

In 1911 an influential article was published by the translator and cultural transmitter, Margaretha Meijboom (1856–1927), arguing for a wider range of Scandinavian literature to be translated into Dutch (see Jiresch 2009). Her essay, entitled 'Skandinavische literatuur in Nederland' ('Scandinavian literature in the Netherlands'), is one of the first articles ever to map the reception of a foreign literature in the Dutch-speaking area. Meijboom noted that many Dutch publishing houses were interested solely in translations of peasant novels and family chronicles from the Nordic countries, thus providing the Dutch audi-ence with a rather unbalanced overview of Scandinavia's many-faceted literature. She was very critical of these commercially driven choices and argued for a clearer distinction between so-called 'highbrow' and 'lowbrow' literature (1911, 47). Meijboom's article was written in the same year that her translation of *Nils Holgersson* was published (Illus. 1).

Margaretha Meijboom was heavily involved in promoting a number of Scandinavian writers and their work in the Netherlands. She met Selma Lagerlöf in 1897 and subsequently gave several lectures about

NIELS HOLGERSSON'S
WONDERBARE REIS

NAAR HET ZWEEDSCH

VAN

SELMA LAGERLÖF

DOOR

MARGARETHA MEIJBOOM

(GEAUTORISEERDE UITGAAF)

EERSTE DEEL

AMSTERDAM
H. J. W. BECHT

Illus. 1. First authorised translation of *Nils Holgersson* into Dutch (1911), by Margaretha Meijboom.

her and published a monograph about her *œuvre* (Meijboom 1919). In this book, *Selma Lagerlöf*, published in the series Scandinavische Bibliotheek (Scandinavian Library), Meijboom painted a vivid picture of the author's life, although parts of it had clearly been dramatised. Meijboom was one of the prime mediators of Scandinavian culture in the Netherlands, but she was not the first scholar to direct her attention to Scandinavia. As early as 1860, a history of Scandinavian literature had been published in Dutch, *Noordsche letteren* ('Nordic Literatures') by C. J. Hansen, providing an early insight into the understanding of Scandinavian literature and culture in the Low Countries (Hansen 1860). Another source of knowledge of the cultural, linguistic, and literary conditions in the Nordic countries was the bilingual journal *Scandia. Maandblad voor Scandinavische Taal en Letteren* ('Scandia. Monthly

Magazine for Scandinavian Language and Literatures'), published in several issues in 1904. This journal featured articles and essays on the Scandinavian countries, the editor-in-chief being Margaretha Meijboom. Well-known authors from Scandinavia submitted essays and original work to be published in *Scandia*, among them Arne Garborg, Herman Bang, Georg Brandes, Jonas Lie, and Juhani Aho. As a follow-up to *Scandia*, Meijboom in 1905 founded yet another journal concerned with the Nordic countries, *Scandinavië–Nederland. Tijdschrift voor Nederlandsche en Scandinavische Taal, Letteren en Kultuur* ('Scandinavia–Netherlands. Journal for Dutch and Scandinavian Language, Literatures and Culture'), published in 1905–1906. These journals provide valuable material for anyone interested in the early representation of Scandinavian literature in the Netherlands and Flanders.

The reception of Scandinavian literature is a relatively new field of research in the Netherlands, the last few decades seeing a number of studies. Translations of Danish literature were mapped by the late Diederik Grit in his 1994 dissertation, while Petra Broomans and Ester Jiresch, *inter alia*, have analysed the reception of Swedish literature and the networks on which their translators were dependent. Jiresch's dissertation (2013) compares Dutch-Flemish and Austrian-German networks of female transmitters of Scandinavian literature. His research was supervised by, among others, Petra Broomans, who herself has published several studies in the field, and who initiated the series Studies on Cultural Transfer and Transmission (SoCTaT).[2]

Dutch translations from the Norwegian have been registered by the bookseller Jos Groen (1994). However, the most extensive Norwegian–Dutch bibliography to date was published in 2013, volume 5 in the SoCTaT series. This book contains details of more than 1,500 works translated from Norwegian into Dutch (De Saeger 2013). A second extensive bibliography has recently being completed at the University of Groningen, listing translations of Swedish literature into Dutch (1491–2007), and also including works by Finland-Swedish authors (Broomans and Kroon 2013). According to a semi-final draft of this bibliography, which covers novels, drama, and short stories, some 26 different works by Selma Lagerlöf have been translated into Dutch, starting with her first novel *Gösta Berlings saga* (1891) as *Gösta Berling* (1901), and ending with the short story 'Meli' (1938). The quality of Selma Lagerlöf's novels, combined with the efforts of cultural mediators such as Margaretha Meijboom, have ensured a great number of translations and reprints. As a result, Lagerlöf's works have a strong position in the Dutch literary field.

Lagerlöf's perhaps best-known work, *Nils Holgersson's Wonderful Journey through Sweden*, has received much attention from Dutch translators. If we take into account all the translations, including the modernised versions, and also count the various reprints, there is a total of 64 versions of *Nils Holgersson* in Dutch.[3] Some of these translations contain both volumes of the original work, some just the first, while others consist of selected chapters only. The first translation, by Margaretha Meijboom, has been revised and reprinted at least 21 times, the 22nd edition having been published in 2000. A completely new translation of *Nils Holgersson* was published as recently as 2010. The Flemish scholar Isabelle Desmidt from the University of Ghent has written a doctoral dissertation on all the translations, comparing them to the translations of *Nils Holgersson* into German (Desmidt 2001).[4] Interestingly, Desmidt points to the combination of national, meaning Swedish, and international elements as being one of the reasons for the popularity of *Nils Holgersson*, both in Sweden and across the world (2001, 433). These national elements will be the focal point of my analysis of the reception of Selma Lagerlöf in Dutch and Frisian.

Scandinavian authors in Frisian

Frisian, officially West Frisian, is the variety of the Frisian language in the Netherlands, otherwise spoken in North Germany. The Frisian language, or Frysk, is spoken in the bilingual province of Friesland and used actively by approximately 400,000 people. Historical connections between the Frisian lands and the Scandinavian countries date back as early as the Viking Age, when the seafaring Frisians traded extensively with Scandinavia. There are also other types of links between Frisians and Scandinavians, including similarities between their languages. According to some, these similarities are strong, while others argue that this does not reflect facts. As recently as the 1960s and 1970s, annual summer camps were organised on the Frisian island of Skylge (Dutch Terschelling) which were attended by both Scandinavian and Frisian teenagers, with lectures being given on their respective cultures. Prior to that, at the height of its nationalist battle between the 1860s and 1880s, numerous articles were published by the separatist Frisian Movement that touched upon the perceived kinship with people in the Scandinavian countries. To the Frisian Movement, the Frisian language was at the heart of the striving for greater cultural independence. Many of these articles thus refer to language debates similar to the Frisian–Dutch one, such as those in Norway, Finland, and the Faroe Islands. The Frisian Movement took a special interest in Norway and the efforts of Ivar Aasen to establish Nynorsk (New Norwegian) as a new literary language, and several articles have been published on this subject. In his lecture from 1916, *Fryslân en de wrâld* ('Friesland and the world'), the leader of the Frisian Movement, Douwe Kalma (1896–1953), elaborated on his familiar image of the bridge, which envisages Friesland as a cultural and linguistic bridge between the English-speaking and the Scandinavian-speaking parts of the world. This Herderian thinking of placing the native tongue at the heart of nationalist movement proved very fertile in Friesland, and may prove interesting when analysing possible nationalist constructions of a given author in a Frisian text corpus.

The interest in Scandinavia greatly stimulated the translation of Scandinavian authors into Frisian, the tales of Hans Christian Andersen being among the first texts to be translated. The first translation from Swedish that I have found dates from 1903 and is a rendition of Selma Lagerlöf's 'Sång för slöjden' ('Song for Handicrafts') from 1895 (Lagerlöf 1930b). According to one critic, the Frisian interest in the works of Lagerlöf was mostly aroused by the idealism found in her writings: 'the ideas of the Christian socialist and pacifist, Selma Lagerlöf, inspired a number of Frisians to explore her works further' (Krol 2007, 37).[5] Some of the texts in *Kristuslegender* (1904, *Christ Legends*) were translated, as well as one tale from *Saga om en saga och andra sagor* (1908, 'A Tale about a Tale and other Tales'). Several other stories would follow, and in total eight works by Lagerlöf have been translated into Frisian. Interestingly, the Frisian translations of Lagerlöf only include short works: no novels have been translated.

Several bibliographies bring up the issue of Frisian translations of Scandinavian literature. Up to 2011, approximately 30 different Swedish authors had been translated into Frisian (including eleven children's books by Barbro Lindgren and nine by Astrid Lindgren).[6] These translations cover a range of genres, such as short stories, drama, children's books, and novels by a number of authors, including August Strindberg, Kaj Söderhjelm, and the Finland-Swedish writers Zacharias Topelius and Johan Ludvig Runeberg. Most of these translations use

Dutch as an intermediary language, but especially in the 1960s and 1970s, several works were translated directly into Frisian.

At the beginning of the twentieth century, Frisian interest in Scandinavia focused mainly on the notion that the Scandinavian countries and Friesland were kindred nations. The nationalist Frisian Movement displayed a marked interest in the language debates in Norway and in the Faroe Islands, and a number of essays were published on these topics. To what extent, then, were potentially national elements in the works of Lagerlöf picked up by Frisian literary criticism?

Constructions of Lagerlöf in the text corpus

The analysis of my corpus concentrates mainly on how the reception of Selma Lagerlöf in Dutch and Frisian may function as a vehicle for language-linked nationalism and regionalism. The spatial theme of narrating the nation, in the first decade of the twentieth century centring on the dissolution of the Swedish-Norwegian union, is a recurrent theme in Lagerlöf's early works, and moves centre stage in *Nils Holgersson*. This focus on the nation in Lagerlöf has been analysed by, among others, Bjarne Thorup Thomsen (2004, 2007). Like Isabelle Desmidt, he concludes that the combination of national elements and elements promoting the transgression of borders, along with the book's success all across the world, ensured that *Nils Holgersson* quickly gained a place in popular consciousness—both in Sweden and abroad (Thomsen 2004). This pedagogical basis of the book, establishing a sense of the nation through literature, will be the focal point when analysing my text corpus, which begins with its first Dutch translation (1911c).

I have collected reviews, travel accounts, literary articles, biographical texts, and other relevant material containing the keyword 'Lagerlöf' from several Dutch and Frisian archives. My main sources include the digital archives of the Royal Dutch Library in The Hague, the digital newspaper archive of the bilingual *Leeuwarder Courant* (1752), Friesland's biggest newspaper as well as the oldest still published in the Netherlands, and the newspaper archive at Tresoar, the Frisian Historical and Literary centre in the county town of Ljouwert (Leeuwarden). I have searched these archives using the term 'Lagerlöf', which gave 89 hits for the archive of the Royal Library, 34 of which I could use, the other texts being mostly advertisements. A search of the *Leeuwarder Courant* archive resulted in 8 texts, all of which could be used for the corpus.

The archive at Tresoar had only one article from the 1911–21 period. I double-checked the total number of hits by using alternative spellings of the term 'Lagerlöf' ('Lagerlof', 'Lagerløf', 'Lagerloef') and also by scanning the same period for articles containing the term 'Holgersson'. This did not yield any new texts relevant to my analysis.

My two main research questions when analysing this Dutch-Frisian corpus were whether the text corpus contains any constructions of Selma Lagerlöf as a nationalist author or references to national elements in her works; and whether there is a marked difference between the Dutch and Frisian material with regard to the depiction of the author. The analytical model I have used has been inspired by the discourse-analytical model in Petra Broomans's doctoral dissertation (1999) on the Swedish author Stina Aronson. Broomans has drawn on the theories of, *inter alia*, Hayden White on the discourse of the historical text, reworking his model into one that can be used for analysing literary-historical material. Applying this model, articles can be subjected to close readings on the basis of a number of so-called features, relevant text characterisations which in their immediate contexts may form an associative series of words, so-called strings. By defining these chains of relevant words—often adjectives or other meaningful words—a model evolves which opens up for a more thorough analysis of the text's internal structure (see Illus. 2).

Dutch articles

The Dutch material comprises 34 texts and makes up the bulk of my text corpus. Here I am going to highlight a selection of these texts.

The first review, from February 1911, is interesting in that it comments on the lack of knowledge of Scandinavian languages among the Dutch. Even major European languages are fairly unknown, a journalist writes in *Algemeen Handelsblad*: 'Who can read Dante and Petrarca in their original language, who can read Ibsen, Lagerlöf, or Bjørnson?' (*Algemeen Handelsblad*, 23 Feb. 1911, 5). This critique fits very well with the growing interest in Scandinavian languages and culture at the beginning of the twentieth century. This was also the time when several Dutch newspapers were reporting on concerts or cultural soirées, especially in Amsterdam and The Hague, at which short stories by Selma Lagerlöf were read by professional storytellers. 'Vogel Roodborst' ('Fågel Rödbröst', 'Robin Redbreast') is mentioned as one of these, as are some of Lagerlöf's Christmas tales.

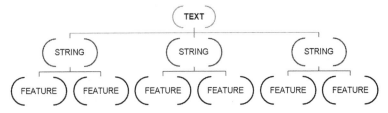

Illus. 2. The analytical structure of the discourse model applied in Broomans 1999.

As part of my text corpus, I have also analysed a number of travel accounts by Dutch journalists visiting Selma Lagerlöf at Mårbacka, her country estate in Värmland. Travel writing is a literary genre well known from Dutch newspapers at the beginning of the twentieth century. The first of these accounts, an extensive narrative of this type of literary tourism, was published in October 1911 in *Het nieuws van den dag*. The beautiful vistas of Värmland are described with great elegance, but nothing is said about what was discussed between Selma Lagerlöf and the Dutch journalist.

Another text in my corpus refers to a journalist meeting Selma Lagerlöf—and actually telling his readers what they spoke about. In July 1917, a Dutch correspondent from the *Nieuwe Rotterdamsche Courant* travelled to Mårbacka and spent some three hours talking to the author. He comments both eloquently and elegantly on their first encounter, and mentions her warm hand resting in his. Her eyes he describes as 'soft but severe', while her gaze is 'thoughtful with a slightly questioning expression'. The two of them enjoy a nice walk through the gardens at Mårbacka and several topics are discussed, including the scenery of Värmland as a backdrop to *Gösta Berling's Saga* and the history of the estate itself. Upon leaving her company, the Dutch journalist comments: 'it felt indeed as if I were leaving the castle of an enchanting fairy' (Anon. 1917). It seems that both Selma Lagerlöf's personality and her books made a big impression, with her appearance described as at once strong and soft. Recurrent features (see Illus. 2) used to describe Lagerlöf's charisma in these travel accounts include adjectives such as 'warm', 'natuurlijk' and 'harmonieus'. It would be interesting to see to what extent the author's physical appearance has been commented on in other, non-Swedish sources too. There are no additional, paratextual features in these articles on

Mårbacka. None of the articles are embellished with illustrations or photographic material, and the texts do not stand out from the other newspaper columns. The article headlines are set in bold, just like the other headlines.

The first reference to the 1911 translation of *Nils Holgersson* in a Dutch newspaper dates from 29 November 1911, and simply states that 'an authorised translation has been published of the renowned Swedish author Selma Lagerlöf'. Almost a month later, in December 1911, *Het nieuws van den dag* featured a review of the book. Here, the critic found it 'curious' that this new book had been written for children, but concluded that grown-ups would like it too. It is a 'fascinating story, filled with beautiful legends and beautiful depictions of Nature, and has a philosophical and pedagogical background', he wrote. The book was in fact 'a deeply moving fairytale, with all the fantastic elements that so characterise the author's later works' (*Het nieuws van den dag*, 27 Dec. 1911). This review would prove to be the first of many of the Dutch translations of *Nils Holgersson*.

Frisian articles

The Frisian part of my corpus comprises nine texts. From this relatively small corpus, a positive image emerges of Selma Lagerlöf as a widely read and much-loved author. The first article dates from October 1911 and is part of a travel account entitled 'Een zomer in het Noorden' ('A summer in Scandinavia'). The correspondent of the *Leeuwarder Courant*, 'Urban', spent several weeks in Scandinavia, and having visited Norway, he returned to Sweden via Värmland (spelled according to its Dutch pronunciation, 'Wermland'), where he visited Mårbacka (spelled 'Marbaeka'). He paints a detailed picture of the vistas and beautiful scenery which form the setting of *Gösta Berling's Saga*. The 'big, blond lads' he encountered were extremely trustworthy, he writes, and they used modern machinery when working the land but, he points out, 'they don't look particularly intelligent'. Selma Lagerlöf he characterises as an 'author of genius', and he considers himself lucky to be able to spend some time with her. Above all, she was 'a child of Värmland, who was guided by real love when composing her breathtakingly beautiful book' (meaning *Gösta Berling's Saga*). Curiously, though, this travel account, just like one of the Dutch articles, does not mention what was discussed between them, only the fact that they met.

In 1918, the leader of the Frisian Movement, Douwe Kalma, published a review of the five short stories from *Christ Legends* in the nationalist *Frisia* magazine. Kalma characterised Lagerlöf as a 'great author' (Kalma 1918, 352). He argued that the value of the work the translator, Sjouke De Zee, had done for the Frisian cause by translating these stories from Swedish was 'undoubtedly high', and he compared the joy they would bring to the enthusiasm of readers of the stories about Raffles, aka Lord Lister, the fictional master thief from Germany, whose adventures were very popular in the Low Countries in the first decades of the twentieth century.[7]

Although too recent to be included in the actual text corpus, a review by Douwe Kalma in the nationalist magazine *It Heitelân* ('The Fatherland') in 1937 mentions Selma Lagerlöf in an interesting context: the article highlights children's love of reading, and the roles of language and literature in constituting an important part of the Frisian people's national sense. Here, we may have found a hint of a nationalist characterisation, in the sense that Lagerlöf is mentioned in a text that puts literature and language centre stage, at the core of the nation. With two out of nine Frisian texts in my corpus having been written by Douwe Kalma, the leader of the Frisian Movement, one might assume that although Lagerlöf's works were not characterised as 'nationalist', her name was often mentioned in a 'nationalist' context, and the publication of her work deemed important for the Frisian cause. It would be interesting, therefore, to pursue further research into the reception of Selma Lagerlöf in Frisian, and of Scandinavian authors in minority languages generally.

Conclusion

In this article, using a discourse-analytical approach to a Dutch-Frisian text corpus, I have explored the reception of Selma Lagerlöf's translations in the Netherlands in the period 1911–1921. The objective of this analysis was to establish to what extent the Lagerlöf *œuvre* has been perceived as containing national elements, and to what extent the notion of *Nils Holgersson* as a work of national unity has rung true in Dutch and Frisian literary criticism.

In my corpus, Selma Lagerlöf is not characterised as a 'nationalist' author, but the Frisian material does suggest that her translated works were important to the Frisian cause. The Frisian texts mention Lagerlöf's name in broader contexts about the importance of language and literature to a given people. Moreover, the Frisian material seems to place some emphasis on the role of a common Scandinavian–Frisian culture. To the Frisian people, whose fate in a true Herderian sense was closely intertwined with their language, translations from countries that could be perceived as kindred nations proved inspiring.

The Dutch material, on the other hand, concentrates mainly on the versatility of Lagerlöf's authorship, including her interests in politics and good causes. The discourse-analytical model I have used for analysing these texts reveals a number of interesting features. Several of the terms used to characterise Lagerlöf recur in the travel accounts from Mårbacka. Adjectives such as 'natural' and 'harmonious' are used to describe the author, and her persona seems to be equally interesting to the journalists as are her novels.

Around 1900, there was a considerable amount of interest in Scandinavian literature in the Netherlands. Many novels were translated into Dutch, and articles and essays in literary journals paid homage to authors from Scandinavia. A number of well-known authors, including Selma Lagerlöf, paved the way for more extensive cultural transmission between the Netherlands and the Scandinavian countries, with mediators such as Margaretha Meijboom forming the pillars of this cultural bridge. In the twenty-first century, this bridge is still firmly in place.

Notes

1 Since 1997, this province is officially referred to by its Frisian name, Fryslân.
2 Up to December 2013, six books have been published in Barkhuis of Groningen's series Studies on Cultural Transfer & Transmission; see <http://www.soctat.org/about>.
3 Number based on Broomans & Kroon 2013 and Desmidt 2001.
4 'En underbar färd på språkets vingar. Selma Lagerlöfs "Nils Holgersson" i tysk och nederländsk översättning/bearbetning', unpublished dissertation, University of Ghent.
5 'de ideeën fan de kristensosjaliste en pasifiste Selma Lagerlöf (wiene) oanlieding foar guon Friezen om harren dêr mear yn te ferdjipjen'.
6 Number based on Dykstra 1962, Heeres 2001, and Krol 2001.
7 Interestingly, the archives at Tresoar mention some correspondence between Kalma and Sjouke De Zee, but I have not been able to assess whether these letters contain any details on De Zee's Frisian translations of Lagerlöf.

CHAPTER 21

Journeys into English

An overview of the English-language versions of
Nils Holgersson and anglophone academic discourse

Charlotte Berry

Published in two volumes during 1906–1907, *Nils Holgerssons under-bara resa genom Sverige* was translated into English by the American Velma Swanston Howard in a London and New York co-edition as *The Wonderful Adventures of Nils* (1907) and *The Further Adventures of Nils* (1911). Written as a geography schoolbook commissioned by the Swedish National Teachers' Society, *Nils Holgersson* (as it is generally known) rapidly established itself as a major work of international children's literature, particularly in Germany.

This essay will briefly consider what academic attention has thus far been given to *Nils Holgersson* in the English-speaking world, highlighting where possible the history of this text's translations into English. The main body of the essay constitutes an innovative overview of the publishing history of the existing English versions: this analysis takes place within the functional and cultural discourses of descriptive translation studies, particularly those relating to contact and transfer studies, with this essay seeking to explore in detail one particular literary 'contact', that of the 'transfer' of *Nils Holgersson* from Sweden to the UK and US. The available editions of the source text are examined in order to construct for the first time a chronological overview of the text's publishing history and to establish a foundation for more detailed research on this topic. Thus, this essay contributes to emerging debates regarding the translation of children's literature and publishing history, as well as demonstrating how these two disciplines can be utilised in tandem in interdisciplinary research.

Nils Holgersson and the anglophone academic discourse

Vivi Edström commented in 1984 that there had been little British critical attention relating to *Nils Holgersson* or regarding the reception of Lagerlöf's books in Sweden and abroad (1984, iii). This gap was partially addressed through Barbara Lide's translation into English of Edström's own volume of literary scholarship on Lagerlöf which contained a chapter entitled 'Nils Holgersson flies over the world'. This chapter gives a useful introductory context of the work, in addition to considering issues such as plot development and characterisation, the journey motif, and the social message of morals.

Suzanne Rahn took up the challenge in her article 'Rediscovering Nils' in the international children's literature journal *The Lion and the Unicorn* in 1986,[1] offering a textual analysis of major themes within Lagerlöf's text, as well as considering the text's potential appeal to English-language readerships. Rahn's article gives very little attention to the quality of Swanston Howard's translation, other than noting that it is 'generally fluent [but] has an old-fashioned flavour that rings oddly in modern ears' (1986, 159); however, she does consider the challenges encountered when translating *Nils Holgersson* for English-speaking audiences, such as the length and complexity of language and plot-structure for the modern child reader, as well as the 'exotic Swedish setting, with its strange names and geography' (1986, 159).[2]

The Swede Björn Sundmark is the only academic to examine *Nils Holgersson* comprehensively in an English-speaking setting. Three articles (2008a, 2008b, 2009a) address broad issues of nationality, world citizenship, children's identity, and Lagerlöf's utopian vision, particularly with reference to *Nils Holgersson* as an educational and ideological text.[3] Sundmark offers a literary assessment of Swanston Howard's English translation of *The Further Adventures of Nils* in the proceedings of the UK's first Nordic translation conference (2009b). Here he draws on the Lagerlöf–Swanston Howard correspondence at the Swedish National Library in Stockholm to re-evaluate the quality and nature of Swanston Howard's translation, concluding that her 'dated' style is 'characterized by a certain flowery wordiness and a predilection for circumlocutions and archaisms that are quite alien to Lagerlöf's effective and direct storytelling technique' (2009b, 171). As Sundmark cites, in the 1911 translator's preface to *The Further Adventures of Nils*, Swanston Howard claims that 'the story itself is intact', having eliminated 'purely geographical matter' and cut only material of 'descriptive [or] local interest' (2009b, 167). However, some chapters have been abridged significantly or wholly deleted. Sundmark focuses his literary analysis on the deletion of two key episodes within the text in the second volume, where Swanston Howard cut 40,000 words in order to make the length of the two volumes similar and make the text and its core themes more marketable to an American juvenile audience. Two chapters relating to the Uppsala student and to the burial of Little Mats are absent from the Swanston Howard translation.[4] Sundmark discusses in literary terms the extent to which the abridgements within Volume Two affect the completeness and the critical and popular reception of the work.

The most recent literary article to appear in English on *Nils Holgersson* is that in *Swedish Book Review* by Paul Binding in 2011. 'Selma Lagerlöf: Nils Holgersson's wonderful journey' considers the early origins of the work, the literary challenges of using the format of geographical reader, the role of Nature within Lagerlöf's works, as well as Nils's own moral and psychological transformation within the text.

Just as the academic study of children's literature has blossomed in recent years within literary circles, children's literature translation studies (CLTS) is becoming an increasingly active field of research within translation studies. In particular, descriptive translation studies (DTS) has proved a fruitful area of scholarship for CLTS, focusing on the 'description of the phenomena of translation' (Munday 2008, 10). In response to the cultural turn of the 1990s, DTS interests have subsequently developed a 'functional orientation' within the broader historical, literary, political, and sociological contexts in which translation takes place.

Emer O'Sullivan has coined the term 'contact and transfer studies' for this area of research which is concerned with 'every form of cultural exchange ... between literature from difference countries, languages and cultures' (2005, 21). Topics include contact, transfer and reception, international mediators, non-translation and delayed translation, and the cross-cultural development of literary traditions. However, little research has been conducted into twentieth-century contact and transfer within the specifically British CLTS context, with David Blamires (1992) and Gillian Lathey (2010) the first to address this issue.

Isabelle Desmidt (2003) is the only translation scholar to publish research on *Nils Holgersson* in a mainstream English-language translation journal, here in a special children's literature issue of *META*. Her research falls within the DTS and 'contact and transfer' camps, and examines the heavy use of adaptation in 52 German versions of *Nils Holgersson* (1906–1999). Desmidt draws on norm studies in particular: she identifies a range of translational norms (literary/educational, pedagogical, and business/economical) which feed into the publishing process and which she shows have contributed to an overall tendency to prioritise the norms of the target rather than source literary culture (2003, 168).

This overview of English-language scholarly treatment of *Nils Holgersson* reveals a body of research which is relatively limited, particularly in translation and publishing history terms. In response, the remainder of this essay will now make preliminary steps in attempting to address the lack of scholarship cited by O'Sullivan and Lathey regarding the historical context of translation, namely through the means of the chronological publishing history of the 'contact and transfer' of *Nils Holgersson* from Sweden to the US and UK. This survey includes a consideration of the principal publishers involved in translating *Nils Holgersson* for the anglophone audience (classed by O'Sullivan as 'international mediators'), as well as occasional references to O'Sullivan's 'delayed' and 'non-translations'. Finally, this essay to some degree also responds to Lathey's discussions relating to the 'erratic phenomenon' of retranslation (2010, 173) by beginning to examine textual elements (for example, deletions, insertions) and especially paratextual factors (for example, illustrations, blurbs, appendices),which are relevant to building a publishing history of *Nils Holgersson*.[5]

English translations, adaptations and retellings

Despite modest levels of scholarly interest in *Nils Holgersson*, the text itself has merited more commercial attention in terms of American and British published translations and adaptations than any other text of modern Scandinavian children's literature translated into English. Swedish *Pippi Longstocking* numbers only three translations since the first into English in 1950 (Berry forthcoming), with most works of Scandinavian children's fiction surviving in a single translation. *Nils Holgersson* proves the exception, demonstrating the ongoing popularity of the text with publishers and readers. As Lathey observes, 'Whatever commercial or personal considerations are at play, retranslation or even republications of translations are rare occurrences largely limited to books that achieve the cachet of "classics"' (2010, 174).

The original US translation of *Nils Holgersson* by Velma Swanston Howard has endured, appearing in a revised British two-volume edition by Dent and used in a 'revised' US version in the early 1990s. Two picture books were published in 1967 (USA) and 1989 (UK). In 2013, the first translation of the complete original Swedish text appeared in the UK.

Translation by Velma Swanston Howard (1907 and 1911 onwards): early US and UK editions[6]

The Wonderful Adventures of Nils appeared in English in 1907, published in New York and London by Doubleday. Volume One was illustrated by Harold Heart and contained an appendix on Swedish pronunciation and a twelve-page translator's introduction. Volume Two included a foreword by Swanston Howard (including mention of Lagerlöf's help in the abridgement) and was illustrated by Astri Heiberg.[7] Doubleday reissues appeared regularly in the US up to *c.*1939, with Harper publishing an edition featuring new illustrations by Mary Hamilton Frye in 1927. From 1947, Pantheon published the title with illustrations by Baumhauer, and continued to do so until the 1960s. In Britain, reprints were issued by London publisher Arthur Bird from 1908 until *c.*1925 when the title went of print. Editions of the second volume, *The Further Adventures of Nils* (1911), are less prolific in English: it was published by Doubleday, New York, and the London publisher Hodder & Stoughton, with a further British Heiberg-illustrated edition reissued by Arthur Bird before the volume then went out of print.[8]

J. M. Dent (1950 onwards): two-volume and omnibus editions

London publisher J. M. Dent, best known for its *Everyman* series of budget classic titles, published a version of Swanston Howard's translation in 1950 using the Baumhauer illustrations. This went on to become the best known British edition, reprinted until the 1970s and still available in second-hand markets. The second volume was issued in 1953 but reissued only in 1957, 1963, and 1970. The Dent edition based on Swanston Howard was partially 'revised', although the precise extent of this adaptation has not been investigated here. The bibliographical page of Volume One states that the Dent version 'has been revised for this edition first published in Great Britain 1950', with a similar acknowledgement in the second volume.[9]

Illus. 1. *The wonderful adventures of Nils* (1950/1975), tr. Velma Swanston Howard (London: J. M. Dent). Cover illustration by H. Baumhauer.

Although the dust jacket and covers vary from edition to edition, each volume contains a colour frontispiece by Baumhauer and a short half-page biography of Lagerlöf. Volume One contains a Table of Pronunciation, revised from the original Swanston Howard glossary. Maps of Sweden are omitted, as are the chapter headings including chronological dates used in the original Swedish version. The volumes contain nearly 300 and 250 pages of text respectively.

Dent issued a one-off paperback omnibus of the two volumes in 1984 as part of their Children's Illustrated Classics Paperback series. This replicated their original two hardback editions, with a colour cover illustration based on Baumhauer's coloured frontispiece from Dent's hardback Volume One. This edition was reissued in 1999 by Puffin.[10] Neither omnibus paperback edition cites the fact that the original translation has been revised.

Dent clearly had considerable commercial interests in the *Nils Holgersson* title, reissuing it regularly and investing in the expense of a paperback omnibus version, activities that only key bestselling products would merit. However, these activities were cut short in 1988 when the publishing house was purchased by Weidenfeld and Nicolson, forming part of the Orion Publishing Group from 1991 and owned by Hachette Livre since 1998. It is surprising that such a successful title has not been exploited by subsequent owners in the form of the reprints, picture books, and simplified versions so prevalent elsewhere with other children's bestsellers.

Adaptation by Tage and Kathrine Aurell and Richard E. Oldenburg (1967)

Following the Swedish colour film of *Nils Holgersson* (1962), the Swedish children's publisher Bonniers Juniorförlag published a picture book version in 1967. The Kenne Fant film used a simplified plot focused on Nils and his journey within a modern Swedish setting: the subsequently shortened edition of the novel was taken on as an international co-edition featuring stills by Hans Malmberg. The American edition was translated by Richard E. Oldenburg and published by Doubleday in New York in 1967: this was not widely available in the UK, and Dent evidently did not think a British edition commercially viable.

The American edition seems to be a direct translation of the Swedish version 'edited' by the Värmland author Tage Aurell and his wife Kathrine Aurell. In order to transform a full-length two-volume novel into a picture book for younger children, considerable changes in length, layout, and readability were required to reduce the work from 55 to 17 chapters, involving extensive rewriting and adaptation. Further research needs to be undertaken to compare the Swedish and American versions and to establish whether further revision occurred during the American translation. Preliminary analyses based on the representation of the first nine chapters of Swanston Howard's Volume One in the picture-book edition show that, despite some rearrangements of the original chapter boundaries, the material in this version remains more or less intact for the opening sequences at least. The episode in Volume Two with the student in Uppsala is included, contrary to its deletion in the original Swanston Howard version. However, it is evident that material later in Volume One and also in Volume Two has been considerably adapted or deleted, given the considerable reduction in length of the complete work.

Uniquely, the first title page contains the translation of an untitled short poem by Lagerlöf: 'The Skåne boy meets many dangers on his journey. | Earth's animals and Heaven's birds can barely keep him safe. | I, who sent the poor thing on his way, | rejoice over every little friend who gives him refuge, | hides him in his heart.'[11] The remainder of the book contains nearly 100 pages of combined photographs and text (as well as full-page photographs) and includes a map and the chronological dates from the original Swedish version.

Adaptation by Rebecca Alsberg and Joan Tate (1992)

A second picture book was published by Bonniers Juniorförlag in 1989, based on the abridged version by the Aurells. Alsberg regarded the Aurell edition of the picture book as 'hopelessly out-of-date' and 'boringly dull' (Desmidt 2003, 178): her edition was therefore lavishly illustrated by Swedish artist/author Lars Klinting.

It was assumed that the text of Alsberg's version would mirror the previous Aurell edition, but this did not prove to be the case in a preliminary analysis of the representation in the Alsberg picture book of the first nine chapters of Swanston Howard's version as compared to the Aurell edition. Contrary to Alsberg's attempts to reintroduce some of the original plotlines and dialogue into the text (such as part one of Chapter 3 in Volume One, 'On the farm', where Nils rescues Sirle the squirrel and its young from a cage), other alterations in the chapter structure and additional deletions result in a text removed further still from Lagerlöf's original structure as presented by Swanston Howard in 1907 and 1911. The original chronological chapter headings are not used in this edition, presumably given the radically altered chapter structure.

The Klinting edition was reissued on several occasions and is still available widely internationally. The front and rear endpapers contain a two-page colour spread of a map of Sweden, and the volume itself contains just under 100 pages. It concludes with a one-page endnote

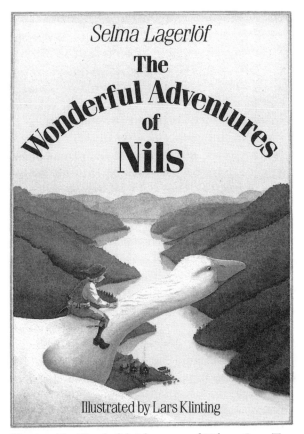

Selma Lagerlöf
The
Wonderful Adventures
of
Nils

Illustrated by Lars Klinting

Illus. 2. *The Wonderful Adventures of Nils*, tr. Joan Tate (Edinburgh: Floris Books, 1992). Cover illustration by Lars Klinting. The text had been adapted by Rebecca Alsberg and Joan Tate, 1992.

by Rebecca Alsberg on Lagerlöf and the history of *Nils Holgersson* as a schoolbook.

Floris Books in Edinburgh capitalised on the Dent takeover and popularity of *Nils Holgersson*, publishing their British co-edition in 1992. Established as a publisher of Swedish children's picture books (including Elsa Beskow), Floris Books had created a strong niche market for the European picture book, particularly within Scandinavian ex-pat communities (Berry 2012). The founder, Christian Maclean, was sufficiently familiar with *Nils Holgersson* to be keen to take the title,[12] and Joan Tate was a prolific British translator of Scandinavian literature already known to both the Scottish and Swedish publishers, later translating four Elsa Beskow titles for Floris during the 1990s. Floris later published a Swanston Howard translation of Lagerlöf's *Christ Legends* as a non-picture book title (1993) and an Ilon Wikland picture book (2004).

Revised version by Nancy Johnson (1991 and 1992)

Skandisk Inc in Minneapolis promotes and sells literature, music, cookery books and other 'gifts with a Scandinavian accent', according to the copyright page of the paperback of *Nils Holgersson* (1991, 2). Primarily a bookseller and distributor of English-language Scandinavian children's books, Skandisk has also published a small amount of Scandinavian literature and music. Their two-volume paperback set of *Nils Holgersson* (1991 and 1992) marked their publishing début within the field of children's literature.

The rear-cover blurb of Volume One celebrates 'one of Sweden's best-loved children's books'. Volume One includes a three-page historical and literary 'Foreword' and comprises about 250 pages, with a two-page black-and-white map. Volume Two is of a similar length, containing Swanston Howard's original 'Table of Pronunciation' and a 'Final note' by Johnson summarising the plot and the work's standing as a 'two-volume treasury of adventure and learning for the entire family' (1992, 211). Unattributed (Baumhauer) black-and-white pencil illustrations taken from the 1947 Pantheon edition are used throughout, including both full-page and smaller illustrations and many which do not appear in the Dent editions, as well as colour covers by an unattributed artist.

The Skandisk edition is not a new translation of the original Lagerlöf text as Swanston Howard's text has largely been kept intact but has been 'revised' by an intermediary editor, Nancy Johnson.[13] Although a detailed analysis has not yet been undertaken in comparison with Swanston Howard, it appears from a preliminary survey that the 'story itself is intact' from the first English translation with plot and chapters complete.[14] Revisions have taken the form of modernisation and updating of Swanston Howard's language (for example, 'The tomten' for 'The elf' in the sub-heading in Chapter 1 in Volume One, and 'earthen' changed to 'clay' in the sub-chapter heading for Chapter 16). Similarly, some of the longer descriptive paragraphs have been split into shorter paragraphs, and the chapter titles include the original chronological dates contained in the original Swedish version.

Illus. 3. *The wonderful adventures of Nils*, tr. Velma Swanston Howard (reprint; New York: Dover Publications, 1995). Cover illustration by Thea Kliros.

Swanston Howard reprint by Dover Publications (1995)

A paperback version *The Wonderful Adventures of Nils* was published in New York in 1995 in the series Dover Children's Books which the blurb announced as an 'inexpensive, unabridged edition [which] will bring new generations of readers under the magical spell of a timeless classic'.

A full reprint of the first volume of Swanston Howard's 1907 translation, the text was reset in this edition 'in easy-to-read type' in 219 pages and with ten new full-page ink illustrations by Thea Kliros as well as a colour front cover by Paul E. Kennedy. No maps are included. According to the 'Bibliographical Note' included in the copyright page, this edition used the original 'unabridged, unaltered' Swanston Howard translation, also retaining the 'Translator's Introduction' (4 pages) and 'Glossary: Table of Pronunciation'. The second volume was not reprinted by Dover, for reasons which remain unclear.

New and complete translation by Norvik Press (2013)
The Swanston Howard translations have had a full and varied life, resulting in numerous editions, reprints, and adaptations since their first appearance in the UK and the US in the early twentieth century. With the passing of time, however, Swanston Howard's translations have inevitably been criticised by critics past and present, not least her rudimentary linguistic errors and textual deletions. Peter Graves observed of *Nils Holgersson* in 2011 that 'Velma Swanson Howard's original is a pretty appalling example of just how slapdash some early 20th-cent. translators and publishers were' (email to the author, 27 February 2011).

Norvik Press (Department of Scandinavian Studies, University College London) seeks to address this issue, and is publishing the 'Lagerlöf in English' series of her most significant works in high-quality new translations. This venture has included the commissioning of a comprehensive translation of *Nils Holgersson*, with the result that the 'intact' text of *Nils Holgersson's Wonderful Journey Through Sweden* became available for the first time to the anglophone community in two volumes in early 2013. As an established literary translator and scholar, Graves himself was well positioned to take on the challenge, with a number of other translations from Swedish published by Norvik Press, and *The Phantom Carriage* already completed for the series. Although the front cover of *Nils Holgersson* fits in with the overall sequence of the other Lagerlöf series titles (designed by Sture Pallarp), new black-and-white textual illustrations by Bea Bonafini have been included in addition to a map of Sweden.

Unfortunately this new translation was published too late for inclusion in this article. However, it offers for the first time an opportunity for a full and detailed analysis of the strategies undertaken during translation and publication. Reviewers, Lagerlöf scholars, and others with an interest in *Nils Holgersson* have welcomed this new translation which will undoubtedly stimulate fresh debate and interest in Lagerlöf and *Nils Holgersson* alike.

Conclusion

This essay has sketched out an innovative publishing history of *Nils Holgersson* in English. As such, it forms part of the current functional and cultural discourses taking place within descriptive translation studies from the perspective of contact and transfer studies. It opened with a brief overview of published scholarship relating to *Nils Holgersson* within an anglophone setting, thus drawing attention to past and current academic explorations of the text. The majority of this research has hitherto taken place within literary or children's literature contexts. However, Desmidt's work (2003) on the body of German translations of *Nils Holgersson* and her analysis of translational norms (literary, pedagogical, and commercial) forms a useful framework for future work on other translations of *Nils Holgersson*. Sundmark's analysis of *The Further Adventures of Nils* (2009b) focuses on deletions and omissions from Lagerlöf's original Swedish text and highlights the overriding literary and textual impacts of this strategy rather than undertaking an in-depth and systematic translation studies analysis of the adaptation and revisionist strategies utilised.

The existing literary focus on *Nils Holgersson* inevitably means that many other central aspects of the text's history, publication, translation, adaptation, and reception as yet remain unexplored. This essay has sought to begin to readdress this balance, by focusing on delivering a chronological and factual publishing history of the text in English. Each American and British edition has been examined in turn in bibliographical terms.

Completeness and adaptation were found to be issues of particular interest, previously highlighted by Lathey (2010) and O'Sullivan (2005) as key factors in their consideration of contact and transfer studies. With the first Swanston Howard translation cutting significant amounts of material, and with subsequent editions adding further revisions, additions and deletions, it quickly became evident throughout this analysis that *Nils Holgersson* in its twentieth-century editions has been inherently unstable as a text. Only with the new 2013 complete translation has the text realised its original form and structure in English for the first time in its history, and it remains to be seen how the translation strategies and norms utilised here as a whole have impacted on the transfer of the text from source to target culture. The full-length English translations following that of Swanston Howard continued to be 'revised', albeit in as yet not fully understood terms, generally taking the form of altered or modernised use of vocabulary. However, the Dent edition did also include some more extensive omissions and deletions. Adaptation and rewriting were unsurprisingly the strategies used in the publication of the two picture book versions in 1967 and 1992, where the original English-language text of nearly 550 pages was reduced to 100 pages including numerous illustrations. In both examples, numerous differences in deletions and omissions of chapters and chapter sections from the original text into often new chapter arrangements make a suitably detailed textual comparison and analysis extremely challenging.

As suggested by Lathey (2010), paratextual features have proved a useful means of unpicking some of the publishing history of *Nils Holgersson*. Comparison of bibliographical data such as text length, blurbs, inclusion or omission of forewords, afterwords and appendices, illustrations, and covers has proved key in building a picture of the (in)completeness and fluidity of the work throughout its lifetime to date. Maps have been used in all editions apart from that of Dent, and the Baumhauer illustrations have proved by far the most popular in the non-picture book editions, although the dust jackets have often been redesigned in order to keep the text fresh and appealing to new audiences.

O'Sullivan's concept of publishing houses as 'international mediators' has also been used beneficially throughout this article, although future research making use of publishing archives may help to answer further questions concerning how the text and its paratexts have been presented in each new edition. Doubleday gets the credit for undertaking the first American and British editions, but quickly lost interest in *Nils Holgersson*, with later mid-century US editions published by Pantheon and little evidence of other versions until the 1990s (Skandisk and Dover). J. M. Dent similarly gets the credit for sustaining British interest in the title over a prolonged period from 1953 up to the house's demise in 1988, after which point Floris Books have published their picture book version (1992). O'Sullivan's notions of 'delayed' and 'non-translations' also feature throughout the publishing history of *Nils Holgersson*, in the non-appearance of a US edition of the Alsberg picture book, the non-appearance of a UK edition of the Aurell picture book, and the inexplicable failure of any UK publisher in the post-Dent era to reissue the work in novel form (other than that of Puffin in 1999) until 2013. In particular, future scholarship within the areas of reception and the text's function within the British and American historical and cultural situations would be welcomed as a means of understanding the reasons for the undeniable and sustained appeal, both commercially and culturally, of transferring this text to new anglophone audiences via British and American publishing houses, past and present.

This essay has demonstrated indisputably the suitability of applying Lathey's term of the 'erratic phenomenon' of retranslation to the example of *Nils Holgersson*, which remains a source of inspiration for future discovery and analysis. It is hoped that this brief study of *Nils Holgersson* in its English guise will help to generate future research interest in the fields of publishing history and translation, as well as contributing further to a broader and in-depth understanding of the complex publishing history of *Nils Holgersson* across the more than 40 languages into which it has now been translated. This essay's emphasis on contact and transfer within the publishing history context has laid the foundations for further strands of research into the cultural, political, historical, and literary depths of this fascinating and challenging text.

Notes

1 Rahn published an updated article in 1995.

2 Another major contribution to anglophone scholarship regarding *Nils Holgersson* is the conference proceedings for the Lagerlöf conference held in Stockholm in September 1997 (Vinge 1998), which contains a range of relevant articles in either Swedish or English by Peter Graves, Bjarne Thorup Thomsen, Sandra L. Beckett, Isabelle Desmidt, and Noriko Thunman.

3 Nation and education, in addition to ecology and nature conservation—all topics which are key to Lagerlöf's writings—are explored in further detail by Oscarson (2009) and Cabanel (2007). They are not discussed here since these articles do not relate directly to the translation and publishing history framework of this chapter.

4 These two episodes nevertheless do appear in a much abridged format in the 1967 and 1989 English-language picture books.

5 Lathey notes that consideration of all these factors is necessary in order to describe fully the (re)translation history of a particular text.

6 Bibliographical research here has been based upon international library catalogues and second-handbook catalogues. Due to the occasional incompleteness of these two sources, some US and UK reprints may have been omitted unintentionally.

7   As no attempts have been made here to compare the Swanston Howard translations with the original Swedish edition, it is recognised that further research is needed in this area in order to assess in detail the scope of omissions and deletions from the source text.

8   There appears to have been little US interest in the title for several decades post 1945, perhaps as the British Dent editions appear to have been available on the American book market from the 1950s onwards.

9   When compared to the Dover 1995 reprint of the original Swanston Howard translation, some of the extent of Dent's revisions rapidly become evident. For example, Americanisms in Swanston Howard's text have been removed and replaced with British equivalents, such as 'father' for 'pop', 'second' for 'jiffy', 'uncommonly industrious' for 'thrifty', 'heap[ing] up the measure of his misfortune' for 'piling it on' etc. in Chapter One.

10 Sundmark regards the Puffin edition as 'Essentially a brushed up and "Britified" version of Swanston Howard's translation' and as the 'most readily available edition today of (almost) the entire work' (2009a, 170). Although this partly seems to be the case in the US, further investigation has revealed that this Puffin edition does not seem to have been readily available in the UK and it is not now available through the major British research libraries or second-hand market. For a title of such prolonged popularity and steady sales, it is perhaps unusual that an edition did not appear in Puffin until this relatively late date. Further research into the publishing history and the completeness of the translation is evidently needed.

11 I have been unable to trace the original Swedish text of this poem.

12 Personal interview, Christian Maclean and Charlotte Berry, Edinburgh, 27 Feb. 2012.

13 Johnson does not seem to be known in the US or elsewhere as an editor, author, or translator apart from a similar contribution to Skandisk's revised edition of the Norwegian Torill Thorstad Hauger's *Captured by Vikings* in 1995.

14 The revised style of narration in this version aside, analysis of the content of the Skandisk edition (taken from the original Swanston Howard translation) can also contribute indirectly to revealing some of the extent of deletions made in the Dent edition. For example, the first part of Skandisk's Chapter Two 'In Närke' recounting the tale of Ysätter-Kaisa the weather-witch is entirely absent from Dent, as are the sections narrating the marking of houses for Death during the Black Plague (II ch. 14) and the replanting of trees on the mountain following a forest fire (II ch. 9).

CHAPTER 22

'Dear Selma'—'Dear Velma'

Velma Swanston Howard's
letters to Selma Lagerlöf

Björn Sundmark

The translation and publication of Selma Lagerlöf's work into English has long remained a relatively unexplored field of research. Peter Graves's analysis of the British reception of Lagerlöf's work (1998) and Steven Sondrup's notes on some of the translations are among the exceptions (1997).[1] However, given the importance of Selma Lagerlöf and her writings—in Sweden and internationally—this does not amount to much, especially in comparison to the studies of the Russian, Polish, German, and French translations of Lagerlöf (Vinge 1998). This essay is an attempt to redress the situation to some extent. The relatively meagre crop of critical writing on Lagerlöf in English cannot be explained by lack of material. Most of her books were translated and published in several editions (albeit small) in both the US and the UK, and are readily available for linguistic as well as literary analyses. Moreover, the Swedish National Library in Stockholm holds the surviving correspondence between Selma Lagerlöf and her main translator into English, Velma Swanston Howard (1868–1937): in all, 543 letters from the period 1908–1935. It is a collection that provides a rich context to many of the translations into English. I have previously tapped this material for a case study of Swanston Howard's translation of the first volume of *Nils Holgersson* (*The Wonderful Adventures of Nils*) (Sundmark 2009a). In another article I have highlighted Lagerlöf's translation instructions to Swanston Howard (2013). Here, however, I will focus on Swanston Howard's letters, and what can be inferred from these about her views on translation. I am also interested in Swanston Howard as Lagerlöf's American connection and mouthpiece.

Until quite recently the role of the translator has as a rule been played down in translation studies. If the author is 'dead', as it were, the translator has not been worthy of consideration at all: s/he has not figured as a corpse, not even a ghost. This has resulted in text-oriented analyses, where the source language text has been compared to the target language text with the help of linguistic and/or literary tools. A central concern for such comparisons has been to find out whether (and to what extent) the target language text retains linguistic and cultural features of the original, or if it fits seamlessly into the target language and culture. In other words, the central concern has been whether a translation is 'invisible', to use Lawrence Venuti's term. Another main issue has been whether a faithful translation is the same thing as a literal one, or one which attempts to reproduce the *effects* of the original. Polysystem theory does not promote either of these positions, but provides an explanatory framework on a macro-level for why accommodation is more common when translating from a lower-status language to a higher-status language, or why higher-status genres/authors retain more source language features than generally permitted in the translation of lower-status genres/authors (Shavit 1986; Toury 2012). In the context of Lagerlöf studies one can note, for instance, that greater liberty has been taken with Lagerlöf into English than with, for instance, Kipling into Swedish (where, for instance, *The Jungle Books* have been translated *in extenso*). Polysystem theory explains this by pointing to the higher status of English compared to Swedish. It is also symptomatic that the one work by Lagerlöf that has been bowdlerized most severely in translation is *The Wonderful Adventures of Nils*—the only book by Lagerlöf that can be labelled children's literature.[2] Again, within the translation system (or economy), children's literature is generally accorded lower status than adult literature (Shavit 1986). In sum, and as far as I can see, there is nothing wrong with the comparative approach outlined above, nor with the issue of accommodation versus faithfulness, nor with polysystem theory—each of these approaches can be justified depending on contexts, aims, and so on—but they are not sufficient. Swanston Howard's experiences, interests, and beliefs, and her relationship with Lagerlöf all have a bearing on the translation process: they are the fruits of the dreams and aspirations and hard work of individuals. As I shall attempt to demonstrate here, it is necessary, therefore, to draw on biography when studying translations.

In this case the biographical information must be pieced together from the letters themselves; there are almost no secondary sources. This is not entirely surprising. In the cases of older texts, translators often remain unacknowledged, or are hidden beneath a pseudonym or indicated only by humble initials. And even when the identity of the translator is no mystery in itself, little may be known about the person anyway. The case of Velma Swanston Howard is typical in many ways. Generally accessible sources such as libraries and online databases provide scant information about her. All that can be gathered from *Who Was Who in America* and comparable sources is that Velma Swanston Howard was born in Sweden on 24 January 1868 and died in New York on 10 March 1937, that she graduated from the Boston School of Oratory in 1888, that she married a Charles Howard, and, finally, that she was a translator of Selma Lagerlöf and August Strindberg. In addition to this, databases such as *Chronicling America* (http://chroniclingamerica.loc. gov/) can provide half a dozen news articles where her name is cited. It is meagre, even if we only consider her translation work—after all, Lagerlöf and Strindberg are major international authors—but Swanston Howard was, moreover, one of the first to stage Ibsen in America, and a pioneer suffragist. Against this background, the lack of information on Velma Swanston Howard is almost provocative.

By reading her translations in tandem with her letters to Lagerlöf, a great deal more can be ascertained. In the following I will provide some clues to Swanston Howard's character gleaned from her letters to Lagerlöf, and show how these traits may be pertinent. I will also provide a sample letter *in extenso*, and demonstrate how many of the identified characteristics surface in this one sample text.

First of all there seems to be a critical consensus that Swanston Howard was not a particularly adept translator (Graves 1998; Sondrup 1997). Yet, she was quite possibly her own harshest critic: indeed, lack of self-confidence is one of her characteristics. Filled with self-doubt she would revise passages over and over again, or she would listen to the advice of academics, editors, and authors and edit accordingly. In a letter to the publisher Henry Holt written early in her career as a translator she writes: 'I realize that my work needs reviewing, & I shall let a good critic go over them hereafter before submitting my MSS' (11 Aug. 1908). Unfortunately the end result was not usually an improvement on the first draft. Lagerlöf even implores her in one letter not to overdo things, asking: 'Isn't the simple English of your letters good enough?' (17 Jan. 1923).[3]

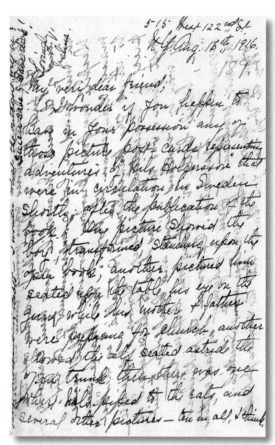

Illus. 1. Letter from Swanston Howard to Lagerlöf, 16 August 1916.

For many years, Swanston Howard was a strong adherent of Christian Science. Positive thinking and the power of prayer are central tenets in Christian Science, and Swanston Howard often mentions how she has healed herself and others through prayer. Her at times quite open proselytising is met with polite interest from Lagerlöf, but nothing more. At least one direct effect of Swanston Howard's Christian Science worldview can be seen in the translation of *The Wonderful Adventures of Nils*, where she added a few lines to the narrative of Mats and Osa (in a sub-plot to the main story about Nils and the flight of the geese). In the original, the two children wander the land, teaching everyone they meet how to battle consumption by observing scrupulous hygiene. For Swanston Howard this was not enough, and she added that 'clean thoughts' are as effective against tuberculosis as bodily cleanliness. Indirectly, too,

one can see the effect of Christian Science in Swanston Howard's dis-
like of descriptions of illness and squalor. Pessimistic literature is not
Swanston Howard's cup of tea. She eventually turned from Christian
Science to Theosophy and the teaching of Madame Blavatsky, but her
literary likes and dislikes remained essentially unchanged. For instance,
after having read Theodore Dreiser (on Lagerlöf's recommendation),
Swanston Howard had to take an antidote in the form of Ernest Renan's
Life of Jesus. And she really could not forgive Lagerlöf and the Swedish
Academy when, in 1930, they awarded the Nobel Prize for Literature
to Sinclair Lewis. It is also characteristic that she preferred translating
Lagerlöf to Strindberg, commenting:

> Selma Lagerlöf on the other hand [compared to Strindberg, that
> is], is vivid, sympathetic and poised in her work. With her the
> translator is not dealing with a mind diseased, nor does he need
> to go thro' heaps of muck and rubbish to find the gems. (Letter to
> Henry Holt, 8 Aug. 1908)

It can be added that the 'gems' she eventually found in Strindberg were
Lycko-Pers resa (*Lucky Pehr* or *Lucky Peter's Travels*) and *Sagor* (*Tales*). In
Swanston Howard's article, 'Selma Lagerlöf, Sweden's Idolized Writer:
A Woman who Has Conquered All Europe with her Pen', it is clear
what it is that attracts her to Lagerlöf's writing:

> Selma Lagerlöf might well be called the founder of a new school
> of literature. She arrived at the psychological moment when the
> literary tendency of Europe was morbidly realistic. She saw what
> other writers had seen—only in another light. Hers was the seer's
> vision rather than the critic's judgment, and so clear was her vision
> that she discovered life where we had seen but dead things and gray.
> (Swanston Howard 1912, 416)

Swanston Howard in fact frequently comes close to idolising Lagerlöf,
something she is keenly aware of herself. On 12 August 1908, she writes:

> It is nearly two years now that I have done little else than working
> on your matter, and it is small wonder that at times I do not know
> whether I am you or myself! I played a dramatic role once which so
> completely possessed me that I had to give it up. I am so sensitive

> I have to guard against the danger of absorption. People think I
> have a strong personality—but I haven't—only strong sympathies.

Her sympathies, however, did not extend to her husband Charles Howard
(always referred to as Mr Howard in her letters). They rarely lived under
the same roof, and their marriage was apparently not very happy. There
were no children, except a grown-up step-daughter. Swanston Howard
even talks in one of her letters about getting a divorce—but this came to
nothing. At least the couple were prosperous in the early years of their
marriage, and Swanston Howard was allowed go to Europe (first class)
almost every year and indulge in her artistic and intellectual hobbies. Mr
Howard was the provider, and it was not for lack of money that she was
afraid that he might not pay for a trip to Sweden, but rather that he 'has
had a green moment', as she calls it, and that he suspected that she had
taken a lover in Sweden. Ironically, many years later, Mr Howard lost his
position, became ill and then lost all his (and his wife's) savings in one
of the bank crashes of the Great Depression. His wife had to take him
in, and eventually all they had to live on was the meagre income from
her translations. For several years Lagerlöf also gave Swanston Howard
an annual sum of money to keep her from destitution.

Politically, Swanston Howard was committed to the campaign for
women's suffrage, belonging to the same circle of activists as Charlotte
Perkins Gilman, and for many years she acted as the Secretary of the
Professional Women's League in New York. In an extract from another
letter she emerges as Lagerlöf's American mouthpiece for women's rights:

> Dear Selma; I just have to sit down and write you about what hap-
> pened this afternoon. At the urgent request of Miss Hay I translated
> your Congress speach [sic]. First I hesitated, thinking that maybe
> another translator would appear; but as none had come to this
> country, at least, I finally decided to go ahead. Spent two weeks
> carefully putting it into concise & clear English.
>
> This afternoon was International Day of The Equal Suffrage League
> of New York and I was down as one of the speakers. So I took this
> opportunity of reading this speech in addition to my own remarks.
>
> Well, my dear, the effect was magical! The women & a few scat-
> tered men positively spellbound from start to finish. It was almost
> like that night in Stockholm—some sobbed & some had tears
> streaming down their cheeks.

When I sat down the applause was deafening. One woman rose and moved that a letter of thanks be sent to you for this beautiful paper, another proposed a note of thanks to the translator and interpreter of the speach [sic].

My ideal is to have it printed in pamphlet form, as in Sweden, and to let the Suffrage leaders spread it as a campaign document, all to help on the Cause here, that is, if you are willing. (3 Nov. 1911)

The speech was published in 1912 under the title 'Woman, the savior of the state: her fundamental achievement in her world, and man's half-success in his, as the basis of the demand for suffrage'. For Swanston Howard, Lagerlöf's political activism was not a side issue to the more important task of writing literature. When she writes about Lagerlöf to an American audience, as she does in the article quoted above, she begins by providing an image of the political Lagerlöf: 'When the International Woman Suffrage Congress met in Stockholm last June, it was the spirit of Selma Lagerlöf that dominated the Congress of Nations' (1912, 416).

However, while Swanston Howard was radical when it came to equal rights for women, she was deeply conservative when it came to most other things, and a staunch royalist at that. Sweden to her was 'a land of song and sagas', as she called it in one of her first letters to Lagerlöf, a country where the old ways were still cherished, in contrast to the 'hurley-burley' of America. Thus nothing upset Swanston Howard more than when she perceived a threat to the social fabric of Sweden. Class struggles were anathema to her. In a letter prompted by the 1909 General Strike in Sweden she wrote:

It is with a sense of pain and sorrow that I read of the labor strife in Sweden! When I think of the many dear friends there, I tremble lest they be swept by this maelström of hatred and blind unreason. These Godless, self-seeking socialist leaders have played upon the worst passions of the workmen until they have turned a quiet, orderly and well paid class into a frenzied mob of destroyers. (11 Aug. 1909)

I have summarised some of the main themes of Swanston Howard's letters, themes that also reflect some of her character traits, opinions and interests. But overviews and summaries and short quotations do not convey the personality of the correspondent as well as a complete letter, nor do they accurately represent the cadences and structure of her writing. The following sample letter, quoted *in extenso*, may serve as a point of entry:

Del Monte, 102 West 75th St, N.Y. Feb 2nd '07
My Dear good friend; Your very welcome letter received, and a few days later came the book [*The Wonderful Adventures of Nils*, I]. I will confess to you that I began reading it in the morning, read all day, & never let go until midnight, and then I was sorry there wasn't more of it. I have not read anything since Hans Christian Andersen so quaint and altogether fascinating. The next day I sat down & wrote Mr Holt about it, got an answer asking me to translate 20 passages from the book, for his consideration.

But I find I'm up against some difficulties: for we have no English to match inimitable Swedish expressions. I should have to substitute American child and bird talk—and it wouldn't be the same.

The book is a classic.

I think it is equally interesting to children of all ages;—say from nine to ninety. I have always loved children's stories, and this one of yours I love best of all. Thank you for sending it. I shall always prize it.

My dear you must write that Swedish-American book. I never could do it. In the first place I have never written a novel, and such a work wants something besides an entire novice's handling. If you only spend six months here, with your keen perception, you'd soon catch on to things. For instance, take the queer way in which Swedes mix American and Swedish idiom—only a thoroughbred would understand the humour of this. I can help you gather together a lot of data, & explain certain American idiosyncracies & take you about where you could see for yourself & get local colour. I can save you a lot wear and tear on detail work; but the real flavor & essence of literary production, you only could handle.

Don't let any doubts as to your physical endurance stand in your way, for I'll keep you well with Christian Science. I help all my friends to get well, & keep well. Even the Norwegian girl who had been sick with heart disease for several years, has been entirely cured. She looks like a new creature; and I'm going to get her a place on the American stage, to play parts where broken English [is] required. And this after the great doctors in Paris, London and

Copenhagen said she never would be able to play again. She does not care to go back to Christiania she says.

What a shame that you should be so ill in bed all thro' the Christmas holidays! I do hope that you are quite well and strong again. Take good care of yourself, do.

Do you know I had a rather trying time of it with 'Brand' [Ibsen's play]. A large and fashionable audience, with not more than ten present who could understand its depth of meaning. The glittering diamonds and gorgeous attire of my hearers nearly took my breath away! I wish American women spent more time cultivating their souls and minds, and gave less attention to studying the fashion plates. One can't do both thoroughly—and it's so hard for an artiste to do all the work, when people simply will not think for themselves.

I hope to take a trip to Chicago before very long, as my husband is out there. I have not seen him since October first. This is American life—the husband away most of the time—wife left to herself. I'll [look] up your sister-in-law when I get there. Seattle, by the way, is a fine place for a rising young man—there are excellent opportunities for every sort of enterprise. You have certainly proved a God send to your people—they are fortunate to have such a loving, generous hearted sister.

I do hope my husband will let me go back to Sweden this summer. It is my one great happiness to which I look forward. You don't know how hard it is here, sometimes. I am such a misfit in this hurley-burley. You mustn't think I'm a great personage here, or a big success—for I'm not. They call me odd and different—they find my work too 'foreign', 'too analytical', 'too full of sentiment', not American—breezy and practical—& prefer to write for Sweden. It [the US] is not a land for me.

On Thursday a newspaper woman interviewed me on prominent Swedish women & what they are doing. This is for a syndicate of 3000 newspapers. She said, she'd give you a fine send off—all these items help bring your name before the public.

As soon as my agent succeeds in selling some more of the Legends [*Christ Legends*], she shall send me a cheque for you. It's slow work getting good work on our market. Americans read such a lot of rot! They have to be educated into a taste for better things. It's only the cultivated few who can appreciate fine art and literature.

By the way, I got a very beautiful letter from Count Celsing, king

Oscar's secretary, in answer to mine. The king was deeply touched by the little incident I related about the school children. What a rare soul is our good old king: so human; so tender hearted! I'm glad he is better. May he live many years yet!

Well, dearie, I think I've told you about all the news. God bless you! Live well & happy & strong. Lovingly yours, Velma Swanston Howard

The letter opens with comments on the first volume of *Nils Holgersson*, published in 1906. Swanston Howard is very enthusiastic and perceptive in her comments. She identifies it as a book for 'children of all ages', and does not hesitate to label it 'a classic', although many (including Lagerlöf herself) initially doubted its appeal outside Sweden.

She mentions that she immediately contacted a publisher (Holt). There was no copyright agreement between the US and Sweden until 1911. In many ways this made translators and authors vulnerable since self-styled translators could pick up any book, translate it, and sell it to a publisher, and neither the author nor the author's original publisher could expect any remuneration. However, it was customary that a serious translator, like Swanston Howard, who was keen to remain on good terms with an author, would split the royalties with the author. In other words, the situation for the translator was precarious in a number of ways. On the other hand, in this pre-copyright period it was often the translator who took the initiative and who had a measure of control. The publisher was dependent on the translator for the contact with the author, and also for suggestions about what to translate. In the letter quoted we see how the process works: Lagerlöf sends a book to Swanston Howard, who likes what she reads; she then contacts a publisher and is asked for a sample translation. One can also infer from this that Swanston Howard was more of an amateur translator than someone translating professionally and/or out of financial necessity. She took on work that inspired her, and where she had a personal relationship with the author.

Swanston Howard voices doubts as to the translatability of the work, mentioning Lagerlöf's 'inimitable Swedish expressions'. Here we find an example of Swanston Howard's lack of self-confidence as a translator. She emphasises the difficulty of the task at hand by implicitly referring to Lagerlöf's genius and, more explicitly, to the richness of the Swedish language, especially in its vernacular forms.

In what follows Swanston Howard tries to persuade Lagerlöf to

Illus. 2. Selma Lagerlöf at Mårbacka.

write 'The Great Swedish-American Immigrant Novel'. It is a topic
that Swanston Howard brings up several times. But since she very
rarely proposes any other book ideas, it is possible that her main
purpose is to persuade Lagerlöf to visit her in the US. In any case,
Lagerlöf never rises to the bait, although the issue is not laid to rest
completely until many years later, when Lagerlöf writes: 'I think I
may have lost my appetite for travel with the death of Sophie Elkan.
She was such a magnificent traveller. I cannot fathom what it would
be like to journey in someone else's company' (25 February 1924).[4]
Interestingly, Lagerlöf had already suggested that Swanston Howard write on the theme of immigration. Two weeks before the letter
quoted above, she wrote to Lagerlöf:

> I am taking the liberty of sending you a type written copy of a little
> story I've just written.—It is the outcome of your suggestion to try
> & write some short tales of 'utvandrare.' This is my first attempt
> in that line.—Please tell me what you think of it? Your judgment

would be of great value to me—and you can be quite frank. (Letter 7 Feb. 1907)

Lagerlöf's opinion is unrecorded, but the resulting text, 'När Maja-Lisa kom till Sverige' ('When Maja-Lisa came to Sweden'), was eventually published in Sweden as part of a series of anti-immigration pamphlets.

In the following section Swanston Howard makes a plea for Christian Science. As I have already shown, this is a recurring theme in her letters to Lagerlöf. She then comments on a performance of Ibsen's *Brand*. Swanston Howard was a great admirer of Ibsen and one of the first to stage his plays in the US. This was at a time when, as she writes, 'only short haired women and long haired men would be seen at an Ibsen lecture or performance' (11 May 1908). In the present example, however, she does not say anything about Ibsen or the play as such, except vaguely talking about its 'depth of meaning'; she seems rather more interested in the play's social function as an occasion for the fashionably intellectual and affluent to be seen. Swanston Howard often criticised contemporary American society for being shallow and materialistic, and tended to regard Sweden, and especially Lagerlöf, as its spiritual and political opposite.

In the subsequent paragraphs Swanston Howard develops this theme, and we can see how this section relates to her own personality and life history, culminating in her self-deprecatory remarks about her sense of alienation in American society. Moreover, in the same passage we get a glimpse of Swanston Howard's conjugal situation. From this letter we understand that husband and wife meet only rarely, and that it was Mr Howard who decided whether his wife could go to Sweden or not.

As we have seen in the passages above, Swanston Howard also engaged herself in Lagerlöf's American concerns, with regard to business as well as more private matters. In this particular letter she promises to visit Lagerlöf's sister-in-law in Chicago and, in what is clearly a reference to Lagerlöf's brother Johan who had been living in Seattle since 1906, recommends the city as good place for a 'rising young man'. She also gives Lagerlöf an update on the sales of *Christ Legends* and (as an explanation for why so few copies have been sold) takes another dig at the lack of sophistication of the American reading public ('they read such a lot of rot'). Swanston Howard also mentions a newspaper feature that she hopes will promote Lagerlöf's work. It is clear that Swanston Howard had multiple roles to fulfil. For her it was certainly not just a question of translating words from one language into another.

The letter ends with a reference to Count Celsing and the King (Oskar II), an indication of Swanston Howard's royalistic and conservative bent.

To sum up, I have endeavoured to shed some light on Velma Swanston Howard's character as it emerges in her correspondence with Selma Lagerlöf. I have also shown that one letter (or a few), read through the lens of the extant corpus of letters, can provide insights into translation practices that would otherwise remain invisible. I believe that analyses carried out on a systemic and meta-literary level are necessary, but they need to be complemented by micro-studies of individual cases. Through the letters we get a glimpse of publishing, marketing and editorial practices. More importantly, we get insights into Swanston Howard's world-view (conservative, religious, feminist, idealistic, anti-modernist), her personality, her financial and marital status, her intellectual and linguistic competence, and her relationship to Lagerlöf. It becomes obvious that all these factors influenced Velma Swanston Howard's work as a translator.

Notes

1 See Forsås-Scott (2010) as well as the volumes in the series 'Lagerlöf in English', each of which has an afterword by the translator (Norvik Press, London, 2011–). See also my articles on Lagerlöf, all more or less concerned with translation issues.
2 Peter Graves's 2013 translation of *Nils Holgersson* (Norvik Press) is the first unabridged version in English—more than a hundred years after the original publication.
3 'Duger inte den enkla engelska du skriver i dina brev?'
4 'Jag har nog också förlorat reslusten, sedan Sophie Elkan dog. Hon var en sådan överdådig resenär. Jag kan inte tänka mig in i hur det skulle vara att resa med ett annat sällskap.'

CHAPTER 23

Selma Lagerlöf in Nazi Germany: Not banned, not forgotten

Lord Arne's Silver as a Nazi Frontbuch

Jennifer Watson

As early as 1933, Selma Lagerlöf, the Nobel Laureate, wrote a met-aphorical protest against Nazi fascism, 'Skriften på jordgolvet' ('The Writing on the Ground'), the royalties and proceeds of which she donated to help Jewish intellectuals escape Nazi Germany. Her letters clearly illustrate the pain and dismay she felt at the state of Europe, and specifically Germany, in the 1930s. And in 1940, essentially on her deathbed, she aided in the flight of the young Jewish poet, Nelly Sachs, and the latter's mother from Nazi Germany to Sweden.

Yet, Lagerlöf continued to be published in Nazi Germany, even through the war years. Goebbels's Propaganda Ministry was respon-sible for the censorship of literature in Germany, including translations. The ministry specifically targeted translations in its attempt to 'cleanse' German society of foreign influences and as early as 1935 required blanket pre-publication censorship of translations. The only other form of writing that was subject to this type of censorship, so early on, was political writing. For a translated text to be approved, a sample of the translation, a summary of the work, a detailed description of the author and his or her racial background, and also a rationale of the work's contribution to the German understanding of the foreign nation had to be provided to the publisher. It was the publisher, though, who essentially regulated the censorship, and hence, the process was not fully formalised nor was it very coherent. Most publishers played it safe in such a climate, publishing translated works that were already in print, and/or avoiding overtly political themes. They also often changed the titles and covers of translations in order to cast the books in a more German and even Nazi light (Sturge 2002, 154).

What is interesting is that the number of translations of fiction published in the 1930s consistently rose until the outbreak of war, from about 9 to 12 per cent of the fiction in Germany (Sturge 2004, 56–7), a phenomenon that indicates the widespread popularity of foreign fiction in Germany. The aspirations of the Propaganda Ministry that 'foreign' literature would be completely overshadowed by German fiction were not fulfilled.

There were shifts, however, in the publication of translations during this decade, in that the proportion of reprints rose in the 1930s compared to first edition publications, for reasons indicated above. Also striking is the shift with regard to source languages, particularly from 1939 onwards. The top source languages during the Weimar period included English, French, Norwegian, Danish, Swedish, Russian, Italian, Flemish, and Dutch. The predominance of English was particularly striking: there were three times as many translations from English than from the next language, French. The only rival to English as a source language, if taken as a group, were the Scandinavian languages. With the outbreak of war, though, French and English completely fell out of favour with the Propaganda Ministry (although not necessarily with German readers), and the Scandinavian languages gained an even greater share of the market, as did Flemish. These languages were praised by the German literary journals of the time as 'Germanic' and 'not truly foreign'. They were considered acceptable as long—of course—as the texts were not 'cheap' and the authors were not critical of the Nazi regime (Sturge 2002, 159–60).

Though Lagerlöf *was* critical of the regime, she still continued to be published in Nazi Germany and never appeared on the 'Liste des schädlichen und unerwünschten Schrifttums' ('Secret list of detrimental and undesirable books') (Ahe 1982, 292–3). In fact, it appears as if her publication figures in Nazi Germany rose later in the period.[1] Moreover, her novella, *Herr Arnes penningar* (*Lord Arne's Silver*) was published as a *Frontbuch* (1943) for German soldiers in Norway.[2]

Other Scandinavian authors, such as Sigrid Undset and Sally Salminen, who were also very popular in pre-Nazi Germany, were banned after having made anti-Nazi statements. Why not Lagerlöf? Because no written files were kept in the censorship offices in Germany outlining the reasons for censorship or promotion of foreign language fiction,[3] one can only make an educated guess.

Clearly the banning of Lagerlöf in Nazi Germany would have hurt publishers commercially, specifically the Langen-Müller Publishing House.[4]
Outside Scandinavia, Germans were Lagerlöf's biggest audience—most of
her major works never went out of print in Germany during her lifetime
(or up to 1944 for that matter) (Watson 2004, 30–1). Ideologically, the
banning of Lagerlöf could have hurt the Nazis because from the start of
her fame in Germany, she had been presented as a Nordic roots writer,
and by the 1930s, she had an almost canonised status in Germany. How
could the Nazis explain her protest against them and their banning of
her? It would have been difficult, and in fact, in Lagerlöf's case, unnecessary. 'Writing on the Ground' was never translated into German, and
according to Nils Afzelius' *Selma Lagerlöfs bibliografi. Originalskrifter* (70),
only one German newspaper, *Die schlesische Zeitung*, even mentioned the
work, and that only briefly. Moreover, from 1933 to her death in 1940,
Lagerlöf was suffering from poor health, and hence made few public
appearances or statements. As a result, the general public in Germany was
essentially unaware of her anti-Nazi sentiments, and in fact, as indicated
by the letters in the Lagerlöf archive, many Nazi sympathisers simply
assumed she shared their beliefs (Watson 2004, 3).

Hence, Lagerlöf continued to be published and held up as a representative Germanic writer, and, in fact, was even used by the Nazi government. For example, *Nils Holgerssons underbara resa genom Sverige* (*Nils
Holgersson's Wonderful Journey through Sweden*) was taught in German
schools as a means of learning about the Germanic lands and people,
with Lagerlöf annually receiving letters from classes of German school
children praising her book;[5] and *Lord Arne's Silver* in 1943 and *Gösta
Berlings saga* (*Gösta Berling's Saga*) in 1944 were made into *Frontbücher*
for the Nazi soldiers in Norway, as source texts on people and landscape.

According to Kate Sturge in her article 'Censorship of Translated
Fiction in Nazi Germany', the types of fiction that were most promoted
by the regime were the historical novel and animal stories, both of
which had to be apolitical and with little or no reference to the outside
world (2002, 161). In the case of a *Frontbuch*, the piece of fiction had
to reflect the true nature of the country and people that were being
occupied, and that Nature would inevitably be Germanic, underlining
why the Germans were there (Sturge 2003, 10).[6] Translators were then
encouraged to accentuate stereotypical gender hierarchies and also the
forces of law and order in the works (Sturge 2002, 164).

Although *Lord Arne's Silver* cannot be categorised as either historical

Illus. 1. Cover of *Herrn Arnes Schatz. Erzählung.* Front-
buchhandelsausg. für die Wehrmacht, Munich, 1943.
Artist unknown.

fiction or an animal story, it does have a historical basis and is apolitical.
Moreover, in the eyes of the Nazis, the novella portrayed the Nature of
the country and people: a rugged landscape of snow and ice, inhabited
by pure and authentic characters whose society appears to contain no
evil, except that which comes from the outside.

Aspects of gender hierarchy and law and order can also be identified
in the original novella and the *Frontbuch* version. It is the women who
are innocent, tender-hearted, and care for others, as demonstrated by
Elsalill's terrible grief at the loss of her loved ones and her openness

with and compassion for Sir Archie.[7] The men are the heads of the household, give orders, and take action, as demonstrated not only in the character of Lord Arne but also in those of the Scottish soldiers.

Gender roles are emphasised even more strongly in the *Frontbuch*, and visually captured in the picture placed on the front cover. Up until the front book edition, the *Frontbuch* covers of the German translations of *Lord Arne's Silver*, entitled *Herrn Arnes Schatz*, did not include pictures. Rather, the covers usually consisted of the title, author, and publisher—written in *Fraktur*—with little decoration. Interestingly, on the *Frontbuch* cover, the *Fraktur* is replaced with writing in broad strokes, indicating action and strength. The picture above it, which dominates the cover, portrays a heroic figure, again of action and strength. He is looking sternly forward, carrying a frail-looking woman who is clearly clinging to him for protection. She looks frightened of something close by and in need of his help.

The picture is a complete stereotype of gender roles, and one, actually, that is not represented in the original work, nor in any of the German-language versions (including the *Frontbuch* text). The man can only be Sir Archie and the woman, Elsalill; yet, the only time that Sir Archie holds Elsalill in his arms—when she is still alive—is when he attempts to flee the men who have come to capture him and uses her as a living shield. She is not afraid of those around her, as it appears on the cover, but rather of Sir Archie. Nor does she cling to him for protection. In the story, she reaches out and guides a spear into her heart so that Sir Archie no longer has protection. Sir Archie is thus not portrayed as a heroic figure in the work.

Clearly, the picture reinforces gender stereotypes but in no way represents the book. As is well known, Sir Archie does not march off with the girl clinging to his neck; the ice around the ship, which is to carry him home, does not break until Sir Archie and his comrades are caught and Elsalill's body is retrieved. The forces of law and order prevail—whether reinforced by God or by Nature—and the criminals will be brought to justice.

Although the book cover and the content do not mesh, they do both fulfil many of the Nazi specifications for books. One has to ask, though, of all the Lagerlöf books, why *Lord Arne's Silver* as a *Frontbuch* for Nazi soldiers in Norway? Fair enough, the novella was one of Lagerlöf's most popular works in Germany—so popular that numerous German writers adapted the story, including the Nobel Prize winning German author, Gerhart Hauptmann[8]—but the work revolves around three 'bad guys' who are depicted as three foreign soldiers in sixteenth-century Bohuslän, at the time part of Denmark. Would this not have been seen as a somewhat parallel situation to the Nazis in Norway?

The only answer that makes sense is no; but then, why not? It is fairly safe to say that Germans at that time saw the Scandinavians as kindred spirits, and in fact, maybe even as the purest representatives of the Germanic race. Hence, the Nazi occupation of Norway did not consist of foreign soldiers in Scandinavia, but rather of Germanic soldiers in a Germanic land. Further, German soldiers were also members of this good and pure society which was protected, by God, Nature or both, from foreign evil doers.

In order to underline the idea of kindred spirits—that Norwegians, Danes, Swedes, Germans: all were Germanic people, and hence the same—the translation of Lagerlöf's work chosen for the *Frontbuch*, although fairly accurate in content, alters the text stylistically. The *Frontbuch* translation was done by Pauline Klaiber-Gottschau and is one that makes the work read much more like a German text.

Interestingly, Langen-Müller did not use the officially-sanctioned German translation of *Lord Arne's Silver*, that of Marie Franzos (under the pseudonym 'Francis Maro'). In 1943, they commissioned a new translation of the work, labelling it the 'officially sanctioned translation', although they most certainly did not have Franzos's or Lagerlöf's permission. Franzos, of course, had no choice in the matter because she was a Jew.[9] Lagerlöf was probably not informed.

One might suspect that Mizi Franzos had forfeited her contract with Müller-Langen in 1933 with the Nazi *Gleichschaltung* (forcible coordination) of publishing contracts.[10] However, the bibliographies from Quandt and Schweitzer, and Ahe's *Rezeption schwedischer Literatur in Deutschland: 1933–1945* clearly indicate that Franzos's translations continued to be published and attributed to her.[11] Even more interesting is the online *Deutsche Nationalbibliographie*, which indicates that even her translation of *Herrn Arnes Schatz* was reprinted at this time.[12]

Hence, the question is why Langen-Müller commissioned a completely new translation of this one specific work, especially in light of the financial hardships in Germany at this time? And why this translation for the *Frontbuch* and not that of Franzos?

The translator they chose for the new translation was Pauline Klaiber-Gottschau, who was the official German translator for Lagerlöf's longer works. The letters in the Lagerlöf archive indicate that Pauline Klaiber (later Klaiber-Gottschau, when she married in 1918) first contacted Lagerlöf in 1901, asking for the rights to translate *Jerusalem*. She was referred to Langen, who had recently become Lagerlöf's publisher in Germany, and by 1903 she had become the official translator of all of Lagerlöf's longer works, while Franzos's role was that of the official translator of the shorter works (Weniger 1994, 46).[13]

Kerstin Weniger in her dissertation, '*Gösta Berling* in deutscher Übersetzung. Studien zur übersetzerischen Rezeption Selma Lagerlöfs', attributes at least some of Lagerlöf's popularity in Germany to Klaiber-Gottschau's translations. In her concluding remarks on Klaiber-Gottschau's translation of *Gösta Berlings Saga*, she writes:

> The reader, who thinks that he is encountering the North in *Gösta Berling* is dealing with a translation that brings the text to him by way of his homeland (Schleiermacher's famous phrase). Hence, it is not surprising that Selma Lagerlöf found such a strong resonance in Germany and that for decades all her works enjoyed such high publication rates. (Weniger 1994, 143)[14]

The translation of *Lord Arne's Silver* that Klaiber-Gottschau produced for Langen-Müller is also very 'germanised', in contrast to Franzos's translation, which remained much truer at every level to the original text.

In contrast to her translation of *Gösta Berlings Saga*, though, and many of her other translations of Lagerlöf, Klaiber-Gottschau did not use existing translations, including Franzos's, as a starting-point. She did, however, use the version of Lagerlöf's text which the Germans knew, for the German version of the text was different from the Swedish one. Distressed that Elsalill was left so alone in death, Lagerlöf decided, after sending the original ending to Bonnier, to change the ending. In the revised ending, Elsalill is retrieved and welcomed into the folds of her ghost family, a resolution that Lagerlöf believed to be more comforting. It was too late for the Swedish version, but it was incorporated into the German version (Watson 2004, 100).[15] Despite the fact that Langen republished the work numerous times, the original ending, which remained the ending in Sweden, was never used—not even in the new translation in 1943.

Yet, it is not just the ending which indicates that the work is aimed at a German audience. Already on the first page of *Herrn Arnes Schatz*, it is obvious that Klaiber-Gottschau is translating the text for the Germans of the 1940s. For example, in the first sentence of the work, she explains what Bohuslän is, whereas Lagerlöf does not.[16] It also becomes clear on the first page that she is creating a text that would seem more recognisable, less foreign, to a German audience. For example, she lengthens sentences by combining a number of Lagerlöf's shorter sentences.[17]

There are numerous examples of this lengthening, but one in particular that is striking for other reasons too can be found in the third section of Chapter 1. Here Lagerlöf has the Branehög neighbour describe his feelings as he watched the three Scotsmen sharpen their knives: 'I felt as though three werewolves had come into my hut. I was glad when they left us at last' (Lagerlöf 2011b, 23).[18] Klaiber-Gottschau combines the sentences: 'Mir war, als seien drei Werewölfe in meine Hütte hereingedrungen, und ich war froh, als sie sich endlich davon machte' (Lagerlöf 1943b, 20).[19] Klaiber-Gottschau not only combines sentences, giving more German texture to the narration, she also infuses the speech of the poor charcoal-burner with greater intensity. Not only does he use Subjunctive I to describe the situation—something even educated Germans do not necessarily use—but he uses descriptive verbs such as *hineindringen* ([had] forced) rather than the direct translation *gekommen* ([had] come) which Franzos has him use (Lagerlöf 1904c, 20). The language of the charcoal-burner is replaced with a much more refined register of speech. Klaiber-Gottschau also reduces this trait in the narrator, creating a narrator who is much less of a storyteller.

To return to the first page, what is perhaps most striking, or in this specific case, shocking, is Klaiber-Gottschau's subtle change to the introduction and description of Torarin, the only character introduced on the first page (besides the dog). He is introduced in the first sentence: 'lived in Marstrand a poor travelling fishmonger, whose name was Torarin' (Lagerlöf 2011b, 15),[20] which Klaiber-Gottschau translates as 'wohnte in Marstrand ein armer Fischhändler, namens Torarin' (5).[21] Not only does the use of 'namens' rather than the direct translation, 'der Torarin hiess'[22] (as Franzos translated it, 5) elevate the language being used, but it also somewhat depersonalises Torarin, making him sound more like an object than a person. The narrator then goes on to describe Torarin:

> He was a weak and lowly man. One of his arms was palsied, so he could neither fish nor row a boat. He could not earn his living at sea, like all the other men of the skerries, but he went round selling salted and dried fish to folk on dry land. (Lagerlöf 2011b, 15)[23]

Klaiber-Gottschau's version reads:

> Er war ein schwächlicher, geringer Mensch. Sein einer Arm war gelähmt, und so taugte er weder zum Fischfang noch zum Rudern. Und deshalb konnte er sich auch nicht, wie alle die anderen Männer auf den Inseln, seinen Unterhalt auf dem Meere verdienen; er zog nur umher und verkaufte gesalzene oder getrocknete Fisch an die Leute auf dem Festland. (Lagerlöf 1943b, 5)[24]

Perhaps the first thing that stands out is Klaiber-Gottschau's translation of the Swedish 'man' as 'Mensch' (Franzos chose 'Mann', 5). She, in a sense, emasculates Torarin as well as depersonalises him. Her use of 'schwächlich' for 'svag' is also an interesting choice. Franzos chose 'schwach' (5) which is much closer to the Swedish word, implying infirm or frail, whereas 'schwächlich', which can indeed mean frail, also implies sickly, weak, even wishy-washy—a much more negative connotation. The same is true of 'gelähmt' for the Swedish 'lam' (Franzos chose 'lahm', 5). Although both German words, 'gelähmt' and 'lahm', mean palsied or paralysed, 'gelähmt' embodies a harsher fate.

Yet, it is not only Klaiber-Gottschau's choice of words that is striking. Her additions and omissions suggest the light in which she wishes to cast Torarin. After the description of Torarin's arm, Klaiber-Gottschau begins the next sentence with 'Und deshalb', which has no equivalent in Lagerlöf's text. Klaiber-Gottschau directly links Torarin's palsied arm to his inability to work like all the other men, whereas Lagerlöf leaves that conclusion up to the reader. In the second clause of the Swedish sentence, Lagerlöf uses 'utan' to connect to the first clause, making it clear that although he could not fish, he did work. Klaiber-Gottschau removes any equivalent of 'utan' and makes a new sentence, connecting the two notions with a semi-colon, and in so doing, stresses the fact that Torarin could not work like all the other men. There is then a pause and she tells the reader what he does do, adding the word 'nur' to the sentence, thereby demeaning what he does—he *just* goes around selling fish.[25] Klaiber-Gottschau's translation creates a harsher judgment on Torarin as the only man in the workforce with an infirmity.

There are other changes to character descriptions throughout the work, although nothing as blatant as in the description of Torarin. Klaiber-Gottschau's translation depicts the character of Elsalill as befitting the visual image on the *Frontbuch* cover. Elsalill and her foster sister are both identified as 'jungfru' ('maid') in the Swedish. Klaiber-Gottschau generally translates the word as 'Mägdlein' or 'Mädchen', dimunitives for 'young girl' (Franzos uses 'Jungfrau' or 'Jungfer'[26]). By choosing dimunitives as translations for 'jungfru', Klaiber-Gottschau underlines their innocence, purity, and helplessness. Klaiber-Gottschau's choice of adjectives for the girls also supports this portrayal. Lagerlöf often describes the girls as 'späd[a]', 'tender' (Lagerlöf 1904b, 40, 41), which Klaiber-Gottschau translates as 'schwach', 'weak' (Lagerlöf 1943b, 32). Franzos has 'zart', meaning 'tender' or 'sweet' (Lagerlöf 1904c, 31).

As on the *Frontbuch* cover, the initial horrific appearance of Sir Archie and his friends is diminished. The Branehög neighbour describes their appearance: 'They looked dreadful, with great beards that had not been trimmed or groomed for many a good day' (Lagerlöf 2011b, 23).[27] Klaiber-Gottschau removes from the men any active responsibility for their appearance—it is not that they had not shaved themselves, as expressed in the Swedish, but rather that they had unshaven faces— and in the first part of the sentence, she changes the description of the men as 'terrible', instead making the whole scene look 'terrible': 'Es sah furchtbar aus. Sie hatten grosse Baerte, die gewiss schon lange nicht mehr geschnitten noch gekämmt waren' (Lagerlöf 1943b, 16).[28]

This reduction of the terribleness of the Scots seems to be an attempt to bring the text in line with the German fairytale, specifically the *Kunstmärchen* (a literary fairytale in contrast to a folk fairytale) (Weniger 1994, 142), which played an important role in New Romanticism in Germany at the turn of the twentieth century (and also played into Nazi ideology). As Weniger points out in her dissertation: 'Appearances, passions, and actions that were too wild were subdued. ... That applied not only to the depiction of people but also to Nature' (1994, 143).[29] Indeed, mirroring the more subdued description of the Scotsmen are the descriptions of Nature. A prime example can be found in the portrayal of the arson attck on Lord Arnes's parsonage, which Lagerlöf's text describes in the following terms: 'The flames had not had time to do more than blacken the good timber of the wall and melt the snow on the thatched roof. But now they were taking hold of the roof straw' (Lagerlöf 2011b, 24).[30] The flames literally bite into the roof, becoming a character in the text, whereas in Klaiber-Gottschau's version they do not even appear in the second sentence: 'denn die Flammen hatten das gute Balkenwerk der Hauswand grade nur geschwärzt und den Schnee auf dem Strohdach zum Schmelzen gebracht. Jetzt aber fing das Stroh auf dem Dach doch zu brennen an' (Lagerlöf 1943b, 17).[31] The strong effect of biting flames is curbed, simply becoming a description of the fire in the *Frontbuch* translation.

Klaiber-Gottschau depersonalises Nature throughout, especially in her choice of verbs. Instead of directly translating the verbs which Lagerlöf uses for actions in Nature, actions that are usually attributed to people, Klaiber-Gottschau replaces them with verbs that do not necessarily point to people. One example, among many, is the description of the ice breaking up at the end of the story. Lagerlöf's text has: 'The sea was running high, and pieces of ice were still dancing on the waves' (Lagerlöf 2011b, 83),[32] which Klaiber-Gottschau translates as: 'Die See ging hoch, und auf den Wogen schaukelten noch Eisstücke' (Lagerlöf 1943b, 88).[33] The drama and activity of the sea have been muted, moving Lagerlöf's novella closer to a *Kunstmärchen*.

Klaiber-Gottschau also reconciled Lagerlöf's text with the *Kunstmärchen* by means of its syntax and narrative style. Lagerlöf's narrator is clearly telling a story in the oral tradition. Sentences are relatively short and are rarely joined together to create longer sentences. Causality of events is implied, not explained with words such as 'therefore' and 'then'. The vocabulary is relatively simple and synonyms are not usually used,[34] as illustrated by the repeated use of 'sade' ('said') to present direct speech; Klaiber-Gottschau, on the other hand, uses 'sagen' ('to say'), 'erwidern' ('to respond'), 'versetzen' ('to alert'), and so on (Lagerlöf 1943b, 13, 15). Finally, there is consistent repetition in the telling of the story, not just in words, but also sentence construction. Lagerlöf repeatedly starts her sentences with the combination subject plus verb, whereas Klaiber-Gottschau removes this repetition, creating more of a written language than a spoken one, as is characteristic of the *Kunstmärchen*.[35]

That Langen-Müller made some very deliberate decisions with regard to the publication of *Lord Arne's Silver* in Nazi Germany is apparent in a number of ways: they kept the German ending of the novella because it would not be foreign to the German audience—it was *the* German ending; and despite the cost at a time of scant resources, they chose to retranslate the work. They clearly wanted a *Herrn Arnes Schatz* that affirmed its German identity. There is no doubt that they were well aware, by this time, of the differences between Franzos and Klaiber-Gottschau, and they clearly felt, or perhaps were told, that the expense was worth it.

Why *Lord Arne's Silver* as a *Frontbuch*? Because in the hands of Klaiber-Gottschau, and the anonymous artist of the front cover, it became a very German text, one that demonstrated the Germanic mindset of the Scandinavians, proving why Germans should be in Norway. It was transformed into a propaganda piece and became a text whose use Selma Lagerlöf would never have condoned.

Notes

1 Sturge, email to Jennifer Watson, 16 September 2007.
2 According to Quandt 1987–8, *Gösta Berling's Saga* was also published as a *Frontbuch* a year after *Lord Arne's Silver* in 1944.
3 Sturge, 16 September 2007.
4 Up to 1931, the Albert Langen Publishing House.
5 National Library of Sweden, Stockholm, Lagerlöf Letter Archive.
6 Sturge, Kate (2003) '"World Literature" in Nazi Germany: Translated Fiction and the Nationalist Agenda', unpublished lecture, Edinburgh Institute for the Advanced Studies of Islam and the Middle East, 27 Feb. Copy with Jennifer Watson.
7 This is not to say that women take no action in *Lord Arne's Silver*. In the end, it is Elsalill who stops Sir Archie through her action. Both Cheri Register (1983) and Helena Forsås-Scott (1997 and elsewhere in this volume) have feminist readings of the work. However, the characters can be—and too often have been—read as stereotypes of passive women and I believe this is how they were interpreted in the Nazi era.
8 Hauptmann adapted the novella in 1917 as a drama, calling it *Winterballade*.
9 By 1939, Franzos was out of work and living off a fund created for her by friends, to which Lagerlöf also contributed. She died in 1941 (Blumesberger, Susanne (2007), 'Ohne Übersetzung keine Weltliteratur. Porträt Mizi Franzos', unpublished lecture, Institut für Wissenschaft und Kunst, Vienna. Copy with Jennifer Watson).
10 *Gleichschaltung* was the Nazi term for bringing everything into line with their doctrine; for Verlag Albert Langen, see www.polunbi.de/inst/langen/html.
11 The bibliographies are not completely reliable, for Schweitzer, Quandt, and Ahe all ascribe published Lagerlöf translations to Franzos after 1933, including the *Frontbuch*. However, WorldCat, a global catalogue of library collections, confirms that other Franzos translations were indeed published after 1933.
12 The German National Bibliography indicates that Franzos's translation was published in 1941.
13 Kerstin Weniger (1994), 'Gösta Berling in deutscher Übersetzung. Studien zu übersetzerischen Rezeption Selma Lagerlöfs', unpublished dissertation, University of Leipzig.
14 'Der Leser, der meint, im *Gösta Berling* dem Norden zu begegnen, hat es mit einer Übersetzung zu tun, die den Text nach seinem Heimatland hin, "auf ihn zu" (Schleiermachers bekannte Formel) bewegt hat. So verwundert es auch nicht, dass Selma Lagerlöf in Deutschland ein derart starkes Echo fand und alle ihre Werke jahrzentenlang so hohe Auflagen erreichten.' All translations are my own.
15 According to Gunnel Weidel in *Helgon och gengångare*, Lagerlöf retained the Swedish ending because of Albert Edelfelt's illustration in the 1904 edition of the women of Marstrand following the bier with Elsalill's body across the ice, back to town (1964, 236).

16 She translates 'På den tiden, då kung Fredrik den andre af Danmark regerade öfver Bohuslän....' (9) as 'Zu der Zeit, da König Friederich II über den schwedischen Bezirk Bohuslän' (5). Interestingly, she is incorrect in attributing Bohuslän to Sweden in 1586, for at the time, it was a province of Denmark, as Lagerlöf's text makes clear by indicating that it was ruled by King Fredrik of Denmark.

17 Lagerlöf: 'Det var alldeles ödsligt och folktomt på vägen, men Torarin behöfde inte därför hålla sig tyst. Han hade bredvid sig på lasset en fullgod vän, med hvilken han kunde språka. Det var en liten svart hund med yfvig päls, som Torarin kallade Grim' (10); Klaiber-Gottschau's introduction: 'Es war sehr öde und menschenleer ringsum; Torarin aber brauchte sich deshalb nicht ganz still und stumm zu verhalten, denn neben ihm auf seinem Wagen hatte er einenn zuverlässigen Freund, mit dem er Zwiesprach halten konnte, nämlich einen kleinen schwarzen Hund mit buschigem Fell, den Torarin Grim nannte' (5). Again, interestingly, she indicates that Torarin is riding in a cart which is incorrect. He uses a horse-drawn sledge because it is winter.

18 'Jag trodde, att det var tre varulfvar, som hade kommit in i stugan. Jag blef glad, då de ändtligen gåfvo sig af' (27).

19 Lit. 'It felt to me as if three werewolves had forced their way into my cottage and I was happy when they finally left.'

20 'bodde i Marstrand en fattig fiskmånglare, som hette Torarin' (9).

21 Lit. 'lived in Marstrand a poor fishmonger of the name Torarin.'

22 Lit. 'who was called Torarin'.

23 'Han var en så svag och ringa man. Hans ena arm var lam, så att han dugde hvarken till fiske eller rodd. Han kunde inte vinna sitt uppehälle på sjön som alla andra skärgårdskarlar, utan han for omkring och sålde saltad och torkad fisk till folk på landbacken' (9).

24 Lit. 'He was a weak and slight person. His arm was palsied and so he was neither good for fishing nor for rowing. And therefore he could not, like all the other men on the island, earn his living on the sea; he just went around and sold salted and dried fish to the people on the mainland.'

25 My emphasis.

26 Both mean 'maid'.

27 'De sågo förfärliga ut, de hade stora skägg, som de inte hade klippt eller ansat på mången god dag' (27).

28 Lit. 'They looked terrible. They had big beards which certainly had not been cut or combed for a long time'.

29 'Allzu wilde Erscheinungen, Leidenschaften und Handlungen werden gedämpft. ... Das gilt nicht nur für die Personenschilderung, sondern auch für die Natur' (143).

30 'Lågorna hade inte hunnit mer än att svärta det goda timret i väggen och smälta snön på halmtaket. Nu höllo de dock på att bita sig fast i takhalmen' (30).

31 Lit. 'because the flames had only just blackened the timber work of the house walls and started to melt the snow on the thatched roof'.

32 'Sjön vräkte hög, och isstycken dansade ännu på vågorna' (141).

33 Lit. 'The waves went up and on the waves bobbed ice pieces'.

34 Weniger, 142–3.

35 Weniger, 142.

Bibliography

Unpublished material
Stockholm, Sweden

National Archives
Pressarkivet: Signaturregister

National Library of Sweden
Ep L45, Letters from Selma Lagerlöf
L 1:1, Letters to Selma Lagerlöf
Ep. L45 (40 letters) and Dep. 266 (76 letters), Letters from Selma Lagerlöf to Velma Swanston Howard
L1:1 and L1:1a, Letters to Selma Lagerlöf from Velma Swanston Howard (427 letters)
Anteckningsbok 11, 55a:11 fragments about train transportation through Sweden of German prisoners of war
L1: 247 Ligg-pf, Sn-Sö. Stämningar från krigsåren, In the compilation of manuscripts: 'Den fridsamme'
L1:335:1:2, Selma Lagerlöf's will (transumt)
ÄA F 1B, 225, Dossier *Stiftelsen Föremålsvård*, Afzelius, Nils (1989–90) 'P.M. för ordnandet av Selma Lagerlöfs brevsamling'
ÄA F 1B, 225, Dossier *Stiftelsen Föremålsvård*, Antonsson, Birgit (1989–90)

Swedish Film Institute
Sjöström, Victor. 'Körkarlen', unpublished manuscript.

Åbo, Finland

Åbo Akademi University Library
Manuscript Collections
Vån.II2:B:4, Hultman, Oskar Fredrik (1912), Diary of Oskar Fredrik Hultman (19 vol.).

Published material
Works by Selma Lagerlöf

Nils Afzelius (1975) *Selma Lagerlöfs bibliografi. Originalskrifter*, ed. Eva Andersson (Selma Lagerlöf-sällskapet Skrifter 11, Acta Bibliothecae regiae Stockholmiensis, 23; Stockholm: Kungliga biblioteket) contains all bibliographical details for the published original works of Selma Lagerlöf from 1886 to 1974.

First editions of all Selma Lagerlöf's major works are available free of charge and as open access as facsimiles, searchable e-texts, PDF files, or EPUB files at Litteraturbanken—The Swedish Literature Bank, <www.litteraturbanken.se>, a collaboration between the Swedish Academy, the National Library of Sweden, and a number of other institutions.

1888   *Officiel Vägvisare vid Verldsutställningen i Landskrona 1888* (Landskrona: H. F. Österberg & Sons Boktryckeri) (pub. anonymously).

1891a   *Ur Gösta Berlings saga. Berättelse från det gamla Värmland. Belönad med högsta priset vid Iduns större pristäfling år 1890* (presentation edn; Stockholm: Frithiof Hellbergs förlag).

1891b   *Gösta Berlings saga* (Stockholm: Frithiof Hellbergs förlag).

1892a   'De fågelfrie', *Svea. Folkkalender* 49, [51]–77.

1892b   'Riddardottern och hafsmannen', *Ord och Bild* 1, [256]–60.

1894a   'Mamsell Fredrika', in *Osynliga länkar* (Stockholm: Bonnier), 155–68.

1894b   'Dunungen', in *Osynliga länkar* (Stockholm: Bonnier), 253–96.

1895a   'Tale Thott: (Efter en folkvisa)', *Svea. Folkkalender* 52, [147]–68.

1895b   'Sång för slöjden. Otto Salomon tillegnad.' Gothenburg.

1896a   'Fiskarringen', *Svea. Folkkalender* 53, [175]–195.

1896b   'Santa Katerina af Siena', *Jul* 9, [3, 5–7].

1897a   *Antikrists mirakler* (Stockholm: Bonnier).

1897b   'Hämnd får man alltid', *Julafton* (Stockholm & Kristiania), 12–13.

1899a   *Drottningar i Kungahälla jämte andra berättelser* (Stockholm: Bonnier).

1899b   *En herrgårdssägen* (Stockholm: Bonnier).

1901a   *Jerusalem*, I: *I Dalarne. Berättelse* (Stockholm: Bonnier).

1901b   *Antikristovy zázraky*, tr. O. S. Vetti (Prague: J. Otto).

1902a   *Jerusalem*, II: *I det heliga landet. Berättelse* (Stockholm: Bonnier).

1902b   'En saga om en saga', in Gustaf af Geijerstam and Karl Warburg (eds.) *När vi började. Ungdomsminnen af svenska författare* (Sveriges författareförening; Stockholm: Ljus), 138–54.

1903a   *Herr Arnes penningar. Berättelse* (Iduns romanbibliotek: 33; Stockholm: Idun).

1903b   'Slöjdsång' [Frisian tr. of 'Sång för slöjden'], tr. Jantsje Terpstra ('Madzy'), *Sljucht en rjucht*, 115.

1904a   *Kristuslegender* (Stockholm: Bonnier).

1904b   *Herr Arnes penningar*, illus. Albert Edelfelt (Nordiskt familjebibliotek, 20; Stockholm: Bonnier).

1904c   *Herrn Arnes Schatz*, tr. Marie Franzos (Munich: Langen).

1904d   'Fågel Rödbröst', in *Kristuslegender* (Stockholm: Bonnier), 173–83.

1904e   'Ljuslågan', in *Kristuslegender* (Stockholm: Bonnier), 201–246.

1906   *Nils Holgerssons underbara resa genom Sverige*, I (Stockholm: Bonnier)

1907a   *Nils Holgerssons underbara resa genom Sverige*, II (Stockholm: Bonnier)

1907b   *The Wonderful Adventures of Nils*, tr. Velma Swanston Howard (New York: Doubleday).

1908a   'Tösen från Stormyrtorpet', in *En saga om en saga och andra sagor* (Stockholm: Bonnier).

1908b   *Christ Legends*, tr. Velma Swanston Howard (New York: Holt).

1909   *Meli. Berättelse. Med illustrationer i färg av Gerda Tirén* (Stockholm: Folkskolans barntidning).

1910a   *The Miracles of Antichrist*, tr. Pauline Bancroft Flach (Boston: Little, Brown).

1910b   *Jerusalem*, I: *V Dalarně*, tr. Emil Miřiovský (Prague: J. Otto).

1911a   *Liljecronas hem: Roman* (Stockholm: Bonnier).

1911b   *The Further Adventures of Nils*, tr. Velma Swanston Howard (New York: Double-day).

1911c   *Niels Holgerssons wonderbare reis*, tr. Margaretha Meijboom (Amsterdam: H. W. J. Becht).

1911d   *Podivuhodná cesta nezbedy Petra s divokými husami*, tr. T. E. Tisovský (Prague: nákladem Zemského ústředního spolku jednot učitelských v království českém)

1911e   *Hem och stat: Föredrag vid Rösträttskongressen den 13 juni 1911* (Stockholm: Bonnier).

1911/   'Home and State', tr. Velma Swanston Howard (Woman's Suffrage Party; [New
1912   York]: [1911]), abridged as 'Woman the saviour of the State: her fundamental achievement in her world, and man's half success in his, a basis of the demand for suffrage', in *The World's Work* (Garden City, NY: Doubleday, Page, 1912), 418–21.

1912   *Körkarlen. Berättelse* (Stockholm: Bonnier).

1913   *Podivuhodná cesta Nilse Holgerssona s divokými husami Švédskem*, tr. Karel V. Rypáček (Prague: Jan Laichter).

1914a   'Gammal fäbodsägen'. *Svenska turistföreningens årsskrift*, [1]–14.

1914b   *Kejsaren av Portugallien. En värmlandsberättelse* (Stockholm: Bonnier).

1915a   *Troll och människor*, I (Stockholm: Bonnier).

1915b   *Legendy o Kristu*, tr. Emil Walter (Prague: Alois Hynek).

1915c   *Podivuhodná cesta Nilse Holgerssona Švédskem*, tr. Emil Walter (Prague: Alois Hynek).

1915d   'Den heliga bilden i Lucca', in *Troll och människor*, I (Stockholm: Bonnier), 155–81.

1916   *Dimman*, illus. G. Sellberg Welamson (2°; Stockholm: Svenska andelsförlaget).

1917a   'Frid på jorden', *Julrosor*, [4–7].

1917b   'Lappland – Schonen', in Selma Lagerlöf, Verner von Heidenstam, Carl G. Laurin, Carl Grimberg, Esaias Tegnér, and Gustaf Fröding, *Schweden* (Stockholm: Norstedt), 3–24.

1918a   'Stämningar från krigsåren. Den lille sjömannen', *Idun* 31, 10–11.

1918b   *Bannlyst. En berättelse* (Stockholm: Bonnier)

1919   *Herr Arnes penningar*, illus. film stills (6th edn., Stockholm: Bonnier).

1921a   'Den lille sjömannen', in *Troll och människor*, II (Stockholm: Bonnier), 185–94.

1921b   'Dimman', in *Troll och människor*, II (Stockholm: Bonnier), 171–83.

1922   *Mårbacka*, I (Stockholm: Bonnier).

1924   *Mårbacka*, tr. Velma Swanston Howard (London: T. Werner Laurie).

1925a   *Löwensköldska ringen* (Stockholm: Bonnier)

1925b   *Charlotte Löwensköld* (Stockholm: Bonnier).

1928   *Anna Svärd* (Stockholm: Bonnier).

1930   *Mårbacka*, II: *Ett barns memoarer* (Stockholm: Bonnier).

1932   *Mårbacka*, III: *Dagbok för Selma Ottilia Lovisa Lagerlöf* (Stockholm: Bonnier).

1933a   *Skriften på jordgolvet* ('Säljes till förmån för insamlingen för landsflyktiga intellektuella' ['Sold for the benefit of the collection for exiled intellectuals']; Stockholm: Bonnier).

1933b 'Den öppnade dörren. Ett Brandes-minne', in *Höst. Berättelser och tal* (Stockholm: Bonnier), 62–71.

1933c 'Sophie Adlersparre (Esselde)', in *Höst. Berättelser och tal* (Stockholm: Bonnier), 31–53.

1933d 'Skriften på jordgolvet. Efter en gammal legend', in *Höst. Berättelser och tal* (Stockholm: Bonnier).

1936 'Hur jag fann ett romanämne', *Svenska Jerusalemsföreningens tidskrift* 35, 124–7.

1943a 'Hämnd får man alltid', in *Från skilda tider. Efterlämnade skrifter*, ed. Nils Afzelius, I (Stockholm: Bonnier), 174–80 (first pub. 1897).

1943b *Herrn Arnes Schatz: Erzählung*, tr. Pauline Klaiber-Gottschau (Wehrmachtausgabe [Wehrmacht *Frontbuch*]; Munich: Albert Langen, Georg Müller).

1943c 'Santa Lucia', in *Från skilda tider. Efterlämnade skrifter*, ed. Nils Afzelius, I (Stockholm: Bonnier), 159–73 (first pub. 1896).

1950/ *The Wonderful Adventures of Nils*, illus. Hans Baumhauer, tr. Velma Swanson
1975 Howard (abridged edn.; London: J. M. Dent).

1953 *The Further Adventures of Nils*, illus. Hans Baumhauer, tr. Velma Swanson Howard (London: J. M. Dent).

1957 *Podivuhodná cesta Nilse Holgerssona Švédskem*, tr. Dagmar Pallasová (Prague: SNDK).

1958 *Poklad pana Arna*, tr. Magda Trhlíková (Prague: Československý spisovatel).

1959 *Gösta Berling*, tr. Břetislav Mencák (Prague: Mladá fronta).

1961 'Patron Ivar Halenius', in Nils Afzelius, Gunnar Ahlström & Bengt Ek, (eds.) *Lagerlöfstudier 2, 1960* (Malmö: Selma Lagerlöf-sällskapet), 11–29.

1962 *Císař z Portugálie*, tr. Dagmar Chvojková-Pallasová (Prague: SNKLU).

1967a *Brev*, I: *1871–1902*, ed. Ying Toijer-Nilsson (Selma Lagerlöf-sällskapet skrifter, 7; Lund: Gleerup).

1967b *The Wonderful Adventures of Nils*, ed. Kathrine Aurell and Tage Aurell, tr. Richard E. Oldenburg (New York: Doubleday).

1971 *Löwensköldův prsten*, tr. Jiřina Vrtišová (Prague: Svoboda).

1984a *Liljecronův domov*, tr. Božena Köllnová-Ehrmannová (Prague: Vyšehrad).

1984b *The Wonderful Adventures, and The Further Adventures of Nils*, illus. Hans Baumhauer, tr. Velma Swanston Howard (London: J. M. Dent).

1991 *The Wonderful Adventures of Nils*, illus. Hans Baumhauer, tr. Velma Swanston Howard, rev. Nancy Johnson (Minneapolis: Skandisk).

1992a *The Wonderful Adventures of Nils*, illus. Lars Klinting, tr. Joan Tate, ed. Rebecca Alsberg (Edinburgh: Floris Books).

1992b *The Further Adventures of Nils*, tr. Velma Swanston Howard, rev. Nancy Johnson (Minneapolis: Skandisk).

1995 *The Wonderful Adventures of Nils*, illus. Thea Kliros, tr. Velma Swanston Howard (New York: Dover Publications).

1999 *The Wonderful Adventures of Nils and Further Adventures of Nils*, illus. Hans Baumhauer, tr. Velma Swanston Howard (Harmondsworth: Puffin).

2005 *Podivuhodná cesta Nilse Holgerssona Švédskem*, tr. Dagmar Hartlová (Prague: Meander)

2009 *The Saga of Gösta Berling*, tr. Paul Norlén (Harmondsworth: Penguin Books).

2011a *The Phantom Carriage*, preface by Helena Forsås-Scott, tr. Peter Graves (London: Norvik Press).

2011b *Lord Arne's Silver*, preface by Helena Forsås-Scott, tr. Sarah Death (London: Norvik Press).

2011c *The Löwensköld Ring*, preface by Helena Forsås-Scott, tr. Linda Schenck (London: Norvik Press).

2012 *Körkarlen: Berättelse*, introduction by Maria Karlsson, ed. Petra Söderlund and Jenny Bergenmar (Stockholm: Svenska vitterhetssamfundet).

2013a *Gösta Berlings saga*, ed. Petra Söderlund (Stockholm: Svenska vitterhetssamfundet).

2013b *Nils Holgersson's Wonderful Journey through Sweden*, preface by Helena Forsås-Scott, illus. Bea Bonafini, tr. Peter Graves (2 vols.; London: Norvik Press).

2014 forthcoming *Charlotte Löwensköld*, preface by Helena Forsås-Scott, tr. Linda Schenck (London: Norvik Press).

Other works

Afzelius, Nils (1961) 'Våld och barmhärtighet. En huvudlinje i Selma Lagerlöfs författarskap', in Nils Afzelius, Gunnar Ahlström & Bengt Ek (eds.) *Lagerlöfstudier 2, 1960* (Malmö: Selma Lagerlöf-sällskapet), 53–67.

—— (1975) *Selma Lagerlöfs bibliografi. Originalskrifter. Färdigställd av Eva Andersson* (Acta Bibliothecae regiae Stockholmiensis, 23; Selma Lagerlöf-sällskapet Skrifter, 1; Stockholm: Kungliga biblioteket).

Ahe, Karl-Rainer (1982) *Rezeption schwedischer Literatur in Deutschland. 1933–1945* (Hattingen: Dr. Bernd Kretschner).

Åhlander, Lars (1982) (ed.) *Svensk filmografi*, II: *1920–1929* (Stockholm: Svenska Filminstitutet).

—— (1986) (ed.) *Svensk filmografi*, I: *1897–1919* (Stockholm: Svenska Filminstitutet).

Ahlström, Gunnar (1942) *Den underbara resan. En bok om Selma Lagerlöfs Nils Holgersson* (Stockholm: Bonnier).

Ahmed, Sara (2004) *The Cultural Politics of Emotion* (New York: Routledge).

Allen, Judith A. (2009) *The Feminism of Charlotte Perkins Gilman: Sexualities, histories, progressivism* (Chicago & London: University of Chicago Press).

Althusser, Louis (2008) [1970] *On Ideology* (London: Verso).

Alù, Giorgia (2008) *Beyond the Traveller's Gaze: Expatriate Ladies Writing in Sicily (1848–1910)* (Bern: Peter Lang).

Anon. (1911a) 'Persoonlijkheden', *Algemeen Handelsblad*, 23 Feb., 5.

Anon. (1911b) 'Kvinnans storverk. Dr Lagerlöfs tal på Operan', *Socialdemokraten*, 14 June.

Anon. (1911c) [untitled review], *Het nieuws van den dag*, 27 Dec., 6.

Anon. (1917) 'Zweden. Op Mårbacka', *Nieuwe Rotterdamsche Courant*, 8–9 July.

Anon. (1919a) 'Ingmarsönerna', *Filmbladet* 5 (1), 16.

Anon. (1919b) ('Chinoise') Ett ståtligt svenskt filmverk', *Stockholms Dagblad*, 2 Jan.

Anon. (1919c) 'Ingmarsönerna', *Filmen* 3, 28.

Anon. (1919d) 'Selma Lagerlöf om "Ingmarssönerna" på filmen', *Stockholms Tidningen*, 2 Jan.

Anon. (1958) 'Selma Lagerlöfová', *Práce*, 23 Nov.

Anttonen, Erkki (2004) 'Edelfelt as an Illustrator', in Leena Ahtola-Moorhouse (ed.) *Albert Edelfelt 1854–1905* (Helsinki: Atheneum Art Museum, Finnish National Gallery), 215–35.

Arvidson, Jens (2007) (ed.) *Changing borders: Contemporary positions in intermediality* (Lund: Intermedia Studies).

Bachmann, Anne (2013) 'Souvenirs from the Selma Lagerlöf Silent Film Adaptations: How 'Beautiful' Book Editions and Prestige Cinema Collaborated in Swedish Visual Culture Around 1920', *Scandinavica* 51 (2), 184–207.

Bal, Mieke (1991) *Reading 'Rembrandt': Beyond the Word–Image Opposition* (Cambridge: CUP).

—— (1999) [1997] *Narratology: Introduction to the Theory of Narrative* (2nd edn., Toronto: University of Toronto Press).

Bannbers, Britta & Bannbers, Ola (1919) '"Ingmarsönernas" kulturvärde', *Dagens Nyheter*, 2 March.

Barthes, Roland (1994) [1975] *Roland Barthes par Roland Barthes* (Berkeley & Los Angeles: University of California Press).

—— (1997) [1971] *Sade, Fourier, Loyola* (Baltimore: Johns Hopkins University Press).

Baudry, Jean-Louis (1974–5) 'Ideological Effects of the Basic Cinematographic Apparatus', *Film Quarterly* 28 (2), 39–47.

Bauer, Adolf (1888) 'Udstillingen 1888 og dens Forgængere', *Nationaløkonomisk Tidsskrift (Ny Række)* 6, 1–52.

Bazin, André (1967) *What is Cinema?* I (Berkeley & Los Angeles: University of California Press).

Beckett, Susan (1998) 'The wonderful adventures of Nils: the "perfect" text for which Michel Tournier strives', in Vinge 1998, 73–86.

Benjamin, Walter (1973) [1955] 'The Work of Art in the Age of Mechanical Reproduction', in id., *Illuminations*, tr. Harry Zohn (London: Collins/Fontana Books, 219–53) (Eng. tr. first pub. 1968).

Bennet, Andrew & Royle, Nicholas (2004) *An Introduction to Literature, Criticism and Theory* (Harlow: Pearson Longman).

Bergenmar, Jenny (1998) 'Bortom kvinnligheten. Kön och identitet i Selma Lagerlöfs självbiografi', *Tidskrift för litteraturvetenskap*, 2, 3–30.

Bergmann, Sven-Arne (1997) *Getabock och gravlilja. Selma Lagerlöfs En herrgårdssägen som konstnärlig text* (Skrifter utgivna av Litteraturvetenskapliga institutionen, 30; Gothenburg: Göteborg University).

Bergström, Maria & Ryan, Emily (2008) *Little Selma from Mårbacka*, tr. Rupert Tansley (Falun: Kulturpoolen i Falun).

Berlant, Lauren (2008) *The Female Complaint: The Unfinished Business of Sentimentality in American Culture* (Durham: Duke University Press).

Berry, Charlotte (2012) 'The wonderful adventures of Floris Books: Swedish children's books from Edinburgh', *Scandinavica* 51 (2), 138–58.

—— (forthcoming) 'Pippi and the dreaming spires: Nordic children's literature and Oxford University Press', in Brett Joyce Epstein (ed.) *True North: Literary Translation in the Nordic Countries* (Newcastle: Cambridge Scholars Press).

Binding, Paul (2011) 'Selma Lagerlöf: Nils Holgersson's Wonderful Journey', *Swedish Book Review* 2, 15–20.

Blamires, David (1992) *Telling Tales: The Impact of Germany on English Children's Books 1780–1918* (Cambridge: Open Book).

Bloom, Harold (1973) *The Anxiety of Influence: A Theory of Poetry* (New York: Oxford University Press).

Boëthius, Ulf (1989) *När Nick Carter drevs på flykten. Kampen mot 'smutslitteraturen' i Sverige 1908–1909* (Hedemora: Gidlund).

Bohlin, Anna (2008) *Röstens anatomi. Läsningar av politik i Elin Wägners Silverforsen,*

Selma Lagerlöfs Löwensköldtrilogi och Klara Johansons Tidevarvskåserier (Umeå: Bokförlaget h:ström).

Bolter, Jay David & Grusin, Richard (1999) *Remediation: Understanding New Media* (Cambridge, MA: MIT).

Bonnevier, Katarina (2007) *Behind Straight Curtains: Towards a Queer Feminist Theory of Architecture* (School of Architecture, Royal Institute of Technology; Stockholm: Axl Books).

Branislav, František (1958) 'Selma Lagerlöf', *Lidová demokracie*, 16 November.

—— & Kejzlar, Radko (1962) Foreword to Selma Lagerlöf, *Císař z Portugálie*, tr. Dagmar Chvojková-Pallasová (Prague: SNKLU).

Bronfen, Elisabeth (1992) *Over her Dead Body: Death, Femininity and the Aesthetic* (Manchester: MUP).

Brooks, Peter (1984) *The Melodramatic Imagination: Balzac, Henry James, Melodrama and the Mode of Excess* (New York: Columbia University Press).

Broomans, Petra (1999) '"Jag vill vara mig själv". Stina Aronson (1892–1956), ett litteraturhistoriskt öde', University of Groningen.

—— & Kroon, Ingeborg (2013) (eds.) *Zweedse Literatuur in Nederland en Vlaanderen en supplement Fins-Zweeds in vertaling* (Groningen: Barkhuis).

Bruhn, Jörgen, Gjelsvik, Anne & Hanssen, Eirik Frisvold (2013) (eds.) *Adaptation studies: New challenges, new directions* (London: Bloomsbury Academic).

Brunius, Celie ('Yvette') (1908) 'Selma Lagerlöf', *Svenska Dagbladet*, 15 Nov.

Brunius, Jan (1963) *Mårbacka. Gårdarnas och släkternas historia* (Skrifter, 4; Sunne: Selma Lagerlöf-sällskapet).

Bryson, Norman (2001) 'Introduction: Art and Intersubjectivity', in Mieke Bal, *Looking In: The Art of Viewing. Essays and Afterword* (Amsterdam: G+B Arts International), 1–39.

Bull, Sofia (2010) 'Artistic Titles in Artistic Films! Investigating Swedish Art-Titles and the Case of Alva Lundin', in Sofia Bull & Astrid Söderbergh Widding (eds.) *Not so Silent: Women in Cinema before Sound* (Stockholm: Stockholm University), 115–24.

Cabanel, Patrick (2007) 'Book, school and nation: Sweden in *The Wonderful Adventures of Nils*', *Nordic Historical Review* 3, 93–112.

Campbell, Karlyn Kohrs (1989a) *Man cannot speak for her*, I: *A Critical Study of Early Feminist Rhetoric* (New York: Grenwood Press).

Campbell, Karlyn Kohrs (1989b) *Man cannot speak for her*, II: *Key Texts of the Early Feminists* (New York: Greenwood Press)

Carbone, Elettra & Forsås-Scott, Helena (forthcoming) 'A fresh start for Selma Lagerlöf: The making of the Norvik Press "Lagerlöf in English" Series', in Brett Joyce Epstein (ed.) *True North: Literary Translation in the Nordic Countries* (Newcastle: Cambridge Scholars Press).

Carlsson, Lena (2009–2010) (ed.) *Selma, Anna och Elise: Brevväxling mellan Selma Lagerlöf, Anna Oom och Elise Malmros åren 1886–1937* (2 vols., Landskrona: Litorina).

Castle, Terry (1995) *The Female Thermometer: Eighteenth-Century Culture and the Invention of the Uncanny* (Oxford: OUP).

Certeau, Michel de (2011) [1984] 'Reading as Poaching', in S. Towheed, R. Crone & K. Halsey (eds.) *The History of Reading* (London: Routledge), 130–9.

Chvojková-Pallasová, Dagmar (1957) Afterword to Selma Lagerlöf, *Podivuhodná cesta Nilse Holgerssona Švédskem*, tr. Dagmar Pallasová (Prague: SNDK).

Claesson Pipping, Git & Olsson, Tom (2010) *Dyrkan och spektakel. Selma Lagerlöfs framträdanden i offentligheten i Sverige 1909 och Finland 1912* (Stockholm: Carlsson).

────── (2011) 'Selma Lagerlöf och den irriterade professorn', in Maria Karlsson & Louise Vinge (eds.) *Spår och speglingar. Lagerlöfstudier 2011* (Hedemora: Gidlund), 216–34.

Claésson, Dick (2002) *The Narratives of the Biographical Legend: The Early Works of William Beckford* (Skrifter utgivna av Litteraturvetenskapliga institutionen, 41; Gothenburg: Gothenburg University).

Collins, Randall (2004) *Interaction ritual chains* (Princeton: PUP).

Connell, Raewyn W. (2005) *Masculinities*, (2nd edn., Cambridge: Polity).

Cowen, Roy C. (1980) *Hauptmann-Kommentar zum dramatischen Werk* (Munich: Winkler).

Cranny-Francis, Anne, et al. (2003). *Gender Studies: Terms and Debates* (Basingstoke: Palgrave-Macmillan).

Crary, Jonathan (1990) *Techniques of the Observer: On Vision and Modernity in the Nineteenth Century* (Cambridge, MA: MIT Press).

Crawford, Elizabeth (2001) *The Women's Suffrage Movement: A Reference Guide 1866–1928* (London: Routledge).

Dahlman, E. (2008) 'Svenska samer på antropologiska bilder och vykort', in Heidi Hansson & Jan-Erik Lundström (eds.) *Looking North: representations of Sámi in visual arts and literature* (Umeå: Bildmuseet, Umeå universitet), 73–9.

Darnton, Robert (1984) 'Readers Respond to Rousseau: The Fabrication of Romantic Sensitivity', in id., *The Great Cat Massacre and Other Episodes in French Cultural History* (London: Allen Lane), 215–56.

────── (2001) [1986] 'First Steps Towards a History of Reading', in J. L. Machor & P. Goldstein (eds.) *Reception Study: From Literary Theory to Cultural Studies* (New York: Routledge), 160–79.

────── (2009) *The Case for Books: Past. Present. Future* (New York: Public Affairs).

de Seta, Cesare (1992) 'La Sicilia del '700 e il "Grand tour" ', in Paolo Chiarini (ed.) *Goethe in Sicilia* (Palermo: Artemide Edizioni), 17–26.

Delblanc, Sven (1999) [1988] 'Den stora berätterskan Selma Lagerlöf', in Lars Lönnroth & Sven Delblanc (eds.) *Den svenska litteraturen*, II: *Genombrottstiden 1830–1920* (Stockholm: Bonnier), 390–5.

Desmidt, Isabelle (1997) *Bilden av Nils Holgerssons underbara resa genom Sverige i ett urval av Selma Lagerlöfs brev till Sophie Elkan* (Gent: Studia Germanica Gandensia).

────── (1998) 'Nils Holgersson i Nederländerna, Flandern och Tyskland', in Vinge 1998, 19–32.

────── (2001) 'En underbar färd på språkets vingar. Selma Lagerlöfs "Nils Holgersson" i tysk och nederländsk översättning/bearbetning', unpub. diss., Ghent: Ghent University.

────── (2003) 'Jetzt bist du in Deutschland, Däumling: Nils Holgersson on foreign soil—subject to new norms', *META* 48 (1–2), 165–81.

Dijkstra, Klaas (1962) *Oersettingen yn it frysk* (Ljouwert [Leeuwarden]: Laverman).

Düben, Gustaf von (1873) *Om Lappland och lapparne, företrädesvis de svenske. Ethnografiska studier* (Stockholm: Norstedt).

Duncan, James & Gregory, Derek (1999) (eds.) *Writes of Passage: Reading Travel Writing* (London: Routledge).

Durkheim, Emile (2002) [1912] 'The Elementary Forms of Religious Life', in Michael Lambek (ed.) *A Reader in the Anthropology of Religion* (Oxford: Blackwell), 34–49.

Edström, Vivi (1984) 'Nils Holgersson flies over the world', in *Selma Lagerlöf* (Twayne's World Authors Series, 741; Boston: Twayne) 58–69.

—— (2001) 'Selma Lagerlöf—en nationell ikon', in Alf W. Johansson (ed.) *Vad är Sverige? Röster om svensk nationell identitet* (Stockholm: Prisma).

—— (2002) *Selma Lagerlöf. Livets vågspel* (Stockholm: Natur & Kultur).

Ek, Bengt (1951) *Selma Lagerlöf efter Gösta Berlings saga. En studie över genombrottsåren 1891–1897* (Stockholm: Bonnier).

Ekecrantz, Jan & Olsson, Tom (1994) *Det redigerade samhället. Om journalistikens, beskrivningsmaktens och det informerade förnuftets historia* (Stockholm: Carlsson).

Elenius, L. (2000) 'En skåning besöker Lappland. Om Selma Lagerlöfs syn på de etniska minoriteterna', in Kjell-Arne Brändström (ed.) *Bilden av det samiska. Samerna och det samiska i skönlitteratur, forskning och debatt* (Umeå: Umeå universitet), 88–99.

—— (2002) 'Selma Lagerlöf och Norrland. Nationella idealbilder i Nils Holgerssons underbara resa', in K. Hatje (ed.) *Sekelskiftets utmaningar. Essäer om välfärd, utbildning och nationell identitet vid sekelskiftet 1900* (Stockholm: Carlsson), 15–41.

—— (2010) 'Symbolic Charisma and the Creation of Nations: The Case of the Sámi', *Studies in Ethnicity and Nationalism* 10 (3), 467–82.

Eliasson, Erik (1958) *Selma Lagerlöf i Landskrona* (Skrifter, 2; Landskrona: Landskrona Museiförening).

Elleström, Lars (2010) (ed.) *Media borders, multimodality and intermediality* (Basingstoke: Palgrave Macmillan).

Elsaesser, Thomas (1985) 'Tales of Sound and Fury', in B. Nichols (ed.) *Movies and Methods: An anthology* (Berkeley & Los Angeles: University of California Press), II 166–89.

Elswijk, Roald van (2012) 'Noarwegen en de wråld. Over de ontwikkeling van het Nynorsk', in Pieter Boersma, Goffe Jensma & Reinier Salverda (eds.) *Philologia Frisica anno 2008. Lêzings fan it achttjinde Frysk Filologekongres fan de Fryske Akademy op 10, 11 en 12 desimber 2008* (Ljouwert [Leeuwarden]: Fryske Akademy), 218–36.

—— (fortcoming) 'Exploring the North. Over de "brêge" tussen Scandinavië en Fryslân', in Janneke Spoelstra & Pieter Boersma (eds.) *Philologia Frisica anno 2012. Lêzings fan it njoggentjinde Frysk Filologekongres fan de Fryske Akademy op 13, 14 en 15 juny 2012* (Ljouwert [Leeuwarden]: Fryske Akademy).

Eriksson, Gunnar (1978) *Kartläggarna* (Umeå: Umeå University Library).

Erlandson-Hammargren, Erik (2006) *Från alpromantik till hembygdsromantik. Natursynen i Sverige från 1885 till 1915, speglad i Svenska Turistföreningens årsskrifter och Nils Holgerssons underbara resa genom Sverige* (Stockholm: Gidlund).

Eyerman, Ron & Jamison, Andrew (1991) *Social Movements: A Cognitive Approach* (Cambridge: Polity).

—— (1998) *Music and Social Movements: Mobilizing Traditions in the Twentieth Century* (Cambridge: CUP).

Flint, Kate (1993) *The Woman Reader 1837–1914* (Oxford: Clarendon).

Florin, Bo (1997) *Den nationella stilen. Studier i den svenska filmens guldålder* (Stockholm: Aura Förlag).

Florin, Christina (2006) *Kvinnor får röst. Kön, känslor och politiska kultur i kvinnornas rösträttsrörelse* (Stockholm: Atlas).

Forsås-Scott, Helena (1997) 'Beyond the Dead Body: Masculine Representation and the Feminine Project in Selma Lagerlöf's *Herr Arnes penningar*', *Scandinavica* 36 (2), 217–38.

—— (1997) *Swedish Women's Writing 1850–1995* (London: Athlone).

—— (1998) 'Text och identitet: Dagbok för Selma Ottilia Lovisa Lagerlöf', in Vinge 1998, 143–53.

—— (2010) ' "Oh children of a later day!" Den problematiske Gösta Berling på engelska', in Claes-Göran Holmberg & Per Erik Ljung (eds.) *Föredrag vid den 28:e studiekonferensen i International Association of Scandinavian Studies (IASS) i Lund 3–7 augusti 2010*, </nile.lub.lu.se/ojs/index.php/IASS2010/>.

—— (2013) 'Nordic, Scottish, Other: Selma Lagerlöf's *Herr Arnes penningar* and Gerhart Hauptmann's *Winterballade* from a Postcolonial and Gendered Perspective', *Journal of the North Atlantic* (special issue, *Across the Sólundarhaf: Connections between Scotland and the Nordic World. Selected Papers from the Inaugural St. Magnus Conference 2011*) 4, 170–6.

Forslund, Bengt (1980) *Victor Sjöström. Hans liv och verk* (Stockholm: Norstedt).

Foucault, Michel (1986) 'Of Other Spaces', *Diacritics* 16 (1), 22–7.

Frascina, Francis (1999) *Art, Politics and Dissent: Aspects of the art left in sixties America* (Manchester: MUP).

Freud, Sigmund (1995) [1955] [1919] 'The Uncanny', tr. James Strachey, in *The Standard Edition of the Complete Psychological Works of Sigmund Freud*, XVII: *1917–1919, An Infantile Neurosis and Other Works* (London: Hogarth Press), 217–53.

Frostegren, Margareta (1979) 'Damernas egen. Idun 1906', in Anita Alveus et al. (eds.) *Veckopressen i Sverige. Analyser och perspektiv* (Löderup: Förlagshuset Mälargården), 11–46.

Fullerton, John (2001) 'Notes on the Cultural Context of Reception: "The Girl from the Marsh Croft", 1917', *Film History* 13 (1), 58–64.

Fur, Gunlög (2006) *Colonialism in the margins: Cultural encounters in New Sweden and Lapland* (Leiden: Brill).

—— & Engsbråten, E. (2009) (eds.) *Svenska möten. Hemma och på resa* (Växjö: VUP).

Furhammar, Leif (1991) *Filmen i Sverige. En historia i tio kapitel* (Stockholm: Wiken).

—— (1998) *Filmen i Sverige* (Stockholm: Bra Böcker).

—— (2003) *Filmen i Sverige. En historia i tio kapitel och en fortsättning* (Stockholm: Dialogos).

—— (2010) 'Selma Lagerlöf and Literary Adaptations', in M. Larsson & A. Marklund (eds.) *Swedish film: An Introduction and Reader* (Lund: Nordic Academic Press), 86–91.

Furuhjelm, Annie (1933) 'Några personliga minnen om Selma Lagerlöf och om hennes eriksgata i Finland', *Astra. Hemmets tidskrift för kulturella och praktiska spörsmål*, 458–60.

Genette, Gérard (1997) [1987] *Paratexts: Thresholds of Interpretation* (Cambridge: CUP).

Gentzler, E. (1993) (ed.) *Contemporary Translation Theories* (London & New York: Routledge).

Gilman, Charlotte Perkins (1903) *The Home: Its Work and Influence* (New York: McClure, Phillips) (unabridged repub. 1970; New York: Source Book Press).

Gledhill, Christine (1987) (ed.) *Home is where the heart is: Studies in melodrama and the Woman's Film* (London: British Film Institute).

Gooskens, Charlotte, Bezooyen, René van & Kürschner, Sebastian (2012) 'Deens is makkelijker voor Friezen dan voor Nederlanders—feit of fabel?', in Pieter Boersma, Goffe Jensma & Reinier Salverda (eds.) *Philologia Frisica anno 2008. Lêzings fan it achttjinde Frysk Filologekongres fan de Fryske Akademy op 10, 11 en 12 desimber 2008* (Ljouwert [Leeuwarden]: Fryske Akademy), 286–98.

Graves, Peter (1998) 'The reception of Selma Lagerlöf in Britain', in Vinge 1998, 9–18.

Grit, Diederik (1994) *Driewerf zalig Noorden. Over literaire betrekkingen tussen de Nederlanden en Scandinavië* (Maastricht: UPM).

Groen, Jos (1994) *250 jaar Noorse literatuur in Nederland en Vlaanderen, 1743–1993. Bibliografie van vertalingen en recensies* (Hoorn: De Noordsche Passage).

Guillory, John (1993) *Cultural Capital: The Problem of Literary Canon Formation* (Chicago: University of Chicago Press).

Gullberg, Helge (1979) 'Selma Lagerlöfs brev till sin översättarinna Maria Franzos', *Lagerlöfstudier 6* (Sunne: Selma Lagerlöf-sällskapet), 115–37.

Hallberg, Kristina (1982) 'Litteraturvetenskapen och bilderboksforskningen', *Tidskrift för litteraturvetenskap* 3–4, 163–8.

Hansen, Constant Jacob (1860) *Noordsche letteren (talen, letterkunden, overzettingen)* (Ghent: Van Doosselaere).

Hansson, Heidi, Lindgren Leavenworth, Maria & Pettersson, Lennart (2010) (eds.) *Regionernas bilder. Estetiska uttryck från och om periferin* (Umeå: Institutionen för språkstudier, Umeå universitet).

Hauptmann, Gerhart (1917) *Winterballade. Eine dramatische Dichtung* (Berlin: S. Fischer).

—— (1919) *Vinterballaden. Dramatisk dikt. Med författarens tillåtelse översatt och bearbetad av Selma Lagerlöf* (Stockholm: Bonnier).

Heeres, Richard (2001) *Frjemdt wurdt eigen. Oersettingen yn en út it Frysk* (Ljouwert [Leeuwarden]: Frysk Letterkundich Museum en Dokumintaasjesintrum).

Heggestad, Eva (2012) 'Nils Holgerssons underbara resa över världen', in Johan Svedjedal (ed.) *Svensk litteratur som världslitteratur. En antologi* (Uppsala: Uppsala universitet), 101–115.

Hendler, Glenn (2001) *Public Sentiments: Structures of Feelings in Nineteenth-Century American Literature* (Chapel Hill: University of North Carolina Press).

Hikl, Karel (1910) 'Selma Lagerlöfová – Jerusalém', *Novina* IV, 570.

Hobsbawm, Eric (1971) [1959] *Primitive Rebels* (Manchester: MUP).

Högman, Ernst (1908) 'Några timmar i Selma Lagerlöfs hem', *Idun* 46, 464–6.

Holm, Birgitta (2008) 'Selma Lagerlöf och Nobelpriset', in Anna Nordlund (ed.) *Selma Lagerlöf 1858–2008* (Stockholm: Kungliga biblioteket), 89–103.

Idestam-Almquist, Bengt (1939) *Den svenska filmens drama. Sjöström och Stiller* (Stockholm: Åhlén & Söner).

—— (1959) *När filmen kom till Sverige. Charles Magnusson och Svenska Bio* (Stockholm: Norstedt).

Jackson, Rosemary (2003) [1981] *Fantasy: The Literature of Subversion* (London: Routledge).

Jameson, Fredric (2004) 'The Politics of Utopia', *New Left Review* 25, 35–54

Jiresch, Ester (2009) 'Margaretha Meyboom (1856–1927)—"Cultural Transmitter", Feminist or Socialist?', in Petra Broomans (ed.) *From Darwin to Weil: Women as Transmitters of Ideas* (Studies on Cultural Transfer and Transmission, 1; Groningen: Barkhuis), 101–119.

—— (2013) *Im Netzwerk der Kulturvermittlung. Sechs Autorinnen und ihre Bedeutung für die Verbreitung skandinavischer Literatur und Kultur in West- und Mitteleuropa um 1900* (Groningen: Barkhuis)

Jones, Michael R. & Olwig, Kenneth (2008) 'Introduction: Thinking Landscape and Regional Belonging on the Northern Edge of Europe', in ead. (eds.) *Nordic Landscapes: Region and Belonging on the Northern Edge of Europe* (Minneapolis: University of Minnesota Press), ix–xxix.

Jordansson, Birgitta & Vammen, Tinne (1998) (eds.) *Charitable Women: Philanthropic Welfare 1780–1930* (Odense: Odense University Press).

Kalma, Douwe (1918) [untitled review], *Frisia. Moanneskrift fen de Jongfryske Mienskip*, 352.

—— (1936) [untitled review], *It Heitelân. Algemien frysk moannebléd*, v. 11, 254.

Kaplan, E. Ann (1987) 'Mothering Feminism and Representation: the maternal melodrama and the Women's Film 1910–40', in Gledhill 1987, 123–35.

Kaplan, Temma (1992) *Red city, blue period: social movements in Picasso's Barcelona* (Berkeley & Los Angeles: University of California Press).

Kaprová, Linda (2009) 'Translating Swedish Literature for Children into Czech in the 20th and 21st Century: Solutions in Translating Proper Names in Selma Lagerlöf's The Wonderful Journey of Nils through Sweden', unpub. MA dissertation, Charles University.

Kåreland, Lena (2008) 'Selma Lagerlöf—det stora undantaget', in Boel Englund & Lena Kåreland, *Rätten till ordet. En kollektivbiografi över skrivande stockholmskvinnor 1880–1920* (Stockholm: Carlsson), 237–76.

Karlgren, Anton (1908) 'Hos Selma Lagerlöf. Ett besök hos författarinnan i hennes hem i Falun', *Dagens Nyheter*, 15 Nov.

Karlsson, Maria (2002) *Känslans röst. Det melodramatiska i Selma Lagerlöfs romankonst* (Stockholm/Stehag: Symposion).

Kittler, Friedrich (2003) *Maskinskrifter. Essäer om medier och litteratur*, ed. Otto Fischer & Thomas Götselius, tr. Tommy Andersson (Gråbo: Antrophos).

Krol, Jelle (2001) 'West Frisian literature in translation', in Horst Haider Munske & Nils Århammar (eds.) *Handbuch des Friesischen/Handbook of Frisian Studies* (Tübingen: Niemeyer), 232–44.

—— (2007) 'Oersettingen út 'e Skandinavyske talen', in Jacob van Sluis (ed.) *De grins oer. Literaire vertalingen in en uit het Fries* (Groningen: Barkhuis), 37–8.

Kuhn, Annette (1994) [1982] *Women's Pictures: Feminism and Cinema* (2nd edn., London: Verso).

Lagerroth, Erland (1958) *Landskap och natur i Gösta Berlings saga och Nils Holgersson* (Stockholm: Bonnier).

—— (1971) 'Selma Lagerlöf som siciliansk hembygdsdiktare', in Bengt Ek, Inge Jonsson & Ying Toijer-Nilsson (eds.) *Lagerlöfstudier 4, 1971* (Sunne: Selma Lagerlöf-sällskapet), 74–109.

Lagerroth, Ulla-Britta (1961) 'Världsbrand i småstadsperspektiv. Kommentar till Patron Ivar Halenius', in Nils Afzelius, Gunnar Ahlström & Bengt Ek (eds.) *Lagerlöfstudier 2, 1960* (Malmö: Selma Lagerlöf-sällskapet), 33–49.

—— (1963) *Körkarlen och Bannlyst. Motiv- och idéstudier i Selma Lagerlöfs 10-talsdiktning* (Stockholm: Bonnier).

—— (2000) 'Nordism i Selma Lagerlöfs liv och författarskap', *Nordisk tidskrift för vetenskap, konst och industri* 76 (2), 129–46.

Langer, Judith (1994) *The Culture of Reading and the Teaching of English* (Manchester: MUP).

—— (2010) *Envisioning Literature: Literary Understanding and Literature Instruction* (New York: Teachers College Press).

Larsson, Lisbeth (1996) 'Att skriva sitt jag i världen', in Elisabeth Møller Jensen & Ebba Witt-Brattström (eds.) *Nordisk kvinnolitteraturhistoria*, III: *Vida världen 1900–1960* (Höganäs: Bra böcker), 233–48, available at <www.nordicwomensliterature.net>.

Lathey, Gillian (2010) *The Role of Translators in Children's Literature: Invisible Storytellers* (London: Routledge).

Ledger, Sally (1997) *The New Woman: Fiction and feminism at the fin de siècle* (Manchester: MUP).

Lefebvre, Henri (1991) [1974] *The Production of Space*, tr. Donald Nicholson-Smith (Oxford: Blackwell).

Lefebvre, Martin (2006) 'Between Setting and Landscape in the Cinema', in id. (ed.) *Landscape and Film* (New York: Routledge), 19–59.

Lewan, Bengt (2001) *Arkadien. Om herdar och herdinnor i svensk dikt* (Nora: Nya Doxa).

Levý, Jiři (1996) *České teorie překladu I* (Prague: Ivo Železný).

Lichtman, Susan A. (1996) *The Female Hero in Women's Literature and Poetry* (Lewiston, NY: Mellen).

Liljedahl, Elisabeth (1975) *Stumfilmen i Sverige—kritik och debatt. Hur samtiden värderade den nya konstarten* (Stockholm: Proprius /Svenska Filminstitutet).

Lindemann, A. (1911) 'Report', in Ida Husted Harper (ed.) (1922), *The History of Women Suffrage*, VI: *1900–1920* (National American Woman Suffrage Association), 846–7, available at <http://www.gutenberg.org/ebooks/30051>.

Lindqvist, Märta ('Quelqu'une') (1919) '"Ingmarssönerna"—en storartad svensk filmskapelse', *Svenska Dagbladet*, 2 Jan.

—— (1923) 'Hos sagoberätterskan på Mårbacka. Den tvåhundraåriga släktgården i nytt skick—en förvandling från idyllisk Värmlandsstuga till en vacker herrgård med gammaldags stil och trevnad', *Svenska Dagbladet*, 17 Nov.

Lindskog, Gerda Helena (2005) *Vid svenskhetens nordliga utposter. Om bilden av samerna i svensk barn- och ungdomslitteratur under 1900–talet* (Lund: BTJ förlag).

Lundström, Gunilla (2001) 'En värld i rubriker och bilder (1897–1919)', in Gunilla Lundström, Per Rydén & Elisabeth Sandlund, *Den svenska pressens historia*, III: *Det moderna Sveriges spegel 1897–1945* (Stockholm: Ekerlids förlag), 22–140.

Lundström, Jan-Erik (2008) 'The anthropometric photograph: popular and scientific gazes at people of the north', in Heidi Hansson & Jan-Erik Lundström (eds.) *Looking North: representations of Sámi in visual arts and literature* (Bildmuseet; Umeå: Umeå universitet), 93–100.

Lury, Celia (1993) *Cultural Rights: Tehnology, Legality and Personality* (London: Routledge).

Lyons, Martyn (2003) [1995] 'New Readers in the Nineteenth Century: Women, Children, Workers', in G. Cavallo & R. Chartier (eds.) *A History of Reading in the West*, tr. Lydia G. Cochrane (Amherst: University of Massachusetts Press), 313–44.

Määttä, Sylvia (1997) *Kön och evolution. Charlotte Perkins Gilmans feministiska utopier 1911–1919* (Nora: Nya Doxa).

McLuhan, Marshall (1964) *Understanding media: The extensions of man* (London: Routledge).

Marshall, P. David (1997) *Celebrity and Power: Fame in Contemporary Culture* (Minnesota: University of Minnesota Press).

Marx, Karl (1997) [1867] *Kapitalet. Kritik av den politiska ekonomin. Första boken*, tr. Ivan Bohman (Lund: A-Z förlag).

Masschelein, Anneleen (2011) *The Unconcept: The Freudian Uncanny in Late-Twentieth-Century Theory* (Albany, NY: Suny).

Mattingly, Carol (1998) *Well-Tempered Women: Nineteenth-Century Temperance Rhetoric* (Carbondale: Southern Illinois University Press).

—— (2002) *Appropriate[ing] Dress: Women's Rhetorical Style in Nineteenth-Century America* (Carbondale: Southern Illinois University Press).

Melberg, Arne (2006) *Resa och skriva. En guide till den moderna reselitteraturen* (Gothenburg: Daidalos).

Mercer, J. & Shingler, M. (2004) *Melodrama: Genre, Style, Sensibility* (New York: Columbia University Press).

Meijboom, Margaretha (1911) 'Skandinavische literatuur in Nederland', *De Boekzaal* 5, 45–9.

—— (1919) *Selma Lagerlöf* (Leiden: Sijthoff).

Miall, David S. (2006) *Literary Reading: Empirical and Theoretical Studies* (New York: Lang).

Miřiovský, Emanuel (1910) Foreword to Selma Lagerlöf, *Jerusalem*, I: *V Dalarně*, tr. Emanuel Miřiovský (Prague: J. Otto).

Mirovitch, Zenéide (1911) [report, 6th IWSA Congress], *Dagens Nyheter*, 14 June.

Mitchell, William J. T. (1994) introduction in id. (ed.) *Landscape and Power* (Chicago: University of Chicago Press).

—— (1995) *Picture Theory: Essays on Verbal and Visual Representation* (Chicago: University of Chicago Press).

Molloy, Gunilla (2011) *Selma Lagerlöf i mångfaldens klassrum* (Lund: Studentlitteratur).

Moretti, Franco (2000) 'Conjectures on World Literature', *New Left Review* 1, 54–68.

—— (2009) [1998] *Atlas of the European Novel* (London: Verso).

Mral, Brigitte (1999) 'The Public Woman: Women Speakers Around the Turn of the Century in Sweden', in Christine Mason Sutherland & Rebecca Sutcliffe (eds.) *The Changing Tradition: Women in the History of Rhetoric* (Calgary: University of Calgary Press), 161–72.

Mulvey, Laura (2000) 'Visual Pleasure and Narrative Cinema', in E. Ann Kaplan (ed.) *Feminism and Film* (Oxford: OUP), 34–47 (first pub. 1975).

Munday, Jeremy (2008) *Introducing Translation Studies: Theories and Applications* (London: Routledge).

Näsström, Gustaf (1937) *Dalarna som svenskt ideal* (Stockholm: Wahlström & Widstrand).

Nathorst, M. T. (1918) 'Selma Lagerlöfs hem i Falun', *Svenska hem i ord och bilder* 6 (3), 564–7.

Nichols, Bill (1985) (ed.) *Movies and Methods: An anthology*, II (Berkeley & Los Angeles: University of California Press).

Nikolajeva, Maria & Scott, Carole (2001) *How picturebooks work* (New York: Garland).

Nochlin, Linda (1991) 'Women, Art, and Power', in Norman Bryson, Michael Ann Holly & Keith Moxey (eds.) *Visual Theory: Painting and Interpretation* (Cambridge: Polity), 13–46.

Nordlund, Anna (2005) *Selma Lagerlöfs underbara resa genom den svenska litteraturhistorien 1891–1996* (Stockholm/Stehag: Symposion).

Nyblom, Andreas (2008) *Ryktbarhetens ansikte. Verner von Heidenstam, medierna och personkulten i sekelskiftets Sverige* (Stockholm: Atlantis).

O'Sullivan, Emer (2005) *Comparative Children's Literature* (London: Routledge).

Olsson, Tom (2006) *Rätten att tala politik. Medieintellektuella och manlig medielogik* (Stockholm: Carlsson).

Olsson, Ulf (2007) 'I det svarta: läsningar av Lagerlöf', in id., *Invändningar. Kritiska artiklar* (Stockholm: Brutus Östlings Bokförlag Symposion), 81–139.

Oscarson, Christopher (2009) '*Nils Holgersson*: Empty maps and the entangled bird's-eye view of Sweden', *Edda* 109, 99–117.

Österberg, Eva (2007) *Vänskap. En lång historia* (Stockholm: Atlantis).

af Petersens, Lovisa (2006) *Formering för offentlighet. Kvinnokonferenser och Svenska Kvinnors Nationalförbund kring sekelskiftet 1900* (Stockholm Studies in History, 87; Stockholm: Acta Universitatis Stockholmiensis).

Peterson, Abby (2012) 'Wounds That Never Heal: On Anselm Kiefer and the Moral Innocence of the West German Student Movements and West German New Left', *Cultural Sociology* 6 (3), 367–85.

Peucker, Brigitte (1980) *Arcadia to Elysium: Preromantic Modes in 18th-Century Germany* (Bonn: Bouvier Verlag Herbert Grundmann).

Pikkarainen, Heidi & Brodin, Björn (2008) *Diskriminering av samer. Samers rättigheter ur ett diskrimineringsperspektiv* (Stockholm: Ombudsmannen mot etnisk diskriminering, DO).

Pollock, Griselda (2003) *Vision and Difference: Feminism, Femininity and the Histories of Art* (London: Routledge).

Poovey, Mary (2008) *Genres of the Credit Economy: Mediating Value in Eighteenth- and Nineteenth-century Britain* (Chicago: University of Chicago Press).

Pym, A. (2009) *Exploring Translation Theories* (London: Routledge).

Quandt, Regina (1987–88) *Schwedischer Literatur in deutscher Übersetzung, 1830–1980. Eine Bibliographie*, ed. Fritz Paul & Heinz-Georg Halbe (7 vols., Göttingen: Vandenhoeck and Ruprecht).

Radway, Janice A. (1987) [1984] *Reading the Romance: Women, Patriarchy and Popular Literature* (London: Verso).

—— (1997) *A Feeling for Books: The Book of the Month Club, Literary Taste, and Middle-Class Desire* (Chapel Hill: University of North Carolina Press).

—— (2008) 'What's the Matter with Reception Study? Some Thoughts on the Disciplinary Origins, Conceptual Constraints and Persistent Viability of a Paradigm', in P. Goldstein & J. L. Machor (eds.) *New Directions in American Reception Study* (New York: OUP), 327–48.

Rahn, Suzanne (1986) 'Rediscovering Nils', *The Lion and the Unicorn* 10, 158–66.

—— (1995) 'The boy and the wild geese: Selma Lagerlöf's *Nils*', in Suzanne Rahn (ed.), *Rediscoveries in Children's Literature* (New York: Garland), 39–50.

Rajewsky, Irina O. (2002) *Intermedialität* (Tübingen: Francke).

—— (2005) 'Intermediality, Intertextuality, and Remediation: A Literary Perspective on Intermediality', *Intermédialités* 6, 43–64.

Ravn, Jørgen (1958a) 'Selma Lagerlöf i Landskrona og København', in Nils Afzelius & Ulla-Britta Lagerroth (eds.) *Lagerlöfstudier [1]* (Malmö: Selma Lagerlöf-sällskapet), 139–56.

—— (1958b) *Menneskekenderen Selma Lagerlöf. Vignetter af forfatteren* (Copenhagen: G. E. C. Gad).

Register, Cheri (1983) 'The Sacrificial Hera: Selma Lagerlöf's *The Treasure* as Feminist Myth', in Karin Westman Berg & Gabriella Åhmansson (eds.) *Mothers–Saviours–Peacemakers: Swedish Women Writers in the Twentieth Century* (Kvinnolitteraturforskning, 4; Uppsala: Uppsala University), 29–73.

Revault d'Allonnes, Fabrice (1991) *La lumière au cinéma* (Paris: Editions Cahiers du cinéma).

Riall, Lucy (2008) *Garibaldi: Invention of a Hero* (New Haven: Yale University Press).

Roberson, Susan L. (2001) (ed.) *Defining travel: Diverse visions* (Jackson: University Press of Mississippi).

Rose, Jonathan (2001) *The Intellectual Life of the British Working Classes* (New Haven: Yale University Press).

Royle, Nicholas (2003) *The Uncanny* (Manchester: MUP).

Runeberg, Johan Ludvig (1954) [1848, 1860] *Fänrik Ståls sägner*, illus. Albert Edelfelt (Lund: C.W.K. Gleerups bokförlag).

Rupp, Leila J. (1997) *Worlds of Women: The making of an International Women's Movement* (Princeton: PUP).

—— (2010) 'Constructing Internationalism: The Case of Transnational Women's Organizations, 1888–1945', in Karen Offen (ed.) *Globalizing feminisms 1789–1945* (London: Routledge), 139–52.

—— & Taylor, Verta (2002) 'Loving Internationalism: The Emotion Culture of Transnational Womens's Organizations 1888–1945', *Mobilization: An International Journal* 7 (2), 141–58.

Ryall, Anka, Schimanski, Johan & Waerp, Henning Howlid (2010) (eds.) *Arctic discourses* (Newcastle upon Tyne: Cambridge Scholars).

Saeger, Raf de (2013) *Noorse auteurs in Nederlandse vertaling 1741–2012 / Norske forfattere oversatt til nederlandsk 1741–2012*, ed. Petra Broomans & Janke Klok (Studies on Cultural Transfer and Transmission, 6; Groningen: Barkhuis).

Sahlberg, Gardar (1961) 'Selma Lagerlöf och filmen', in Nils Afzelius, Gunnar Ahlström & Bengt Ek (eds.) *Lagerlöfstudier 2, 1960* (Malmö: Selma Lagerlöf-sällskapet), 189–205.

Šalda, F. X. (1893) 'J. P. Jacobsen', *Rozhledy*, 28.

—— (1899) 'Literatura překladová', *Lumír* 27, 253.

Sandberg, Mark (1995) 'Effigy and Narrative: Looking into the Nineteenth-Century Folk Museum', in Leo Charney & Vanessa R. Schwartz (eds.) *Cinema and the Invention of Modern Life* (Berkeley & Los Angeles: University of California Press).

Sandell, Klas & Sörlin, Sverker (2008) [2000] (eds.) *Friluftshistoria. Från 'härdande friluftslif' till ekoturism och miljöpedagogik. Teman i det svenska friluftslivets historia* (2nd rev. edn., Stockholm: Carlsson).

Schaffer, Barbro (1989) 'Att göra fantasin autentisk—om Selma Lagerlöf och hennes illustratörer', in Vivi Edström et al. (eds.) *Selma Lagerlöf och bildkonsten* (Stockholm: Nationalmuseum, Selma Lagerlöf-sällskapet), 47–76.

Schiedermair, Joachim (2005) 'Melodramatic Unveiling as Aesthetic Disguise: Selma Lagerlöf's *Dagbok* (1932) as Aesthetic Confession', *Scandinavica* 44 (1), 29–53.

Schweitzer, Sibylle (1990) *Selma Lagerlöf. Eine Bibliographie*, ed. Gunilla Rising Hintz (Marburg: Marburg Universitätsbibliothek).

Segerberg, Ebba (1998) 'Silent Stories: Film, Modernity, and the Storyteller', in Vinge 1998, 105–119.

—— (1999) *Nostalgia, Narrative, and Modernity in Swedish Silent Cinema* (Berkeley & Los Angeles: University of California).

Shavit, Zohar (1986) *The Poetics of Children's Literature* (Atlanta: University of Georgia Press).

Showalter, Elaine (1978) [1977] *A Literature of Their Own: British Women Novelists from Brontë to Lessing* (London: Virago).

Sjöberg, Maria (2001) *Kvinnors jord, manlig rätt. Äktenskap, egendom och makt i äldre tid* (Hedemora: Gidlund).

Sjöholm, Carina (2003) *Gå på bio. Rum för drömmar i folkhemmets Sverige* (Stockholm/Stehag: Brutus Östlings Bokförlag Symposion).

Sjöström, Viktor (1938) *Viktor Sjöström om respekten för Selma inför ett möte om filmmanus* (Sveriges radio, 20 November, available from SR Minnen/Radiofynd as <http://t.sr.se/102yvPw>) [radio talk].

—— (1941) 'Selma Lagerlöf och filmen', in Sven Thulin (ed.) *Mårbacka och Övralid. Minnen av Selma Lagerlöf och Verner von Heidenstam* (Uppsala: J. A. Lindblads förlag), II, 175–88.

—— (2008) [1941] 'Selma Lagerlöf och filmen', in Anna Nordlund (ed.) *Selma Lagerlöf 1858–2008* (Stockholm: Kungl. Biblioteket), 119–135.

Smedberg Bondesson, Anna (2012), 'Nils Holgerssons resa genom seklet och runt jordklotet', in S. Kärrholm & P. Tenngart (eds.) *Barnlitteraturens värden och värderingar* (Lund: Studentlitteratur), 135–46.

Snickars, Pelle (2001) *Svensk film och visuell masskultur 1900* (Stockholm: Aura förlag).

Söderbergh Widding, Astrid (2001) 'Tio teman ur Herr Arnes pengar', in Bo Florin (ed.) *Moderna motiv—Mauritz Stiller i retrospektiv* (Stockholm: Cinemateket Svenska filminstitutet), 30–36.

Soila, Tytti (1997a) 'På spaning efter ett kvinnligt subjekt', in ead. (ed.) *Dialoger. Feministisk filmteori i praktik* (Stockholm: Aura förlag), 22–37.

—— (1997b) 'Thalias magra bröd', in ead. (ed.) *Dialoger. Feministisk filmteori i praktik* (Stockholm: Aura förlag), 152–72.

—— (2000) 'Desire Disavowed in Victor Sjöström's "The Phantom Carriage"', in Ann-Charlotte Gavel Adams & Terje I. Leiren (eds.) *Stage and Screen: Studies in Scandinavian Drama and Film: Essays in honor of Birgitta Steene* (Seattle: DreamPlay Press Northwest), 159–75.

Sondrup, Steven P. (1997) 'Three Stories: Scandinavian Kings and Queens: Astrid, Sigrid Storrade, and The Silver Mine', *Scandinavian Studies* 69 (4), 88–90.

Sörlin, Sverker (2013) (ed.) *Science, geopolitics and culture in the Polar region: Norden beyond borders* (Farnham: Ashgate).

Sporrong, Ulf (2008) 'The Province of Dalecarlia (Dalarna): Heartland or Anomaly?', in Michael Jones & Kenneth R. Olwig (eds.) *Nordic Landscapes: Region and Belonging on the Northern Edge of Europe* (Minneapolis: University of Minnesota Press), 192–219.

Stanton, Elizabeth Cady (1989) 'Speech at the Seneca Falls Convention, 1848', in Karlyn Kohrs Campbell (1989b) *Man cannot speak for her*, II: *Key Texts of the Early Feminists* (New York: Grenwood Press), 41–70.

Steinfeld, Thomas (2011) 'Drömmen om något fast utanför tiden', *Svenska Dagbladet*, 2 Sept.

—— & Lamm, Staffan (2006) *Das Kollektivhaus. Utopie und Wirklichkeit eines Wohnexperiments* (Frankfurt am Main: S. Fischer).

Stenberg, Lisbeth (1995) 'Nationen som hem. Idyll, utopi och reella kontradiktioner i Selma Lagerlöfs *Jerusalem*', *Tidskrift för litteraturvetenskap* 3/4, 47–69.

—— (2001) *En genialisk lek. Kritik och överskridande i Selma Lagerlöfs tidiga författarskap* (Skrifter utgivna av Litteraturvetenskapliga institutionen, 40; Gothenburg: Gothenburg University).

—— (2009) *I kärlekens namn… Människosynen, den nya kvinnan och framtidens samhälle i fem litteraturdebatter 1881–1909* (Stockholm: Normal).

Stenkvist, Jan (1987) 'Sven Hedin och bondetåget', in Kurt Johannesson et. al. (eds.) *Heroer på offentlighetens scen. Politiker och publicister i Sverige 1809–1914* (Stockholm: Tidens förlag), 246–347.

Stiller, Mauritz (1923) 'Gunnar Hedes saga. Filmskådespel med motiv från *En herr-gårdssägen* av Selma Lagerlöf', *Filmnyheter* 8 (15), 10–11.

Sturge, Kate (1999) 'A danger and a veiled attack: Translating into Nazi Germany', in Jean Boase-Beier and Michael Holman (eds.) *The Practice of Literary Translation: Constraints and Creativity* (Manchester: St Jerome), 135–46.

—— (2002) 'Censorship of Translated Fiction in Nazi Germany', *Études sur le texte et ses transformations* 15 (special issue, ed. Denise Merkle), 153–69.

—— (2004) *'The Alien Within': Translation into German during the Nazi Regime* (Munich: Idicum)

Sundmark, Björn (2008a) 'Lagerlöf's legacy: a hundred years of writing the nation', *Bookbird* 46 (3), 14–20.

—— (2008b) 'Of Nils and nation: Selma Lagerlöf's The Wonderful Adventures of Nils', *International Research in Children's Literature* 1 (2), 168–86.

—— (2009a) '"But the Story Itself Is Intact" (or is it?): the Case of the English Translations of *The Wonderful Adventures of Nils*', in Brett Epstein (ed.) *Nordic Lights: Translation in the Nordic Countries* (Oxford: Peter Lang), 167–80.

—— (2009b) 'Citizenship and children's identity in *The Wonderful Adventures of Nils* and *Scouting for Boys*', *Children's Literature in Education* 40 (2), 109–119.

—— (2013) '"Dear Selma"—"Dear Velma": Selma Lagerlöf's Translation Instructions to Velma Swanston Howard', in Hanne Jansen and Anna Wegener (eds.) *Authorial and Editorial Voices in Translation*, I: *Collaborative Relationships between Authors, Translators, and Performers* (Montréal: Éditions québécoises de l'œuvre, collection Vita Traductiva), available at <http://yorkspace.library.yorku.ca/xmlui/handle/10315/26596>.

Surmatz, Astrid (2004) 'Konfrontationen med det andra och genderdiskursen i valda beskrivningar av samerna under 1600– och 1700–talet', in J. Kusmenko (ed.) *The Sámi and the Scandinavians: Aspects of 2000 years of contact* (Hamburg: Kovac), 113–28.

—— (2006) 'Det dubbla tilltalet i Hans Christian Andersens "Sneedronningen": etnicitet, kön och oskuld', in Elisabeth Oxfeldt (ed.) *H. C. Andersen: Eventyr, kunst og modernitet* (Bergen: Fagboksforlaget), 93–113.

Svedjedal, Johan (1997) [1990] 'Den svenska bokmarknaden', in Lars Lönnroth & Hans-Erik Johannesson (eds.) *Den svenska litteraturen*, VII: *Bokmarknad. Bibliografier. Samlingsregister* (Stockholm: Bonnier Alba), 11–37.

Swanston Howard, Velma (1908) *När Maja-Lisa kom hem från Amerika* (Folkskrifter, 1; Stockholm: Nationalföreningen mot emigration).

Swanston Howard, Velma (1912) 'Selma Lagerlöf, Sweden's Idolized Writer: A Woman who Has Conquered All Europe with her Pen', *The World's Work* (Feb.), 416–17.

Tegnér, Esaias (1919) [1812] 'Svea 1812', in id., *Samlade skrifter*, II: *1808–1816*, ed. Ewert Wrangel & Fredrik Böök (Stockholm: Norstedt).

Thacker, Andrew (2003) *Moving through Modernity: Space and Geography in Modernism* (Manchester: MUP).

Thomashevsky, Boris (1978) [1923] 'Literature and biography', in L. Matejka & K. Pomorska (eds.) *Readings in Russian Poetics: Formalist and Structuralist Views* (Ann Arbor: MIT), 47–55.

Thomsen, Bjarne Thorup (1997) 'Aspects of Topography in Selma Lagerlöf's *Jerusalem*, Vol. 1', *Scandinavica* 36 (1), 23–41.

—— (1998) 'Terra (In)cognita. Reflections on the search for the sacred place in Selma Lagerlöf's *Jerusalem* and *Nils Holgerssons underbara resa genom Sverige*', in Vinge 1998, 131–42.

—— (2004) 'Nordic national borderlands in Selma Lagerlöf', in id. (ed.) *Centring on the Peripheries: Studies in Scandinavian, Scottish, Gaelic and Greenlandic Literature* (Norwich: Norvik Press), 79–93.

—— (2007) *Lagerlöfs litterære landvinding: Nation, mobilitet og modernitet i Nils Holgersson og tilgrænsende tekster* (Amsterdam Contributions to Scandinavian Studies, 3; Amsterdam: Scandinavisch Instituut, Universiteit van Amsterdam).

—— (2011) 'Comparative considerations: Lagerlöf, Andersen and the British perspective', *Northern Studies. Journal of the Scottish Society for Northern Studies* (special issue in honour of Peter Graves) 42, 41–54.

Thunman, Noriko (1998) 'Selma Lagerlöf i Japan', in Vinge 1998, 41–59.

Tickner, Lisa (1987) *The Spectacle of Women: Imagery of the Suffrage Campaign 1907–14* (London: Chatto & Windus).

Tisovský, T. E. (1911) Foreword to Selma Lagerlöf, *Podivuhodná cesta nezbedy Petra s divokými husami*, tr. T. E. Tisovský (Prague: Zemský Ústředni Spolek Jednot Učitelských v královstvi Českém).

Todorov, Tzvetan (1975) [1970] *The Fantastic: A Structural Approach to a Literary Genre*, tr. Richard Hower (Ithaca NY: Cornell University Press).

Toijer-Nilsson, Ying (1992) (ed.) *Du lär mig att bli fri. Selma Lagerlöf skriver till Sophie Elkan* (Stockholm: Bonnier).

—— (2006) (ed.) *En riktig författarhustru. Selma Lagerlöf skriver till Valborg Olander* (Stockholm: Bonnier).

Torpe, Ulla (1996) 'En enda lång variation över ordet vilja. Om Selma Lagerlöf', in Elisabeth Møller Jensen & Ebba Witt Brattström (eds.) *Nordisk kvinnolitteraturhistoria*, III: *Vida världen 1900–1960* (Höganäs: Bra Böcker), 113–25, available at <www.nordicwomensliterature.net>.

Toury, Gideon (2012) *Descriptive Translation Studies—and Beyond* (2nd edn., Amsterdam: John Benjamins).

Uddgren, Gustaf ('Sancho Pansa') (1911) 'Dem man möter', *Stockholms Dagblad*, 18 June.

'Urban' (1911) 'Een zomer in het Noorden', *Leeuwarder Courant*, 3 Oct., 9–10.

Vardac, A. Nicholas (1993) [1949] *Stage To Screen: Theatrical Origins of Early Film: David Garrick to D. W. Griffith* (New York: Da Capo).

Venuti, Lawrence (1998) *The Scandals of Translation: Towards an Ethics of Difference* (London: Routledge).

Vimr, Ondřej (2006–07) 'Když železná opona spadne. Hugo Kosterka (1867–1956). Dějiny překladu ze skandinávských jazyků 1890–1950, pars pro toto', *Plav*.

Vinge, Louise (1998) (ed.) *Selma Lagerlöf Seen from Abroad/ Selma Lagerlöf i utlandsperspektiv. Ett symposium i Vitterhetsakademien den 11 och 12 september 1997* (Conferences, 44; Stockholm: Kungl. Vitterhets historie och antikvitets akademien).

—— (2000) 'Selma Lagerlöf läser högt', in Arne Jönsson & Anders Piltz (eds.) *Språkets speglingar. Festskrift till Birger Bergh* (Lund: Klassiska institutionen, Lunds universitet), 146–54.

Vodák, V. (1984) 'Plodný návrat Selmy Lagerlöfové', *Lidová demokracie*, 18 May.

Wacklin, Sara (1919) *Hundrade minnen från Österbotten jämte Österbottniska anekdoter. En efterskörd efter Sara Wacklin*, ed. Helena Westermarck (Helsinki: Schildt).

Wacklin, Sara (1974) [1844, 1846] *Hundrade minnen från Österbotten* (Vitterhetskommissionens utgivning, 6; Helsinki: Schildt).

Wägner, Elin (1942) *Selma Lagerlöf*, I: *Från Mårbacka till Jerusalem* (Stockholm: Bonnier).

333

—— (1943) *Selma Lagerlöf,* II: *Från Jerusalem till Mårbacka* (Stockholm: Bonnier).
Waldekranz, Rune (1976) *Så föddes filmen. Ett massmediums uppkomst och genombrott* (Stockholm: PAN/Norstedt).
—— (1985) *Filmens historia,* I: *Pionjäråren* (Stockholm: Norstedt).
Watson, Jennifer (2004) *Swedish Novelist Selma Lagerlöf, 1858–1940, and Germany at the Turn of the Century: O du Stern ob meinem Garten* (Lewiston, NY: E. Mellen).
Weber, Brenda R. (2012) *Women and Literary Celebrity in the Nineteenth Century: The Transatlantic Production of Fame and Gender* (Farnham: Ashgate).
Weidel, Gunnel (1960) 'Kring Herr Arnes penningar', in Nils Afzelius, Gunnar Ahlström & Bengt Ek (eds.), *Lagerlöfstudier 2, 1960* (Malmö: Selma Lagerlöf-sällskapet) , 69–95.
—— (1964) *Helgon och gengångare. Gestaltningen av kärlek och rättvisa i Selma Lagerlöfs diktning* (Lund: C. W. K. Gleerup).
Weniger, Kerstin (1994) '*Gösta Berling* in deutscher Übersetzung. Studien zur übersetzerischen Rezeption Selma Lagerlöfs', dissertation, University of Leipzig.
Werner, Gösta (1978) *Den svenska filmens historia* (Stockholm: Norstedt).
—— (1979) *Herr Arnes pengar. En filmvetenskaplig studie och dokumentation av Mauritz Stillers film efter Selma Lagerlöfs berättelse* (Stockholm: Norstedt).
—— (1991) *Mauritz Stiller. Ett livsöde* (Stockholm: Prisma).
Wijkmark, Sofia (2009) *Hemsökelser. Gotiken i sex berättelser av Selma Lagerlöf* (Karlstad University Studies, 20; Karlstad: Estetisk-filosofiska fakulteten, Litteraturvetenskap).
Willems, Gottfried (2001) 'Der Weg ins Offene als Sackgasse. Zur jüngsten Kanon-Debatte und zur Lage der Literaturwissenschaft', in Gerhard R. Kaiser & Stefan Matuschek (eds.) *Begründungen und Funktionen des Kanons* (Jenaer germanistische Forschungen, 9; Heidelberg: Winter).
Williams, Anna (1997) *Stjärnor utan stjärnbilder. Kvinnor och kanon i litteraturhistoriska översiktsverk under 1900–talet* (Hedemora: Gidlund).
Williams, Raymond (1977) *Marxism and Literature* (Oxford: OUP).
Witt-Brattström, Ebba 2003 (ed.) *The New Woman and the Aesthetic Opening: Unlocking Gender in Twentieth-Century Texts* (Huddinge: Södertörns högskola).
—— (2009) 'Den sista balen. Arvet efter Sara Wacklin', *Svenska akademiens handlingar,* 191–203.
Wittman, Reinhard. (2003) [1995] 'Was there a Reading Revolution at the End of the Eighteenth Century?', in G. Cavallo & R. Chartier (eds.) *A History of Reading in the West,* tr. Lydia G. Cochrane (Amherst: University of Massachusetts Press), 284–312.
Wivel, Henrik (1988) *Snedronningen. En bog om Selma Lagerlöfs kærlighed* (Copenhagen: Gad).
Wolf, Werner (2002) 'Towards a Functional Analysis of Intermediality: The Case of Twentieth-Century Musicalized Fiction', in Erik Hedling and Ulla-Britta Lagerroth (eds.) *Cultural Functions of Intermedial Exploration* (Amsterdam: Rodopi), 15–34.
Zackarias Linberg, Johannes ('Z–k–s') (1919) 'Ingmarssönernas premier', *Stockholms Tidningen,* 2 Jan.

Filmography

Berg-Ejvind och hans hustru (1918) (*Eyvind of the Hills|You and I*), dir. Victor Sjöström, AB Svenska Biografteatern.
Bilder från Fryksdalen (1907) (*Gösta Berlings land*) ('Pictures from Fryksdalen (The Land of Gösta Berling)'), dir. Charles Magnusson, AB Biokronan.

Dunungen (1919) (*In Quest of Happiness*), dir. Ivan Hedqvist, AB Svenska Biografteatern.

En resa genom Dalarne (1907) ('A Trip through Dalarna'), dir. Charles Magnusson, AB Biokronan.

Gösta Berlings saga, 1–2 (1924) (*The Atonement of Gösta Berling\The Story of Gosta Berling*), dir. Mauritz Stiller, AB Svensk Filmindustri.

Gunnar Hedes saga (1923) (*Snowbound\The Blizzard*), dir. Mauritz Stiller, AB Svensk Filminspelning.

Herr Arnes pengar (1919) (*Sir Arne's Treasure*), dir. Mauritz Stiller, AB Svenska Biografteatern.

Ingeborg Holm (1913) (*Margaret Day*), dir. Victor Sjöström, AB Svenska Biografteatern.

Ingmarssönerna, 1–2 (1919) (*Sons of Ingmar\Dawn of Love*), dir. Victor Sjöström, AB Svenska Biografteatern.

Karin Ingmarsdotter (1920) (*God's Way*), dir. Victor Sjöström, AB Svenska Biografteatern.

Klostret i Sendomir (1920) (*The Monastery of Sendomir*), dir. Victor Sjöström, AB Svenska Biografteatern.

Körkarlen (1921) (*The Phantom Carriage*), dir. Victor Sjöström, AB Svensk Filmindustri.

Nils Holgerssons underbara resa (1962) (*Nils Holgersson's Wonderful Journey*), dir. Kenne Fant, Svenska AB Nordisk Tonefilm, Kenne Fant & Co.

Synnøve Solbakken (1919), dir. John W. Brunius, Filmindustri AB Skandia.

Terje Vigen (1917) (*A Man There Was*), dir. Victor Sjöström, AB Svenska Biografteatern.

Tösen från Stormyrtorpet (1917) (*The Girl from the Marsh Croft*), dir. Victor Sjöström, AB Svenska Biografteatern.

The Wonderful Adventures of Nils (1980) (*Nirusu no Fushigi na*), dir. Studio Pierrot, [Japanese animated series].

Illustrations

The Editors would like to thank all the providers of the images included in this book. With great expertise and kindness they have helped us identify, retrieve, and reproduce a priceless compilation of photographs, drawings, and other types of artwork. Every effort has been made to trace the copyright of the illustrations included. The publisher would be grateful for information about any errors or omissions.

Contributors

Jenny Bergenmar is Senior Lecturer in Comparative Literature at the University of Gothenburg. She has been technical editor of the series The Selma Lagerlöf Archive, and, in collaboration with Maria Karlsson (Uppsala University), researcher in a project about the letters from the Swedish general public to Selma Lagerlöf, 1890–1940, funded by *Riksbankens Jubileumsfond* (the Swedish Foundation for the Humanities and Social Sciences).

Charlotte Berry read English Language and Scandinavian Studies at the University of Edinburgh. Since graduating she has worked as an archivist and curator, specialising in literary and business collections. In 2013 she completed a Ph.D. at the University of Edinburgh, 'Publishing, Translation, Archives: Nordic Children's Literature in the United Kingdom, 1950–2000'.

Anna Bohlin has been a lecturer at Uppsala University, Stockholm University, and Södertörn University. The title of her doctoral dissertation is *Anatomy of Voice. Readings of Politics in Silverforsen by Elin Wägner, the Löwensköld trilogy by Selma Lagerlöf and Klara Johanson's Causeries in Tidevarvet* (2008; in Swedish). She is currently working on a study of Fredrika Bremer.

Elettra Carbone is a Teaching Fellow in Norwegian at University College London. She co-edited *Lyset kommer fra Sør* (2011) and *Nordic Publishing and Book History* (2013), and has published on the representation of Italy in Nordic literature. She is currently working on the cultural mobility of Thorvaldsen's sculptures in print culture, and the reception of the Norwegian constitution in literature. She is an editorial assistant for Norvik Press.

Git Claesson Pipping is General Secretary of the Swedish University Teachers' Association and has been Reader in Gender Studies at Södertörn University since 2009. Her recent research concerns the use of structures of feelings to convey political messages in public celebrations of Selma Lagerlöf, including the monograph *Dyrkan och spektakel* (2010, 'Worship and Spectacle') with Tom Olsson.

Roald van Elswijk read Scandinavian Studies and Early Germanic at the University of Groningen, the Netherlands. His research interests include literary criticism, sociolinguistics, and Nynorsk. He also takes a keen interest in translation and has translated poetry, short stories, and children's literature from Icelandic, Norwegian, and Faroese.

Helena Forsås-Scott was Professor of Swedish and Gender Studies at University College London and retired in 2010. She has published on Swedish literature and especially women's writing, including *Re-Writing the Script: Gender and Community in Elin Wägner* (2009; new edition 2014). She is currently working on a study of Kerstin Ekman. She is a director of Norvik Press, London, and co-ordinator of 'Lagerlöf in English'.

Dagmar Hartlová, translator, specialises in Swedish and Norwegian literature. She has published on the reception of Swedish literature in Czech, and her publications include an anthology of modern Swedish poetry (1999); participation in the edition of August Strindberg's selected works (2004); and the *Lexicon of Nordic literatures* (2004) as editor and co-author. Since 1989 she has taught modern Swedish literature at the Charles University, Prague.

Maria Karlsson is Senior Lecturer in Comparative Literature at Uppsala University. She has been one of the editors of the series The Selma Lagerlöf Archive and, in collaboration with Jenny Bergenmar (University of Gothenburg) researcher in a project about the letters from the Swedish general public to Selma Lagerlöf 1890–1940, funded by *Riksbankens Jubileumsfond* (the Swedish Foundation for the Humanities and Social Sciences).

Anna Nordlund is Senior Lecturer at Uppsala University. She has been one of the editors of the series The Selma Lagerlöf Archive. Her doctoral thesis on Lagerlöf in Swedish literary history was published in 2005. She is currently working on a study of Lagerlöf in the emerging Swedish media industry.

Tom Olsson was Professor of History at Södertörn University and retired in 2011. He has published on Swedish labour history, twentieth-century Swedish journalism, men's fashion in sixteenth- and seventeenth-century Europe, and, together with Git Claesson Pipping, Selma Lagerlöf's public performances.

Christopher 'Chip' Oscarson is an Associate Professor of Interdisciplinary Humanities at Brigham Young University, and director of the university's Scandinavian Studies Program. His research interests include early Swedish cinema, turn-of-the-twentieth-century Nordic literature, and ecocriticism.

Kristina Sjögren completed her Ph.D. in Gender Studies at University College London in 2010, with a dissertation investigating gender in novels from the Scandinavian Modern Breakthrough (1880–1905). She was a Lecturer in Gender Studies at Lund University, 2010–2012. The author of several works of fiction for young adults, she is currently a full-time writer. She also teaches creative writing.

Tytti Soila is Professor of Cinema Studies and Associate Dean of the Faculty of Humanities at Stockholm University. She has published on Nordic cinema, women film-makers, and stardom, and has been editor of *The Cinema of Scandinavia* (2005) and *Stellar Encounters: Stardom in Popular European Cinema* (2009). She is currently working on the formation of public images and the work of film actors.

Lisbeth Stenberg is Reader in Comparative Literature at the University of Gothenburg. Her doctoral thesis (2001) offered a queer–feminist approach to Selma Lagerlöf's early writings. She has subsequently contextualised and outlined an emancipatory aesthetics used by Lagerlöf's mentors. Forthcoming with Ulla-Britta Lagerroth is an annotated edition of Lagerlöf's theatre sonnets, portraying actors in plays she attended during her years in Stockholm, 1881–5.

Björn Sundmark is Associate Professor of English at Malmö University. His publications include *Alice in the Oral-Literary Continuum* (Lund University Press), the co-edited volume *The Nation in Children's Literature* (Routledge) as well as articles on Selma Lagerlöf, Lewis Carroll, Andrew Lang, Walter Scott, and Hesba Stretton. He currently serves on the children's literature committee of the Swedish Arts Council.

Astrid Surmatz is Assistant Professor in Scandinavian Literature and Swedish at the University of Amsterdam, and Associate Professor at the Linnaeus University, Sweden, where she is involved in the research project 'Concurrences'. A fellow of the Linnean Society and board member of the International Research Society for Children's Literature, she has published and edited books on the international and intermedial reception of Astrid Lindgren and on Scandinavian postcolonialism.

Bjarne Thorup Thomsen is Reader in Scandinavian Literature in the Division of European Languages and Cultures at the University of Edinburgh. His work is primarily focused on regional, national, and transnational dimensions of Scandinavian novel and travel writing. He has also published on Danish literary history and working-class autobiographies. He has an additional interest in the relationship between literature and Scandinavian silent cinema. His books include *Centring on the Peripheries* (2007, editor) and *Lagerlöfs litterære landvinding* (2007).

Jennifer Watson is an Associate Professor of German and Scandinavian Studies and Associate Dean of the Humanities at University of Wisconsin–Milwaukee. Her research has centred on the literary relationship between Germany and Sweden at the turn of the twentieth century, with specific focus on Selma Lagerlöf and Germany. Her current research project is an English-language biography of Lagerlöf.

Sofia Wijkmark is Senior Lecturer in Comparative Literature at Karlstad University, Sweden. She wrote her doctoral dissertation on gothic elements in Selma Lagerlöf's short stories (2009). Her current research focuses on fictional violence and the uncanniness of Nature in contemporary fiction.

Ebba Witt-Brattström is Professor of Nordic Literature at the University of Helsinki. She has published chiefly on Swedish and Finland-Swedish authors of the nineteenth and twentieth centuries. Forthcoming in 2014, *Stå i bredd—1970-talets kvinnor, män och litteratur* ('Side by Side: Women, Men, and Literature in the 1970s'). She is Swedish editor of the second and third volumes of *Nordisk kvinnolitteraturhistoria* (*The History of Nordic Women's Literature*) (1993–6).

Index of works
by Selma Lagerlöf

This index covers works referred to in the book, including translations, and also films inspired by Lagerlöf's texts. Page references to films are given in *italics*.

Index of names